W9-BTL-608

Travel Planner's
WEATHER GUIDE

Travel Planner's
WEATHER GUIDE

Russell & Penny Jennings

OPEN ROAD PUBLISHERS
Vancouver, BC, Canada

ISBN 0–9691363–3–1

First edition, 1999
Second edition, 2003

Text copyright © 2003 Russell and Penny Jennings
Maps copyright © 2003 ITMB Publishing Ltd.

No part of this book may be reproduced in any form without permission in writing from the publisher, except by a reviewer who may quote weather descriptions for review.

Every effort has been made to ensure the accuracy of the information in this weather guide. The authors and publishers disclaim any liability to any party for any loss, inconvenience, injury or travel disruption caused by errors or omissions in this book.

National Library of Canada Cataloguing in Publication Data

Jennings, Russell, 1943–
    Travel planner's weather guide

    Includes index.
    ISBN 0–9691363–3–1

1. Climatology – Handbooks, manuals, etc.
2. Travel – Guidebooks.

I. Jennings, Penny, 1941 –   II. Title.

QC981.J46 2003   551.6   C2002–910609–5

OPEN ROAD PUBLISHERS
3316 West 8th Avenue
Vancouver, BC, V6R 1Y4, Canada

Fax: +1 604 734 1586

E–mail: info@worldweatherguide.com

Website: www.worldweatherguide.com

Printed in Canada

CONTENTS

ACKNOWLEDGMENTS

To the World Meteorological Organization, Geneva, Switzerland and the National Oceanic and Atmospheric Administration, National Climatic Data Center, Asheville, North Carolina, USA, for weather records and their permission to reproduce them.

To Mark Hoffmann at Babblefish Design (www.babblefishdesign.com) for Art Direction, Cover Design, Page Layout, Scanning, and Prepress preparation.

To Galina Korobova for preparing the maps.

AN INVITATION

We invite you to contact us.
If you have any comments concerning amendments, additions, deletions or complaints,
please contact us.

Russell and Penny Jennings
OPEN ROAD PUBLISHERS
3316 West 8th Avenue,
Vancouver, BC, V6R 1Y4, Canada

Fax: +1 604 734 1586
E–mail: info@worldweatherguide.com
Website: http://www.worldweatherguide.com

PREFACE

What prompted this weather guide?

Basically, a need.

As travel agents we advised numerous people about the best time to visit a country or region to find the sun, to go on safari, to go trekking, to go skiing, or sailing, or cruising or cycling…

Tourist literature published by government agencies promotes their country's attractions but mention of weather is often confined to one paragraph or nothing at all. Similarly, brochures of tour operators promote their tours and destinations but little information, if any, is given about weather. This weather guide is designed to fill the information gap.

Increasing numbers of people are travelling for business and pleasure and many are booking on the Internet. It is important that travel planners are aware of the weather to be expected at their destination. Reduced airfares and low hotel rates may be appealing but if you are booking a holiday in a wet season you should be aware of it in advance. In compiling this weather guide we have described year–round weather and have suggested the best time to travel. To us, the best time is when the weather is sunny, warm and dry.

Over the years we have taken long trips lasting many months, so visiting each country at the "best time" has not always been possible. But it is wise to be aware of the "best time" before you leave.

We have often been in places when it has been far from the best time. We travelled in India during the intense heat of summer, journeyed down the Amazon River during the rainy season, camped in central Australia in May and almost froze in the unseasonably cold weather, and travelled through the Indonesian islands of Bali, Java and Sumatra during the monsoon season. We visited Kenya on a photographic safari in the normally dry month of January when rainstorms bogged us down in the game reserves. We journeyed to the grasslands of Inner Mongolia in late September when freezing Arctic winds chilled us to the bone. We travelled in Mali during a drought when one of our major concerns became seeking water, and we stayed on one of Fiji's small islands in the middle of the cyclone season. A cyclone roared across the island, flattened vegetation, snapped the trunks of palm trees as if they were toothpicks, hurled coconuts through the air and tossed boats onto the beaches.

However, we have also travelled during the "best times" and have enjoyed festivals, animal migrations, beaches, sailing, trekking, wildflower seasons and colorful foliage changes.

Your experiences will be different according to when you travel but the rewards, many.

We hope that this comprehensive, easy–to–read weather guide will help you choose your destination or plan your journey. Enjoy your travels!

Russell and Penny Jennings

WHAT IS... WEATHER? CLIMATE? GLOBAL WARMING? THE OZONE LAYER?

Weather is the condition of the atmosphere at a **specific place and time**. The variables of temperature, precipitation and wind are used to describe weather.

Climate is the general meteorological condition of a **region**. The basic factors that determine climate are latitude, the average temperature, precipitation and prevailing winds. Other factors are warm or cold ocean currents.

Global warming. In our atmosphere are gases — carbon dioxide, methane and nitrous oxide — which are called greenhouse gases because they act like a greenhouse by forming a blanket or shield around the Earth, preventing the sun's heat from escaping into space. The result is a warm place to live. Without the gases the Earth would be too cold to support life as we know it.

The burning of fossil fuels such as oil and coal to power our industries, homes and vehicles releases carbon dioxide, methane and nitrous oxide into the atmosphere. Carbon dioxide is the most abundant heat–trapping gas. The emission of excessive greenhouse gases can be harmful. What is happening these days is an increase in the gases which results in a thickening of the blanket that insulates the Earth. Each year the rate of increase accelerates. The conclusion is that the world's temperatures will continue rising.

The effect of global warming is to cause mountain snow lines and glaciers to contract, coral reefs to die as the water warms up, migration patterns of animals on the land and in the sea to change, and lakes and rivers in colder climes to freeze later and thaw earlier.

Global warming affects weather. Higher temperatures can bring heat waves, induce droughts, generate tornadoes, bring thunderstorms and cause sea levels to rise to erode coastlines, flood coastal plains and submerge low islands.

Ozone layer. The ozone layer is a shield of ozone gas that encircles our world in the stratosphere, a region from 10 to 50km (6 to 30 miles) above the Earth's surface. The ozone layer protects life on earth from the sun's deadly ultraviolet rays that can harm DNA of humans, plants and animals. The rays can cause skin cancer and cataracts.

Human–made gases such as chlorofluorocarbons (CFCs) have been used as refrigerants and solvents. Air currents carry the used gases into the stratosphere where they "eat" the ozone, thus depleting it. A depleting ozone layer allows more ultraviolet rays to reach us. However, provided countries reduce their emissions, the ozone in the stratosphere should eventually recover.

The sun's ultraviolet rays are strongest between 10am and 4pm, a time when vacationers are more likely to be sightseeing or engaging in sporting activities.

Preventative measures should be taken such as wearing a wide–brimmed hat, sunglasses, covering exposed skin during prolonged periods in the sun, and using sunscreen with a sun protection factor (SPF) of at least 15 to block the UV rays.

HOW TO USE THIS BOOK

Our explanation is in three sections: **TEXT, MAPS, and WEATHER TABLES.**

ABOUT THE TEXT
Every country in the world is listed as well as island dependencies.
For each of these we suggest the **best time to visit** which, in our opinion, is when the weather is sunny, warm, relatively dry and with low humidity, if any. However, you should not confine your visit only to the best time. Quite often the months before and after the best time are good, and we often mention this fact. The accompanying text describes the other months.
Sometimes weather is described with overlapping months as follows:
May to October
October to March
March to May
When months overlap it indicates that the transitional months, in this example October, March and May, have a weather mix of both seasons.

When we mention **humidity**, we describe it simply as high, medium or low. High humidity indicates an uncomfortable, damp heat which causes "stickiness" when perspiration will not evaporate and clothes are slow to dry. Low humidity indicates a measure of comfort without perspiration. Medium humidity indicates a mix of high and low. See Humidity in the Glossary.

Technical and foreign terms are explained in the Glossary.

Some main **Natural Attractions, Cultural Events and Activities** for visitors are listed in the text.

ABOUT THE MAPS
A map is provided for each country. If a country has more than one weather region, the weather regions are separated by broken lines and are given numbers that correspond to the descriptions in the text. Cities mentioned in the text are shown on the maps.

ABOUT THE WEATHER TABLES
The figures in the Weather Tables are a monthly average of readings taken over, usually, a 30–year period. Note that when temperature figures in the Weather Tables are compared with those in the text, the figures may differ slightly. This is because the figures in the text apply to a region if it is a large country or to an entire country if the country is small, whereas a Weather Table pertains to a specific city.

Altitude: This is the altitude above sea level of the weather station expressed in metres and feet.

Temperatures: These are temperatures read in the shade and expressed in Celsius (°C) and Fahrenheit (°F). Sunrise temperatures are read one hour either side of sunrise. Mid–afternoon temperatures are read between 2pm and 4pm.
Temperatures are affected by altitude. Temperatures decrease by 0.6°C (1°F) for every 100m (330 ft) increase in altitude.

Days with precipitation: These days also include days with snowfalls when applicable. Be aware that in the countries within 5 degrees of the equator, heavy tropical rain can fall almost daily throughout the year but usually only for a short time – an hour or so daily, thus interrupting sightseeing only temporarily. Away from the tropics light rains can be continuous for days on end. This column should be read with the type of rainfall in mind. In the text, when necessary, we have described the type of rainfall.

HOW TO USE THIS BOOK (continued)

Precipitation: Precipitation includes rain, snow, sleet and hail. Measurements are in millimetres and inches.

Snow: When monthly snowfall figures are available they are listed separately. Be aware that the figures have already been included in the Precipitation figures after the snowfall has been converted to the "melted equivalent of rain."

The ratio used to convert snow to the "melted equivalent of rain" varies from region to region. With heavy, wet snow the ratio may be 5 to 1. That is, 5 parts of snow equates to 1 part of rain water. With light, powdery snow the ratio may be 20 parts of snow to 1 part of rain water. A generally accepted but inaccurate ratio is 10 parts of snow to 1 part of water. This can also be expressed as 10mm of snowfall equals 1 mm of rain, or 10 inches of snowfall equals 1 inch of rain.

CRUISING: WHEN TO GO

The best time to cruise is when the weather is cool in hot climates, warm in cool climates, and when there is less rain.

Africa
East Africa: October to March.
Red Sea: October to March.

Antarctica
November to early March.

Asia
Southeast Asia: October to March.

Australia's east coast and New Zealand
Year–round, especially November to April, but in December and January the weather is unpredictable because of potential cyclones in the Pacific Ocean.

Caribbean Sea
December to May. Weather from June to November is unpredictable because of potential hurricanes, particularly between late August and mid–October. However, with the ability of today's modern weather equipment to track a storm, a captain can move the ship to calmer waters. This allows for cruising year–round.

Central America
Year–round.
Panama Canal: September to April.

Egypt and Israel
October to April.

Europe
Arctic Ocean: July.
Around Great Britain: May to early October.
Black Sea: April to August.
Norway's fjords and North Cape: June to August.
Greenland: July.
Iceland: June to August.
Mediterranean Sea: April to October.

Indian Ocean
October to March

South America
Around South America: Mostly year–round but November through March is best for the southern region.
Amazon River, Brazil: Anytime, but be aware the rainy season is January to April.
Panama Canal: September to April.

Continued on page 406

DIVING: WHEN TO GO

The "best time" is when water is calm, clear and warm according to most divers. Be aware that during the "best time" you could be disappointed by inclement weather. Because we are dealing with weather the first and last months of the "best time" must be considered flexible.

Anguilla Year–round.

Antigua Year–round.

Aruba Year–round, but wind is strongest January through April.

Australia
Queensland (Great Barrier Reef): Best, July to November. September and October are usually superb.
South Australia: Best, February to March.
Western Australia: Best, March. (Coral spawning.)

Baja California (see Mexico)

Bahamas Year–round except June to September, the hurricane season.

Barbados April to November. (Calm seas and good visibility.)

Belize Year–round. Best months are April, May, and September through November. In winter, December through February, unpleasant northers (cold fronts) come in. Summer, June through August, is the hurricane season.

Bermuda Best months are mid–March through November. (Warmer water temperature.)
Winter months, December to March, have better visibility but the water is cooler.

Bonaire (Netherlands Antilles) Good year–round. Popular time is October to April. (Bonaire is outside the hurricane belt.)

Bora Bora (see French Polynesia)

Brazil September to March. (Warm weather.) January and February have rainstorms but they are brief.

Canary Islands Year–round. Best months to see the breeding of angel sharks are January to April.

Cayman Islands Year–round. Best is October through April. (Calm, warm, better visibility.) The rainy season starts in May and peaks in October. Rains are brief and do not adversely affect water clarity.

Costa Rica
Caribbean coast: Best visibility is March to early May, and mid–August to mid–November.
Pacific coast: May is the best month. (No rain, no wind.) June to November is also good despite it being the rainy season. Visibility may be better in the dry season, December to April, but it is windy, making boating difficult.

Continued on page 407

CULTURAL EVENTS

Thousands of colourful cultural events are held annually around the world. Following are some events we consider to be spectacular and of superb photographic interest. The dates of many cultural events change each year because they are based on the lunar calendar. Therefore we will only give months in which the dates will fall.

Brazil
• Carnival. Parades and costumed balls. Rio de Janeiro, Recife, Salvador (Bahia). February or March.

Canada
• Calgary Exhibition and Stampede. Rodeo in Calgary in early July.
• Carnaval de Quebec (The Winter Carnival). Quebec City. February.

China
• Tin Hau. Birthday celebration of Tin Hau, Goddess of the Sea. Hundreds of colourful boats with shrines. Hong Kong. Around May.
• Naadam. A New Year festival that features horse riding, wrestling and archery. Inner Mongolia. July 20 to 26. (See also Mongolia.)

Ethiopia
• Timkat. Feast of the Epiphany. Colourful religious procession. In Addis Ababa, Gondar, Lalibela and elsewhere. January 18 and 19.

France
• Fête des Saintes Maries (Festival of the Holy Maries). Gypsy festival. Parades and bull sports at Les Saintes Maries de–la–Mer, south of Marseilles. May 24 and 25.

Germany
• Munich hosts the world's biggest beer festival, the Oktoberfest. It runs mid–September to early October.

India
• Rath Yatra (also called Jagannath Festival). Tall chariots are pulled through the streets by hundreds of devotees. Puri, Orissa state. July/August.
• Meenakshi Kalyanam. Chariots containing images from the temple are processed through the streets. Madurai, Tamil Nadu state. April.
• Pushkar Camel Fair. Hindu religious festival and livestock sales. At Pushkar in Rajasthan state. October/November.

Malaysia
• Thaipusam. Procession of devotees, many with their upper bodies pierced by hooks and skewers. Pinang and Kuala Lumpur. January or February.

Malta
• Carnival. Parade of floats, folk dancing, brass bands. Valletta. Runs for the 5 days before Lent. February or March.

CULTURAL EVENTS (continued)

Mexico
- Carnival. Parades, fireworks, music and dance. Acapulco, Ensenada, La Paz, Mazatlan, Merida, Vera Cruz. February or March. (Before Lent).
- Semana Santa. Plays, music, dance. Held throughout Mexico during Easter week, March or April.

Mongolia
- Naadam. A New Year festival which features horse racing, archery and wrestling at Ulaanbaatar. July 7 to 11. See also Inner Mongolia, China.

Morocco
- Camel Market at Goulimine, held annually usually in July.
- Rose festival. Parade of floats. Folk dancing competitions between different Berber clans. At El Kelãa, April or May.

Nepal
- Bisket Jatra (New Year festival). A tall chariot or wagon containing religious images is pulled through the streets of Bhaktapur, near Kathmandu, in mid–April.
- Indra Jatra. Golden chariots are pulled through the streets, starting from the palace of the Living Goddess who also makes an appearance. Held in Kathmandu in September or October.
- A tall chariot or wagon containing a temple image is pulled through the streets during White Machhendranath in Kathmandu in March or April, and during Red Machhendranath in Patan, near Kathmandu, in April or May.

Papua New Guinea
- Highland shows, or Sing–sings. Different tribal groups wearing their colourful traditional garb gather for chanting, dancing, drumming and competitions. Held in Mt Hagen in August and Goroka in September.

Peru
- Inti Raymi Fiesta. This colourful festival is held at Sacsayhuaman, a high point overlooking Cuzco, the ancient Inca capital. June 24.

Scotland
- Edinburgh International Festival. Pipe bands from all over the world perform. A highlight is the Military Tattoo performed each night at Edinburgh Castle. Held during the last 2 weeks of August and the first week of September.

Singapore
- Thaipusam. Devotees walk in procession, their flesh pierced with hooks and skewers as a sign of penance.

Spain
- San Fermin Festival or "Running of the Bulls." Young men risk their lives running through the narrow streets ahead of bulls being herded to the bullring for the bullfights. In Pamplona, July 7 to 14.

CULTURAL EVENTS (continued)

Sri Lanka
• Esala Perahera. For nine nights processions of elephants, dancers, drummers, horn blowers and torch bearers parade to the Temple of the Tooth which is believed to house a tooth of Buddha. Held at Kandy during the full moon during the month of Asadha, between mid–June and mid–July.

Thailand
• Elephant Round–up. Elephant trainers demonstrate the elephants' abilities in a tug–of–war with 200 men, log–pulling contests, a soccer game between two teams of elephants and parading as if preparing for battle. Additionally, there are folk dance performances. At Surin, third weekend in November.

Trinidad and Tobago
• Carnival. Marching bands and hundreds of marchers parade on the two carnival days, the Monday and Tuesday before Ash Wednesday. Held in Port of Spain in February or March.

United States of America
• Mardi Gras carnival in New Orleans. For the two weeks leading up to Ash Wednesday there are street parades with jazz bands and floats with costumed and masked 'Krewe' members who toss gifts to the crowds. Held in February or March.

For more cultural events, check www.bugbog.com/festivals

NAME CHANGES OF COUNTRIES

Current Name	Former Name(s)
Bangladesh	East Pakistan
Belarus	Bylerussia, Belorussia
Belize	British Honduras
Benin	Dahomey
Bosnia and Herzegovina	Was part of Yugoslavia
Botswana	Bechuanaland
Burkina Faso	Upper Volta, Haute Volta
Cambodia	Kampuchea, Khmer Republic
Congo, Democratic Republic of (Unofficially Congo–Kinshasa)	Zaire, Belgian Congo
Congo, Republic of (Unofficially Congo–Brazzaville)	French Congo
Croatia	Was part of Yugoslavia
Czech Republic	Was part of Czechoslovakia
East Timor	Was part of Indonesia
Eritrea	Was part of Ethiopia
Ethiopia	Abyssinia
Ghana	Gold Coast
Guinea–Bissau	Portuguese Guinea
Guyana	British Guiana
Iran	Persia
Kiribati	Gilbert Islands
Lesotho	Basutoland
Madagascar	Malagasy Republic
Malawi	Nyasaland
Myanmar	Burma
Macedonia	Was part of Yugoslavia
Moldova	Moldavia
Namibia	South West Africa
Oman	Muscat and Oman
Samoa	Western Samoa
Serbia and Montenegro	Was part of Yugoslavia
Slovakia	Was part of Czechoslovakia
Slovenia	Was part of Yugoslavia
Sri Lanka	Ceylon
Suriname	Netherlands Guiana
Tanzania	Tanganyika
Thailand	Siam
Tuvalu	Ellice Islands
Western Sahara	Spanish Sahara
Zambia	Northern Rhodesia
Zimbabwe	Rhodesia, Southern Rhodesia

NAME CHANGES OF COUNTRIES

Former Name	Current Name(s)
Abyssinia	Ethiopia
Basutoland	Lesotho
Bechuanaland	Botswana
Belgian Congo	Congo, Democratic Republic of
Belorussia	Belarus
British Guiana	Guyana
British Honduras	Belize
Burma	Myanmar
Ceylon	Sri Lanka
Czechoslovakia	Separated into Czech Republic, and Slovakia
Dahomey	Benin
Dutch Guiana	Suriname
East Pakistan	Bangladesh
Ellice Islands	Tuvalu
French Congo	Congo, Republic of
Gilbert Islands	Kiribati
Gold Coast	Ghana
Haute Volta	Burkina Faso
Kampuchea	Cambodia
Khmer Republic	Cambodia
Malagasy Republic	Madagascar
Moldavia	Moldova
Muscat and Oman	Oman
Netherlands Guiana	Suriname
New Hebrides	Vanuatu
Northern Rhodesia	Zambia
Nyasaland	Malawi
Persia	Iran
Portuguese Guinea	Guinea–Bissau
Rhodesia	Zimbabwe
Siam	Thailand
Southern Rhodesia	Zimbabwe
South West Africa	Namibia
Spanish Sahara	Western Sahara
Tanganyika	Tanzania
Upper Volta	Burkina Faso
Western Samoa	Samoa
Yugoslavia	Separated into Bosnia and Herzegovina, Croatia, Macedonia, Serbia and Montenegro, and Slovenia
Zaire	Congo, Democratic Republic of

NAME CHANGES OF ISLANDS, PROVINCES AND CITIES

Current Name	Former Name
Almaty, Kazakhstan	Alma Ata
Banjul, Gambia	Bathurst
Beijing, China	Peking
Bioko Island, Equatorial Guinea	Fernando Po
Chennai, India	Madras
Chongqing, China	Chungking
Chuuk, Micronesia	Truk
Dhaka, Bangladesh	Dacca
Guangzhou, China	Canton
Hagatña, Guam	Agana
Hangzhou, China	Hangchow
Ho Chi Minh City, Vietnam	Saigon
Iqaluit, Canada	Frobisher Bay
Kashi, China	Kashgar
Kochi, India	Cochin
Kolkata, India	Calcutta
Maluku, Indonesia	Moluccas
Melaka, Malaysia	Malacca
Mumbai, India	Bombay
Nanjing, China	Nanking
Nunavut, Canada	Was part of Northwest Territories
Nuuk, Greenland	Godthab
Pinang, Malaysia	Penang
Pohnpei, Micronesia	Ponape
St Petersburg, Russia	Leningrad
Sulawesi, Indonesia	Celebes
Suzhou, China	Soochow
Toamasina, Madagascar	Tamatave
Urumqi, China	Urumchi
Xian, China	Sian
Xizang, China	Tibet
Yangon, Myanmar	Rangoon, Burma

NAME CHANGES OF ISLANDS, PROVINCES AND CITIES

Former Name	Current Name
Agana, Guam	Hagatña
Alma Ata, Kazakhstan	Almaty
Bathurst, Gambia	Banjul
Bombay, India	Mumbai
Calcutta, India	Kolkata
Canton, China	Guangzhou (pronounced Guang–joe)
Celebes, Indonesia	Sulawesi
Chungking, China	Chongqing (pronounced Chongching)
Cochin, India	Kochi
Dacca, Bangladesh	Dhaka
Fernando Po, Equatorial Guinea	Bioko Island
Frobisher Bay, Canada	Iqaluit
Godthab, Greenland	Nuuk
Hangchow, China	Hangzhou (pronounced Hang–joe)
Kashgar, China	Kashi
Leningrad, Russia	St Petersburg
Madras, India	Chennai
Malacca, Malaysia	Melaka
Moluccas, Indonesia	Maluku
Nanking, China	Nanjing
Peking, China	Beijing
Penang, Malaysia	Pinang
Ponape, Micronesia	Pohnpei
Rangoon, Burma	Yangon, Myanmar
Saigon, Vietnam	Ho Chi Minh City
Sian, China	Xian (pronounced She–ahn)
Soochow, China	Suzhou (pronounced Soo–joe)
Tibet, China	Xizang (pronounced She–jang)
Truk, Micronesia	Chuuk (pronounced Chuke)
Urumchi, China	Urumqi (pronounced Urumchi)

BAGGAGE LIST

The less baggage you carry, the better.
In addition to putting a tag on your luggage, put your name and address inside. Never overpack. After packing, check again and remove 20% or more of the weight.

The following list is a rough guide only. What you take depends on your type of holiday.

Basic Items
Suitcase with a strap to go around it to prevent it popping open, or a backpack with an internal frame which doubles as a soft–sided suitcase.
Shoulder bag (for camera, maps).
Camera and more film than you think you will need.
Camera batteries and lens–cleaning tissue.
Money belt or neck pouch.

Documents
Passport.
Travellers cheques.
Credit cards.
Airline ticket.
International Driver's License (if required).
International Certificates of Vaccinations (if required).
Hostelling International membership card if you plan on using the worldwide network of "Youth" hostels which are open to all ages.

Clothes
Sturdy walking shoes.
Sandals (optional).
Rubber thongs (wear in showers to prevent foot diseases).
2 pairs of trousers for men; 2 pairs of slacks for women plus a drip dry skirt.
1 sweater.
1 jacket.
3 shirts for men; 3 blouses for women.
T–shirts.
3 changes of underwear.
3 handkerchiefs.
1 hat (crushable).
Bathing suit.
Towel.
Shorts (optional).
Sleep wear.

BAGGAGE LIST (continued)

Toilet Articles

Soap in plastic container, toothbrush and paste, shampoo, shave cream, razor blades, nail scissors, comb or brush, small packs of paper tissues, aspirin, cold remedies, women's sanitary requisites, moisture lotion, package of moistened tissues to wipe face and hands, mosquito repellent, adhesive plasters, ointment for bites, needle and thread, lip salve, sunscreen, water purifying tablets, half–roll of toilet paper, tablets for stomach upsets and constipation, possibly sleeping pills and vitamin tablets, and electrolytes.

Electrolytes replace minerals lost through diarrhea. Take packages of electrolytes containing glucose, sodium chloride, sodium bicarbonate, potassium and chloride.

Odds and ends

Spare plastic bags for laundry, film, fruit, odds and ends.
Sunglasses.
Spare set of reading glasses (if applicable).
Lightweight travelling alarm clock.
Clothes pins and clothesline (for use in your hotel room).
Swiss Army knife with corkscrew, bottle opener.
Knife or vegetable peeler (to peel fruit before eating).
Small flashlight.
Wash basin plug (universal type).
Water bottle (1 quart or litre capacity).
Immersion heater and cup (for tea or coffee in your hotel room).
Guidebook and map.
Writing paper, envelopes, pen, journal or diary.
Food rations: A can of food in case restaurants are closed.
Duct tape in the event that your luggage is damaged.

Optional extras could include

Sleeping bag liner (for use in budget hotels if the sheets are unclean).
Empty soft–sided bag in which to carry home purchases.
Fold–up umbrella.
Gloves.
Lightweight binoculars (for game viewing or bird watching).
Trading items or giveaways for Africa or South America: pens, T–shirts, postcards of your city, or lapel pins of your country's flag.
Camping equipment if applicable: tent, sleeping bag, sleeping mat and cooking and eating utensils.

Notes regarding prescriptions

1. Prescription glasses. Take an extra pair or take the prescription.
2. Prescription drugs. If you are taking prescription drugs ensure that you have an adequate supply. Ask your doctor for the generic name of the drug and carry the name with you, plus directions for use.

BARGAINING TIPS

Bargaining is a normal way of doing business in most developing countries. Do not accept the first price asked otherwise you undermine the system upon which the trading economy is based.

The process can be fun for both sides. Sometimes after we have completed a bargaining session and paid for our purchases the vendor has added a "sweetener," a handkerchief, fan or bottle of perfume as a token of his appreciation. Or was it because he felt guilty about the high prices we paid? Maybe we should have bargained lower? We'll never know!

You will encounter young girls and boys selling single cigarettes or cheap items they have made themselves, things you possibly do not really want. Consider buying them anyway to encourage them in their work. It is better to encourage trade than to have them beg.

In some countries, items such as T–shirts can be offered in addition to some money.

When you go to bargain, dress casually. It is better not to show your wealth.

Before you go, place known amounts of money in your various pockets. If you bargain down the merchant to a price of say $10, you do not want to have to pull out a twenty and ask for change. (To simplify our discussion we will talk in dollars.)

The seller has techniques that work for him. He may invite you into his shop for a cup of tea and/or invite you into a back room to watch craftsmen making items for sale. You could accept these offers but remember you are not under any obligation to buy.

Maintain a poker face. If you appear enthusiastic about the item you want to buy it will be difficult to bargain him down. Disregard the seller's first offer. Show your lack of interest to get him to start lower.

Carry a pen and paper to write down your offer if language is a problem. If the seller meets your price you must buy from him.

There are various techniques you can try:
Technique A:

When you see something you really want, do not point to it immediately. Point to something nearby and ask how much. When he tells you, shake your head and point to something else, then again shake your head. Your disinterest in his prices could cause him to lower them. When you point to what you really want, the bargaining will be starting at a lower figure.

The amount you first offer varies from country to country, but generally you offer one third of his asking price and the bargaining will creep up from there.

Technique B:

You could decide how much you want to pay and put the money on the counter saying, "To me it is worth this much."

If he won't accept your offer you could say you will think about it and start making your way to the door. He may then come down further.

If you agree on a price but you still think it should be lower there are two techniques available.

Technique C:

If you have bargained him down to the equivalent of say $22 you then go to a pocket and extract exactly $20 which you count out slowly. Because you are short, you mention that you must go back to the hotel to get more. Rather than lose a sale he should accept $20.

BARGAINING TIPS (continued)

Technique D:
The second technique after settling on a price in local currency is to ask what he will sell it to you for if you pay in hard currency such as U.S. dollars. His favourable exchange rate could reduce the real cost even further.

Before going shopping for expensive items such as carpets, jewelry or intricate carvings, visit city stores to establish prices and quality.

Street sellers abound in many cities frequented by tourists and can be quite persistent. If you do not want what they have, do not say it is too small, too big, the wrong colour, or too expensive because they will produce an alternative. Simply say, "I have one." If you learn to say "No thank you" in their own language, use it. These two methods usually work.

If they persist, take the object they are offering and place it on the ground, then walk away. This method has never been known to fail in getting across the message that you are not buying.

Do remember, however, that these people must be respected. They are doing a difficult job for usually little reward. Do not be rude to them; you are a guest in their country.

GLOSSARY of TERMS

Aurora borealis: Also called the Northern Lights, this is a phenomenon in north polar regions when the sky is illuminated with many–coloured streamers or waves of light. It is thought to be caused by the capture of charged particles from solar wind by the Earth's magnetic field. A similar phenomenon occurs in the southern hemisphere called aurora australis.

Blizzard: A combination of snow and strong winds.

Chinook: A warm wind that blows from the Pacific and descends the eastern slopes of the Rocky Mountains, raising the temperature and melting the snow in winter and spring (December to May).

Cyclone: A stormy, destructive mass of air that revolves rapidly around a calm centre as it moves forward.

Dog days: The Northern Hemisphere's hot, sultry period between mid–July and September.

El Niño: Many weather patterns are upset by the irregular occurrence of El Niño, the warm ocean current from the western Pacific that warms the central and eastern Pacific Ocean. It appears unexpectedly off the Peruvian coast every few years. Because it appears around Christmas it has been dubbed El Niño, 'The Boy Child' or 'The Christ Child.' Weather far beyond Peru is affected. The results include floods, droughts, tropical storms, ice–storms and extreme temperature fluctuations in different parts of the world.

Flash flood: When a thunderstorm drops a heavy rainfall in a small area in a very short time, the rapid rise of water could quickly flood an area.

Föhn: A warm, dry wind that blows from the Mediterranean Sea. As it descends a mountainside it can melt snow quickly.

Global warming: See page 8.

Gulf Stream: A warm ocean current in the North Atlantic Ocean. It flows from the Gulf of Mexico through the Straits of Florida, northeast along the U.S. coast, then east towards Europe where it is influential in keeping coastal temperatures mild from Britain to Norway.

Haboob: A powerful wind that picks up sand and dust from the desert. It often precedes a rainstorm which will then clear the air of sand and dust. The term is common to Sudan.

Harmattan: A dry, dust–laden wind that blows from the Sahara across West Africa. It blows during the dry season, usually November to February. When it reaches the humid Gulf of Guinea its dryness is refreshing. The skies of most West African countries are grey with dust at this time and remain so until the coming of the rains, about May.

Hurricane: A violent, stormy cyclone of thunder and heavy rains that originates in the Caribbean Sea or the Gulf of Mexico and travels north, northeast or northwest.

GLOSSARY of TERMS (continued)

Humidity and Relative humidity: When it is humid there is water vapour, or moisture, in the air. The hotter the air the more water vapour it can hold. Relative humidity is the ratio of the amount of water vapour in the air at a given temperature to the maximum capacity which could exist at that temperature. In this book, the ratio is expressed as a percentage. Thus, a relative humidity of 100 percent means the vapour content of the air at a given temperature has reached maximum capacity at that temperature.

When the percentage ratio of relative humidity is high, body perspiration is slow to evaporate and clothing is slow to dry. Conversely, when the percentage is low, evaporation is faster and clothes dry quicker.

Khamsin: A hot, dry wind that blows from the Sahara into Egypt and the Middle East from March through May. It brings heat and dust and makes the sky hazy.

Land breeze: This breeze blows at night from the land to the sea or onto a lake. It occurs when the air temperature over water is warmer than that over land.

La Niña: Spanish for 'The Girl Child' refers to extensive cooling of the central and eastern Pacific Ocean. It also disrupts weather patterns.

Mistral: A cold, dry wind from the north that blows in squalls through the Rhône Valley of southern France towards the Mediterranean coast. It may blow at any time of year.

Monsoon rains: The heavy rains brought by winds from the southwest that fall on the Indian sub–continent and other regions of southeast Asia.

Monsoon wind: A seasonal wind of the Indian Ocean and southeast Asia. Between April and October it blows from the southwest, predominantly across the Indian Ocean, bringing heavy rain to the Indian sub–continent and southeast Asia. For the rest of the year it reverses, blowing from the northeast, across land, bringing a dry season.

Ozone layer: See page 8.

Sea breeze: This breeze blows in the daytime from the sea to land. It occurs when the air temperature over the land is warmer than that over the sea.

Sirocco (also Scirocco): A wind that originates in the Sahara as a dry, dusty wind. It blows north over the Mediterranean Sea and captures moisture and is humid by the time it reaches Greece, Italy and the Mediterranean islands.

Soroche: Thin air at high elevations can bring on "soroche," altitude sickness, which leaves a person with nausea and shortness of breath. People with heart or lung problems should be aware of this.

Tornado: An extremely violent and destructive rotating column of air. It moves forward as a whirling funnel extending down from the mass of dark, cumulonimbus cloud.

GLOSSARY of TERMS (continued)

Tradewinds: Consistent systems of winds that blow over the oceans in the tropics. In the northern hemisphere they blow towards the equator from the northeast hence they are the northeast tradewinds and, in the southern hemisphere, they blow towards the equator from the southeast (the southeast trades).

Transitional month: This is a month between seasons when the weather is a mix of the preceding month and the following month.

Typhoon: An intense tropical storm or cyclone that occurs in the western Pacific or the China Sea.

Wind direction: A wind is named for the direction from which it blows.

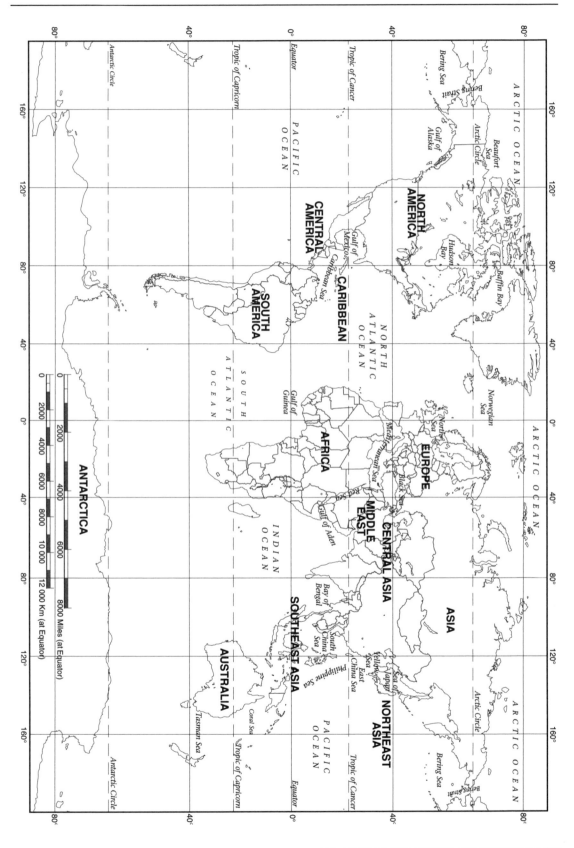

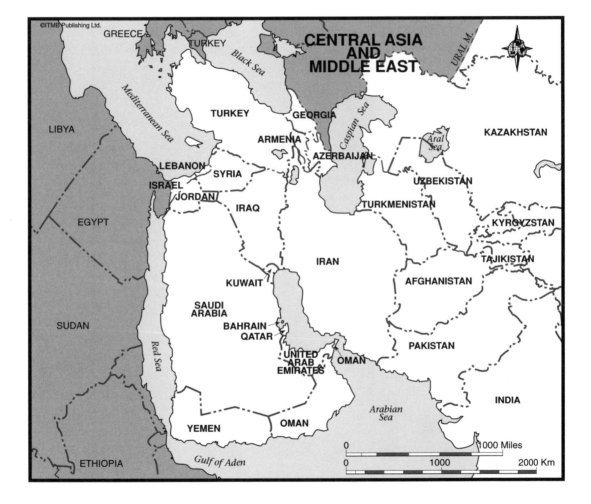

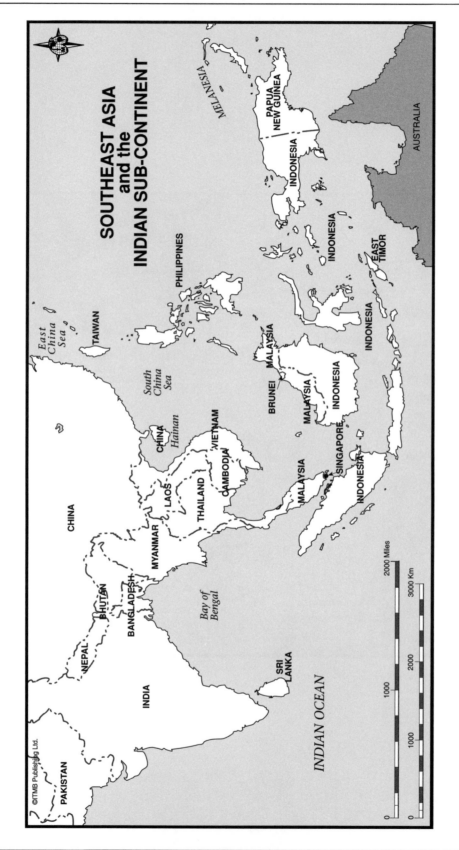

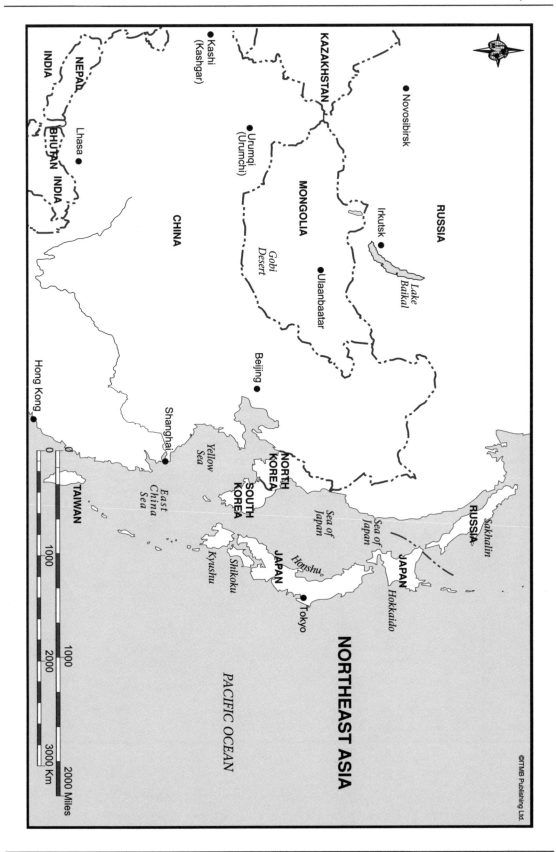

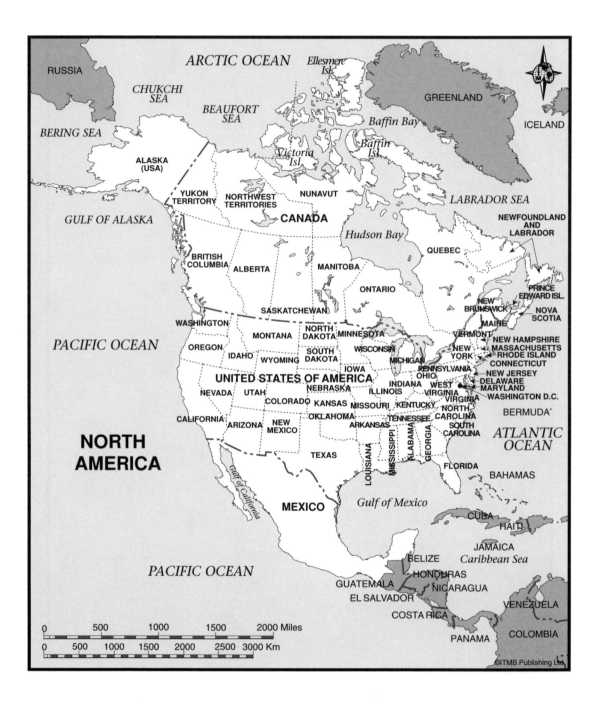

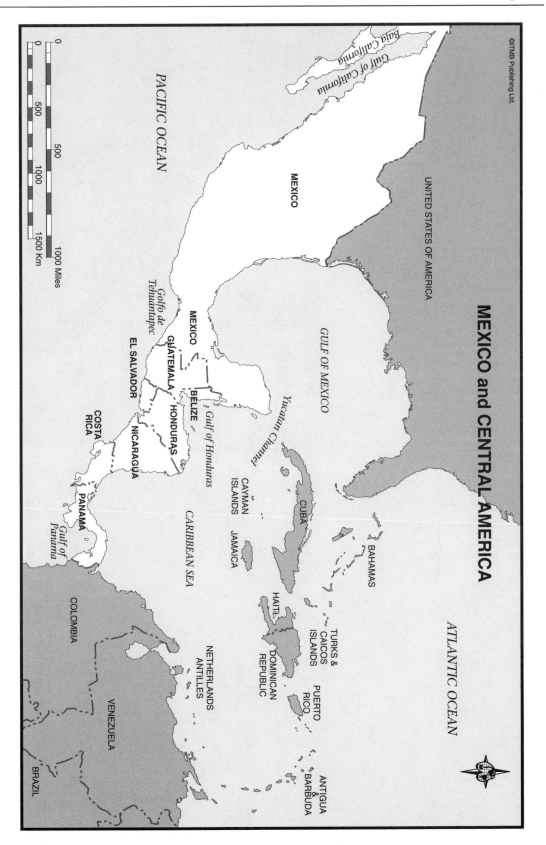

MEXICO and CENTRAL AMERICA

UNITED STATES OF AMERICA

PACIFIC OCEAN

MEXICO

Baja California

Gulf of California

©ITMB Publishing Ltd.

0
500
1000
1500 Km

0
500
1000 Miles

GULF OF MEXICO

MEXICO

GUATEMALA

BELIZE

EL SALVADOR

HONDURAS

NICARAGUA

COSTA RICA

PANAMA

Golfo de Tehuántepec

Gulf of Honduras

Gulf of Panama

Yucatan Channel

CARIBBEAN SEA

CAYMAN ISLANDS

JAMAICA

CUBA

BAHAMAS

HAITI

TURKS & CAICOS ISLANDS

DOMINICAN REPUBLIC

PUERTO RICO

NETHERLANDS ANTILLES

ANTIGUA & BARBUDA

ATLANTIC OCEAN

COLOMBIA

VENEZUELA

BRAZIL

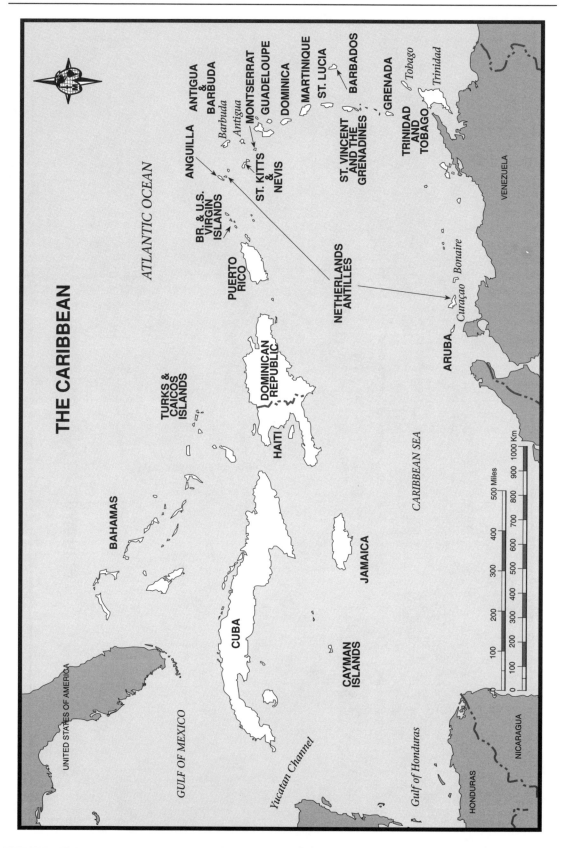

THE CARIBBEAN

UNITED STATES OF AMERICA

GULF OF MEXICO

ATLANTIC OCEAN

BAHAMAS

TURKS & CAICOS ISLANDS

CUBA

Yucatan Channel

CAYMAN ISLANDS

JAMAICA

HAITI

DOMINICAN REPUBLIC

PUERTO RICO

BR. & U.S. VIRGIN ISLANDS

ANGUILLA

ANTIGUA & BARBUDA

Barbuda

Antigua

ST. KITTS & NEVIS

MONTSERRAT

GUADELOUPE

DOMINICA

MARTINIQUE

ST. LUCIA

BARBADOS

ST. VINCENT AND THE GRENADINES

GRENADA

Tobago

Trinidad

TRINIDAD AND TOBAGO

NETHERLANDS ANTILLES

Curaçao

Bonaire

ARUBA

VENEZUELA

CARIBBEAN SEA

Gulf of Honduras

NICARAGUA

HONDURAS

500 Miles

1000 Km

0   100   200   300   400   500   600   700   800   900

0   100   200   300   400   500

CARIBBEAN SEA

COSTA
RICA
PANAMA

NETHERLANDS
ANTILLES

TRINIDAD
& TOBAGO

Gulf of
Panama

VENEZUELA

GUYANA   SURINAME

FRENCH GUIANA

COLOMBIA

ATLANTIC OCEAN

ECUADOR

BRAZIL

PERU

BOLIVIA

PARAGUAY

CHILE

PACIFIC OCEAN

ATLANTIC OCEAN

ARGENTINA

URUGUAY

SOUTH AMERICA

FALKLAND
ISLANDS
(U.K.)

Strait of Magellan

| 0 | 500 | 1000 | 1500 | 2000 Miles |

| 0 | 500 | 1000 | 1500 | 2000 | 2500 | 3000 Km |

©ITMB Publishing Ltd.

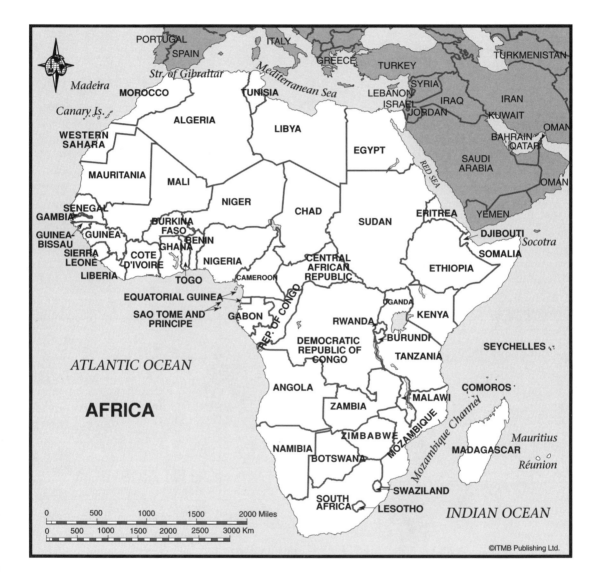

AFGHANISTAN
Official Name: Islamic State of Afghanistan

Capital: Kabul
Languages: Pashto, Dari, Turkic languages

Afghanistan is a relatively dry country. About three–fourths consists of mountainous uplands. The lowlands contain river valleys and desert.

Best time: April and May, and September and October.

December to February: Winter. Cold, especially in the north. Light rains.
March to May: Spring. Mild, light rains.
June to August: Summer. Dry, hot. Strong winds, 180 km/h (110 mph), can blow June to September.
September to November: Autumn. Mild.
Rains: Light rains October to April. Negligible rain falls June to October.

Kabul, Afghanistan: Altitude 1827m (5994ft)

	Jan	Feb	Mar	Apr	May	Jun
Sunrise ºC(ºF)	–7(19)	–6(21)	1(33)	6(42)	9(48)	12(53)
Mid–afternoon ºC(ºF)	5(41)	6(42)	13(55)	19(66)	24(75)	30(86)
Days with precipitation	2	3	7	6	2	1
Precipitation mm	34	60	68	72	23	1
Precipitation inches	1.3	2.4	2.7	2.8	0.9	0.04
Daily hours of sunshine	6	6	7	8	10	12

	Jul	Aug	Sep	Oct	Nov	Dec
Sunrise ºC(ºF)	15(59)	14(57)	9(48)	4(39)	–1(30)	–5(23)
Mid–afternoon ºC(ºF)	32(89)	32(89)	29(84)	22(72)	15(59)	8(46)
Days with precipitation	1	0	0	1	2	1
Precipitation mm	6	2	2	4	19	22
Precipitation inches	0.2	0.08	0.08	0.1	0.7	0.9
Daily hours of sunshine	11	11	10	9	8	6

ALBANIA

Official Name: Republic of Albania

Capital: Tirana
Languages: Albanian, Greek

Most of Albania is mountainous but it has a broad belt of coastal lowlands interspersed with hilly ridges.

Best time: June to September.

There are two regions: the coast and the hilly interior.
June to September: Warm months. Sunny, warm and humid on the coast. Sea breezes temper the coastal heat. Thunderstorms occur inland and on the coast, but it is mostly dry. Ten hours of sunshine daily. Average afternoon temperature is 30°C (86°F).
October and November, and April and May: Cool months. Mild, rainy. Afternoon average, 20°C (68°F).
December to March: Cold months. Heavy rains along coast. Rain and snow in interior mountains.

Tirana, Albania: Altitude 89m (292ft)

	Jan	Feb	Mar	Apr	May	Jun
Sunrise ºC(ºF)	2(35)	3(37)	4(39)	8(46)	12(53)	16(60)
Mid–afternoon ºC(ºF)	12(53)	13(55)	16(60)	19(66)	24(75)	28(82)
Days with precipitation	13	13	14	13	12	7
Precipitation mm	135	152	128	117	122	86
Precipitation inches	5.3	6.0	5.0	4.6	4.8	3.4
Daily hours of sunshine	4	4	5	7	8	10

	Jul	Aug	Sep	Oct	Nov	Dec
Sunrise ºC(ºF)	17(62)	17(62)	14(57)	10(50)	6(42)	3(37)
Mid–afternoon ºC(ºF)	31(87)	31(87)	27(80)	22(72)	12(53)	13(55)
Days with precipitation	5	4	6	9	16	16
Precipitation mm	32	32	60	105	211	173
Precipitation inches	1.3	1.3	2.4	4.1	8.3	6.8
Daily hours of sunshine	11	11	9	7	3	2

ALGERIA

Official Name: Democratic and Popular Republic of
Algeria

Capital: Algiers
Languages: Arabic, French, Berber

More than 90 percent of Algeria is desert but there is an
arable hilly section extending 80 to 200km (50 to 120
miles) inland from the Mediterranean coast.

**Best time: March and April, and October and
November.**
There are three regions: the coast, the Atlas Mountains in
the north, and the desert.
March and April: Spring, and **October and November:** Autumn. Coast is warm; average afternoon
temperature, 20°C (68°F). Six to 7 hours of sunshine daily. On coast, expect an average of seven rainy
days per month. In mountains and desert: negligible rain.
June to September: Summer. Hot and humid in coastal region. Afternoon temperatures range from 27
to 32°C (80 to 89°F). Summer in the desert is dry and hot in daytime, 40°C (104°F), but cold at night,
5°C (40°F), with frequent cold winds. Hot, dry winds (the sirocco, also called the chehili) bring swirls
of dust from the Sahara in summer (July and August). The coast is affected for only about 20 days.
December to February: Winter. Coast is mild. Afternoon average, 15°C (59°F). Expect 5 hours
of sunshine per day. Main rainy season on coast is November to February with average of 11 rainy
days per month. Saharan Atlas mountains receive snow. Desert is virtually rainless with an afternoon
average of 21°C (70°F).

Recreational activity: In the Hoggar Mountains in southern Algeria, climbing is possible from
October to March.
The best time to travel in the Sahara is October and November.

Algiers, Algeria: Altitude 59m (194ft)

	Jan	Feb	Mar	Apr	May	Jun
Sunrise °C(°F)	9(48)	10(50)	11(51)	13(55)	15(59)	18(65)
Mid–afternoon °C(°F)	15(59)	16(61)	18(65)	20(68)	23(73)	26(78)
Days with precipitation	11	9	9	5	5	2
Precipitation mm	112	84	74	41	46	15
Precipitation inches	4.4	3.3	2.9	1.6	1.8	0.6
Daily hours of sunshine	5	6	7	7	8	9

	Jul	Aug	Sep	Oct	Nov	Dec
Sunrise °C(°F)	21(69)	22(71)	20(68)	17(63)	13(55)	11(51)
Mid–afternoon °C(°F)	28(83)	29(85)	27(80)	23(74)	19(66)	16(61)
Days with precipitation	1	1	4	7	11	12
Precipitation mm	0	5	41	79	130	137
Precipitation inches	0	0.2	1.6	3.1	5.1	5.4
Daily hours of sunshine	10	10	8	6	5	4

AMERICAN SAMOA
Official Name: Territory of American Samoa
(Dependent Territory of the U.S.A.)

Capital: Pago Pago (pronounced Pango Pango)
Languages: Samoan and English

Most of the islands are volcanic. Tutuila, on which
Pago Pago is situated, is the largest island with densely
forested, rugged, mountainous terrain.

**Good time to visit: April to November, with June and
July being the best.** (Cooler.)

April to November: Temperate season. Warm, humid,
but tempered by cool southeast tradewinds.
December to March or April: Wet season. Hot, humid. Cyclones may occur.
Sunshine throughout the year averages 7 hours per day.
Rain: When it occurs, usually comes late afternoon, and humidity increases.

Pago Pago, American Samoa: Altitude 3m (10ft)

	Jan	Feb	Mar	Apr	May	Jun
Sunrise ºC(ºF)	23(74)	23(74)	23(74)	23(74)	22(71)	22(71)
Mid–afternoon ºC(ºF)	33(91)	33(91)	33(91)	33(91)	32(89)	31(88)
Precipitation mm	297	339	332	350	271	230
Precipitation inches	11.7	13.3	13.1	13.7	10.7	9.1

	Jul	Aug	Sep	Oct	Nov	Dec
Sunrise ºC(ºF)	21(70)	21(70)	22(71)	22(71)	23(73)	23(73)
Mid–afternoon ºC(ºF)	31(88)	31(88)	31(88)	32(89)	32(89)	32(90)
Precipitation mm	200	201	146	331	253	377
Precipitation inches	7.9	7.9	5.7	13.1	10.0	14.8

ANDORRA
Official Name: Principality of Andorra

Capital: Andorra la Vella
Languages: Catalan, French, Spanish

Andorra is in a valley encircled by high peaks of the
Pyrenees mountains.

Best time: June to August.

June to August: Summer. Cool to warm, reasonably
dry; afternoon temperature, 25ºC (77ºF). The days from
May to September are tempered by cool mountain air.
Evenings can become cold.

December to February: Winter. Cold, reasonably dry; afternoon temperature, 6°C (43°F). The days from mid–November to May are cold with snow.

Recreational activity: Skiing from November to May.

ANGOLA

Official Name: People's Republic of Angola

Capital: Luanda
Languages: Portuguese, Bantu languages

There are two main regions: coastal plains, and inland hills. The small enclave of Cabinda also belongs to Angola. It is situated on the coast between Congo Republic and Congo Democratic Republic.

Best time: June to September.

April to September: Dry season. Coast is cooled by the cold Benguela current from the south. Average afternoon temperature on coast, 23°C (74°F).
October to early May: Wet season. About 4 rainy days per month around Luanda. Afternoon temperature averages 29°C (85°F).
Inland hills' temperatures are 2°C (4°F) lower than the coast because of their elevation.

Luanda, Angola: Altitude 70m (230ft)

	Jan	Feb	Mar	Apr	May	Jun
Sunrise °C(°F)	24(75)	25(77)	25(77)	24(75)	23(73)	20(68)
Mid–afternoon °C(°F)	30(86)	30(86)	31(87)	30(86)	29(84)	26(78)
Days with precipitation	3	3	6	8	2	0
Precipitation mm	25	36	76	117	13	0
Precipitation inches	1.0	1.4	3.0	4.6	0.5	0
Daily hours of sunshine	7	7	7	6	7	7

	Jul	Aug	Sep	Oct	Nov	Dec
Sunrise °C(°F)	19(66)	19(66)	20(68)	22(72)	23(73)	23(73)
Mid–afternoon °C(°F)	24(76)	24(76)	25(77)	27(80)	28(82)	29(84)
Days with precipitation	0	0	1	2	4	3
Precipitation mm	0	0	3	5	28	20
Precipitation inches	0	0	0.1	0.2	1.1	0.8
Daily hours of sunshine	5	5	5	5	6	6

ANGUILLA
Official Name: Anguilla (pronounced An–gwi–la)
(Dependent Territory of the United Kingdom)

Capital: The Valley
Language: English

The island's interior is flat and dry with scrub and salt pans. It is ringed by sandy beaches of white coral.

Best time: January to May.
Peak season for tourism is January and February.

January to March: Winter. Dry season.
April to September: Summer. Wet season.
October to December can also have rain. Humidity is higher than in the dry season.
Sunshine: Expect 8 hours per day throughout year.
Tradewinds: The northeast tradewinds keep the islands relatively cool, between 23 and 29°C (73 and 84°F).
Hurricanes: Possible, June to October.

Note: See under Caribbean Islands for general weather information.

The Valley, Anguilla: Altitude 9m (30ft)

	Jan	Feb	Mar	Apr	May	Jun
Sunrise °C(°F)	23(75)	23(75)	23(75)	25(77)	25(77)	26(80)
Mid–afternoon °C(°F)	28(83)	28(83)	28(83)	28(84)	30(86)	31(88)
Days with precipitation	11	9	8	8	11	10
Precipitation mm	70	49	49	79	90	70
Precipitation inches	2.9	1.9	1.9	3.1	3.6	2.8

	Jul	Aug	Sep	Oct	Nov	Dec
Sunrise °C(°F)	26(80)	26(80)	26(80)	26(80)	25(78)	24(76)
Mid–afternoon °C(°F)	31(89)	31(88)	31(88)	30(87)	29(85)	28(83)
Days with precipitation	12	14	13	14	14	13
Precipitation mm	80	110	110	100	110	90
Precipitation inches	3.3	4.3	4.3	3.9	4.3	3.6

ANTARCTICA

No capital.
No country has sovereignty over Antarctica.

Best time: December and January.

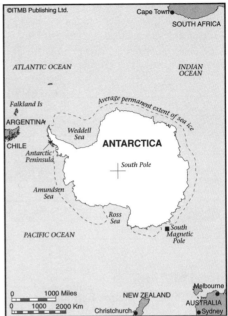

December and January: Summer. Warmer weather.
Summer temperatures on the Antarctic Peninsula: Average
daily low is –4°C (25°F); average daily high is 7°C
(45°F). Windchill is a factor. Winds may blow suddenly,
carrying snow to produce a blizzard–like effect. Daylight
hours in summer: up to 20 hours. Penguins' eggs are
hatching; chicks are being fed.
February and March: Late part of summer season. Adult
penguins are ashore, molting. Penguin chicks are fledging.
This is a good time for whale watching. Numbers peak
between January and April.
Mid–March to September: Winter. No tourism allowed.
Sunless days. Darkness lasts 4 months, May to August.
Temperature drops to below –40°C (–40°F). Pack ice
expands around continent.
October and November: Early part of summer season. Penguins, and other birds, are courting and
mating. The pack ice is breaking up.

Access: Cruise ships from Ushuaia, Argentina visit Antarctic Peninsula for shore excursions.
There are no docks in Antarctica. To transfer passengers for shore excursions inflatable rubber rafts
(Zodiacs) are used.

ANTIGUA and BARBUDA

Official Name: Antigua and Barbuda
(Independent nation; formerly a British possession)

Capital: Saint John's
Languages: English, local dialects

Antigua, pronounced Anteega, has hills of volcanic origin
in the southwest section. The rest of the island has dry,
scrubby, undulating plains. Barbuda, pronounced Bar–
bew–da, is a relatively flat coral island.

Best time: January to May.
Peak season for tourism is January and February. These
islands are generally dry and pleasant all year. Hottest
months are September and October, 30°C (86°F).

January to March: Winter. Dry season.
April to September: Summer. Wet season.
October to December: Some rain. Humidity is higher
than in the dry season.

Rain: Annual rainfall is 1070mm (42 inches). Most falls in summer, April to September.
Sunshine: Expect 8 hours per day throughout the year.
Hurricanes: Possible, June to October.
Note: See under Caribbean Islands for general weather information.
 St John's, Antigua: Altitude 19m (62ft)

	Jan	Feb	Mar	Apr	May	Jun
Sunrise ºC(ºF)	22(72)	22(72)	22(72)	23(74)	24(75)	25(77)
Mid–afternoon ºC(ºF)	27(81)	27(81)	28(82)	28(82)	29(84)	29(85)
Days with precipitation	7	4	3	4	6	7

	Jul	Aug	Sep	Oct	Nov	Dec
Sunrise ºC(ºF)	25(77)	25(77)	24(76)	24(75)	24(75)	23(73)
Mid–afternoon ºC(ºF)	30(86)	30(86)	30(86)	30(86)	29(84)	28(83)
Days with precipitation	7	9	7	9	8	7

ARGENTINA
Official Name: Argentine Republic

Capital: Buenos Aires
Languages: Spanish, English, Italian, German

The Andes mountain range in the west forms a natural border between Argentina and Chile. East of the mountains the terrain consists of flat or rolling plains.

Good months for the whole country: October to April. Best months are October, November and April because December to March can be uncomfortably humid. However, because there is little rain Argentina is a year–round destination.

We have divided the weather into four regions. Refer to map for corresponding numbers.
1. Pampas region (includes Buenos Aires).
October and November: Pleasant afternoon temperatures, 20 to 26ºC (69 to 79ºF). Six to 8 hours of sunshine daily. Light rains. (Rains are spaced fairly evenly throughout the year.)
December to February: Summer. Hot season. The coast is moderated by cold ocean currents. Average afternoon temperature in Buenos Aires is 29ºC (84ºF). Expect 9 hours of sunshine daily. This season receives sudden, heavy downpours on just a few days. Humidity increases after the rain.
March and April: Pleasant afternoon temperatures, 20 to 26ºC (69 to 79ºF). Six to 8 hours of sunshine daily. Light rains. (Rains are spaced fairly evenly throughout the year.)
June to August: Winter. Afternoon temperatures are a mild 14ºC (57ºF). Expect 4 hours of sunshine daily. Rain is light, and diminishes the farther westward (inland) you go.

Buenos Aires, Argentina: Altitude 25m (82ft)

	Jan	Feb	Mar	Apr	May	Jun
Sunrise ºC(ºF)	20(68)	19(67)	17(63)	13(55)	10(50)	8(46)
Mid–afternoon ºC(ºF)	30(86)	29(84)	26(79)	23(73)	19(67)	16(61)
Days with precipitation	7	6	7	8	7	7
Precipitation mm	119	118	134	97	74	63
Precipitation inches	4.7	4.6	5.3	3.8	2.9	2.5
Daily hours of sunshine	9	9	7	7	6	4

	Jul	Aug	Sep	Oct	Nov	Dec
Sunrise ºC(ºF)	8(46)	8(46)	10(50)	13(55)	15(59)	18(64)
Mid–afternoon ºC(ºF)	15(59)	17(62)	19(66)	22(71)	25(77)	28(82)
Days with precipitation	8	9	8	9	9	8
Precipitation mm	66	70	73	119	109	105
Precipitation inches	2.6	2.8	2.9	4.7	4.3	4.1
Daily hours of sunshine	5	6	6	7	8	9

2. Patagonia region (includes Trelew, Sarmiento, Ushuaia).
October to April: Cool, cloudy, dry.
May to September: Cold. Although there are snowfalls, the influence of the ocean reduces the severity of winter. Temperatures rarely average less than 0ºC (32ºF), even in the south in mid–winter. In the south, e.g. Ushuaia, violent thunderstorms occur in winter, June to August.

Natural attractions:
1. Peninsula Valdes: Habitat of sea elephants which breed August to October and molt in December. Best time to visit: September and October. Right whales can be seen. They arrive in July and depart in November.
2. Punta Loma: Habitat of seals and sea lions. Best time: September and October.
3. Punta Tombo: Penguin habitat of thousands. See them from arrival time, September, to departure time, April. The young take to the water December to January.

Trelew, Argentina: Altitude 43m (141ft)

	Jan	Feb	Mar	Apr	May	Jun
Sunrise ºC(ºF)	14(57)	13(55)	11(51)	7(44)	4(39)	1(33)
Mid–afternoon ºC(ºF)	30(86)	28(82)	25(77)	21(69)	16(60)	12(53)
Precipitation mm	12	17	19	17	20	14
Precipitation inches	0.5	0.7	0.7	0.7	0.8	0.6
Daily hours of sunshine	10	10	8	7	5	5

	Jul	Aug	Sep	Oct	Nov	Dec
Sunrise ºC(ºF)	1(33)	2(35)	4(39)	7(44)	10(50)	13(55)
Mid–afternoon ºC(ºF)	12(53)	15(59)	18(64)	21(69)	25(77)	27(81)
Precipitation mm	19	14	11	17	14	14
Precipitation inches	0.7	0.6	0.4	0.7	0.6	0.6
Daily hours of sunshine	4	6	7	8	9	10

3. Western Argentina region (includes Mendoza).
October to April: Afternoon temperatures range from a mild 22°C (72°F) to a hot 30°C (86°F).
January is hottest. Expect 8 to 10 hours of sunshine daily. Rain is light, but frequent. Snow melts on
the mountains from November to February.
May to September: Cool. Afternoons are 10 to 18°C (50 to 65°F). Expect 6 to 7 hours of sunshine
daily. Light snow falls on the Andes peaks. Drought can occur in the lowlands.

Recreational activity: Skiing is possible, July to October, at San Carlos de Bariloche, which is known
locally as Bariloche.

Mendoza, Argentina: Altitude 801m (2628ft)

	Jan	Feb	Mar	Apr	May	Jun
Sunrise °C(°F)	18(64)	17(62)	14(57)	10(50)	6(42)	2(35)
Mid–afternoon °C(°F)	32(89)	31(87)	27(80)	24(76)	19(66)	16(61)
Days with precipitation	10	9	8	7	6	6
Precipitation mm	36	34	27	13	6	4
Precipitation inches	1.4	1.3	1.1	0.5	0.2	0.1
Daily hours of sunshine	8	7	7	7	6	6

	Jul	Aug	Sep	Oct	Nov	Dec
Sunrise °C(°F)	2(35)	4(40)	6(42)	11(51)	14(57)	17(62)
Mid–afternoon °C(°F)	15(59)	19(67)	21(69)	26(78)	29(85)	32(89)
Days with precipitation	6	7	8	8	10	10
Precipitation mm	7	3	8	11	16	24
Precipitation inches	0.3	0.1	0.3	0.4	0.6	0.9
Daily hours of sunshine	6	6	7	8	8	8

4. Northeastern region (includes Santiago del Estero, and Iguassu Falls).
October to April: Hot. Afternoon temperatures peak in January, 36°C (97°F). Expect 6 to 8 hours of
sunshine daily. Most rain falls in summer, particularly December to March, causing uncomfortable
humidity.
May to September: Dry and mild. Afternoon temperatures range 20 to 27°C (70 to 80°F). Expect 5 to
7 hours of sunshine daily.

Natural attraction:
Iguassu Falls (Cataratas del Iguazú) on the Argentina–Brazil border: Has 275 falls, frontage of 2.5km
(1.5 miles), 65m (200ft) high. Most of the falls are on the Argentinean side where there are many
catwalks.
Best months are August to November. Flood months are May to July when some catwalks are not
usable. Possible months to avoid are December to March (extremely hot) and July (local holidays).
Because of the light, photography is best from the Brazilian side in the morning and the Argentinean
side in the afternoon.

Santiago del Estero, Argentina: Altitude 199m (653ft)

	Jan	Feb	Mar	Apr	May	Jun
Sunrise ºC(ºF)	20(68)	20(68)	18(64)	14(57)	11(51)	7(44)
Mid–afternoon ºC(ºF)	34(94)	33(92)	30(86)	27(80)	24(75)	20(68)
Days with precipitation	6	6	6	4	2	2
Precipitation mm	136	111	83	37	17	6
Precipitation inches	5.4	4.4	3.3	1.5	0.7	0.2
Daily hours of sunshine	7	7	6	5	5	4

	Jul	Aug	Sep	Oct	Nov	Dec
Sunrise ºC(ºF)	6(42)	7(44)	10(50)	15(59)	18(64)	20(68)
Mid–afternoon ºC(ºF)	21(69)	24(75)	27(80)	30(86)	32(89)	34(93)
Days with precipitation	1	1	2	4	5	5
Precipitation mm	4	5	14	33	68	96
Precipitation inches	0.1	0.2	0.6	1.3	2.7	3.8
Daily hours of sunshine	6	7	7	7	7	8

ARMENIA

Official Name: Republic of Armenia

Capital: Yerevan
Languages: Armenian, Russian

Armenia is mountainous and has a high plateau. About half of the country is above 2000m (6500ft). Mountains block the moderating influence of the Mediterranean Sea and the Black Sea. This results in wide temperature variations between summer and winter.

Best time: May and June, and September and October. July and August are also good, but they are hotter.

May and June: Warm, humid and rainy.
July and August: Dry, sunny and hot, about 35ºC (95ºF) in the afternoons.
September and October: Warm, humid and mostly dry.
November to April: Cool in November and April but cold and snowy with freezing temperatures on the plateau and mountains from December to March. Expect light rain.

Yerevan, Armenia: Altitude 907m (2975ft)

	Jan	Feb	Mar	Apr	May	Jun
Sunrise °C(°F)	−9(15)	−8(18)	−1(30)	6(42)	10(50)	14(57)
Mid–afternoon °C(°F)	−2(29)	1(34)	10(50)	19(66)	24(76)	31(87)
Days with precipitation	5	5	6	7	8	5
Precipitation mm	21	24	32	37	43	21
Precipitation inches	0.8	0.9	1.3	1.5	1.7	0.8
Daily hours of sunshine	3	4	5	6	8	10

	Jul	Aug	Sep	Oct	Nov	Dec
Sunrise °C(°F)	17(63)	18(64)	13(55)	7(45)	1(34)	−3(26)
Mid–afternoon °C(°F)	34(93)	33(92)	28(83)	21(69)	10(50)	3(38)
Days with precipitation	2	2	2	5	4	5
Precipitation mm	10	7	10	27	22	23
Precipitation inches	0.4	0.3	0.4	1.1	0.9	0.9
Daily hours of sunshine	11	11	9	7	5	3

ARUBA

Official Name: Aruba
(Dependent Territory of the Netherlands)

Capital: Oranjestad
Languages: Dutch is official. Papiamento is the colloquial tongue. English and Spanish are widely understood.

This rather barren, flat, rocky island is the top of a submerged mountain linked to the Andes chain.

Best time: All year round but the drier months, February to October, are preferable.

February to October: Driest are April and May. Warmest are August and September.
November to January: Wet season. Expect 16 rainy days each month.
Sunshine: Expect 8 hours daily throughout the year.
Winds: Pleasant, cooling, northeasterly tradewinds blow all year.
Hurricanes: The island is outside the hurricane belt.

For a Weather Table see under Netherlands Antilles – Curaçao.

ASCENSION ISLAND

(A dependency of St Helena, a British possession)
Main town: Georgetown
Language: English

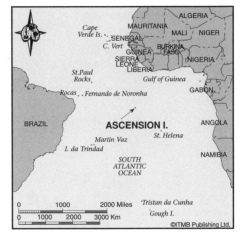

Ascension Island is a remote mountain peak that rises to
859m (2817 ft) above the South Atlantic Ocean. It is dry,
dusty and almost barren and has an area of 88 sq km (34
sq miles).

Best time: Any time of year.

Georgetown, located on the leeside of the mountain
mass, is virtually rainless throughout the year. Rain
falls on the heights of Green Mountain, brought by the
prevailing southeast tradewinds. January to April is the period of slightly heavier rains. The afternoon
temperatures throughout the year are a consistent 30°C (86°F) in Georgetown, but at higher elevations
they drop to 25°C (77°F).

AUSTRALIA

Official Name: Commonwealth of Australia

Capital: Canberra
Language: English

Along the eastern seaboard is a coastal plain about 65km (40 miles) wide. Running parallel to the east
coast is a mountain range that separates the coastal plain from vast inland plains on the western side of
the range. Farther west is a large arid plateau containing deserts and eroded mountain ranges.

Best time for the southern part of Australia, in general terms: September to April.
Best time for the north and centre: May to October.

Seasons: December to February: Summer.
        March to May: Autumn.
        June to August: Winter.
        September to November: Spring.

We have divided the weather into six regions. Refer to map for corresponding numbers.
1. North Queensland (includes Townsville and Cairns) and **Northern Territory** (includes Darwin).
Best time: May to October. (Warm, mostly dry.)

May to October: Dry season. Almost cloudless skies. Cool nights, warm days. Daytime temperatures
range 24 to 31°C (75 to 87°F). This is a good time to visit Cairns for the Great Barrier Reef, and good
for Darwin. May can experience occasional, end–of–wet–season storms.
October is the pre–wet season with occasional storms in the afternoons.
November to April: Wet season. Cyclonic rain. Heaviest, January to March. December to February
daytime temperatures range 30 to 35°C (86 to 96°F). Humidity is high. Cyclones may occur at the
"Top End" of Australia and along the Queensland coast in the wet season, November to April.
Sunshine: Expect 9 to 10 hours per day in the dry season, and 7 in the wet season.

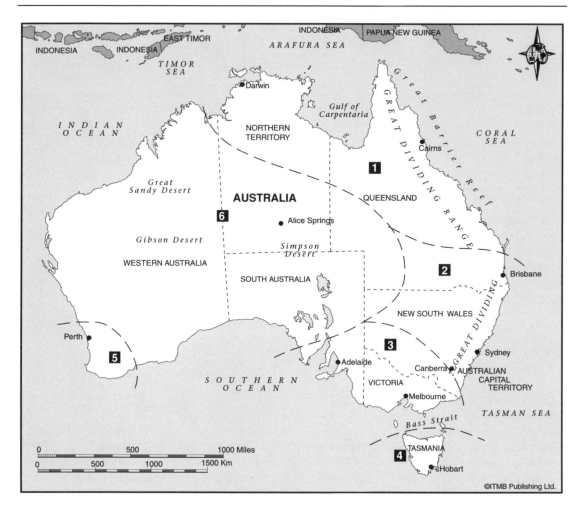

Darwin, Northern Territory: Altitude 30m (98ft)

	Jan	Feb	Mar	Apr	May	Jun
Sunrise ºC(ºF)	25(77)	25(77)	24(75)	24(75)	22(72)	20(68)
Mid–afternoon ºC(ºF)	32(89)	31(87)	32(89)	33(91)	32(89)	31(87)
Days with precipitation	20	18	17	6	1	1
Precipitation mm	437	343	342	85	29	2
Precipitation inches	17.2	13.5	13.5	3.4	1.1	0.08
Daily hours of sunshine	6	6	7	9	9	10

	Jul	Aug	Sep	Oct	Nov	Dec
Sunrise ºC(ºF)	19(67)	21(70)	23(73)	25(77)	25(77)	25(77)
Mid–afternoon ºC(ºF)	30(86)	31(87)	33(91)	33(91)	33(91)	33(91)
Days with precipitation	0	0	2	5	10	15
Precipitation mm	1	8	19	76	131	234
Precipitation inches	0.04	0.3	0.7	3.0	5.2	9.2
Daily hours of sunshine	10	10	10	10	8	7

Townsville, northern Queensland: Altitude 15m (49ft)

	Jan	Feb	Mar	Apr	May	Jun
Sunrise ºC(ºF)	24(76)	24(76)	23(73)	21(70)	18(64)	15(59)
Mid–afternoon ºC(ºF)	31(87)	31(87)	31(87)	29(84)	27(80)	25(77)
Days with precipitation	15	12	10	6	5	4
Precipitation mm	244	232	176	61	41	21
Precipitation inches	9.6	9.1	6.9	2.4	1.6	0.8
Daily hours of sunshine	8	7	7	8	7	8

	Jul	Aug	Sep	Oct	Nov	Dec
Sunrise ºC(ºF)	14(57)	15(59)	17(62)	21(70)	23(73)	24(76)
Mid–afternoon ºC(ºF)	25(77)	26(78)	28(82)	29(84)	31(87)	31(87)
Days with precipitation	3	3	2	4	5	12
Precipitation mm	11	14	10	25	55	148
Precipitation inches	0.4	0.6	0.4	1.0	2.2	5.8
Daily hours of sunshine	8	9	9	10	9	9

2. New South Wales (includes Sydney) and southern Queensland (includes Brisbane). For Canberra see Footnote.
Best time: September to May. (Warm to hot.)

September to May: Sunny. Warm to hot, in the 20s°C (70s°F) in the afternoons. Rain falls, expecially March to May.
June to August: Winter. Cool. Rain. Snow falls in the Snowy Mountains in southern New South Wales where skiing is popular.

Footnote for Canberra in the A.C.T. (Australian Capital Territory).
Best time: September to November (spring) and **March to May** (autumn). Summers (December to February) are very hot, and winters (June to August) are extremely cold.

Brisbane, southern Queensland: Altitude 42m (137ft)

	Jan	Feb	Mar	Apr	May	Jun
Sunrise ºC(ºF)	21(69)	20(68)	19(66)	16(61)	13(56)	11(51)
Mid–afternoon ºC(ºF)	29(85)	29(85)	28(82)	26(79)	23(74)	21(69)
Days with precipitation	13	14	15	12	10	8
Precipitation mm	169	148	140	104	97	74
Precipitation inches	6.7	5.8	5.5	4.1	3.8	2.9
Daily hours of sunshine	8	7	7	7	7	7

	Jul	Aug	Sep	Oct	Nov	Dec
Sunrise ºC(ºF)	9(49)	10(50)	13(55)	16(60)	18(64)	19(67)
Mid–afternoon ºC(ºF)	20(68)	22(71)	24(76)	27(80)	28(82)	29(85)
Days with precipitation	8	7	8	9	10	12
Precipitation mm	68	46	33	105	110	132
Precipitation inches	2.7	1.8	1.3	4.1	4.3	5.2
Daily hours of sunshine	7	8	8	8	8	9

Sydney, New South Wales: Altitude 40m (131ft)

	Jan	Feb	Mar	Apr	May	Jun
Sunrise ºC(ºF)	19(66)	19(66)	18(64)	15(59)	12(54)	10(50)
Mid–afternoon ºC(ºF)	26(78)	26(78)	25(77)	23(73)	20(68)	18(64)
Days with precipitation	14	13	14	14	13	12
Precipitation mm	131	126	164	133	101	140
Precipitation inches	5.2	5.0	6.5	5.2	4.0	5.5
Daily hours of sunshine	7	7	6	6	6	6

	Jul	Aug	Sep	Oct	Nov	Dec
Sunrise ºC(ºF)	8(46)	9(48)	11(51)	14(57)	16(60)	18(64)
Mid–afternoon ºC(ºF)	17(62)	18(64)	20(68)	22(72)	24(75)	26(78)
Days with precipitation	12	11	12	12	12	13
Precipitation mm	56	99	65	88	116	85
Precipitation inches	2.2	3.9	2.6	3.5	4.6	3.4
Daily hours of sunshine	6	7	7	7	8	8

3. Victoria (includes Melbourne) and **South Australia** (includes Adelaide).
Best time: November to March. (Warm to hot.)

November to March: Sunny. Warm to hot, sometimes 38ºC (100ºF), especially in January. Expect light rain every month.
April to October: Cooler months. June to August is the dull winter when most rain falls, much of it as showers and drizzle. Snow falls in the Victorian Alps where skiing is popular, June to August.

Melbourne, Victoria: Altitude 113m (371ft)

	Jan	Feb	Mar	Apr	May	Jun
Sunrise ºC(ºF)	15(59)	15(59)	14(57)	12(53)	9(48)	7(44)
Mid–afternoon ºC(ºF)	26(78)	26(78)	24(75)	20(68)	17(62)	14(57)
Days with precipitation	9	8	9	13	14	16
Precipitation mm	47	46	44	53	68	43
Precipitation inches	1.9	1.8	1.7	2.0	2.7	1.7
Daily hours of sunshine	9	8	7	5	4	3

	Jul	Aug	Sep	Oct	Nov	Dec
Sunrise ºC(ºF)	6(42)	7(44)	8(46)	9(48)	10(50)	12(54)
Mid–afternoon ºC(ºF)	13(56)	15(59)	17(63)	19(67)	22(71)	24(75)
Days with precipitation	17	17	15	14	13	11
Precipitation mm	49	57	53	65	57	58
Precipitation inches	1.9	2.2	2.1	2.6	2.2	2.3
Daily hours of sunshine	4	4	6	6	7	7

Adelaide, South Australia: Altitude 43m (140ft)

	Jan	Feb	Mar	Apr	May	Jun
Sunrise ºC(ºF)	16(60)	16(60)	14(57)	12(53)	10(50)	8(47)
Mid–afternoon ºC(ºF)	28(82)	28(82)	26(78)	22(72)	19(66)	16(61)
Days with precipitation	5	5	5	10	13	15
Precipitation mm	19	20	22	38	57	50
Precipitation inches	0.7	0.8	0.9	1.5	2.2	2.0
Daily hours of sunshine	10	10	9	8	5	5

	Jul	Aug	Sep	Oct	Nov	Dec
Sunrise ºC(ºF)	7(45)	8(46)	9(48)	11(51)	13(55)	14(57)
Mid–afternoon ºC(ºF)	15(59)	16(60)	18(64)	21(70)	24(75)	26(78)
Days with precipitation	16	16	13	10	8	6
Precipitation mm	67	51	41	37	23	25
Precipitation inches	2.6	2.0	1.6	1.5	0.9	1.0
Daily hours of sunshine	5	6	7	8	9	9

4. Tasmania (includes Hobart).
Best time to visit: November to March. (Warm.)

November to March: Sunny and warm but the four seasons may be experienced on the same day. Temperatures may change from say 27ºC (80ºF) to freezing in a matter of hours, or much less. Tasmania is situated in latitudes known for their stormy conditions. Light rains fall in every month. **April to October:** Cool. Light rains with most falling in winter, June to August. Snow falls in the highlands.
Rain falls year–round with most falling on the west coast.

Hobart, east coast of Tasmania: Altitude 57m (187ft)

	Jan	Feb	Mar	Apr	May	Jun
Sunrise ºC(ºF)	12(53)	12(53)	11(51)	10(50)	7(44)	5(41)
Mid–afternoon ºC(ºF)	22(71)	22(71)	20(68)	18(64)	15(59)	13(55)
Days with precipitation	13	10	13	14	14	16
Precipitation mm	41	39	45	44	46	37
Precipitation inches	1.6	1.5	1.8	1.7	1.8	1.5
Daily hours of sunshine	8	7	6	5	4	4

	Jul	Aug	Sep	Oct	Nov	Dec
Sunrise ºC(ºF)	4(40)	5(41)	7(44)	8(46)	10(50)	11(51)
Mid–afternoon ºC(ºF)	12(53)	13(55)	15(59)	17(63)	19(66)	20(68)
Days with precipitation	17	18	17	18	16	14
Precipitation mm	60	60	50	58	53	54
Precipitation inches	2.4	2.4	2.0	2.3	2.1	2.1
Daily hours of sunshine	4	5	6	7	7	7

5. Southwest corner of Western Australia (includes Perth).
Best time: September to April. (Warm to hot.)

September to April: Sunny, dry, warm to hot. Mid–summer (January) can exceed 32°C (90°F). Very little rain falls during these months. Wildflowers bloom August to November, after the winter rains.
May to August: Winter rains. Mild. Coolest month is July, 17°C (63°F) in the afternoons.

Perth, Western Australia: Altitude 60m (197ft)

	Jan	Feb	Mar	Apr	May	Jun
Sunrise °C(°F)	17(63)	17(63)	16(61)	14(57)	12(53)	10(50)
Mid–afternoon °C(°F)	29(85)	29(85)	27(81)	24(76)	21(69)	18(64)
Days with precipitation	3	3	5	8	15	17
Precipitation mm	8	10	20	43	130	180
Precipitation inches	0.3	0.4	0.8	1.7	5.1	7.1
Daily hours of sunshine	10	10	9	7	6	5

	Jul	Aug	Sep	Oct	Nov	Dec
Sunrise °C(°F)	9(48)	9(48)	10(50)	12(53)	14(57)	16(61)
Mid–afternoon °C(°F)	17(63)	18(64)	19(67)	21(70)	24(76)	27(81)
Days with precipitation	19	19	15	12	7	5
Precipitation mm	170	145	86	56	20	13
Precipitation inches	6.7	5.7	3.4	2.2	0.8	0.5
Daily hours of sunshine	5	6	7	8	10	10

6. The Centre (includes Alice Springs).
Best time: May to October. (Warm, mostly dry.)
This is a good time to visit Alice Springs and Uluru (formerly Ayers Rock).

May to September: Cool season. Average afternoon temperatures range 19 to 27°C (67 to 81°F). In the desert "outback," early morning temperatures can be below freezing point. Rainfall is negligible. Humidity is low.
October is a warmer month with a small increase in rainfall, temperature and humidity.
November to April: Hot season. Afternoons average 32 to 36°C (90 to 96°F). Mid–summer (January and February) can be scorchingly hot. Slight increase in rainfall and humidity. Expect 10 hours of sunshine daily.

Alice Springs, Northern Territory: Altitude 547m (1795ft)

	Jan	Feb	Mar	Apr	May	Jun
Sunrise ºC(ºF)	21(70)	21(69)	17(63)	12(54)	8(46)	5(41)
Mid–afternoon ºC(ºF)	36(97)	35(95)	32(90)	28(82)	23(73)	20(68)
Days with precipitation	4	3	3	2	2	2
Precipitation mm	42	37	52	17	18	14
Precipitation inches	1.6	1.5	2.0	0.7	0.7	0.6
Daily hours of sunshine	10	10	10	9	8	9

	Jul	Aug	Sep	Oct	Nov	Dec
Sunrise ºC(ºF)	4(39)	6(43)	9(49)	14(58)	18(64)	20(68)
Mid–afternoon ºC(ºF)	19(67)	22(72)	27(81)	31(88)	34(93)	36(96)
Days with precipitation	1	2	1	3	4	4
Precipitation mm	16	12	11	19	27	36
Precipitation inches	0.6	0.5	0.4	0.7	1.1	1.4
Daily hours of sunshine	9	10	10	10	10	10

AUSTRIA

Official Name: Federal Republic of Austria

Capital: Vienna
Language: German

Austria's terrain is predominently mountainous with most ranges extending in an east–west direction. The east and north regions which are outside the Alps have rolling uplands.

Best time: May to September.

May to September: Sunny, mild, 20 to 25ºC (68 to 77ºF). Rain, which often comes as brief thunderstorms, can fall as many as one day out of three. July and August are the rainiest months.

October to April: Cool to severely cold. Temperatures drop to freezing. Snow falls. On the mountains it can stay all year. Cold winds from the northeast can bring the coldest temperatures. Alpine ski resorts are popular December to March.

Rain: Because of the mountainous terrain, humid winds from the Adriatic Sea and the Atlantic easily condense their vapour, bringing rain all year round.

Föhn wind: During spring (March to May) and autumn (September to November) winds from the Mediterranean blow across the mountains and flow down the northern slopes. This warm dry wind, the föhn, can melt snow quickly, causing avalanches.

Innsbruck, Austria: Altitude 207m (679ft)

	Jan	Feb	Mar	Apr	May	Jun
Sunrise ºC(ºF)	−7(20)	−5(24)	0(32)	4(39)	8(46)	11(52)
Mid–afternoon ºC(ºF)	1(34)	4(40)	11(51)	16(60)	20(68)	24(74)
Days with precipitation	8	7	9	9	11	13
Precipitation mm	46	38	46	59	88	105
Precipitation inches	1.8	1.5	1.8	2.3	3.5	4.1
Daily hours of sunshine	3	4	5	5	6	6

	Jul	Aug	Sep	Oct	Nov	Dec
Sunrise ºC(ºF)	13(55)	12(54)	10(49)	5(40)	0(32)	−4(24)
Mid–afternoon ºC(ºF)	25(77)	24(75)	21(69)	15(58)	8(46)	2(36)
Days with precipitation	14	13	9	7	8	8
Precipitation mm	128	120	76	52	57	49
Precipitation inches	5.0	4.7	3.0	2.0	2.2	1.9
Daily hours of sunshine	7	7	6	5	3	2

Vienna, Austria: Altitude 200m (656ft)

	Jan	Feb	Mar	Apr	May	Jun
Sunrise ºC(ºF)	−4(25)	−3(28)	−1(30)	6(42)	10(50)	14(56)
Mid–afternoon ºC(ºF)	1(34)	3(38)	8(47)	15(58)	19(67)	23(73)
Days with precipitation	8	8	8	8	9	9
Precipitation mm	38	42	41	51	61	74
Precipitation inches	1.5	1.6	1.6	2.0	2.4	2.9
Daily hours of sunshine	2	3	4	6	7	7
Snow mm	330	255	50	0	0	0
Snow inches	13	10	2	0	0	0

	Jul	Aug	Sep	Oct	Nov	Dec
Sunrise ºC(ºF)	15(60)	15(60)	11(53)	7(44)	3(37)	−1(30)
Mid–afternoon ºC(ºF)	25(76)	24(75)	20(68)	14(56)	7(45)	3(37)
Days with precipitation	9	8	7	6	8	8
Precipitation mm	63	58	45	41	50	43
Precipitation inches	2.5	2.3	1.8	1.6	2.0	1.7
Daily hours of sunshine	8	7	6	4	2	2
Snow mm	0	0	0	25	0	101
Snow inches	0	0	0	1	0	4

AZERBAIJAN

Official Name: Azerbaijan Republic

Capital: Baku
Languages: Azeri, Russian, Armenian

Azerbaijan is a mountainous country with peaks rising to 2700m (9000ft). Azerbaijan also includes the Naxçivan (or Nakhichevan) Autonomous Republic which is separated from Azerbaijan–proper by Armenia.

Best time: May and June, and September and October.

June to September: Dry, hot, 30°C (86°F) in the afternoon. This weather applies to Baku on the lowlands along the Caspian Sea and to the Azerbaijan steppe which covers half the country.

November to April or May: Wet and mild but temperature can drop to freezing in January. Mountain temperatures are cooler for longer, especially November to March.

Winds: Baku, located on the Caspian Sea, is in a region that is subject to violent wind gusts coming off the Caspian, from inland regions and from the north.

Baku, Azerbaijan: 17m (56ft) below sea level

	Jan	Feb	Mar	Apr	May	Jun
Sunrise °C(°F)	2(35)	2(35)	4(39)	9(48)	15(59)	20(68)
Mid–afternoon °C(°F)	7(44)	6(42)	10(50)	16(60)	22(72)	27(80)
Days with precipitation	6	6	5	4	3	2
Precipitation mm	21	20	21	18	18	8
Precipitation inches	0.8	0.8	0.8	0.7	0.7	0.3
Daily hours of sunshine	3	3	4	7	8	10

	Jul	Aug	Sep	Oct	Nov	Dec
Sunrise °C(°F)	22(72)	23(73)	19(66)	14(57)	9(48)	5(41)
Mid–afternoon °C(°F)	31(87)	30(86)	26(78)	20(68)	14(57)	10(50)
Days with precipitation	1	2	2	6	6	6
Precipitation mm	2	6	15	25	30	26
Precipitation inches	0.08	0.2	0.6	1.0	1.2	1.0
Daily hours of sunshine	10	9	7	5	3	3

AZORES
(A territory of Portugal)

Capital: Ponta Delgada (on São Miguel island)
Language: Portuguese

The Azores consists of nine hilly islands in an archipelago stretching for 650km (400 miles).

Best time: April to September, but the islands are good year–round.

June to September: Warm, 24°C (75°F) in the afternoons. This is the dry season although rain will fall and storms are possible. Expect 7 days with rain per month.

October to May: Mild to cool. Midday temperatures average 17°C (62°F) in the winter months, December to March. Expect storms with strong winds. This is the rainy season with an average of 13 days with rain per month.

Ponta Delgada, Azores: Altitude 36m (118ft)

	Jan	Feb	Mar	Apr	May	Jun
Sunrise °C(°F)	12(53)	11(51)	12(53)	12(53)	13(55)	15(59)
Mid–afternoon °C(°F)	17(62)	17(62)	17(62)	18(64)	20(68)	22(72)
Days with precipitation	15	13	12	10	8	7
Precipitation mm	133	107	100	72	53	37
Precipitation inches	5.2	4.2	3.9	2.8	2.1	1.5
Daily hours of sunshine	3	4	4	5	6	5

	Jul	Aug	Sep	Oct	Nov	Dec
Sunrise °C(°F)	17(62)	18(64)	18(64)	16(60)	14(57)	13(55)
Mid–afternoon °C(°F)	24(75)	26(79)	25(77)	22(72)	20(68)	18(64)
Days with precipitation	6	6	10	12	13	14
Precipitation mm	30	38	86	113	130	127
Precipitation inches	1.2	1.5	3.4	4.4	5.1	5.0
Daily hours of sunshine	7	7	6	5	4	3

BAHAMAS

Official Name: Commonwealth of the Bahamas
(Independent nation; formerly a British possession)

Capital: Nassau
Languages: English, Creole

The Bahamas consists of about 700 islands and islets of
which less than 30 are inhabited. The islands have formed
from coral deposits and are long with flat surfaces and
some rounded hills.

Best time: December to April.

December to April: Winter. Dry season. Average
afternoon temperature, 26°C(78°F).
May to November: Summer. Wet season. Afternoon average, 31°C(87°F). High humidity.
Winds: Atlantic breezes cause a pleasant, mild climate.
Hurricanes: Possible, June to November.

Note: See under Caribbean Islands for general weather information.

Nassau, Bahamas: Altitude 7m (23ft)

	Jan	Feb	Mar	Apr	May	Jun
Sunrise °C(°F)	18(65)	18(65)	19(66)	21(69)	22(71)	23(74)
Mid–afternoon °C(°F)	25(77)	25(77)	26(79)	27(81)	29(84)	31(87)
Days with precipitation	6	5	5	6	9	12
Precipitation mm	36	38	36	64	117	163
Precipitation inches	1.4	1.5	1.4	2.5	4.6	6.4
Daily hours of sunshine	7	8	9	9	9	8

	Jul	Aug	Sep	Oct	Nov	Dec
Sunrise °C(°F)	24(75)	24(75)	24(75)	23(74)	21(70)	19(67)
Mid–afternoon °C(°F)	31(87)	32(89)	31(87)	29(85)	27(81)	26(79)
Days with precipitation	14	14	15	13	9	6
Precipitation mm	147	135	175	165	71	33
Precipitation inches	5.8	5.3	6.9	6.5	2.8	1.3
Daily hours of sunshine	9	9	7	7	7	7

BAHRAIN
Official Name: State of Bahrain

Capital: Manama
Languages: Arabic, English, Farsi (Persian), Urdu

Bahrain, an independent state in the Persian Gulf, consists
of 33 low desert islands of which Bahrain Island is the
largest.

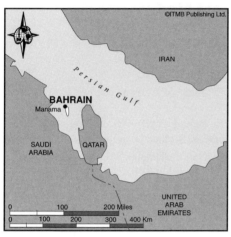

Best time to visit: October to April.

November to March: Mild, warm, humid days. Cool
nights. Cold winds from the north, from Iran, can bring
chilly weather particularly during the winter months,
December to February. Light rains fall from November to March, but the total is only 80mm (less than
4 inches).
April is a transitional month.
May to September: Uncomfortably hot and humid. Some days exceed 40°C (over 100°F). Hot, dry
winds and dust storms add to the discomfort.
October is a transitional month.

Manama, Bahrain: Altitude 2m (7ft)

	Jan	Feb	Mar	Apr	May	Jun
Sunrise °C(°F)	14(57)	15(59)	18(64)	21(70)	26(78)	29(84)
Mid–afternoon °C(°F)	20(68)	21(70)	25(77)	29(84)	34(94)	36(96)
Days with precipitation	2	2	2	1	0	0
Precipitation mm	15	16	14	10	1	0
Precipitation inches	0.6	0.6	0.6	0.4	0.04	0
Daily hours of sunshine	7	8	8	9	10	11

	Jul	Aug	Sep	Oct	Nov	Dec
Sunrise °C(°F)	30(86)	30(86)	29(84)	26(78)	21(69)	16(60)
Mid–afternoon °C(°F)	38(100)	38(100)	36(96)	33(91)	28(82)	22(71)
Days with precipitation	0	0	0	0	1	2
Precipitation mm	0	0	0	1	4	11
Precipitation inches	0	0	0	0.04	0.1	0.4
Daily hours of sunshine	11	11	11	10	9	7

BALEARIC ISLANDS
(Spanish Province of Baleares)
Includes Mallorca, Menorca, Ibiza, Formentera.

Capital: Palma, on Mallorca
Language: Spanish

Mallorca is mountainous, up to 1445m (4741ft), with
plains and a steep, rocky coastline with some good
beaches. Menorca is a tableland with low hills and with
beaches on the southern shore. Ibiza has a rough stony
landscape with many low peaks and white sand beaches.
Formentera is largely flat except for a precipitous
mountain in the east. There are many sandy beaches.

Best time to visit: June to August.
Other good months are April, May, September and October.

June to August: All islands are dry and hot with 11 hours of sunshine daily. This is the peak season
for tourism. Mallorca's afternoon temperatures reach 30°C (86°F). Mallorca's mountain region in the
north is cooler. Menorca is influenced by winds which cool it in summer. Ibiza (pronounced Ebeetha)
and Formentera are the warmest, driest islands.
September to November: Autumn. The average afternoon temperature in September and early
October is 27°C (81°F) and the water temperature is pleasantly warm for swimming. Expect 8 to 10
hours of sunshine. By November, afternoon temperatures drop to 18°C (65°F) and daily sunshine to 5
hours. Expect light rains in autumn.
December to February: Winter. Average afternoon temperature is a mild 14°C (58°F) with 5 hours of
sunshine daily. Expect 7 rainy days per month. Mallorca's mountains in the north are wetter and have
occasional snowfalls.
March to May: Spring. Afternoon temperatures begin to rise from 17°C (62°F) in March to 19°C (66°F)
in April and to 23°C (73°F) in May. By May there are 9 to 10 hours of sunshine daily. Expect light rains.

Palma de Mallorca, Balearic Islands, Spain: Altitude 8m (26ft)

	Jan	Feb	Mar	Apr	May	Jun
Sunrise °C(°F)	6(42)	6(42)	8(46)	10(50)	13(55)	17(62)
Mid–afternoon °C(°F)	14(57)	15(59)	17(62)	19(66)	22(72)	26(78)
Days with precipitation	8	7	7	7	5	3
Precipitation mm	37	35	36	39	30	14
Precipitation inches	1.5	1.4	1.4	1.5	1.2	0.6
Daily hours of sunshine	5	6	6	7	9	10

	Jul	Aug	Sep	Oct	Nov	Dec
Sunrise °C(°F)	20(68)	20(68)	18(64)	14(57)	10(50)	8(46)
Mid–afternoon °C(°F)	28(82)	29(84)	27(80)	23(73)	18(64)	15(59)
Days with precipitation	1	3	5	8	8	8
Precipitation mm	9	20	50	63	47	44
Precipitation inches	0.4	0.8	2.0	2.5	1.9	1.7
Daily hours of sunshine	11	10	8	7	6	5

BANGLADESH

Official Name: People's Republic of Bangladesh

Capital: Dhaka
Languages: Bengali, English

Bangladesh is comprised of a broad, lowland plain which is subject to flooding, and small hilly regions.

Best time to visit: November to February.

October to March: Winter. Dry and cool with winds from the north and northwest. January is the coolest month with an afternoon average of a pleasant 25°C (77°F).

March to June: Summer. Humid and hot with temperatures ranging 32 to 38°C (90 to 100°F). April is the warmest month. March to May experiences violent thunderstorms.

June to September or October: Southwest monsoon. Main rainy season. Severe cyclonic storms are possible with winds of 100 to 150km/h (60 to 90 mph). Humidity is high. Skies are cloudy with only 3 to 4 hours of sunshine daily, compared with 5 to 9 in other months. Afternoon temperatures average 32°C (89°F). About 80% of the annual rainfall falls in the monsoon season. Floods caused by heavy rainfall are a characteristic of Bangladesh.

Dhaka, Bangladesh: Altitude 8m (26ft)

	Jan	Feb	Mar	Apr	May	Jun
Sunrise °C(°F)	12(54)	13(55)	16(61)	23(73)	25(77)	26(79)
Mid–afternoon °C(°F)	25(77)	28(82)	33(91)	35(95)	34(93)	32(90)
Days with precipitation	1	1	3	6	11	16
Precipitation mm	18	31	58	103	194	321
Precipitation inches	0.7	1.2	2.3	4.1	7.6	12.6
Daily hours of sunshine	9	8	7	6	5	3

	Jul	Aug	Sep	Oct	Nov	Dec
Sunrise °C(°F)	26(79)	26(79)	26(79)	24(75)	18(64)	13(55)
Mid–afternoon °C(°F)	31(88)	31(88)	31(88)	31(88)	29(84)	26(79)
Days with precipitation	12	16	12	7	1	0
Precipitation mm	437	305	254	169	28	2
Precipitation inches	17.2	12.0	10.0	6.7	1.1	0.1
Daily hours of sunshine	2	2	3	6	8	9

BARBADOS

Official Name: Barbados
(Independent nation; formerly a British possession)

Capital: Bridgetown
Language: English

The island has a hilly interior, is flat around the coast and is surrounded by coral reefs.

Best time: December to May.

December to June: Winter. Dry season. Average afternoon temperature is a relatively cool 28°C(83°F).
July to November: Wet season with 16 rainy days per month. Average afternoon temperature is a warm 31°C (87°F) with high humidity.
Hurricanes: Possible July to November, but a touchdown is rare.

Note: See under Caribbean Islands for general weather information.

Bridgetown, Barbados: Altitude 55m (181ft)

	Jan	Feb	Mar	Apr	May	Jun
Sunrise °C(°F)	21(70)	21(69)	21(70)	22(72)	23(73)	23(73)
Mid-afternoon °C(°F)	28(83)	28(83)	29(85)	30(86)	31(87)	31(87)
Days with precipitation	13	8	8	7	9	14
Precipitation mm	66	28	33	36	58	112
Precipitation inches	2.6	1.1	1.3	1.4	2.3	4.4
Daily hours of sunshine	9	9	9	9	9	8

	Jul	Aug	Sep	Oct	Nov	Dec
Sunrise °C(°F)	23(73)	23(73)	23(73)	23(73)	23(73)	22(71)
Mid-afternoon °C(°F)	30(86)	31(87)	31(87)	30(86)	29(85)	28(83)
Days with precipitation	18	16	15	15	16	14
Precipitation mm	147	147	170	178	206	97
Precipitation inches	5.8	5.8	6.7	7.0	8.1	3.8
Daily hours of sunshine	9	9	8	8	8	8

BELARUS
Official Name: Republic of Belarus

Capital: Minsk
Languages: Belarusian, Russian

Belarus is largely flat. About one third is forested.

Best time: May to September.

May to September: For cool, pleasant weather the preferred months are May and September, 10 to 15°C (50 to 59°F) in the afternoons. June to August are warmer, 20°C (70°F), but are the wettest months when sunny days can be marred by overcast skies and short cloudbursts.

October to April: Both October and April are a mild 10°C (50°F) in the afternoons. Winter is November to March when frosts are experienced. Temperatures stay below freezing point from December to February and snow cover prevails from December to March. Cold winds from Russia blow at this time.

Minsk, Belarus: Altitude 231m (757ft)

	Jan	Feb	Mar	Apr	May	Jun
Sunrise ºC(ºF)	−10(14)	−9(16)	−5(23)	2(35)	8(46)	11(51)
Mid–afternoon ºC(ºF)	−4(25)	−3(27)	2(35)	11(51)	18(64)	21(69)
Days with precipitation	10	9	10	9	9	11
Precipitation mm	40	34	42	42	62	83
Precipitation inches	1.6	1.3	1.6	1.6	2.4	3.3
Daily hours of sunshine	1	3	4	6	8	9

	Jul	Aug	Sep	Oct	Nov	Dec
Sunrise ºC(ºF)	13(55)	12(53)	8(46)	3(37)	−1(30)	−6(21)
Mid–afternoon ºC(ºF)	22(72)	22(72)	17(62)	10(50)	3(37)	−2(29)
Days with precipitation	11	9	9	9	11	12
Precipitation mm	88	72	60	49	52	53
Precipitation inches	3.5	2.8	2.4	1.9	2.0	2.1
Daily hours of sunshine	8	8	6	3	1	1

BELGIUM
Official Name: Kingdom of Belgium

Capital: Brussels
Languages: Flemish, French, German

Belgium consists of three geographical regions: the densely wooded plateau of the Ardennes highlands, the central rolling plain with fertile valleys, and the low–lying coastal region, much of which is land reclaimed from the sea.

Best time: May to August.
May to August: Temperatures are increasing from 16°C (60°F) in May to 23°C (73°F) in July and August, the warmest months. The north is slightly warmer than the forested, hilly south. Throughout the entire country summer temperatures rarely exceed 24°C (75°F). Precipitation is spread fairly evenly over the year. July and August are the wettest months in the interior; stormy weather is common.
September to April: Cool, 20°C (68°F), in September to freezing point in December. Most temperatures do not go lower than freezing point, except in the south. Snow falls November to March especially in the Ardennes in the hilly south. Winter winds which keep Belgium's weather comfortable from November to March are the westerlies. They also bring rain which falls every month of the year. From March to May winds from the east occasionally bring cold days with blue skies to the hilly south.
Rain: Rainfall, which is fairly evenly distributed throughout the year, is low. The central and coastal regions receive 600mm (24in) per year, and the hilly south, 900mm (36in).

Brussels, Belgium: Altitude 100m (328ft)

	Jan	Feb	Mar	Apr	May	Jun
Sunrise °C(°F)	0(32)	0(32)	2(35)	5(41)	8(46)	11(51)
Mid–afternoon °C(°F)	5(41)	6(42)	9(48)	13(55)	17(62)	20(68)
Days with precipitation	12	10	11	12	10	11
Precipitation mm	67	54	73	57	70	78
Precipitation inches	2.6	2.1	2.9	2.2	2.8	3.1
Daily hours of sunshine	2	3	3	5	6	6
Snow mm	101	75	25	0	0	0
Snow inches	4	3	1	0	0	0

	Jul	Aug	Sep	Oct	Nov	Dec
Sunrise °C(°F)	13(55)	13(55)	11(51)	8(46)	3(37)	1(33)
Mid–afternoon °C(°F)	22(72)	22(72)	19(67)	14(57)	9(48)	6(42)
Days with precipitation	11	11	10	12	12	13
Precipitation mm	75	63	59	71	78	76
Precipitation inches	3.0	2.5	2.3	2.8	3.1	3.0
Daily hours of sunshine	6	6	5	4	2	1
Snow mm	0	0	0	0	51	128
Snow inches	0	0	0	0	2	5

BELIZE

Official Name: Belize
(Independent nation; formerly British Honduras)

Capital: Belmopan
Languages: English, Spanish, Mayan, Carib

The broad coastland is a belt of mangrove swamps and
jungle with the occasional beach. Beyond that to the west
are arable plains. The northern terrain is low and flat. The
south is mountainous and forested. Coral reefs and islets
(cays, pronounced keys) with sandy beaches and clear
water vary from 15 to 65km (10 to 40 miles) off the coast.

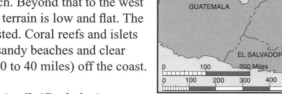

Best time: Late November to April. (Cool, dry.)

Late November to April: Dry season. Cool, pleasant but high humidity. Light rains are possible in
November, December and into January. By January these light rains in northern Belize peter out.
The dry season in the south runs only from February to April.
February and March are the driest months throughout the country.
November to February can have cold spells.
The hotter months are March to May, with April and May the hottest. Maximum temperatures on the
coast range from 27 to 30°C (81 to 86°F). Inland temperatures can reach 38°C (100°F), and nighttime
temperatures can drop to near freezing in the highlands.
May or June to October: Wet season. Hot and humid. Sea breezes moderate the heat on the coast.
Storms blow in from the sea, drop their rain then disperse quickly. Rain rarely falls all day. Rainfall
increases from north to south. For example, annual rainfall for Corozal in the north is 1270mm (50in);
Belize City, 1900mm (75in); Dangriga, 2400mm (95in); Punta Gorda, 4000mm (160in). The extreme
south has a longer wet season with heavier rainfall. July to October is when hurricanes are possible,
but they are rare. Winds are generally calm in mid–summer (August). Hot, dense air hovers overhead
to produce a 2–week period of dog days in August of hot, dry, uncomfortable weather. Rain then
follows to bring some relief.

Natural attractions: Parallel to the mainland are scores of small islands, or cays. They are used as
bases by scuba divers and snorkelers for exploring the nearby coral reefs. Water temperature in winter,
December to March, is 23°C (73°F) and in summer, June to September, it is 29°C (84°F). The waters
are clearest, March and April.

Belize City, Belize: Altitude 5m (17ft)

	Jan	Feb	Mar	Apr	May	Jun
Sunrise °C(°F)	20(68)	21(69)	22(72)	23(73)	25(77)	25(77)
Mid–afternoon °C(°F)	28(82)	29(84)	30(86)	31(87)	32(89)	32(89)
Days with precipitation	24	6	4	6	9	15
Precipitation mm	140	73	59	52	106	258
Precipitation inches	5.5	2.9	2.3	2.0	4.2	10.2
Daily hours of sunshine	6	7	8	9	9	7

Belize City, Belize: (continued)

	Jul	Aug	Sep	Oct	Nov	Dec
Sunrise ºC(ºF)	24(75)	24(75)	24(75)	23(73)	22(72)	21(69)
Mid–afternoon ºC(ºF)	31(88)	32(89)	31(88)	30(86)	29(84)	28(82)
Days with precipitation	13	13	14	19	16	29
Precipitation mm	244	187	278	255	183	176
Precipitation inches	9.6	7.4	10.9	10.0	7.2	6.9
Daily hours of sunshine	8	8	6	6	6	6

BENIN

Official Name: Republic of Benin

Capital: Porto–Novo (official), Cotonou (seat of government)
Languages: French, Fon, other African languages

The short coastline has low, sandy barriers that have formed a series of lagoons. The interior terrain is largely flat except for the Atakora mountain range in the northwest.

Best time: November to February.

There are two weather regions:
1. Coastal region. (Flat plains in the south. Includes Cotonou.)
Beginning of November to mid–March: Dry.
Late March to mid–July: Rainy, heaviest in June.
July to September: Dry.
Mid–September to beginning of November: Rain.

2. Northern region. (Forested plateau in the centre and north.)
The north is drier than the coastal region in the south.
Mid–October to mid–May: Dry. From December to March hot harmattan winds blow from the northeast, from the Sahara Desert. (The coast is not affected.) March and April are the hottest, driest months when afternoon temperatures can exceed 40ºC (104ºF).
Late May to early October: Rainy season.
For similar weather conditions in the north, refer to the table for Kano, Nigeria.

Cotonou, coast of Benin: Altitude 9m (30ft)

	Jan	Feb	Mar	Apr	May	Jun
Sunrise ºC(ºF)	24(76)	25(77)	26(78)	26(78)	25(77)	24(76)
Mid–afternoon ºC(ºF)	31(87)	32(89)	32(89)	32(89)	31(87)	29(84)
Days with precipitation	1	2	4	7	11	15
Precipitation mm	9	37	74	137	197	356
Precipitation inches	0.4	1.5	2.9	5.4	7.8	14.0
Daily hours of sunshine	7	8	7	7	7	5

Cotonou, coast of Benin: (continued)

	Jul	Aug	Sep	Oct	Nov	Dec
Sunrise ºC(ºF)	24(76)	23(73)	24(75)	24(75)	24(75)	24(75)
Mid–afternoon ºC(ºF)	28(82)	28(82)	28(82)	30(86)	31(87)	31(87)
Days with precipitation	8	5	8	8	4	2
Precipitation mm	147	65	99	127	41	20
Precipitation inches	5.8	2.6	3.9	5.0	1.6	0.8
Daily hours of sunshine	4	5	6	7	8	7

BERMUDA

Official Name: Commonwealth of Bermuda
(Dependent Territory of the United Kingdom)

Capital: Hamilton
Language: English

The island group includes about 150 islands and islets
of which only six are important. The most important is
Bermuda, also called Great Bermuda and Main Island.

Best time: April to June. (Sunny, mild.) Other months
are good because of the warm Gulf Stream which flows
between Bermuda and the U.S.A. and keeps the climate
mild, except for July and August which are hot.

May to mid–November: Warmer months. July and August are the most humid and the hottest, 30ºC (86ºF).
December to April: Cooler months. Average afternoon temperatures are a mild 20ºC (68ºF). February
is the coolest.
Winds: Strong winds moving north from the Caribbean may bring heavy rainstorms in September.

Hamilton, Bermuda: Altitude 46m (151ft)

	Jan	Feb	Mar	Apr	May	Jun
Sunrise ºC(ºF)	14(58)	14(57)	14(57)	15(59)	18(64)	21(69)
Mid–afternoon ºC(ºF)	20(68)	20(68)	20(68)	22(71)	24(76)	27(81)
Days with precipitation	14	13	12	9	9	9
Precipitation mm	112	119	122	104	117	112
Precipitation inches	4.4	4.7	4.8	4.1	4.6	4.4
Daily hours of sunshine	5	5	6	8	8	8

	Jul	Aug	Sep	Oct	Nov	Dec
Sunrise ºC(ºF)	23(73)	23(73)	22(72)	21(69)	17(63)	16(60)
Mid–afternoon ºC(ºF)	29(85)	30(86)	29(84)	26(79)	23(74)	21(70)
Days with precipitation	10	13	10	12	13	15
Precipitation mm	114	137	132	147	127	119
Precipitation inches	4.5	5.4	5.2	5.8	5.0	4.7
Daily hours of sunshine	10	9	8	6	6	5

BHUTAN

Official Name: Kingdom of Bhutan

Capital: Thimphu
Languages: Dzonkha, Tibetan, Nepali

Bhutan, in the eastern Himalaya, is completely
mountainous. Peaks rise above 7300m (24000ft).

**Best time to visit: March to May, and September to
November.**

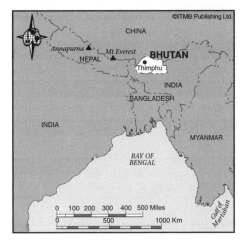

March to May: Spring. Cool to warm sunny days. Light
rains start in March, 20mm (0.8 inches), and increase
gradually to a maximum of 220mm (8.7 inches) in
August. Flowers, including rhododendrons, are in bloom. Bird life is abundant. Snowcapped peaks are
clearly visible.

June to August: Summer. Monsoon rains occur, starting in mid–June and continuing into September.
August is the wettest month with 220mm (8.7 inches). Rain generally falls in the afternoons and
evenings. Temperatures are pleasantly mild.

September to November: Autumn. Cool to warm, sunny days.

Mid–November to February: Winter. Cool to warm days, blue skies, good visibility. Nights are cold.
Almost rainless but expect snowfalls at the end of December which can make some roads impassable.

Note: The weather patterns of Bhutan are similar to those of Darjeeling, India.

Recreational activity: Trekking. Popular times to trek in the mountains are March to May, and
September to November. Best views of the Himalayas are from October to March. Note that many
trekking routes are closed in winter, December to February.

Events: Colourful religious festivals are held March to May, and September to November.

Thimphu, Bhutan: Altitude 2200m (7218ft)

	Jan	Feb	Mar	Apr	May	Jun
Sunrise ºC(ºF)	3(37)	0(32)	5(41)	9(48)	9(48)	15(59)
Mid–afternoon ºC(ºF)	12(54)	13(55)	14(57)	19(66)	19(66)	24(75)

	Jul	Aug	Sep	Oct	Nov	Dec
Sunrise ºC(ºF)	18(64)	17(63)	16(61)	11(52)	6(43)	5(41)
Mid–afternoon ºC(ºF)	29(84)	25(77)	21(70)	19(66)	17(63)	15(59)

BOLIVIA

Official Name: Republic of Bolivia

Capital: La Paz (seat of government)
        Sucre (legal capital and seat of judiciary)
Languages: Spanish, Quechua, Aymara (all official)

More than half of Bolivia is mountainous. In the west are
the Andes which divide into two parallel ranges. Between
them lies the altiplano, a high plateau 3700 to 4000m
(12000 to 13000ft) above sea level. Low plains cover the
rest of the country.

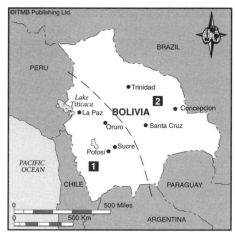

**Best time: Good all year round, but better March to
May (autumn) and September to November (spring).**
Other good months are June to August (dry but cold) and December to February (warm but wet).
Variations in altitude provide Bolivia with contrasting patterns of climate. Note that thin air at high
elevations can bring on "soroche," altitude sickness, which leaves you with nausea and shortness of
breath. People with heart or lung problems should be aware of this.

We have divided the weather into two regions. Refer to map for corresponding numbers.
1. Altiplano region. (Includes the high plateau where La Paz is situated.)
April to October: Warm. Afternoon temperatures average 17°C (63°F). Overnight temperatures can
drop to –3°C (27°F), particularly June to August. This is the dry season; June is the driest month.
November to March: Warm to hot. Afternoon temperatures average 19°C (66°F) but temperatures can
fall quickly after sunset to 6°C (42°F) and lower. This is the rainy season; most rain falls December to
February. Afternoons are often cloudy, but sun usually shines for several hours. Expect 5 to 6 hours of
sunshine daily.

Recreational activity: Skiing is possible, December to March, at Chacaltaya, the highest ski run in
the world, just 36km (22 miles) from La Paz. Ski equipment can be rented in La Paz.

La Paz, Bolivia: Altitude 3658mm (12001ft)

	Jan	Feb	Mar	Apr	May	Jun
Sunrise °C(°F)	6(42)	6(42)	6(42)	4(39)	3(37)	1(33)
Mid–afternoon °C(°F)	17(63)	17(63)	18(64)	18(65)	18(64)	17(62)
Days with precipitation	21	18	16	9	5	2
Precipitation mm	114	107	66	33	13	8
Precipitation inches	4.5	4.2	2.6	1.3	0.5	0.3
Daily hours of sunshine	6	5	5	6	8	9

	Jul	Aug	Sep	Oct	Nov	Dec
Sunrise °C(°F)	1(33)	2(35)	3(38)	4(40)	6(42)	6(42)
Mid–afternoon °C(°F)	17(62)	17(63)	18(64)	19(66)	19(66)	18(64)
Days with precipitation	2	4	9	9	11	18
Precipitation mm	10	13	28	41	48	94
Precipitation inches	0.4	0.5	1.1	1.6	1.9	3.7
Daily hours of sunshine	9	8	7	6	6	6

2. Lowlands region. (Includes the Amazon basin in eastern part of Bolivia.)
April to October: Hot and humid. Season of little rain. Afternoon temperatures range 27 to 32°C (80 to 90°F). Night temperatures can drop sharply to a few degrees above freezing when cold winds blow from the Argentine pampa, particularly May to August.
November to March: Hot and humid. Average afternoon temperature averages 30°C (86°F). This is the rainy season; most rain falls December to February.

BOSNIA and HERZEGOVINA

Official Name: Republic of Bosnia and Herzegovina

Capital: Sarajevo
Language: Serbo–Croat (Bosnian)

The northern region consists of flat, fertile plains. The remainder is mountainous.

Best time: Late April to September.

April to September: Warm days, mild nights. Rain falls year–round.
October to March: Cool to cold days. Snow falls in this season and can lie until April in the higher elevations of this mountainous country.

Sarajevo, Bosnia and Herzegovina: Altitude 638m (2093ft)

	Jan	Feb	Mar	Apr	May	Jun
Sunrise °C(°F)	–4(25)	–3(27)	1(33)	4(40)	8(47)	12(53)
Mid–afternoon °C(°F)	3(37)	6(42)	11(51)	17(62)	21(69)	24(75)
Days with precipitation	10	9	10	10	10	11
Precipitation mm	71	67	70	74	82	91
Precipitation inches	2.8	2.6	2.8	2.9	3.2	3.6
Daily hours of sunshine	2	3	4	5	6	7
Snow mm	635	582	329	126	25	0
Snow inches	25	23	13	5	1	0

	Jul	Aug	Sep	Oct	Nov	Dec
Sunrise °C(°F)	13(55)	13(55)	11(51)	6(42)	2(36)	–2(29)
Mid–afternoon °C(°F)	26(78)	26(78)	22(72)	17(62)	10(50)	4(39)
Days with precipitation	8	8	8	8	10	11
Precipitation mm	80	71	70	77	94	85
Precipitation inches	3.2	2.8	2.8	3.0	3.7	3.4
Daily hours of sunshine	8	8	6	5	3	1
Snow mm	0	0	0	75	431	560
Snow inches	0	0	0	3	17	22

BOTSWANA
Official Name: Republic of Botswana

Capital: Gaborone
Languages: English, Setswana, other African languages

Most of Botswana is arid. It consists of a tableland which averages 1000m (3300ft) above sea level. The southwestern part of the country is covered by the Kalahari Desert.

Good time to visit: April to October.

April and May: Sunny, dry, pleasantly warm, 27°C (80°F) in afternoons. Light rain is possible, more so in the northern regions. Temperatures begin to drop.
June and July: Sunny and dry. Cold mornings, 5°C (41°F), mild afternoons, 23°C (74°F). Night frosts are not uncommon in June, July and August.
August and September: Sunny, clear skies, dry, pleasantly warm. Mild mornings, 10°C (50°F) and warm afternoons, 27°C (80°F). Nights are cold, zero to 5°C (32 to 41°F). September is the height of the dry season, good for animal viewing.
October and November: Sunny, very hot, over 32°C (90°F), sometimes 38°C (100°F). Dry, but clouds are building prior to the rains, and the temperature is rising.
December to March: Sunny. This is the rainy season and the hottest season, sometimes over 40°C (104°F), with high humidity. Rain is heaviest in the north but less towards the west and south. Animals are hard to spot in the national parks in the rainy season. In some years the Kalahari Desert in the south does not receive any rain.

Natural attractions:
1. Okavango Delta – a vast wetlands area containing wildlife and birds.
Good time: April to October, in the dry season. The best time is July to September when the water level is high. This results in animals congregating on high spots of a reduced land area, making them more easily visible. **Bird watching** is good year–round but the best time is November to April when flocks of migrating birds arrive from the north.

2. Chobe National Park.
Best time to visit the Chobe River area of Chobe National Park, known for its thousands of elephants, is **June to October,** during the dry season.

Gaborone, Botswana: Altitude 1007m (3303ft)

	Jan	Feb	Mar	Apr	May	Jun
Sunrise °C(°F)	18(64)	18(64)	15(60)	11(52)	5(42)	2(35)
Mid–afternoon °C(°F)	32(90)	31(88)	30(86)	28(83)	25(77)	22(72)
Days with precipitation	7	7	5	3	1	1
Precipitation mm	96	84	72	41	12	4
Precipitation inches	3.8	3.3	2.8	1.6	0.5	0.2
Daily hours of sunshine	8	8	9	9	10	10

Gaborone, Botswana: (continued)

	Jul	Aug	Sep	Oct	Nov	Dec
Sunrise ºC(ºF)	1(34)	4(39)	9(48)	14(58)	16(61)	17(63)
Mid–afternoon ºC(ºF)	22(72)	25(77)	29(84)	32(89)	32(89)	33(91)
Days with precipitation	0	0	2	3	5	7
Precipitation mm	3	4	14	43	67	89
Precipitation inches	0.1	0.2	0.6	1.7	2.6	3.5
Daily hours of sunshine	10	10	10	9	8	8

BRAZIL

Official Name: Federative Republic of Brazil

Capital: Brasilia
Languages: Portuguese, Spanish, English

More than one–third of Brazil consists of Amazon lowlands. They cover most of northern Brazil and comprise rainforests, floodplains and swamps. South of the Amazon lowlands is a vast hilly region called the Brazilian highlands or plateau. Along the coast are narrow plains.

Best time to visit: All year round. The most pleasant weather (i.e. cooler) is in the winter months, June to August. Other months are hot and humid, particularly the summer months, January and February.

Short tropical rainstorms occur throughout the year, but they should not adversely affect travel plans.

We have divided the weather into five regions. Refer to map for corresponding numbers.

1. Southeastern region (where Rio de Janeiro is located).
Includes southern coast of Bahia, coast of Espiritu Santo, Rio de Janeiro state and northern coast of São Paulo state.
Best time: April to October (less rain) but other months are good despite rain.
April to October: Warm and humid with pleasant afternoon temperatures averaging 25°C (77°F). Six hours of sunshine daily. Expect some rain each month although this is not the rainy season. Tradewinds cool the air, giving Rio a pleasant climate. Winter, June to August, are the coolest months, 24°C (76°F).
November to March: Rainy season. Hot and humid. Average afternoon temperatures range from 26 to 29°C (78 to 85°F). January and February are the hottest months with oppressive humidity. Six hours of sunshine daily.

Event: Carnival, the pre–Lenten extravaganza in Rio, culminates on Tuesday, the day before Ash Wednesday. The main evenings are the preceding Sunday and Monday. Rehearsals can be seen from December onwards. Carnival is held in February or March; the dates vary each year. Salvador and Recife also have carnivals. (Salvador is also called Bahia.)

Rio de Janeiro, Brazil: Altitude 61m (201ft)

	Jan	Feb	Mar	Apr	May	Jun
Sunrise °C(°F)	23(73)	23(73)	23(73)	22(72)	20(68)	19(66)
Mid–afternoon °C(°F)	29(84)	30(86)	29(84)	28(82)	26(78)	25(77)
Days with precipitation	13	11	12	10	10	7
Precipitation mm	114	105	103	137	86	80
Precipitation inches	4.5	4.1	4.1	5.4	3.4	3.2
Daily hours of sunshine	6	7	7	6	6	5

	Jul	Aug	Sep	Oct	Nov	Dec
Sunrise °C(°F)	18(64)	19(66)	19(66)	20(68)	21(70)	22(72)
Mid–afternoon °C(°F)	25(77)	26(78)	25(77)	26(78)	27(80)	29(84)
Days with precipitation	7	7	11	13	13	14
Precipitation mm	56	51	87	88	96	169
Precipitation inches	2.2	2.0	3.4	3.5	3.8	6.7
Daily hours of sunshine	6	6	5	5	6	5

2. Plateau region (An area of tablelands and low hills. Includes Goias and Brasilia.)
Includes states of Mato Grosso do Sul, Mato Grosso, Goias, Tocantins, Minas Gerais, Federal District of Brasilia, southern Maranhão, and the following states but excluding their coastlines: Piaui, Ceará, Rio Grande do Norte, Paraiba, Pernambuco, Algoas, Bahia, Espiritu Santo, São Paulo.

Best time to visit: April to October.
Best time to visit the Pantanal (see Natural attraction): May to October. April is also good.

April to September: Hot. Average afternoon temperature, 33°C (91°F). Dry season. High humidity.
October to March: Hot. Average afternoon temperature, 33°C (91°F). This is the wet season with 13 to 15 rainy days per month, and high humidity.

Natural attraction: Pantanal wetlands in Mato Grosso and Mato Grosso do Sul is a sanctuary for capybaras, monkeys, reptiles and birds and is best visited in the dry season, **April to October.** Wildlife is attracted to water in the roadside ditches along the Transpantaneira dirt roadway. Bird life is best seen July to September when they are nesting in their hundreds. During the heavy rains, November to March, flooding makes travel difficult.

Goias, Brazil (Brasilia is similar): Altitude 520m (1706ft)

	Jan	Feb	Mar	Apr	May	Jun
Sunrise °C(°F)	21(69)	21(69)	21(69)	20(68)	19(66)	17(62)
Mid–afternoon °C(°F)	31(87)	31(87)	32(89)	32(89)	32(89)	32(89)
Days with precipitation	16	14	15	7	1	0
Precipitation mm	357	269	237	105	41	4
Precipitation inches	14.1	10.6	9.3	4.1	1.6	0.1
Daily hours of sunshine	4	5	6	7	8	8

	Jul	Aug	Sep	Oct	Nov	Dec
Sunrise °C(°F)	17(62)	19(66)	21(69)	21(69)	21(69)	21(69)
Mid–afternoon °C(°F)	32(89)	34(93)	35(95)	33(91)	31(87)	31(87)
Days with precipitation	0	1	4	8	13	13
Precipitation mm	4	11	38	159	248	313
Precipitation inches	0.1	0.4	1.5	6.3	9.8	12.3
Daily hours of sunshine	8	8	5	6	5	5

3. Northern region (Amazon basin area. Includes Manaus and Belem.)
Includes states of Amazonas, Roraima, Amapa, Pará, central Maranhão, Acre, Rondonia.
Best time: June to December. (Less rain.)

May and June to December: Hot, humid. Average afternoon temperature, 32 to 33°C (89 to 91°F). Seven to 8 hours of sunshine daily. Many days have rain showers.
January to April and May: Hot and humid. Average afternoon temperature, 31°C (87°F). Three to 5 hours of sunshine daily. January to April has the heaviest rainfall, mostly as violent thunderstorms which fall in the late afternoon or overnight, but rain falls throughout year. Winds are almost totally absent. Rivers are rising, January to June.

The Amazon River in Brazil
The water level is low from August or September to December then starts to rise during the rains. The river is highest from April through June, then it starts to fall in July. By September it is low again. The river is 8km (5 miles) wide at some sections. For a close–up look at the jungle and the possible viewing of wildlife you need to go on an excursion along a tributary or backwater. These are available at Manaus and Iquitos (Peru). Photography hint: Use high speed film or a flash for better pictures in the shady jungle.

Manaus, Brazil: Altitude 44m (144ft)

	Jan	Feb	Mar	Apr	May	Jun
Sunrise ºC(ºF)	23(73)	23(73)	23(73)	23(73)	23(73)	23(73)
Mid–afternoon ºC(ºF)	30(86)	30(86)	31(87)	31(87)	31(87)	31(87)
Days with precipitation	20	19	20	19	18	11
Precipitation mm	260	288	314	300	256	114
Precipitation inches	10.2	11.3	12.4	11.8	10.1	4.5
Daily hours of sunshine	4	3	3	4	5	6

	Jul	Aug	Sep	Oct	Nov	Dec
Sunrise ºC(ºF)	23(73)	23(73)	23(73)	24(75)	24(75)	23(73)
Mid–afternoon ºC(ºF)	31(87)	33(91)	33(92)	33(91)	32(90)	31(87)
Days with precipitation	8	6	7	11	12	16
Precipitation mm	88	58	83	126	183	217
Precipitation inches	3.5	2.3	3.3	5.0	7.2	8.5
Daily hours of sunshine	7	7	5	6	5	4

Belem, Brazil: Altitude 13m (42ft)

	Jan	Feb	Mar	Apr	May	Jun
Sunrise ºC(ºF)	22(72)	22(72)	22(72)	22(72)	23(73)	22(72)
Mid–afternoon ºC(ºF)	31(87)	30(86)	30(86)	31(87)	31(87)	32(89)
Days with precipitation	27	26	28	27	24	22
Precipitation mm	367	418	436	360	304	140
Precipitation inches	14.5	16.5	17.2	14.2	12.0	5.5
Daily hours of sunshine	4	4	3	4	6	8

	Jul	Aug	Sep	Oct	Nov	Dec
Sunrise ºC(ºF)	22(72)	22(72)	22(72)	22(72)	22(72)	22(72)
Mid–afternoon ºC(ºF)	32(89)	32(89)	32(89)	32(89)	32(89)	32(89)
Days with precipitation	19	16	16	15	12	19
Precipitation mm	152	131	141	116	112	216
Precipitation inches	6.0	5.2	5.6	4.6	4.4	8.5
Daily hours of sunshine	8	8	8	7	7	6

4. Northeastern region (where Recife and Salvador, also called Bahia, are located). Includes the coast of Pará south of Belem, coasts of Maranhão, Piaui, Ceará, Rio Grande do Norte, Paraiba, Pernambuco, Algoas, Sergipe and northern coast of Bahia.
Best time: September to April (dry) but other months are good, although they are rainy.

September to April: Hot, humid. Afternoon temperatures average 29ºC (85ºF) with 7 to 9 hours of sunshine daily. Comparatively dry, although it rains all year.
May to August: Hot, humid. Afternoon temperature, 27 to 28ºF (80 to 83ºF), with 6 to 7 hours of sunshine daily. This is the rainy season. Humidity is high on the coast.

Recife, Brazil: Altitude 30m (98ft)

	Jan	Feb	Mar	Apr	May	Jun
Sunrise ºC(ºF)	22(72)	23(73)	23(73)	23(73)	22(72)	22(72)
Mid–afternoon ºC(ºF)	30(86)	30(86)	30(86)	30(86)	29(84)	29(84)
Days with precipitation	10	12	14	17	21	21
Precipitation mm	103	144	265	326	329	390
Precipitation inches	4.1	5.7	10.4	12.8	13.0	15.4
Daily hours of sunshine	8	8	7	6	6	6

	Jul	Aug	Sep	Oct	Nov	Dec
Sunrise ºC(ºF)	21(69)	21(69)	21(69)	21(69)	22(72)	22(72)
Mid–afternoon ºC(ºF)	27(80)	27(80)	28(82)	29(84)	30(86)	30(86)
Days with precipitation	22	19	11	8	7	6
Precipitation mm	386	214	123	66	48	65
Precipitation inches	15.2	8.4	4.8	2.6	1.9	2.6
Daily hours of sunshine	5	3	7	8	9	8

5. Southern region (where Porto Alegre is located). Includes states of Parana, Santa Catarina and Rio Grande do Sul.
Best time: October to March (less rain). However, any time of year is good.

October to March: Warm and humid. Seven to 8 hours of sunshine daily. Rain falls each month.
April to September: Cool season with 5 to 6 hours of sunshine daily. This is the rainy season with increasing humidity, particularly January and February.

Porto Alegre, Brazil: Altitude 10m (33ft)

	Jan	Feb	Mar	Apr	May	Jun
Sunrise ºC(ºF)	20(68)	21(70)	19(66)	16(60)	13(55)	11(51)
Mid–afternoon ºC(ºF)	30(86)	30(86)	29(84)	25(77)	22(72)	19(66)
Days with precipitation	8	9	8	9	9	10
Precipitation mm	100	109	104	86	95	133
Precipitation inches	3.9	4.3	4.1	3.4	3.8	5.2
Daily hours of sunshine	8	7	6	6	6	5

	Jul	Aug	Sep	Oct	Nov	Dec
Sunrise ºC(ºF)	11(51)	11(51)	13(55)	15(59)	17(62)	19(66)
Mid–afternoon ºC(ºF)	20(68)	20(68)	22(72)	24(75)	27(80)	29(84)
Days with precipitation	9	11	10	10	8	7
Precipitation mm	122	140	140	114	104	101
Precipitation inches	4.8	5.5	5.5	4.5	4.1	4.0
Daily hours of sunshine	5	5	5	7	7	8

Natural attraction:

Iguassu (Iguaçu) Falls on the Brazil–Argentina border: 275 cascades; length 2.5km (1.5 miles), 65m (200ft) high. Although Argentina has most of the falls, the panoramic views of the falls are best seen from the Brazil side, preferably in the morning when the light is better for photography. The afternoon is the best time to photograph the falls from the Argentina side.

Best months are August to November. Flood months are May to July when some catwalks for viewing cannot be used. Possible months to avoid are December to March (very hot) and July (local holidays).

BRUNEI

Official Name: Negara Brunei Darussalam

Capital: Bandar Seri Begawan
Languages: Malay, English, Chinese

Brunei is on the island of Borneo which it shares with Indonesia and Malaysia. Brunei comprises two parts separated by the Malaysian state of Sarawak. The terrain consists of rocky hills in the east, swamps in the west and thick forests in the interior.

Best time: March to September (less rain). However, all other months are good for travel.

March to September is outside the monsoon season but rain can be expected on any day. Morning temperatures are 23°C (73°F) throughout the year, and afternoon temperatures, 32°C (89°F). Humidity is a high 79% year–round. Seven hours of sunshine daily.
October to January: Wet season of heavy, sudden downpours. More rain falls in the interior than on the coast. Annual rainfall in the interior is 7600mm (300in), and 2500mm (100in) on the coast. Temperatures, humidity and hours of sunshine are the same as March to September.

Bandar Seri Begawan, Brunei: Altitude 15m (49ft)

	Jan	Feb	Mar	Apr	May	Jun
Sunrise °C(°F)	23(73)	23(73)	23(73)	23(73)	23(73)	23(73)
Mid–afternoon °C(°F)	30(86)	31(87)	32(89)	32(89)	32(89)	32(89)
Days with precipitation	15	10	9	12	15	13
Precipitation mm	308	158	129	177	228	201
Precipitation inches	12.1	6.2	5.1	7.0	9.0	7.9
Daily hours of sunshine	7	7	7	8	8	7

	Jul	Aug	Sep	Oct	Nov	Dec
Sunrise °C(°F)	23(73)	23(73)	23(73)	23(73)	23(73)	23(73)
Mid–afternoon °C(°F)	32(89)	32(89)	32(89)	32(89)	31(87)	31(87)
Days with precipitation	13	12	16	18	20	18
Precipitation mm	219	198	285	304	359	343
Precipitation inches	8.6	7.8	11.2	12.0	14.1	13.5
Daily hours of sunshine	7	7	7	7	7	7

BULGARIA
Official Name: Republic of Bulgaria

Capital: Sofia
Language: Bulgarian

More than half of Bulgaria is mountainous. There are major lowlands in the north and southeast.

Bulgaria's weather is influenced by winds from the Russian steppes and the exposure to the Black Sea.

Best time: June to September.

June to August: Summer. Hot, reaching 27°C (80°F) in the mountains in the daytime, and 29°C (85°F) on the Black Sea coast. Expect short, violent cloudbursts, sometimes with hail. Rain is spread fairly evenly throughout the year but summer has the heaviest downpours.
September to November: Autumn. Summer can extend into September because of winds from the Russian steppes which pick up warmth from the Black Sea. October and November are transitional months when temperatures decrease. Expect rain in all months.
December to February: Winter. Cold northeast winds from Russia can introduce bitterly harsh conditions. Snow falls in mountainous western Bulgaria, e.g. Sofia. Snow permanently covers the highest peaks. In eastern Bulgaria, e.g. Varna on the Black Sea, heavy rains fall, especially in December.
March to May: Spring. Changeable with warm and cold days. Snow is possible in early spring. Snow may last until June at the higher elevations, e.g. in western and south–western Bulgaria.

Sofia, Bulgaria: Altitude 550m (1805ft)

	Jan	Feb	Mar	Apr	May	Jun
Sunrise °C(°F)	–5(23)	–3(27)	0(32)	5(41)	9(48)	12(53)
Mid–afternoon °C(°F)	2(35)	5(41)	10(50)	15(59)	20(68)	24(75)
Days with precipitation	9	10	10	12	13	12
Precipitation mm	31	34	37	49	78	75
Precipitation inches	1.2	1.3	1.5	1.9	3.1	3.0
Daily hours of sunshine	2	4	4	6	7	8

	Jul	Aug	Sep	Oct	Nov	Dec
Sunrise °C(°F)	14(57)	14(57)	11(51)	6(42)	1(33)	–3(27)
Mid–afternoon °C(°F)	26(78)	26(78)	23(73)	17(62)	10(50)	4(39)
Days with precipitation	10	9	7	11	10	12
Precipitation mm	55	49	38	35	53	44
Precipitation inches	2.2	1.9	1.5	1.4	2.1	1.7
Daily hours of sunshine	9	9	7	5	3	2

BURKINA FASO

Official Name: Burkina Faso
(Independent nation; formerly Republic of Upper Volta.
Burkina Faso means Country of the Upright People.)

Capital: Ouagadougou (pronounced Wugga–doo–goo)
Languages: French, African languages

This landlocked country is on a plateau, the southern half
of which is covered in small trees and grass. Much of the
north is semi–desert, being on the fringe of the Sahara.

Best time: November to March.

November to February: Sunny, warm, dry. Harmattan
winds from the northeast bring dry air, sometimes dust–laden, which cause the sky to be hazy.
March to June: Sunny, hot season with temperatures exceeding 40ºC (104ºF). Humidity is low.
June to September and into October: Hot, humid, mix of cloud and sun with 6 hours of sunshine
daily. This is the rainy season with the heaviest falls in July and August. Rain often comes as
afternoon or evening thunderstorms but continuous rainy spells occur.

Ouagadougou, Burkina Faso: Altitude 302m (991ft)

	Jan	Feb	Mar	Apr	May	Jun
Sunrise ºC(ºF)	16(60)	20(68)	23(73)	26(79)	26(79)	24(76)
Mid–afternoon ºC(ºF)	33(92)	37(98)	40(104)	39(103)	38(101)	36(96)
Days with precipitation	0	0	1	2	6	9
Precipitation mm	0	3	13	15	84	122
Precipitation inches	0	0.1	0.5	0.6	3.3	4.8
Daily hours of sunshine	9	9	9	8	9	8

	Jul	Aug	Sep	Oct	Nov	Dec
Sunrise ºC(ºF)	23(74)	22(72)	23(73)	23(74)	22(71)	17(62)
Mid–afternoon ºC(ºF)	33(91)	31(87)	32(89)	35(95)	36(96)	35(95)
Days with precipitation	12	14	11	3	0	0
Precipitation mm	203	277	145	33	0	0
Precipitation inches	8.0	10.9	5.7	1.3	0	0
Daily hours of sunshine	7	6	7	9	9	8

BURMA, see MYANMAR

BURUNDI

Official Name: Republic of Burundi

Capital: Bujumbura
Languages: French, Kirundi, Swahili

Burundi is mainly a mountainous country whose elevation gives it a pleasantly mild climate, often with days having a maximum of 20°C (68°F). The lower land near Lake Tanganyika is more humid and hotter, 30°C (86°F).

There are two dry seasons and two wet seasons although some rain can fall every month.
Best time: June to mid–September. (Dry.)

June to September: Long dry season.
October to December: Short wet season.
December to February: Short dry season.
March to May: Long wet season.

Bujumbura, Burundi: Altitude 805m (2640ft)

	Jan	Feb	Mar	Apr	May	Jun
Sunrise °C(°F)	19(66)	19(66)	19(66)	19(66)	19(66)	18(64)
Mid–afternoon °C(°F)	28(82)	28(82)	28(82)	28(82)	28(82)	29(64)
Days with precipitation	15	14	17	18	10	3
Precipitation mm	94	109	121	125	57	11
Precipitation inches	3.7	4.3	4.8	4.9	2.2	0.4
Daily hours of sunshine	5	5	6	6	7	8

	Jul	Aug	Sep	Oct	Nov	Dec
Sunrise °C(°F)	17(63)	18(64)	19(66)	20(68)	19(66)	19(66)
Mid–afternoon °C(°F)	29(84)	30(86)	31(88)	30(86)	28(82)	28(82)
Days with precipitation	1	2	8	12	19	19
Precipitation mm	5	11	37	64	100	114
Precipitation inches	0.2	0.4	1.5	2.5	3.9	4.5
Daily hours of sunshine	9	8	7	6	5	5

CAMBODIA
Official Name: Kingdom of Cambodia

Capital: Phnom Penh
Languages: Khmer, French

A large alluvial, low–lying plain covers much of the north, centre and south. Through it runs the Mekong River. In the east is an undulating plateau and in the west, a hilly region.

There are two seasons: Dry, November to April and wet, May to October and November. (November is a transitional month.)

Best time: December to February. November is also good.

December to February: Dry, comparatively cool. January is the "coolest" month with average afternoon temperature, 31°C (87°F). Nine hours of sunshine daily in each month. Humid.
March and April: Dry. Temperatures become progressively hotter. April is the hottest month of the year with average afternoon temperature, 35°C (94°F). Eight to 9 hours of sunshine daily. High humidity.
May to November: Rainy season. September and October are the wettest. Cloudy and high humidity and about 6 hours of sunshine daily.

Phnom Penh, Cambodia: Altitude 12m (39ft)

	Jan	Feb	Mar	Apr	May	Jun
Sunrise ºC(ºF)	21(70)	22(72)	23(74)	24(76)	24(76)	24(76)
Mid–afternoon ºC(ºF)	31(87)	32(90)	34(92)	35(94)	34(92)	33(91)
Days with precipitation	1	1	3	6	14	15
Precipitation mm	7	10	40	77	134	155
Precipitation inches	0.3	0.4	1.6	3.0	5.3	6.0
Daily hours of sunshine	9	9	9	8	7	6

	Jul	Aug	Sep	Oct	Nov	Dec
Sunrise ºC(ºF)	24(75)	25(76)	25(76)	24(76)	23(74)	22(71)
Mid–afternoon ºC(ºF)	32(89)	32(89)	31(88)	30(87)	30(86)	30(86)
Days with precipitation	16	16	19	17	9	4
Precipitation mm	171	160	224	257	127	45
Precipitation inches	6.7	6.3	8.8	10.1	5.0	1.8
Daily hours of sunshine	6	6	5	7	8	9

CAMEROON
Official Name: Republic of Cameroon

Capital: Yaoundé
Languages: French, English, African languages

The centre of the country is on a plateau which reaches 1400m (4500ft) above sea level. In the west are high, forested mountains; in the south lies a coastal plain of dense rainforests. The north has savanna plains.

Best time: November to February (drier). **October and March and April** are also good months. Average daily maximum temperature is a fairly constant 28°C (82°F), and humidity is high. Cameroon has different weather regions. The wet and dry months are shown below.

1. Southern coastal region (includes Douala).
November to February: Drier season.
March and April: Light rains.
May to October: Rainy season.

2. South and east of Yaoundé (terrain consists of tropical forests).
November to March: Long dry season.
March to June: Short rainy season.
June to August: Short dry season.
August to November: Long rainy season.

3. Central Uplands (includes Ngaoundere).
November to March: Dry season. Afternoon temperatures rise to 35°C (95°F) in March.
April to October: Rainy season. Afternoons average 28°C (82°F).

4. Northern Plains and Desert (includes Maroua).
October to April: Dry and very hot. Afternoon temperatures can exceed 40°C (104°F).
May to September: Rainy season.

Douala, coast of Cameroon: Altitude 8m (26ft)

	Jan	Feb	Mar	Apr	May	Jun
Sunrise ºC(ºF)	23(73)	24(75)	24(75)	23(73)	23(73)	23(73)
Mid–afternoon ºC(ºF)	32(89)	32(89)	32(89)	32(89)	31(87)	29(84)
Days with precipitation	5	9	16	18	21	23
Precipitation mm	36	64	168	230	272	429
Precipitation inches	1.4	2.5	6.6	9.1	10.7	16.9
Daily hours of sunshine	6	6	6	6	5	4

	Jul	Aug	Sep	Oct	Nov	Dec
Sunrise ºC(ºF)	23(73)	23(73)	23(73)	23(73)	23(73)	23(73)
Mid–afternoon ºC(ºF)	28(82)	27(80)	29(84)	30(86)	31(87)	31(87)
Days with precipitation	27	30	27	25	13	6
Precipitation mm	695	755	626	410	134	35
Precipitation inches	27.3	29.7	24.6	16.1	5.3	1.4
Daily hours of sunshine	2	2	3	4	5	6

Yaoundé, southern interior of Cameroon: Altitude 760m (2493ft)

	Jan	Feb	Mar	Apr	May	Jun
Sunrise ºC(ºF)	17(62)	20(68)	20(68)	20(68)	20(68)	19(67)
Mid–afternoon ºC(ºF)	31(87)	31(87)	30(86)	30(86)	29(85)	28(82)
Days with precipitation	2	5	12	16	18	16
Precipitation mm	17	51	140	180	220	162
Precipitation inches	0.7	2.0	5.5	7.1	8.7	6.4
Daily hours of sunshine	6	6	5	5	5	4

	Jul	Aug	Sep	Oct	Nov	Dec
Sunrise ºC(ºF)	19(66)	19(66)	19(66)	19(66)	19(66)	19(66)
Mid–afternoon ºC(ºF)	26(78)	26(78)	27(80)	28(82)	28(82)	28(82)
Days with precipitation	11	14	22	24	11	3
Precipitation mm	70	102	254	296	111	25
Precipitation inches	2.8	4.0	10.0	11.7	4.4	1.0
Daily hours of sunshine	3	3	3	4	6	6

CANADA

Official Name: Canada

Capital: Ottawa
Languages: English, French (both official languages)

Canada's terrain is described here from west to east, a distance of 6500km (4000 miles).
- British Columbia and Yukon are mountainous with numerous ranges including the Canadian Rockies on the British Columbia–Alberta border.
- Southern and eastern Alberta and the southern halves of Saskatchewan and Manitoba have flat prairies interspersed with low mountain ranges.
- Northern and central Ontario have rocky, undulating uplands with rivers and lakes.
- Southern Ontario and southern Quebec are on a generally level plain.
- Eastern Quebec is mountainous.
- Inland and northern Quebec are rugged and hilly with extensive forests.
- New Brunswick is generally flat except for the rugged, hilly northwest.
- Nova Scotia has low hills.
- Prince Edward Island has flat and undulating terrain.
- Newfoundland is rugged and hilly while Labrador is on an undulating, lakestrewn plateau.
- Northern Saskatchewan, northern Manitoba, Northwest Territories and Nunavut consist of rocky, undulating uplands with rivers and lakes.

We have divided Canada into 6 regions. Refer to map for corresponding numbers.

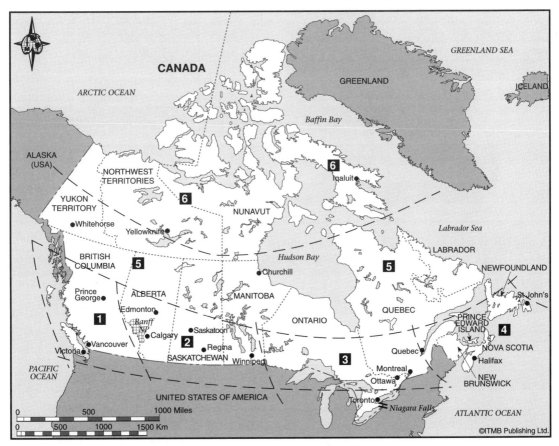

Region 1. Pacific Region
British Columbia (Includes Prince George, Vancouver and Victoria.)
Best time for general travel: Mid–May to mid–September.

Mid–May to mid–September: Summer. Warm. July is the most pleasant month with little rain, long periods of sunshine, and moderate temperatures, 23°C (74°F). The pleasant weather extends to mid–September but there could be intermittent rainy days. In the interior valleys of southern British Columbia, summers (July and August) are hot, rising occasionally above 40°C (104°F). North of central British Columbia summer is short and mild, 24°C (75°F). At Victoria on Vancouver Island, summer is normally sunny, dry and warm.

Mid–September to mid–November: Autumn. September and October sometimes continue to have summer–like weather. Rainy season begins in October.

Mid–November to mid–March: Winter. Mild on the coast. These are the rainiest months. Snow falls in the mountains. Grey clouds reduce sunlight. Fog occurs along the coast. In most places the mid–winter temperature will stay above 7°C (45°F), being kept above freezing by the warm Pacific current. January is usually the most severe month. The higher you go in the mountains, the cooler it gets. Winter sports are popular in the Coast Mountains, e.g. at Whistler, 2 hours by road north of Vancouver. Winter at Victoria, on Vancouver Island, experiences more rain than snow although sometimes there are no snowfalls.

Mid–March to mid–May: Spring. Cool. Rainy. Grey clouds may linger, mixed with blue sky.

Prince George, British Columbia: Altitude 691m (2267ft)

	Jan	Feb	Mar	Apr	May	Jun
Sunrise °C(°F)	−14(7)	−10(14)	−6(21)	−1(30)	3(37)	6(42)
Mid–afternoon °C(°F)	−6(21)	0(32)	5(41)	11(51)	16(60)	20(68)
Precipitation mm	54	35	34	28	52	65
Precipitation inches	2.1	1.4	1.3	1.1	2.0	2.6
Daily hours of sunshine	2	3	5	7	8	9

	Jul	Aug	Sep	Oct	Nov	Dec
Sunrise °C(°F)	8(46)	8(46)	4(39)	0(32)	−7(19)	−12(11)
Mid–afternoon °C(°F)	22(72)	21(69)	16(60)	10(50)	1(33)	−5(23)
Precipitation mm	60	60	59	59	53	54
Precipitation inches	2.4	2.4	2.3	2.3	2.1	2.1
Daily hours of sunshine	9	8	5	4	2	2

Vancouver, British Columbia: Altitude 14m (46ft)

	Jan	Feb	Mar	Apr	May	Jun
Sunrise °C(°F)	0(32)	1(33)	3(37)	5(41)	8(46)	11(51)
Mid–afternoon °C(°F)	6(42)	8(46)	10(50)	13(55)	16(60)	19(66)
Days with precipitation	20	17	17	14	12	11
Precipitation mm	150	124	109	75	62	46
Precipitation inches	5.9	4.9	4.3	3.0	2.4	1.8
Daily hours of sunshine	2	3	4	6	8	8
Snow mm	304	152	75	0	0	0
Snow inches	12	6	3	0	0	0

Vancouver, British Columbia: (continued)

	Jul	Aug	Sep	Oct	Nov	Dec
Sunrise °C(°F)	13(55)	13(55)	10(50)	6(42)	3(37)	1(33)
Mid–afternoon °C(°F)	22(72)	22(72)	18(64)	13(55)	9(48)	6(42)
Days with precipitation	7	8	9	16	19	22
Precipitation mm	36	38	64	115	170	179
Precipitation inches	1.4	1.5	2.5	4.5	6.7	7.0
Daily hours of sunshine	10	9	6	4	1	1
Snow mm	0	0	0	0	50	152
Snow inches	0	0	0	0	2	6

Victoria, British Columbia: Altitude 69m (226ft)

	Jan	Feb	Mar	Apr	May	Jun
Sunrise °C(°F)	0(32)	1(33)	2(35)	4(39)	6(42)	9(48)
Mid–afternoon °C(°F)	6(43)	8(46)	10(50)	13(56)	16(61)	18(65)
Days with precipitation	19	15	15	11	9	8
Precipitation mm	141	99	72	42	33	27
Precipitation inches	5.6	3.9	2.8	1.6	1.3	1.1
Daily hours of sunshine	2	3	5	6	8	9
Snow mm	151	126	25	0	0	0
Snow inches	6	5	1	0	0	0

	Jul	Aug	Sep	Oct	Nov	Dec
Sunrise °C(°F)	11(53)	11(53)	8(46)	5(41)	3(37)	0(32)
Mid–afternoon °C(°F)	20(68)	20(68)	18(64)	14(57)	9(49)	7(45)
Days with precipitation	4	5	9	14	19	19
Precipitation mm	18	24	37	74	139	152
Precipitation inches	0.7	0.9	1.5	2.9	5.5	6.0
Daily hours of sunshine	10	9	7	4	3	2
Snow mm	0	0	0	0	25	25
Snow inches	0	0	0	0	1	1

Region 2. Prairie Region
Southern halves of Alberta, Saskatchewan and Manitoba (Includes Calgary, Edmonton, Regina and Winnipeg.)

Good time for travelling is mid–May to mid–September. Best is August and September.

June to August: Summer is a short season with hot days reaching 30°C (86°F). July is the hottest summer month. Because the air is dry, the temperature is bearable because of the lack of humidity. Rain is moderate, often falling as heavy showers.
September to November: Autumn. September is chilly, snow starts in October and by November the long winter has begun.
December to February: Winter has daytime temperatures regularly below freezing. The air is cold and dry but is not like the less bearable damp, cold air along the coast. The harsh, cold temperatures are often accompanied by sunny, blue skies. Winter snow can stay until mid–March. Temperatures can

be raised by the chinook wind, a wind that comes from the west across the Rocky Mountains. When it descends the eastern flank, the warm wind quickly melts the snow.

March to May: Spring is chilly with some snow.

Calgary, Alberta: Altitude 1080m (3543ft)

	Jan	Feb	Mar	Apr	May	Jun
Sunrise ºC(ºF)	−16(3)	−12(11)	−9(16)	−2(29)	3(37)	7(44)
Mid–afternoon ºC(ºF)	−4(25)	−1(30)	3(37)	11(51)	16(60)	21(70)
Days with precipitation	7	8	10	8	11	12
Precipitation mm	12	10	15	25	53	77
Precipitation inches	0.5	0.4	0.6	1.0	2.1	3.0
Daily hours of sunshine	4	5	6	7	8	10
Snow mm	126	126	202	152	126	25
Snow inches	5	5	8	6	5	1

	Jul	Aug	Sep	Oct	Nov	Dec
Sunrise ºC(ºF)	9(48)	9(48)	4(39)	−1(30)	−9(16)	−14(7)
Mid–afternoon ºC(ºF)	23(73)	23(73)	17(62)	13(55)	3(38)	−2(29)
Days with precipitation	10	10	8	7	5	5
Precipitation mm	70	49	48	16	12	13
Precipitation inches	2.8	1.9	1.9	0.6	0.5	0.5
Daily hours of sunshine	10	9	7	6	4	3
Snow mm	0	0	75	101	177	152
Snow inches	0	0	3	4	7	6

Event: Calgary Exhibition and Stampede is a 10–day rodeo with a parade, held in the second week of July.

Natural attraction: Banff National Park in the Rocky Mountains is open year–round. Busiest months for sightseeing and hiking are July and August (summer). There are three world class ski resorts in the Park. Snow covers the ground from November to May. High season for skiing is March.

Edmonton, Alberta: Altitude 671m (2201ft)

	Jan	Feb	Mar	Apr	May	Jun
Sunrise ºC(ºF)	–20(–4)	–17(1)	–11(13)	–3(27)	3(37)	7(44)
Mid–afternoon ºC(ºF)	–9(16)	–5(23)	0(32)	10(50)	17(62)	21(70)
Days with precipitation	12	9	10	8	12	15
Precipitation mm	23	16	16	22	43	76
Precipitation inches	0.9	0.6	0.6	0.9	1.7	3.0
Daily hours of sunshine	3	4	5	7	8	9
Snow mm	228	177	177	126	50	0
Snow inches	9	7	7	5	2	0

	Jul	Aug	Sep	Oct	Nov	Dec
Sunrise ºC(ºF)	9(48)	8(46)	3(37)	–2(29)	–11(13)	–18(–1)
Mid–afternoon ºC(ºF)	22(72)	22(72)	17(62)	11(51)	0(32)	–7(19)
Days with precipitation	14	12	9	9	11	12
Precipitation mm	101	70	48	18	16	19
Precipitation inches	4.0	2.8	1.9	0.7	0.6	0.7
Daily hours of sunshine	10	9	6	5	3	2
Snow mm	0	0	25	101	202	202
Snow inches	0	0	1	4	8	8

Regina, Saskatchewan: Altitude 577m (1893ft)

	Jan	Feb	Mar	Apr	May	Jun
Sunrise ºC(ºF)	–22(–8)	–19(–3)	–12(11)	–3(27)	4(39)	9(48)
Mid–afternoon ºC(ºF)	–11(13)	–8(18)	–1(30)	10(50)	19(67)	24(75)
Precipitation mm	19	13	17	21	50	61
Precipitation inches	0.7	0.5	0.7	0.8	2.0	2.4
Daily hours of sunshine	3	4	5	7	9	10

	Jul	Aug	Sep	Oct	Nov	Dec
Sunrise ºC(ºF)	11(52)	10(50)	4(39)	–3(27)	–11(13)	–20(–4)
Mid–afternoon ºC(ºF)	26(78)	25(77)	18(64)	11(51)	0(32)	–9(16)
Precipitation mm	59	39	34	21	13	19
Precipitation inches	2.3	1.5	1.3	0.8	0.5	0.7
Daily hours of sunshine	11	10	6	5	4	3

Winnipeg, Manitoba: Altitude 240m (787ft)

	Jan	Feb	Mar	Apr	May	Jun
Sunrise ºC(ºF)	–24(–12)	–21(–6)	–12(11)	–2(29)	5(41)	10(50)
Mid–afternoon ºC(ºF)	–13(8)	–10(14)	–2(29)	10(50)	19(66)	23(73)
Days with precipitation	12	11	9	9	10	12
Precipitation mm	19	15	23	36	60	84
Precipitation inches	0.7	0.6	0.9	1.4	2.4	3.3
Daily hours of sunshine	4	5	6	8	9	10
Snow mm	228	202	253	101	25	0
Snow inches	9	8	10	4	1	0

	Jul	Aug	Sep	Oct	Nov	Dec
Sunrise ºC(ºF)	13(55)	12(53)	6(42)	0(32)	–9(16)	–19(–3)
Mid–afternoon ºC(ºF)	26(78)	25(77)	19(66)	11(51)	0(32)	–10(14)
Days with precipitation	10	10	9	6	9	11
Precipitation mm	72	75	51	30	21	19
Precipitation inches	2.8	3.0	2.0	1.2	0.8	0.7
Daily hours of sunshine	10	9	6	5	3	3
Snow mm	0	0	0	75	228	228
Snow inches	0	0	0	3	9	9

Region 3. Great Lakes Region
Southern Ontario and southern Quebec (Includes Montreal, Niagara Falls, Ottawa, Quebec City, Toronto.)
Good time for travelling is mid–May to mid–September. Best are August and September.

June to August: Summer. Warm and pleasant. Hot days can be sultry because of the accompanying humidity. Occasional thunderstorms.
September to November: Autumn. Rainy with grey skies. Foliage is a blaze of colour when it changes in September. The colours can last into November. First snow arrives in November and can last until late April.
December to February: Winter. Long, cold, snowy, although many hours of sunshine are experienced. Some bitterly cold temperatures are accompanied by howling winds.
March to May: Spring. Mild and short, from end of March to end of May. Snow ends in April. Early spring (March) is one of the rainiest times of the year.

Sporting activities: Best time for winter sports is mid–November to end of March. E.g. skiing, snowboarding, ice skating, snowmobiling.

Montreal, Quebec: Altitude 57m (187ft)

	Jan	Feb	Mar	Apr	May	Jun
Sunrise ºC(ºF)	−15(5)	−14(7)	−7(19)	1(33)	7(44)	13(55)
Mid–afternoon ºC(ºF)	−6(21)	−4(25)	2(35)	11(51)	18(64)	23(73)
Days with precipitation	15	14	14	12	12	13
Precipitation mm	63	56	68	75	68	83
Precipitation inches	2.5	2.2	2.7	3.0	2.7	3.3
Daily hours of sunshine	3	4	5	6	7	8
Snow mm	711	584	508	152	0	0
Snow inches	28	23	20	6	0	0

	Jul	Aug	Sep	Oct	Nov	Dec
Sunrise ºC(ºF)	15(59)	14(57)	9(48)	4(39)	−2(29)	−11(13)
Mid–afternoon ºC(ºF)	26(78)	25(77)	20(68)	13(55)	5(41)	−3(27)
Days with precipitation	12	11	12	13	14	15
Precipitation mm	86	100	87	75	93	86
Precipitation inches	3.4	3.9	3.4	3.0	3.7	3.4
Daily hours of sunshine	9	8	6	5	3	3
Snow mm	0	0	0	25	279	609
Snow inches	0	0	0	1	11	24

Niagara Falls, Ontario: Altitude 99m (324ft)

	Jan	Feb	Mar	Apr	May	Jun
Sunrise ºC(ºF)	−8(18)	−7(19)	−4(25)	3(37)	7(45)	13(56)
Mid–afternoon ºC(ºF)	−1(30)	0(32)	4(39)	13(56)	19(66)	24(76)
Days with precipitation	18	17	16	12	12	11
Precipitation mm	75	70	73	75	78	43
Precipitation inches	3.0	2.8	2.9	3.0	3.1	1.7
Snow mm	484	406	279	50	0	0
Snow inches	19	16	11	2	0	0

	Jul	Aug	Sep	Oct	Nov	Dec
Sunrise ºC(ºF)	16(60)	16(60)	11(52)	6(43)	1(33)	−5(23)
Mid–afternoon ºC(ºF)	27(81)	26(79)	21(71)	16(61)	8(47)	2(35)
Days with precipitation	10	9	11	13	15	19
Precipitation mm	58	114	68	65	65	73
Precipitation inches	2.3	4.5	2.7	2.6	2.6	2.9
Snow mm	0	0	0	0	177	380
Snow inches	0	0	0	0	7	15

Ottawa, Ontario: Altitude 103m (338ft)

	Jan	Feb	Mar	Apr	May	Jun
Sunrise ºC(ºF)	–15(5)	–14(7)	–7(19)	1(33)	7(44)	12(53)
Mid–afternoon ºC(ºF)	–6(21)	–5(23)	2(35)	11(51)	19(66)	24(76)
Days with precipitation	13	12	12	11	11	10
Precipitation mm	51	50	57	65	77	84
Precipitation inches	2.0	2.0	2.2	2.6	3.0	3.3
Daily hours of sunshine	3	4	5	6	7	8
Snow mm	558	431	355	126	0	0
Snow inches	22	17	14	5	0	0

	Jul	Aug	Sep	Oct	Nov	Dec
Sunrise ºC(ºF)	15(59)	14(57)	10(50)	4(39)	–2(29)	–11(13)
Mid–afternoon ºC(ºF)	26(78)	25(77)	20(68)	13(55)	5(41)	–4(25)
Days with precipitation	11	10	11	12	12	14
Precipitation mm	87	88	84	75	81	73
Precipitation inches	3.4	3.5	3.3	3.0	3.2	2.9
Daily hours of sunshine	9	8	6	4	3	2
Snow mm	0	0	0	25	152	431
Snow inches	0	0	0	1	6	17

Quebec City, Quebec: Altitude 74m (243ft)

	Jan	Feb	Mar	Apr	May	Jun
Sunrise ºC(ºF)	–17(2)	–16(4)	–10(15)	–2(29)	5(41)	10(50)
Mid–afternoon ºC(ºF)	–8(18)	–6(21)	1(33)	8(46)	17(62)	22(72)
Days with precipitation	14	14	14	12	13	14
Precipitation mm	90	74	85	76	100	110
Precipitation inches	3.6	2.9	3.4	3.0	3.9	4.3
Daily hours of sunshine	3	4	5	6	7	8
Snow mm	736	584	533	228	25	0
Snow inches	29	23	21	9	1	0

	Jul	Aug	Sep	Oct	Nov	Dec
Sunrise ºC(ºF)	13(55)	12(54)	7(44)	2(35)	–4(25)	–13(9)
Mid–afternoon ºC(ºF)	25(77)	23(73)	18(64)	11(51)	3(37)	–5(23)
Days with precipitation	13	12	13	13	14	17
Precipitation mm	119	120	124	96	106	109
Precipitation inches	4.7	4.7	4.9	3.8	4.2	4.3
Daily hours of sunshine	8	7	5	4	3	3
Snow mm	0	0	0	50	355	635
Snow inches	0	0	0	2	14	25

Event: The Winter Carnival (Carnaval de Québec) in Quebec City starts on the first Thursday in February and lasts for ten days. Includes parades, snow sculpture competitions, fireworks, canoe races and grand balls.

Toronto, Ontario: Altitude 116m (381ft)

	Jan	Feb	Mar	Apr	May	Jun
Sunrise ºC(ºF)	–11(13)	–11(13)	–5(23)	1(33)	6(42)	11(51)
Mid–afternoon ºC(ºF)	–2(29)	–2(29)	4(39)	11(51)	18(64)	24(75)
Days with precipitation	16	12	13	12	13	11
Precipitation mm	46	46	57	64	66	69
Precipitation inches	1.8	1.8	2.2	2.5	2.6	2.7
Daily hours of sunshine	2	4	4	6	7	9
Snow mm	406	380	279	75	0	0
Snow inches	16	15	11	3	0	0

	Jul	Aug	Sep	Oct	Nov	Dec
Sunrise ºC(ºF)	14(57)	13(55)	9(48)	4(39)	–1(30)	–7(19)
Mid–afternoon ºC(ºF)	27(80)	25(77)	21(69)	14(57)	7(44)	0(32)
Days with precipitation	10	9	12	11	13	13
Precipitation mm	77	84	74	63	70	66
Precipitation inches	3.0	3.3	2.9	2.5	2.8	2.6
Daily hours of sunshine	9	8	7	5	3	2
Snow mm	0	0	0	25	101	304
Snow inches	0	0	0	1	4	12

Region 4. East Coast Region
New Brunswick, Nova Scotia, Prince Edward Island, and Newfoundland. (Includes Halifax and St. John's.)
Good time: Mid–May to mid–October. Best is early July to early October.

Mid–June to mid–September: Summer. Clear, sunny, warm days, but nights are cool, sometimes close to freezing point. Summer weather is changeable. Even the same day can have howling winds, sunshine and rain.
Mid–September to mid–December: Autumn. Cool. The presence of the Gulf Stream helps moderate the winter temperatures. Foliage changes colour at this time.
Mid–December to mid–March: Winter. Cold with severe storms and snowfalls.
Mid–March to mid–June: Spring. Damp and cool in early spring. Muggy and warm at end of spring. The coast can be foggy in May and June, but inland at the same time can be sunny.

Halifax, Nova Scotia: Altitude 30m (99ft)

	Jan	Feb	Mar	Apr	May	Jun
Sunrise ºC(ºF)	−10(14)	−11(13)	−6(21)	−1(30)	4(39)	9(48)
Mid–afternoon ºC(ºF)	−1(30)	−1(30)	3(37)	8(46)	15(59)	20(68)
Days with precipitation	17	14	15	14	14	14
Precipitation mm	147	119	123	124	111	98
Precipitation inches	5.8	4.7	4.8	4.9	4.4	3.9
Daily hours of sunshine	3	4	5	5	6	7

	Jul	Aug	Sep	Oct	Nov	Dec
Sunrise ºC(ºF)	13(55)	13(55)	9(48)	4(39)	−1(30)	−7(19)
Mid–afternoon ºC(ºF)	23(73)	23(73)	19(66)	13(55)	7(44)	1(33)
Days with precipitation	13	12	12	13	14	15
Precipitation mm	97	110	95	129	154	167
Precipitation inches	3.8	4.3	3.8	5.1	6.1	6.6
Daily hours of sunshine	8	7	6	5	3	3

St. John's, Newfoundland: Altitude 140m (459ft)

	Jan	Feb	Mar	Apr	May	Jun
Sunrise ºC(ºF)	−8(18)	−9(16)	−6(21)	−2(29)	1(33)	6(42)
Mid–afternoon ºC(ºF)	0(32)	−1(30)	1(33)	5(41)	10(50)	16(60)
Days with precipitation	15	15	15	15	15	13
Precipitation mm	148	134	127	110	101	97
Precipitation inches	5.8	5.3	5.0	4.3	4.0	3.8
Daily hours of sunshine	2	3	3	4	5	6

	Jul	Aug	Sep	Oct	Nov	Dec
Sunrise ºC(ºF)	11(51)	11(51)	8(46)	3(37)	0(32)	−5(23)
Mid–afternoon ºC(ºF)	20(68)	19(66)	16(60)	11(51)	6(42)	1(33)
Days with precipitation	13	13	14	16	17	17
Precipitation mm	78	122	125	152	145	144
Precipitation inches	3.1	4.8	4.9	6.0	5.7	5.7
Daily hours of sunshine	7	6	5	4	2	2

Region 5. Northern Region
Yukon, northern regions of Alberta, Saskatchewan, Manitoba, Ontario, Quebec and all of Labrador. (Includes Churchill and Whitehorse.)

Best time: July to mid–September.

Mid–June to mid–September: Summer. Cool, 9 to 14ºC (48 to 57ºF). Expect rain every month.
October to May: Cold, snowy. Blizzards, December to March. Temperatures can drop to −40ºC (−40ºF). Snowfalls along the shores of Hudson Bay can total 183cm (72 inches).

Churchill, Manitoba: Altitude 29m (95ft)

	Jan	Feb	Mar	Apr	May	Jun
Sunrise ºC(ºF)	–31(–24)	–30(–22)	–25(–13)	–15(5)	–5(23)	1(33)
Mid–afternoon ºC(ºF)	–23(–10)	–21(–6)	–15(5)	–5(23)	3(37)	11(52)
Days with precipitation	5	6	6	6	7	9
Precipitation mm	17	13	18	23	31	45
Precipitation inches	0.7	0.5	0.7	0.9	1.2	1.8
Daily hours of sunshine	2	4	6	7	6	8

	Jul	Aug	Sep	Oct	Nov	Dec
Sunrise ºC(ºF)	7(44)	7(44)	2(35)	–4(25)	–16(3)	–27(–17)
Mid–afternoon ºC(ºF)	17(62)	16(60)	9(48)	1(33)	–9(16)	–19(–3)
Days with precipitation	10	12	11	12	9	8
Precipitation mm	51	61	53	47	36	20
Precipitation inches	2.0	2.4	2.1	1.9	1.4	0.8
Daily hours of sunshine	9	8	4	2	2	2

Natural attractions:
1. Polar bears at Churchill, Manitoba, on the western shore of Hudson Bay: Polar bears migrate to the ice–covered coastline of Hudson Bay and venture onto the ice in search of seals. See them from late–October to after the middle of November. Be aware that global warming is thinning the ice and the migratory routes and times may change.
2. Northern Lights (aurora borealis) can be seen September to April.

Whitehorse, Yukon: Altitude 704m (2310ft)

	Jan	Feb	Mar	Apr	May	Jun
Sunrise ºC(ºF)	–23(–10)	–18(–1)	–13(8)	–5(23)	0(32)	5(41)
Mid–afternoon ºC(ºF)	–14(7)	–8(18)	–1(30)	6(42)	13(55)	18(64)
Precipitation mm	17	12	12	8	14	31
Precipitation inches	0.7	0.5	0.5	0.3	0.6	1.2
Daily hours of sunshine	1	3	5	8	8	9

	Jul	Aug	Sep	Oct	Nov	Dec
Sunrise ºC(ºF)	8(46)	6(42)	2(35)	–3(27)	–14(7)	–20(–4)
Mid–afternoon ºC(ºF)	20(68)	18(64)	12(53)	4(39)	–6(21)	–12(11)
Precipitation mm	39	39	35	23	19	19
Precipitation inches	1.5	1.5	1.4	0.9	0.7	0.7
Daily hours of sunshine	8	7	5	3	2	1

Natural attraction at Whitehorse: The **Northern Lights** (aurora borealis) can be seen during the winter months, September to April.

Region 6. Arctic and subarctic region
Northwest Territories and Nunavut. (Includes Iqaluit and Yellowknife.)
Best time to visit: Mid–July to end of August.

June to mid–September: Summer can be pleasantly dry and warm. From mid–July to late August expect 20 hours of sun and 4 hours of twilight. Afternoon temperatures can reach 24°C (75°F), but nights are cool. July afternoon temperatures reach 21°C (70°F) in Yellowknife in Northwest Territories and 12°C (53°F) in Iqaluit on Baffin Island, Nunavut.
October through May is cold with temperatures continually below freezing. Blizzards are common in October and November, and February through April. The sun does not rise for days. As you travel to higher latitudes the sun is below the horizon for months. E.g. 3 months, early November to early February, at Resolute.

Iqaluit, Nunavut: Altitude 34m (111ft)

	Jan	Feb	Mar	Apr	May	Jun
Sunrise °C(°F)	–30(–22)	–31(–24)	–28(–18)	–20(–4)	–8(18)	0(32)
Mid–afternoon °C(°F)	–22(–8)	–22(–8)	–19(–3)	–10(14)	0(32)	6(42)
Precipitation mm	22	19	22	28	30	37
Precipitation inches	0.9	0.7	0.9	1.1	1.2	1.5
Daily hours of sunshine	1	3	5	7	6	6

	Jul	Aug	Sep	Oct	Nov	Dec
Sunrise °C(°F)	4(39)	3(37)	0(32)	–8(18)	–17(1)	–26(–15)
Mid–afternoon °C(°F)	12(53)	10(50)	5(41)	–2(29)	–9(16)	–18(–1)
Precipitation mm	58	64	52	42	31	20
Precipitation inches	2.3	2.5	2.0	1.6	1.2	0.8
Daily hours of sunshine	7	5	3	2	2	1

Yellowknife, Northwest Territories: Altitude 206m (676ft)

	Jan	Feb	Mar	Apr	May	Jun
Sunrise °C(°F)	–32(–27)	–29(–19)	–25(–13)	–12(11)	0(32)	8(46)
Mid–afternoon °C(°F)	–24(–12)	–20(–4)	–13(8)	0(32)	10(50)	18(64)
Precipitation mm	15	13	11	10	17	23
Precipitation inches	0.6	0.5	0.4	0.4	0.7	0.9
Daily hours of sunshine	1	1	6	9	11	13

	Jul	Aug	Sep	Oct	Nov	Dec
Sunrise °C(°F)	12(53)	10(50)	3(37)	–4(25)	–19(–3)	–28(–18)
Mid–afternoon °C(°F)	21(70)	18(64)	10(50)	1(33)	–11(13)	–20(–4)
Precipitation mm	35	42	29	35	24	15
Precipitation inches	1.4	1.6	1.1	1.4	0.9	0.6
Daily hours of sunshine	12	9	5	2	2	1

Natural attraction: Yellowknife is well–known as a place to view the Northern Lights (aurora borealis) in the winter months, September to April.

CANARY ISLANDS
(A territory of Spain)

Capital: Santa Cruz de Tenerife
Language: Spanish

The Canary Islands consist of seven main islands which
are peaks of a volcanic mountain range. The islands of
Tenerife, Gran Canaria, La Palma, El Hierro and La
Gomera are mountainous. The islands of Lanzarote and
Fuerteventura are comparatively flat.

Weather in general: Temperatures are always warm, rain
is minimal and the sun is always shining on all or part of
each island.

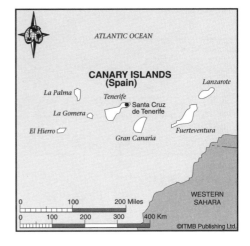

We have divided the weather into two regions, the Mountainous islands and the Flat islands.

Best time to visit: Year–round.

1. Mountainous islands.
December to February: Winter. Warm, afternoon average, 22°C (72°F). Sunny with an average of 6
to 7 hours daily. Most of the annual rainfall falls in winter, brought by the northeast tradewinds. When
they hit the northern slopes of the mountains they drop their moisture, causing the northern half of
these islands to be overcast and wet for days at a time. However, the southern half of these islands
enjoys sunshine year–round with hardly a drop of rain. The main tourist islands are Tenerife and Gran
Canaria. If the north is rainy, just head to the dry south, a drive of an hour or so. These months are part
of the peak season for visitors from Europe who are escaping the northern winter. The peak season
stretches from November to April.
March to May: Spring. Warm, sunny and dry. Popular time to visit.
June to August: Summer. Summer temperatures are a little higher than winter. Afternoon
temperatures average 25°C (77°F) but some days can be in the 30s°C (over 90°F). Days are sunny with
an average of 9 or 10 hours daily. Winds from North Africa can arrive with desert dust and sand, but
this is rare.
September to November: Autumn. Warm, sunny and dry. Popular time to visit.

2. Flat islands (Lanzarote and Fuerteventura).
Year–round: Dry, sunny and warm. In summer, June to August, there is a slight chance of desert
dust and sand blowing across the water from the Sahara. The African coast is only 100km (60 miles)
distant.

Las Palmas, Canary Islands (Spain): Altitude 6m (20ft)

	Jan	Feb	Mar	Apr	May	Jun
Sunrise °C(°F)	14(57)	14(57)	15(59)	15(60)	17(62)	18(64)
Mid–afternoon °C(°F)	21(69)	21(69)	22(72)	22(72)	23(73)	24(75)
Days with precipitation	7	5	4	2	0	0
Precipitation mm	17	22	10	6	2	0
Precipitation inches	0.7	0.9	0.4	0.2	0.08	0
Daily hours of sunshine	6	7	7	7	8	9

Las Palmas, Canary Islands (Spain): (continued)

	Jul	Aug	Sep	Oct	Nov	Dec
Sunrise ºC(ºF)	19(66)	20(68)	21(69)	19(66)	18(64)	16(60)
Mid–afternoon ºC(ºF)	25(77)	26(78)	26(78)	25(77)	24(75)	22(72)
Days with precipitation	0	0	1	3	7	7
Precipitation mm	0	0	9	10	21	21
Precipitation inches	0	0	0.4	0.4	0.8	0.8
Daily hours of sunshine	9	9	8	7	6	6

CAPE VERDE

Official Name: Republic of Cape Verde

Capital: Praia (on the island of São Tiago)
Language: Portuguese

The Republic of Cape Verde in the Atlantic Ocean
consists of ten hilly islands and five islets. They are stark
and dry with only 10 percent of the land being arable.

Best time: Pleasant all year round, but take note of
August to October.

Late August to early October: Season of light rains.
Expect cloudy conditions. Rain is irregular. Rainfall
is light on the coasts, but increases at higher elevations. This is also the hottest period with high
humidity, and afternoon temperatures reach 29ºC (85ºF). Sea breezes tend to temper the climate.
November to September is dry and pleasant. Although there is no defined cool season, December
to March are the coolest months. A warm sweater is advisable. December to February is when the
harmattan winds carry dust from the Sahara and cause low visibility.

Sal, Cape Verde: Altitude 55m (180ft)

	Jan	Feb	Mar	Apr	May	Jun
Sunrise ºC(ºF)	20(68)	19(66)	20(68)	20(68)	20(68)	21(69)
Mid–afternoon ºC(ºF)	24(75)	24(75)	25(77)	25(77)	25(77)	26(78)
Days with precipitation	1	1	0	0	0	0
Precipitation mm	5	4	1	0	0	0
Precipitation inches	0.2	0.1	0.04	0	0	0
Daily hours of sunshine	6	6	6	7	7	6

	Jul	Aug	Sep	Oct	Nov	Dec
Sunrise ºC(ºF)	22(72)	24(75)	24(75)	24(75)	22(72)	22(71)
Mid–afternoon ºC(ºF)	27(80)	29(84)	29(84)	29(84)	27(80)	25(77)
Days with precipitation	0	8	7	3	1	0
Precipitation mm	1	14	34	7	3	2
Precipitation inches	0.04	0.6	1.3	0.3	0.1	0.08
Daily hours of sunshine	5	5	6	6	6	5

CARIBBEAN ISLANDS

For individual islands, see list below.

There are more than 7000 islands in the Caribbean Sea but many are small or uninhabited.

Most popular time to visit: November to April.
Best time: January to April.

February to April: Generally dry. These winter months are the driest and sunniest. Temperatures are kept down by sea breezes. Humidity is lower. Expect 8 hours of sunshine daily. (December and January are also relatively dry.)

May to November: Generally wet. September is the rainiest. Rain often falls as thunderstorms late in the day. Expect 8 hours of sunshine daily, but with higher humidity.

Tradewinds: Tradewinds from the northeast bring a higher rainfall to the northern and eastern slopes of the islands' mountains. The leeward slopes on the southern and western sides receive less rain.

Hurricanes: Hurricane season runs June through November, peaking in September. Some islands escape hurricanes for several years. Other islands on the fringe of a hurricane's path may receive heavier–than–normal rains.

Note: For weather of each island see under separate headings: Anguilla, Antigua and Barbuda, Aruba, Bahamas, Barbados, Cayman Islands, Cuba, Dominica, Dominican Republic, Grenada, Guadeloupe, Haiti, Jamaica, Martinique, Monserrat, Netherlands Antilles (St Eustatius, Saba, Sint Maarten, Bonaire, Curaçao), Puerto Rico, St Kitts and Nevis, St Lucia, St Vincent and the Grenadines, Trinidad and Tobago, Turks and Caicos, Virgin Islands (British), Virgin Islands (U.S.).

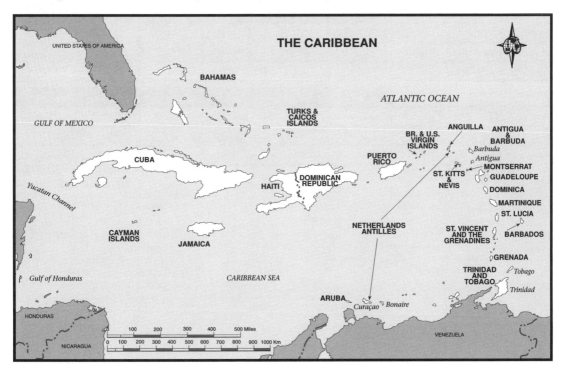

CAYMAN ISLANDS

Official Name: Cayman Islands
(United Kingdom Crown Colony)

Capital: Georgetown
Language: English

Three islands comprise the group of Grand Cayman, Little
Cayman and Cayman Brac. They are of coral formation,
topped with fertile soil.

Best time: December to April.
Pleasant temperature year round.

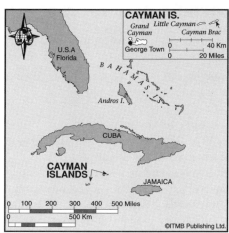

December to April: Dry season. Winter. Afternoon
average, 28°C (83°F). This is the peak tourist season.
June to September: Wet season. Summer. Afternoon average, 32°C (89°F).
Rain: May to October, but only as short showers.
Humidity: High throughout year.

Note: See under Caribbean Islands for general weather information.

Georgetown, Cayman Islands: Altitude, sea level.

	Jan	Feb	Mar	Apr	May	Jun
Sunrise °C(°F)	21(69)	21(69)	21(69)	21(69)	22(72)	24(75)
Mid–afternoon °C(°F)	28(82)	28(82)	29(84)	30(86)	31(87)	31(87)
Days with precipitation	5	4	4	4	7	7

	Jul	Aug	Sep	Oct	Nov	Dec
Sunrise °C(°F)	24(75)	24(75)	23(74)	23(74)	22(72)	21(70)
Mid–afternoon °C(°F)	32(89)	32(89)	32(89)	31(87)	29(84)	28(83)
Days with precipitation	7	8	9	10	9	6

CENTRAL AFRICAN REPUBLIC

Official Name: Central African Republic

Capital: Bangui
Languages: French, Sango

Most of the country is on a plateau 600 to 750m (2000 to 2500ft) above sea level. The south has dense rainforests while most of the country has open grassland, expecially the north.

Best time to visit: November to March. (Dry.)

There are two weather regions.
1. North.
November to March: Sunny, dry season. Hot, 32°C (90°F).
March to May: Sunny. Light rain falls as the rainy season approaches. Humidity increases and daytime temperatures climb to 40°C (104°F).
May to October: Rainy season. Sunny with high humidity. Hot, 30 to 37°C (86 to 99°F).

2. South (includes Bangui).
December to February: Sunny, dry, hot, 32°C(90°F). Humidity is high.
March to November: Rains start in March but the main rainy season is June to October with the wettest months being July and August. Humidity is high. Afternoon temperatures remain fairly constant, about 32°C (90°F).

Bangui, Central African Republic: Altitude 387m (1270ft)

	Jan	Feb	Mar	Apr	May	Jun
Sunrise °C(°F)	20(68)	21(70)	22(71)	22(71)	21(70)	21(70)
Mid–afternoon °C(°F)	32(90)	34(93)	33(91)	33(91)	32(89)	31(87)
Days with precipitation	3	5	11	10	15	12
Precipitation mm	25	43	127	135	188	114
Precipitation inches	1.0	1.7	5.0	5.3	7.4	4.5
Daily hours of sunshine	7	7	6	6	6	6

	Jul	Aug	Sep	Oct	Nov	Dec
Sunrise °C(°F)	21(69)	21(69)	21(69)	21(69)	20(68)	19(66)
Mid–afternoon °C(°F)	29(85)	29(85)	31(87)	31(87)	31(87)	32(90)
Days with precipitation	17	19	16	19	11	2
Precipitation mm	226	206	150	201	125	5
Precipitation inches	8.9	8.1	5.9	7.9	4.9	0.2
Daily hours of sunshine	4	4	5	5	6	7

CHAD
Official Name: Republic of Chad

Capital: N'Djamena
Languages: French, Arabic, African languages

The country sits on a plateau that slopes upward from Lake Chad, about 275m (900ft), to heights of 900 to 1200m (3000 to 4000ft). The northern half of the country is in the Sahara Desert. In the north are the Tibesti Mountains, 3400m (11200ft).

Best time to visit: November to February.

November to February: Sunny, dry, medium humidity.
This is the relatively cool season. Afternoon temperatures reach 28 to 33°C (82 to 91°F). Hot, dry, dust–laden harmattan winds from the northeast can cause haziness in the sky from November to March.
March to May: Sunny, dry, humid and very hot with daytime maximums exceeding 40°C (104°F). The excessive heat makes travelling uncomfortable.
June to September: Rainy season. July and August are the rainiest months with high humidity. The reliability of rain decreases from south to north. The northern region is rainless.

N'Djamena, Chad: Altitude 295m (968ft)

	Jan	Feb	Mar	Apr	May	Jun
Sunrise ºC(ºF)	14(57)	17(62)	21(69)	25(77)	26(78)	25(77)
Mid–afternoon ºC(ºF)	32(89)	35(95)	39(102)	41(105)	40(104)	37(98)
Days with precipitation	0	0	0	1	4	6
Precipitation mm	0	0	0	10	26	50
Precipitation inches	0	0	0	0.4	1.0	2.0
Daily hours of sunshine	10	10	9	9	9	9

	Jul	Aug	Sep	Oct	Nov	Dec
Sunrise ºC(ºF)	23(73)	22(72)	23(73)	22(72)	18(64)	15(59)
Mid–afternoon ºC(ºF)	34(93)	32(89)	34(93)	37(98)	36(96)	34(93)
Days with precipitation	12	15	10	3	0	0
Precipitation mm	144	174	84	20	0	0
Precipitation inches	5.7	6.9	3.3	0.8	0	0
Daily hours of sunshine	7	6	8	9	10	10

CHILE
Official Name: Republic of Chile

Capital: Santiago
Language: Spanish

(**Easter Island,** part of Chile, is listed separately under **E.**)

The Andes Mountains extend along the eastern side in a north–south direction. Between the mountains and the ocean is a plateau which is a rainless desert in the north and fertile in the south.

Best months for travelling are, in general, October to March.
Best months for skiing are June to early October.

We have divided the weather into four regions.
Refer to map for corresponding numbers.
1. Northern Chile, between Peruvian border and Rio Aconcagua. (Includes Antofagasta.)
Good time: Anytime of year.
May to October: Dry, warm days with average afternoon temperature of 18°C (64°F). Mornings can be bitterly cold in this desert climate. Six hours of sunshine daily. There is no rain.
November to April: Dry, sunny, warm days. Afternoon temperatures are fairly constant, 21 to 24°C (70 to 76°F). Mornings are cold. In summer months, December to February, expect 10 hours of sunshine daily. No rain.

Antofagasta, Chile: Altitude 94m (308ft)

	Jan	Feb	Mar	Apr	May	Jun
Sunrise °C(°F)	17(63)	17(63)	16(61)	14(58)	13(55)	11(52)
Mid–afternoon °C(°F)	24(76)	24(76)	23(74)	21(70)	19(67)	18(65)
Days with precipitation	0	0	0	0	0	0
Precipitation mm	0	0	0	0	0	3
Precipitation inches	0	0	0	0	0	0.1
Daily hours of sunshine	11	10	8	4	6	6

	Jul	Aug	Sep	Oct	Nov	Dec
Sunrise °C(°F)	11(51)	11(52)	12(53)	13(55)	14(58)	16(60)
Mid–afternoon °C(°F)	17(63)	17(62)	18(64)	19(66)	21(69)	22(72)
Days with precipitation	0	0	0	0	0	0
Precipitation mm	5	3	0	3	0	0
Precipitation inches	0.2	0.1	0	0.1	0	0
Daily hours of sunshine	6	6	6	6	7	9

2. Central Chile, between Rio Aconcagua and Concepcion. (Includes Santiago.)
Best time: October to March.

October to March: Summer. Dry. Afternoon temperatures reach 29°C (85°F) in mid–summer (January).
April to September: Winter. Afternoon temperatures are 15 to 20°C (59 to 69°F). Evenings are cold. Rainy months are May to August. Snow and frost occur inland but are rare on the coast.

Recreational activity: Skiing. June to early October is the skiing season. E.g. at Farellones and Portillo.

Santiago, Chile: Altitude 520m (1706ft)

	Jan	Feb	Mar	Apr	May	Jun
Sunrise ºC(ºF)	12(53)	11(52)	9(49)	7(45)	5(41)	3(37)
Mid–afternoon ºC(ºF)	29(85)	29(85)	27(80)	23(74)	18(65)	14(58)
Days with precipitation	0	0	1	1	5	6
Precipitation mm	3	3	5	13	64	84
Precipitation inches	0.1	0.1	0.2	0.5	2.5	3.3
Daily hours of sunshine	11	9	9	6	4	3

	Jul	Aug	Sep	Oct	Nov	Dec
Sunrise ºC(ºF)	3(37)	4(39)	6(42)	7(45)	9(48)	11(51)
Mid–afternoon ºC(ºF)	15(59)	17(62)	19(66)	22(72)	26(78)	28(83)
Days with precipitation	6	5	3	3	1	0
Precipitation mm	76	56	31	15	8	5
Precipitation inches	3.0	2.2	1.2	0.6	0.3	0.2
Daily hours of sunshine	3	4	5	6	9	10

3. Southern region between Concepcion and Puerto Montt. (Includes Valdivia.)
Best time: November to March.

November to March: Summer. Afternoon temperatures are a pleasant 18 to 23°C (65 to 73°F). In the Lake District, between Temuco and Puerto Montt, cold winds can blow around the mountains and across the lakes. Stormy weather and fog are possible. Expect 6 to 8 hours of sunshine daily. The best season to visit the Lake District is mid–December to mid–March.
April to October: Winter. Cool. Afternoon temperatures range around 13°C (55°F). Expect 2 to 4 hours of sunshine. Most rain falls during the winter months, April to September, and snow falls on the high ground of the Lake District.

Valdivia, Chile: Altitude 5m (16ft)

	Jan	Feb	Mar	Apr	May	Jun
Sunrise ºC(ºF)	11(52)	11(51)	9(49)	8(46)	6(43)	6(42)
Mid–afternoon ºC(ºF)	23(73)	23(73)	21(69)	17(62)	13(56)	11(52)
Days with precipitation	7	7	11	12	21	21
Precipitation mm	66	74	132	234	361	550
Precipitation inches	2.6	2.9	5.2	9.2	14.2	17.7
Daily hours of sunshine	8	8	7	4	2	2

	Jul	Aug	Sep	Oct	Nov	Dec
Sunrise ºC(ºF)	5(41)	4(40)	5(41)	7(44)	8(46)	10(50)
Mid–afternoon ºC(ºF)	11(52)	12(54)	14(58)	17(63)	18(65)	21(69)
Days with precipitation	20	18	13	13	10	10
Precipitation mm	394	328	208	127	125	104
Precipitation inches	15.5	12.9	8.2	5.0	4.9	4.1
Daily hours of sunshine	2	3	4	4	6	7

4. Chilean Archipelago from Puerto Montt to Cape Horn. (Includes Punta Arenas.)
Best time: January and February.

December to February: Summer. Cool days, cold nights. Afternoon temperatures, 14ºC (58ºF). Mostly misty and cloudy. Expect cold wind gusts even on sunny summer days.
March to April: Autumn. Wet, windy, cloudy. Afternoon temperatures decline from 12ºC (54ºF) in March to 5ºC (41ºF) in May.
June to August: Winter. Cold days. Afternoon temperature, 5ºC (41ºF). Cloudy. Heavy winter rains.
September to November: Spring. Strong, bitterly cold winds blow, reaching a velocity of 80km/h (50mph).

Natural attraction: Torres del Paine National Park in Chile's Patagonia region. Best time to visit is January to April, before snowfalls.

Punta Arenas, Chile: Altitude 8m (26ft)

	Jan	Feb	Mar	Apr	May	Jun
Sunrise ºC(ºF)	7(45)	7(44)	5(41)	4(39)	2(35)	1(33)
Mid–afternoon ºC(ºF)	14(58)	14(58)	12(54)	10(50)	7(45)	5(41)
Days with precipitation	6	5	7	9	6	8
Precipitation mm	38	23	33	36	33	41
Precipitation inches	1.5	0.9	1.3	1.4	1.3	1.6

	Jul	Aug	Sep	Oct	Nov	Dec
Sunrise ºC(ºF)	−1(31)	1(33)	2(35)	3(38)	4(40)	6(43)
Mid–afternoon ºC(ºF)	4(40)	6(42)	8(46)	11(51)	12(54)	14(57)
Days with precipitation	6	5	5	5	5	8
Precipitation mm	28	31	23	28	18	36
Precipitation inches	1.1	1.2	0.9	1.1	0.7	1.4

For Easter Island see under Easter Island.

CHINA

Official Name: People's Republic of China

Capital: Beijing
Languages: Mandarin, other Chinese languages, Tibetan, Uigur, Mongol and others

Along the coast are lowlands and plains. To the west is a series of north–south mountain ranges and extensive uplands. Farther west are the highlands of Tibet.

Best time:
1. China proper:
    First choice: Sept. and October.
    Second choice: April and May.
2. Grasslands of Inner Mongolia:
June to mid–September.
3. Silk route through Xinjiang province: April and September.
4. Tibet: May to October.
5. Yunnan province: Year–round.
6. Hong Kong and the southeastern provinces: Mid–September to December, and March and April.

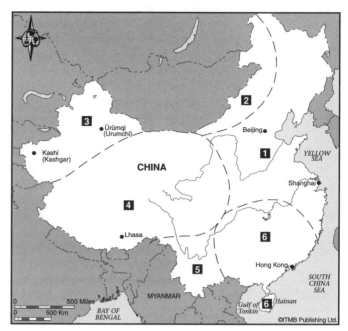

We have divided the weather into 6 regions as listed above. Refer to map for corresponding numbers.

1. China proper. (Includes Beijing and Shanghai.)
Best time: First choice: September and October.
Second choice: April and May.

September and October: Autumn. Best time to travel. Pleasantly cool in the north in Beijing. Pleasantly warm in the south in Shanghai with light rains.
November to March: Winter. Cold, expect light snowfalls. Dry in the north in Beijing. Mild and dry in the south in Shanghai, but no snow.
April and May: Spring. Dry in the north. Dust storms can occur at this time. Expect 8 hours of sunshine daily in Beijing. Average afternoon temperatures in Beijing are a mild 21 to 27°C (69 to 81°F). In the south, e.g., Shanghai, there is more rain. Afternoon temperatures are a mild 19 to 25°C (66 to 77°F), a pleasant time for Shanghai.
June to August: Summer. Uncomfortably hot, humid and rainy. July usually has the heaviest rains.

Beijing, China: Altitude 55m (180ft)

	Jan	Feb	Mar	Apr	May	Jun
Sunrise ºC(ºF)	–9(16)	–7(19)	–1(30)	7(44)	13(55)	18(64)
Mid–afternoon ºC(ºF)	2(35)	4(39)	11(51)	20(68)	26(78)	30(86)
Days with precipitation	1	2	2	3	4	6
Precipitation mm	3	6	9	26	29	71
Precipitation inches	0.1	0.2	0.4	1.0	1.1	2.8
Daily hours of sunshine	6	7	8	8	9	9

	Jul	Aug	Sep	Oct	Nov	Dec
Sunrise ºC(ºF)	22(72)	20(68)	14(57)	7(44)	–1(30)	–7(19)
Mid–afternoon ºC(ºF)	31(87)	29(84)	26(78)	19(66)	10(50)	3(37)
Days with precipitation	10	9	4	3	1	1
Precipitation mm	176	182	49	19	6	2
Precipitation inches	6.9	7.2	1.9	0.7	0.2	0.08
Daily hours of sunshine	7	7	8	7	6	6

Shanghai, China: Altitude 7m (23ft)

	Jan	Feb	Mar	Apr	May	Jun
Sunrise ºC(ºF)	1(33)	1(33)	5(41)	11(51)	16(60)	20(68)
Mid–afternoon ºC(ºF)	8(46)	9(48)	13(55)	19(66)	23(73)	27(80)
Days with precipitation	6	7	9	10	10	10
Precipitation mm	39	59	81	102	115	152
Precipitation inches	1.5	2.3	3.2	4.0	4.5	6.0
Daily hours of sunshine	4	4	5	5	6	5

	Jul	Aug	Sep	Oct	Nov	Dec
Sunrise ºC(ºF)	25(77)	25(77)	20(68)	15(59)	9(48)	2(35)
Mid–afternoon ºC(ºF)	32(89)	31(87)	27(80)	22(72)	17(62)	11(51)
Days with precipitation	9	8	9	6	5	5
Precipitation mm	128	133	156	61	51	35
Precipitation inches	5.0	5.2	6.1	2.4	2.0	1.4
Daily hours of sunshine	7	8	5	5	5	5

2. Grasslands of Inner Mongolia.

Best time to travel: June to mid–September. Warm with average afternoon temperature of 20ºC (68ºF) with little rain. Clear, blue skies predominate throughout the year.

September and October: Cold winds from the north blow across the flat terrain.
December to March or April: Winter. Light snow and frost.

3. Silk route through Xinjiang province. (Includes Kashi and Urumqi.)
Good time to travel: April and September.

April: Dry and pleasant with an average afternoon temperature of 22°C (72°F).
May and June: Dry and pleasant, 26°C (79°F).
July and August: Dry and oppressively hot, 33°C (91°F).
September: Dry and pleasant. Good time to visit. Average afternoon temperature, 22°C (72°F).
November to February: Dry, and cold to freezing.

Kashi (Kashgar), China: Altitude 1291m (4235ft)

	Jan	Feb	Mar	Apr	May	Jun
Sunrise °C(°F)	−11(13)	−6(21)	2(35)	9(48)	13(55)	16(60)
Mid–afternoon °C(°F)	1(33)	5(41)	14(57)	22(72)	26(78)	30(86)
Days with precipitation	1	1	1	1	1	2
Precipitation mm	3	6	6	6	11	7
Precipitation inches	0.1	0.2	0.2	0.2	0.4	0.3
Daily hours of sunshine	5	5	5	7	8	10

	Jul	Aug	Sep	Oct	Nov	Dec
Sunrise °C(°F)	19(66)	17(62)	12(53)	5(41)	−2(29)	−8(18)
Mid–afternoon °C(°F)	32(89)	31(87)	26(78)	20(68)	10(50)	2(35)
Days with precipitation	1	2	1	1	0	0
Precipitation mm	8	8	6	3	2	1
Precipitation inches	0.3	0.3	0.2	0.1	0.08	0.04
Daily hours of sunshine	10	9	9	8	7	5

Urumqi (Urumchi), China: Altitude 906m (2972ft)

	Jan	Feb	Mar	Apr	May	Jun
Sunrise °C(°F)	−22(−7)	−19(−3)	−11(12)	2(36)	8(47)	12(54)
Mid–afternoon °C(°F)	−11(13)	−8(17)	−1(31)	16(60)	22(72)	26(78)
Days with precipitation	17	14	14	9	5	11
Precipitation mm	15	8	13	38	28	38
Precipitation inches	0.6	0.3	0.5	1.5	1.1	1.5
Daily hours of sunshine	6	5	6	7	10	9

	Jul	Aug	Sep	Oct	Nov	Dec
Sunrise °C(°F)	14(58)	13(56)	8(47)	−1(31)	−11(13)	−13(8)
Mid–afternoon °C(°F)	28(82)	27(80)	21(69)	10(50)	−1(30)	−8(17)
Days with precipitation	5	4	4	10	14	18
Precipitation mm	18	25	15	43	41	10
Precipitation inches	0.7	1.0	0.6	1.7	1.6	0.4
Daily hours of sunshine	9	9	9	7	5	5

4. Tibet, or Xizang province. (Includes Lhasa.)
Best weather for general travel and trekking: May to October. (Warmer temperatures.)

May and June: Relatively dry.
July and August: Rainy, with about 15 days a month of rain.
September and October: Relatively dry.
November to April: Cool to very cold. Virtually rainless.

Lhasa, Tibet, China: Altitude 3650m (11975ft)

	Jan	Feb	Mar	Apr	May	Jun
Sunrise ºC(ºF)	–10(14)	–7(19)	–3(27)	1(33)	5(41)	9(48)
Mid–afternoon ºC(ºF)	7(44)	9(48)	12(53)	16(60)	19(66)	23(73)
Days with precipitation	0	0	1	1	5	10
Precipitation mm	1	1	2	5	27	72
Precipitation inches	0.04	0.04	0.08	0.2	1.1	2.8
Daily hours of sunshine	8	8	8	8	9	9

	Jul	Aug	Sep	Oct	Nov	Dec
Sunrise ºC(ºF)	10(50)	9(48)	7(44)	1(33)	–5(23)	–9(16)
Mid–afternoon ºC(ºF)	22(72)	21(69)	20(68)	16(60)	11(51)	8(46)
Days with precipitation	15	15	10	2	0	0
Precipitation mm	119	123	58	10	2	1
Precipitation inches	4.7	4.8	2.3	0.4	0.08	0.04
Daily hours of sunshine	7	7	8	9	9	8

5. Yunnan province. (Includes Kunming.)
Good for travelling year–round.

May to September: Rainy season with a constant afternoon temperature of 24ºC (75ºF). July and August are the rainiest with 16 wet days each per month. May, June and September average 13 rainy days each.
Mid–October to April: Negligible rain. Mild to warm.

Kunming, Yunnan, China: Altitude 1892m (6207ft)

	Jan	Feb	Mar	Apr	May	Jun
Sunrise ºC(ºF)	2(35)	3(37)	5(41)	9(48)	14(57)	16(60)
Mid–afternoon ºC(ºF)	15(59)	17(62)	20(68)	23(73)	25(77)	24(75)
Days with precipitation	2	3	3	4	9	14
Precipitation mm	12	12	16	27	92	173
Precipitation inches	0.5	0.5	0.6	1.1	3.6	6.8
Daily hours of sunshine	7	8	9	8	7	5

Kunming, Yunnan, China: (continued)

	Jul	Aug	Sep	Oct	Nov	Dec
Sunrise ºC(ºF)	17(62)	16(60)	14(57)	11(51)	7(44)	2(35)
Mid–afternoon ºC(ºF)	24(75)	24(75)	22(72)	20(68)	17(62)	15(59)
Days with precipitation	16	16	12	11	5	2
Precipitation mm	205	206	122	89	40	14
Precipitation inches	8.1	8.1	4.8	3.5	1.6	0.6
Daily hours of sunshine	5	5	5	5	6	7

6. Hong Kong and the southeastern provinces.
Best time to visit: First choice is mid–September to December. (Mild, dry.)
Second choice is March and April.
Wet season is May to September.

January and February: Damp and drizzly with a cold wind that sweeps west to east out of the Chinese mainland.
March and April: Warm. Negligible rain. Haze and low–altitude cloud can prevail for weeks, particularly February, March or April. Reasonable humidity. Climate gets stickier as summer (June to August) approaches.
May to September: Hot, humid and rainy. June is usually the rainiest month. From July to September coastal regions can expect typhoons to blow in from the South China Sea, accompanied by lashing rains.
October to December: Warm but less humid. Light rains only.

Cultural event: Tin Hau festival in Hong Kong. Twenty–third day of the third moon (around May). Hundreds of boats are colourfully decked, carrying shrines which are paraded to temples.

Hong Kong, China: Altitude 33m (108ft)

	Jan	Feb	Mar	Apr	May	Jun
Sunrise ºC(ºF)	13(55)	14(57)	16(60)	20(68)	24(75)	26(78)
Mid–afternoon ºC(ºF)	19(66)	19(66)	21(70)	25(77)	28(82)	30(86)
Days with precipitation	4	6	6	8	11	16
Precipitation mm	24	47	68	160	314	378
Precipitation inches	0.9	1.9	2.7	6.3	12.4	14.9
Daily hours of sunshine	5	3	3	4	5	5

	Jul	Aug	Sep	Oct	Nov	Dec
Sunrise ºC(ºF)	26(78)	26(78)	25(77)	23(73)	19(66)	15(59)
Mid–afternoon ºC(ºF)	31(87)	31(87)	30(86)	28(82)	24(75)	20(68)
Days with precipitation	14	14	12	6	4	2
Precipitation mm	327	395	305	145	34	27
Precipitation inches	12.9	15.6	12.0	5.7	1.3	1.1
Daily hours of sunshine	7	7	6	6	6	6

COLOMBIA
Official Name: Republic of Colombia

Capital: Bogota
Language: Spanish

Three high, parallel ranges of the Andes Mountains, separated by deep river valleys, extend through the western part of Colombia. About two thirds of the country is covered by lowlands. They are the coastal plains along the Caribbean and Pacific coasts and, in the east, the vast grassy plains of the Llanos, and in the southeast the densely forested Amazon lowlands.

Temperatures vary with altitude. Lowlands are hot, mountains are cooler. Some peaks, especially those above 4500m (15000ft) receive snow.

Best time to visit in general: December to March. (Dry.)

We have divided Colombia into 5 regions.
1. Mountain plateaus and basins. (Includes Bogota.)
Best time to visit: December to March.

December to March: Comparatively dry, pleasant weather, 19°C (67°F) in the afternoons. Five hours of sunshine daily.
April to June: Rainy, but pleasant weather, 19°C (67°F), in the afternoons. April is wettest with 20 rainy days per month. Three to four hours of sunshine daily during this 3–month period.
July to September: Partly dry with 16 rainy days per month. Average afternoon temperature is 18°C (65°F). Expect 4 hours of sunshine daily.
October and November: Wet. Most rain falls in October. 19°C (66°F) in afternoons. Three hours of sunshine daily.

Bogota, Colombia: Altitude 2548m (8359ft)

	Jan	Feb	Mar	Apr	May	Jun
Sunrise °C(°F)	5(41)	6(42)	7(44)	8(46)	8(46)	8(46)
Mid–afternoon °C(°F)	20(68)	20(68)	20(68)	19(66)	19(66)	18(64)
Days with precipitation	6	7	13	20	17	16
Precipitation mm	33	43	66	111	94	57
Precipitation inches	1.3	1.7	2.6	4.4	3.7	2.2
Daily hours of sunshine	6	5	5	4	4	4

	Jul	Aug	Sep	Oct	Nov	Dec
Sunrise °C(°F)	7(44)	7(44)	7(44)	8(46)	8(46)	6(42)
Mid–afternoon °C(°F)	18(64)	18(64)	19(66)	19(66)	19(66)	19(66)
Days with precipitation	18	16	13	20	16	15
Precipitation mm	41	49	73	115	88	54
Precipitation inches	1.6	1.9	2.9	4.5	3.5	2.1
Daily hours of sunshine	5	4	4	4	4	5

2. Caribbean coast. (Includes Cartagena, Barranquilla and Santa Marta, and off–shore islands e.g. San Andrés.) Weather is hot and humid all year with temperatures ranging from a morning low of 25°C (77°F) to an afternoon high of approximately 36°C (97°F).
Best months: February and March.

Mid–December to April: Dry, humid, hot. The cooling tradewinds lower the temperature by 2°C (4°F).
May and June: Rainy, humid, hot.
July to September: Partly dry, humid, hot.
October and November: Rainy, humid, hot.

San Andrés Island, Colombia: Altitude 6m (20ft)

	Jan	Feb	Mar	Apr	May	Jun
Sunrise °C(°F)	25(77)	24(75)	25(77)	25(77)	26(78)	25(77)
Mid–afternoon °C(°F)	29(84)	29(84)	30(86)	30(86)	30(86)	30(86)
Precipitation mm	96	41	22	34	121	224
Precipitation inches	3.8	1.6	0.9	1.3	4.8	8.8
Daily hours of sunshine	8	8	9	9	8	6

	Jul	Aug	Sep	Oct	Nov	Dec
Sunrise °C(°F)	25(77)	25(77)	25(77)	25(77)	25(77)	25(77)
Mid–afternoon °C(°F)	30(86)	30(86)	30(86)	30(86)	30(86)	29(84)
Precipitation mm	204	200	234	302	296	173
Precipitation inches	8.0	7.9	9.2	11.9	11.7	6.8
Daily hours of sunshine	6	7	7	6	6	7

3. Pacific coast.
Wet season is year–round. Rain falls almost daily, coming as afternoon cloudbursts but mainly at night. Humidity is high. Average afternoon temperature year–round is a constant 32°C (89°F).

4. Grassy plains. (Includes Los Llanos, i.e. the savanna grasslands, for which Villavicencio is a gateway city.)
Best time: December to March.

December to March: Dry.
April to November: Wet.

5. Amazon lowlands. (Includes Leticia on the Amazon River.)
Region is hot and damp all year. Afternoon temperatures year–round range 31 to 34°C (88 to 94°F).
Good time to visit Leticia is May to October. Best time is July and August, the early months of the dry season.

June to November: Dry, hot.
December and January: Wet, hot.
February and March: Dry, hot.
April and May: Wet, hot.

COMOROS

Official Name: Union of the Comoros, formerly the
Federal Islamic Republic of the Comoros

Capital: Moroni, on Grand Comoro
Languages: Arabic, French, Comoran

The country includes islands of volcanic origin: Grand
Comoro, also called Njazidja, which has an active
volcano, and Anjouan (Nzwani) and Mohéli (Mwali), and
many coral islets. Mayotte, a nearby island, is claimed by
Comoros but is administered by France.

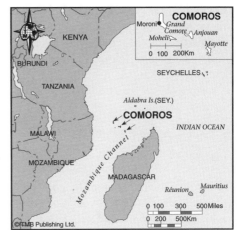

Best time: May to October.

May to October: Season of less rain, 11 to 12 rainy days per month. Cooler season, average afternoon
temperature, 28°C (82°F).
November to April: Wet, hot, humid. Expect 16 to 19 rainy days per month. Average afternoon
temperature, 30°C (87°F).
Cyclones: Between November and April Comoros is subject to cyclones, but these only occur every
three years or so.

Moroni, Comoros: Altitude 12m (39ft)

	Jan	Feb	Mar	Apr	May	Jun
Sunrise °C(°F)	23(73)	23(73)	23(73)	23(73)	21(70)	20(68)
Mid–afternoon °C(°F)	30(86)	30(87)	31(87)	30(87)	29(85)	28(83)
Days with precipitation	18	17	17	19	13	12
Precipitation mm	345	311	300	296	233	215
Precipitation inches	13.6	12.2	11.8	11.7	9.2	8.5
Daily hours of sunshine	6	6	7	6	7	8

	Jul	Aug	Sep	Oct	Nov	Dec
Sunrise °C(°F)	19(66)	19(66)	19(66)	20(68)	22(72)	23(73)
Mid–afternoon °C(°F)	28(82)	27(81)	28(82)	29(84)	31(87)	31(87)
Days with precipitation	12	11	11	12	12	16
Precipitation mm	194	118	117	91	102	220
Precipitation inches	7.6	4.6	4.6	3.6	4.0	8.7
Daily hours of sunshine	8	7	7	8	8	7

CONGO DEMOCRATIC REPUBLIC

Official Name: Democratic Republic of Congo
Unofficial name: Congo (Kinshasa). The country was
formerly known as Belgian Congo and later, Zaire. It
should not be confused with the former French Congo to
the north now known as Republic of the Congo, or Congo
Republic.

Capital: Kinshasa
Languages: French, Lingala, Kingwana

The dominant feature is the Congo River basin, a vast
forested depression that covers much of the country. There
is a high grassland plateau in the south and mountains
in the east and west. In the west and centre, in the vast
forested basin or depression, humidity is high. Year–round temperatures range from 20ºC (68ºF) in the
mornings to 30ºC (86ºF) in the afternoons. In the east, where there is a high plateau of mountains and
lakes, humidity is high and year–round daily temperatures range from 15ºC (59ºF) in the mornings to
25ºC (77ºF) in the afternoons. The country straddles the equator. The wet and dry seasons north and
south of the equator differ.

Best time for region north of the equator (includes Kisangani) is November to March. (Dry.)
Best time for region south of the equator (includes Kinshasa) is July to September. (Dry.)

The two regions are:
1. North of the equator.
Best time: November to March.

November to March: Main dry season.
April to June: Rainy.
July and August: Short dry season.
September and October: Rainy.

2. South of the equator.
Best time: July to September.

June to September: Dry season.
October to May: Rainy.

Kinshasa, Democratic Rep. of Congo: Altitude 322m (1056ft)

	Jan	Feb	Mar	Apr	May	Jun
Sunrise ºC(ºF)	21(70)	22(71)	22(71)	22(71)	22(71)	19(67)
Mid–afternoon ºC(ºF)	31(87)	31(87)	32(89)	32(89)	31(88)	29(84)
Days with precipitation	11	11	12	16	12	1
Precipitation mm	135	145	196	196	159	8
Precipitation inches	5.3	5.7	7.7	7.7	6.2	0.3
Daily hours of sunshine	4	5	5	5	4	4

	Jul	Aug	Sep	Oct	Nov	Dec
Sunrise ºC(ºF)	18(64)	18(64)	20(68)	21(70)	22(71)	21(70)
Mid–afternoon ºC(ºF)	27(81)	29(84)	31(87)	31(87)	31(87)	30(86)
Days with precipitation	0	1	5	11	16	15
Precipitation mm	3	3	30	119	222	142
Precipitation inches	0.1	0.1	1.2	4.7	8.7	5.6
Daily hours of sunshine	4	5	4	5	5	4

Kisangani, Democratic Rep. of Congo: Altitude 418m (1371ft)

	Jan	Feb	Mar	Apr	May	Jun
Sunrise ºC(ºF)	21(69)	21(69)	21(69)	21(70)	21(69)	21(69)
Mid–afternoon ºC(ºF)	31(87)	31(87)	31(87)	31(87)	31(87)	30(86)
Days with precipitation	6	9	11	10	10	9
Precipitation mm	53	84	178	158	137	114
Precipitation inches	2.1	3.3	7.0	6.2	5.4	4.5
Daily hours of sunshine	6	6	6	6	5	5

	Jul	Aug	Sep	Oct	Nov	Dec
Sunrise ºC(ºF)	19(66)	20(68)	20(68)	20(68)	20(68)	20(68)
Mid–afternoon ºC(ºF)	29(84)	28(82)	29(84)	30(86)	29(84)	30(86)
Days with precipitation	10	11	13	14	15	10
Precipitation mm	132	165	183	218	198	84
Precipitation inches	5.2	6.5	7.2	8.6	7.8	3.3
Daily hours of sunshine	4	4	5	6	5	5

CONGO REPUBLIC

Official Name: Republic of the Congo
Unofficial name: Congo (Brazzaville). This country was once French Congo and should not be confused with the Congo Democratic Republic to the south formerly known as Belgian Congo, and later Zaire.

Capital: Brazzaville
Languages: French, Lingala, Kikongo, other African languages

The coastal plain is treeless. The rest of the country is mostly a forested plateau.

The country straddles the equator. The wet and dry seasons differ north and south of the equator.

Best time for region north of the equator is November to March. (Dry, lower temperatures, lower humidity.)
Best time for region south of the equator (includes Brazzaville) is June to September. (Dry, lower temperatures, lower humidity.)

The two regions are:
1. North of the equator.
Best time: November to March.

Early November to late March: Dry season.
April to late October: Rainy season.

2. South of the equator.
Best time: June to September.

May to September: Dry season.
October to mid–December: Short rainy season.
December to mid–January: Short dry season.
Mid–January to May: Main rainy season.

Brazzaville, Republic of the Congo: Altitude 318m (1043ft)

	Jan	Feb	Mar	Apr	May	Jun
Sunrise ºC(ºF)	21(69)	21(70)	21(70)	22(71)	21(70)	18(65)
Mid–afternoon ºC(ºF)	31(87)	32(89)	33(91)	33(91)	32(89)	29(84)
Days with precipitation	2	5	6	6	4	0
Precipitation mm	160	125	188	178	109	15
Precipitation inches	6.3	4.9	7.4	7.0	4.3	0.6
Daily hours of sunshine	5	5	5	6	5	5

Brazzaville, Republic of the Congo: (continued)

	Jul	Aug	Sep	Oct	Nov	Dec
Sunrise ºC(ºF)	17(63)	18(65)	20(68)	21(70)	21(70)	21(70)
Mid–afternoon ºC(ºF)	28(82)	29(85)	31(87)	32(89)	31(87)	31(87)
Days with precipitation	0	0	1	5	9	5
Precipitation mm	0	0	56	137	292	213
Precipitation inches	0	0	2.2	5.4	11.5	8.4
Daily hours of sunshine	4	5	4	5	5	5

COOK ISLANDS

Official Name: Cook Islands
(Self–governing Territory in free association with New Zealand)

Capital: Avarua on Rarotonga Island
Languages: Cook Islands Maori, and English

There are 15 islands in the group. Rarotonga is the largest and highest; it has a towering volcanic rock formation in the middle of the island. The other islands are low; they are mostly coral islands.

Good time to visit: April to November.

April to November: Temperate season. Warm, humid, but tempered by cool southeast tradewinds. Average afternoon temperature, 27ºC (80ºF).
December to March: Wet season. Hot, humid, sometimes cloudy. Cyclones may occur. Afternoon temperature, 29ºC (84ºF).
Sunshine throughout the year averages 7 hours per day.
Rain, when it occurs, usually comes late afternoon, and humidity increases.

Rarotonga, Cook Islands

	Jan	Feb	Mar	Apr	May	Jun
Sunrise ºC(ºF)	23(73)	23(73)	23(73)	22(72)	20(68)	19(66)
Mid–afternoon ºC(ºF)	29(84)	29(84)	29(84)	28(82)	27(81)	26(79)
Precipitation mm	250	225	270	185	170	105
Precipitation inches	9.8	8.9	10.6	7.3	6.7	4.1

	Jul	Aug	Sep	Oct	Nov	Dec
Sunrise ºC(ºF)	19(66)	18(64)	19(66)	20(68)	21(70)	22(72)
Mid–afternoon ºC(ºF)	25(77)	25(77)	25(77)	26(79)	27(81)	28(82)
Precipitation mm	100	130	105	125	145	230
Precipitation inches	3.9	5.1	4.1	4.9	5.7	9.1

COSTA RICA
Official Name: Republic of Costa Rica

Capital: San José
Languages: Spanish, English

Most of the country is comprised of a hilly plateau 900 to 1800m (3000 to 6000ft) above sea level. Narrow lowlands extend along the Pacific coast. Wide lowlands extend along the virtually uninhabited Caribbean coast.

Best time: December to January. (Clear skies; foliage still green after the May to November rains.) November, and February to April, are also very good. December to March is good for birdwatching. (Less rain.)

There are three weather regions.
1. Highlands. (Includes San José and most of the country.)
Good months: November to April. Best are December to January.

November to April: Dry, especially January to end of April. Pleasant days, about 22 to 25°C (72 to 77°F). Nights drop to a comfortable 15°C (60°F). Six to 8 hours of sunshine daily.
May to November: Wet, especially May to October. Mornings are clear; rain comes as afternoon downpours, and sometimes continues into the night. Four to 5 hours of sunshine daily.

San José, inland Costa Rica: Altitude 1146m (3760ft)

	Jan	Feb	Mar	Apr	May	Jun
Sunrise ºC(ºF)	17(62)	17(62)	18(64)	18(64)	18(64)	18(64)
Mid–afternoon ºC(ºF)	28(82)	29(84)	30(86)	30(86)	29(84)	27(80)
Days with precipitation	3	1	2	7	19	22
Precipitation mm	6	11	14	80	277	290
Precipitation inches	0.2	0.4	0.6	3.2	10.9	11.4
Daily hours of sunshine	9	9	9	8	6	5

	Jul	Aug	Sep	Oct	Nov	Dec
Sunrise ºC(ºF)	18(64)	18(64)	17(62)	17(62)	17(62)	17(62)
Mid–afternoon ºC(ºF)	28(82)	28(82)	27(80)	27(80)	27(80)	28(82)
Days with precipitation	23	24	24	25	14	6
Precipitation mm	188	286	381	342	136	34
Precipitation inches	7.4	11.3	15.0	13.5	5.4	1.3
Daily hours of sunshine	5	5	5	5	6	8

2. Pacific coast.
Good months: November to April.

November to April: Dry. Seven to 9 hours of sunshine daily. Humidity is high.
End of May to November: Wet. Rainiest are September and October. Average daily sunshine during these six months is 6 hours. Humidity is high. Hot throughout year, 32°C (90°F) in the afternoon.

Puntarenas, Costa Rica's Pacific coast: Altitude 3m (10ft)

	Jan	Feb	Mar	Apr	May	Jun
Sunrise °C(°F)	23(73)	23(73)	23(73)	23(73)	22(72)	24(75)
Mid–afternoon °C(°F)	34(94)	35(95)	35(95)	35(95)	33(91)	32(89)
Precipitation mmn	6	2	6	30	189	223
Precipitation inches	0.2	0.08	0.2	1.2	7.4	8.8
Daily hours of sunshine	8	9	9	9	7	5

	Jul	Aug	Sep	Oct	Nov	Dec
Sunrise °C(°F)	23(73)	23(73)	23(73)	23(73)	23(73)	22(72)
Mid–afternoon °C(°F)	32(89)	33(91)	32(89)	32(89)	32(89)	33(91)
Precipitation mm	176	227	291	248	117	32
Precipitation inches	6.9	8.9	11.5	9.8	4.6	1.3
Daily hours of sunshine	5	5	5	5	6	7

3. Caribbean coast.
Can rain at any time throughout year. Storms come and go quickly.
Wettest months are November to January.
Lightest rain is February to April, and September.
Coast is hot all year, topping 32°C (90°F) in afternoons.

Puerto Limon, Costa Rica's Caribbean coast: Altitude 3m (10ft)

	Jan	Feb	Mar	Apr	May	Jun
Sunrise °C(°F)	20(68)	20(68)	21(69)	22(72)	22(72)	22(72)
Mid–afternoon °C(°F)	30(86)	30(86)	30(86)	31(87)	31(87)	31(87)
Precipitation mm	319	201	193	287	281	276
Precipitation inches	12.6	7.9	7.6	11.3	11.1	10.9
Daily hours of sunshine	5	6	6	6	5	4

	Jul	Aug	Sep	Oct	Nov	Dec
Sunrise °C(°F)	22(72)	22(72)	22(72)	22(72)	22(72)	21(69)
Mid–afternoon °C(°F)	30(86)	30(86)	30(86)	31(87)	30(86)	30(86)
Precipitation mm	408	289	163	198	367	402
Precipitation inches	16.1	11.4	6.4	7.8	14.5	15.8
Daily hours of sunshine	4	5	5	5	5	5

CÔTE D'IVOIRE

Official Name: Republic of Côte d'Ivoire
(Also called Ivory Coast)

Capital: Yamoussoukro (Abidjan is the administrative
centre)
Languages: French, African languages

From the coast a dense forest extends inland for a distance
varying from 100 to 260km (60 to 165 miles), then it
gives way to grasslands. In the west are mountains that
rise beyond 1500m (5000ft).

**Best months for both regions: Mid–November to
February.** (Drier and cooler.)

The regions are:
1. South. (Includes Abidjan.)
December to mid–May: Long dry season. Seven hours of sunshine daily. Humid and hot with daily
maximum of 32°C (90°F).
Mid–May to mid–July: Season of the great rains. Humid, hot, 29°C (85°F).
Mid–July to September: Short dry season. Humid, hot, 28°C (83°F).
October and November: Short rainy season. Humid, hot, 30°C (86°F).

2. North.
November to May: Long dry season. During December to February hot, dry,
dust–laden harmattan winds blow from the northeast, causing hazy skies. Temperatures reach the high
30s°C (high 90s°F).
Late May to early October: Rainy season. The north receives less rain than the south. Daily
maximum temperatures average 30°C (86°F).

Abidjan, Côte d'Ivoire: Altitude 20m (65ft)

	Jan	Feb	Mar	Apr	May	Jun
Sunrise °C(°F)	23(73)	24(75)	24(75)	24(75)	24(75)	23(73)
Mid–afternoon °C(°F)	31(88)	32(90)	32(90)	32(90)	31(88)	29(85)
Days with precipitation	3	4	6	9	16	18
Precipitation mm	41	53	99	125	361	495
Precipitation inches	1.6	2.1	3.9	4.9	14.2	19.5
Daily hours of sunshine	6	7	7	7	6	4

	Jul	Aug	Sep	Oct	Nov	Dec
Sunrise °C(°F)	23(73)	22(71)	23(73)	23(74)	23(74)	23(74)
Mid–afternoon °C(°F)	28(83)	28(82)	28(83)	29(85)	31(87)	31(88)
Days with precipitation	8	7	8	13	13	6
Precipitation mm	213	53	71	168	201	79
Precipitation inches	8.4	2.1	2.8	6.6	7.9	3.1
Daily hours of sunshine	4	4	4	6	7	7

CROATIA
Official Name: Republic of Croatia

Capital: Zagreb
Language: Serbo–Croat

The western part of the country has the Dalmatian coast, a strip of land along the Adriatic Sea. It has many offshore islands which are crests of submerged mountains. The eastern, inland, part of Croatia is a low–lying agricultural region drained by the Drava and Sava rivers.

Best time for both regions: Late May to mid–September.

The two main weather regions are Coastal and Inland.

1. Coastal region.
May to September: Dry, hot summer. Average afternoon temperatures range 25 to 29°C (77 to 85°F). In spring and early summer (March to June), sea breezes which blow throughout the morning and afternoon help keep down the temperature. Ten to 12 hours of sunshine daily. A warm, northward flowing sea current along the coast makes swimming possible from early May to late September. The sea temperature can top 25°C (77°F) in August.
October to April: Rainy, cloudy, mild winters, about 14°C (58°F) in the afternoons. High mountains protect the coast and islands from severe winter weather and the warm, north–flowing sea current maintains the sea temperature above 10°C (50°F). Expect 4 to 5 hours of sunshine daily.

Split, on Croatia's Dalmatian coast: Altitude 128m (420ft)

	Jan	Feb	Mar	Apr	May	Jun
Sunrise °C(°F)	5(41)	6(42)	8(46)	11(51)	15(59)	19(66)
Mid–afternoon °C(°F)	10(50)	11(51)	13(55)	17(62)	22(72)	27(80)
Days with precipitation	9	8	8	8	6	6
Precipitation mm	83	68	75	66	56	51
Precipitation inches	3.3	2.7	3.0	2.6	2.2	2.0
Daily hours of sunshine	4	5	6	7	9	10

	Jul	Aug	Sep	Oct	Nov	Dec
Sunrise °C(°F)	21(70)	21(70)	18(64)	14(57)	10(50)	6(42)
Mid–afternoon °C(°F)	30(86)	29(85)	25(77)	20(68)	15(59)	11(51)
Days with precipitation	3	4	5	7	10	10
Precipitation mm	28	50	61	79	108	100
Precipitation inches	1.1	2.0	2.4	3.1	4.3	3.9
Daily hours of sunshine	11	10	8	6	4	4

Dubrovnik, Croatia's Dalmatian coast: Altitude 49m (161ft)

	Jan	Feb	Mar	Apr	May	Jun
Sunrise ºC(ºF)	6(42)	6(43)	8(47)	11(52)	14(58)	18(65)
Mid–afternoon ºC(ºF)	12(53)	13(55)	14(58)	17(63)	21(70)	25(78)
Days with precipitation	13	13	11	10	10	6
Precipitation mm	139	125	104	104	75	48
Precipitation inches	5.5	4.9	4.1	4.1	3.0	1.9
Daily hours of sunshine	4	5	5	6	8	10

	Jul	Aug	Sep	Oct	Nov	Dec
Sunrise ºC(ºF)	21(69)	21(69)	18(64)	14(57)	10(51)	8(46)
Mid–afternoon ºC(ºF)	29(83)	28(82)	25(77)	21(69)	17(62)	14(56)
Days with precipitation	4	3	7	11	16	15
Precipitation mm	26	38	101	162	198	178
Precipitation inches	1.0	1.5	4.0	6.4	7.8	7.0
Daily hours of sunshine	12	11	9	7	4	3

2. Inland region.

May to September: Wet, warm, 20 to 23ºC (68 to 73ºF) in the afternoons. Rain falls throughout year.
October to April: Wet, cold. Main snowfalls in the high regions of the hilly interior are in January and February. This winter snow lies for long periods in the mountains.

Zagreb, inland Croatia: Altitude 162m (531ft)

	Jan	Feb	Mar	Apr	May	Jun
Sunrise ºC(ºF)	–2(29)	1(33)	4(39)	8(46)	12(53)	15(59)
Mid–afternoon ºC(ºF)	3(37)	6(42)	11(51)	16(60)	21(69)	24(75)
Days with precipitation	7	7	8	9	10	11
Precipitation mm	53	47	58	65	83	101
Precipitation inches	2.1	1.9	2.3	2.6	3.3	4.0
Daily hours of sunshine	2	3	4	5	7	7

	Jul	Aug	Sep	Oct	Nov	Dec
Sunrise ºC(ºF)	17(62)	16(61)	13(55)	9(48)	4(39)	–1(30)
Mid–afternoon ºC(ºF)	26(79)	25(77)	21(70)	16(60)	9(48)	4(39)
Days with precipitation	8	8	7	7	8	8
Precipitation mm	87	91	81	70	85	62
Precipitation inches	3.4	3.6	3.2	2.8	3.4	2.4
Daily hours of sunshine	9	8	6	4	2	2

CUBA

Official Name: Republic of Cuba

Capital: Havana
Language: Spanish

Mountainous or hilly regions cover about half of Cuba.
The rest of the country consists of flat or undulating
terrain.

Best time: December to April. November and May are
also good.

December to April: Dry. Average afternoon temperature,
28°C (82°F). Light rains.
May to November: Wet. Afternoon average, 31°C (88°F). Hottest are July and August. Humidity
increases in the hot, wet months, particularly May to September.
Hurricanes: June to November, but touchdowns are rare.

Havana, Cuba: Altitude 50m (164ft)

	Jan	Feb	Mar	Apr	May	Jun
Sunrise °C(°F)	18(65)	18(65)	19(67)	21(69)	22(72)	23(74)
Mid–afternoon °C(°F)	26(79)	26(79)	27(81)	29(84)	30(86)	31(88)
Days with precipitation	6	4	4	4	7	10
Precipitation mm	71	46	46	58	119	165
Precipitation inches	2.8	1.8	1.8	2.3	4.7	6.5
Daily hours of sunshine	6	6	7	7	8	6

	Jul	Aug	Sep	Oct	Nov	Dec
Sunrise °C(°F)	24(75)	24(75)	24(75)	23(73)	21(69)	19(67)
Mid–afternoon °C(°F)	32(89)	32(89)	31(88)	29(85)	27(81)	26(79)
Days with precipitation	10	10	11	11	7	6
Precipitation mm	125	135	150	173	79	58
Precipitation inches	4.9	5.3	5.9	6.8	3.1	2.3
Daily hours of sunshine	6	6	5	5	5	5

CYPRUS

Official Name: Republic of Cyprus
Capital: Nicosia, also called Lefkosia
Languages: Greek, Turkish, English

There are two mountain ranges, Kyrenia in the north and Troödos in the south. Between them in the interior is a flat, treeless plain. There are no major rivers in Cyprus, only lakes.
Good time to visit: March to November. Best time is March to May.
March to May: Spring. Warm. March can be wet with six rainy days. Occasional rainstorms occur in April and May but they are short, then sunny blue skies return. March and April are colourful months with citrus trees and flowers in bloom.
June to August: Summer. Rainless. Warm to hot. July and August are the hottest months. Coastal temperatures are tempered by breezes from the sea that cool the land but make the nights balmy. Temperatures in the hills, where there are resorts, are cooler than the lowlands. In late summer the vegetation is brownish.
September to November: Autumn. September is rainless. Although occasional rain may fall in October, the wet season starts in November and continues through to March. Evenings are chilly from October to March. The island's vegetation is brownish until the rains start.
December to February: Winter. The island is sunny, even in winter. December and January are the rainiest months; January and February are the coldest. Snow falls in the mountains; skiing is possible.
Sea temperatures:

	Jan	Feb	Mar	Apr	May	Jun
Average sea temperatures ºC(ºF)	11(51)	12(54)	14(57)	19(66)	21(71)	24(75)

	Jul	Aug	Sep	Oct	Nov	Dec
Average sea temperatures ºC(ºF)	26(78)	27(81)	26(79)	23(73)	14(57)	11(52)

Larnaca, Cyprus: Altitude 2m (7ft)

	Jan	Feb	Mar	Apr	May	Jun
Sunrise ºC(ºF)	7(44)	7(44)	8(46)	11(52)	15(59)	18(64)
Mid–afternoon ºC(ºF)	16(60)	17(62)	19(66)	22(72)	26(78)	30(86)
Days with precipitation	8	7	6	3	1	0
Precipitation mm	62	52	42	12	9	1
Precipitation inches	2.4	2.0	1.6	0.5	0.4	0.04
Daily hours of sunshine	6	7	7	9	11	12

	Jul	Aug	Sep	Oct	Nov	Dec
Sunrise ºC(ºF)	21(69)	21(69)	19(66)	16(60)	12(53)	9(48)
Mid–afternoon ºC(ºF)	32(89)	32(89)	30(86)	27(80)	22(72)	18(64)
Days with precipitation	0	0	0	3	4	7
Precipitation mm	0	0	0	19	43	80
Precipitation inches	0	0	0	0.7	1.7	3.2
Daily hours of sunshine	12	12	11	9	7	6

CZECH REPUBLIC
Official Name: Czech Republic

Capital: Prague
Languages: Czech, Slovak

Hilly and mountainous terrain is the country's main topographical feature. Much of the area rises beyond 1000m (3300ft).

Best time to visit: April to end of September.

April and May: Pleasant, mild temperatures in the daytime, 15°C (60°F) in the afternoons, cooler at night, frequent light rains, blue skies are common, 8 hours of sunshine daily.
June to August: Summer. Afternoon temperatures can be over 27°C (80°F). Thunderstorms bring heavy rain, especially from late June into August. However, expect 8 hours of sunshine daily. July is usually the rainiest month.
September: Afternoon temperatures average 18°C (65°F). Occasional light rain, blue skies, 6 hours of sunshine daily.
October to March: Cold with light rains. In winter, December, January and February skies are often overcast and temperatures are at freezing point. Low temperatures may stay for several days if easterly winds from Russia prevail. Snow falls in the lowlands and in the mountains where there are ski resorts.

Prague (Praha), Czech Republic: Altitude 365m (1197ft)

	Jan	Feb	Mar	Apr	May	Jun
Sunrise °C(°F)	–5(23)	–4(25)	–1(30)	2(35)	7(44)	10(50)
Mid–afternoon °C(°F)	0(32)	3(37)	8(46)	13(55)	18(64)	21(69)
Days with precipitation	7	6	7	8	10	10
Precipitation mm	24	23	28	38	77	73
Precipitation inches	0.9	0.9	1.1	1.5	3.0	2.9
Daily hours of sunshine	2	3	4	6	7	7

	Jul	Aug	Sep	Oct	Nov	Dec
Sunrise °C(°F)	12(53)	12(53)	9(48)	4(39)	0(32)	–3(27)
Mid–afternoon °C(°F)	23(73)	23(73)	19(66)	13(55)	6(42)	2(35)
Days with precipitation	9	9	7	6	7	7
Precipitation mm	66	70	40	31	32	25
Precipitation inches	2.6	2.8	1.6	1.2	1.3	1.0
Daily hours of sunshine	7	7	5	4	2	1

DEMOCRATIC REPUBLIC OF CONGO, see CONGO DEM. REPUBLIC

DENMARK
Official Name: Kingdom of Denmark

Capital: Copenhagen
Language: Danish

The country consists of the mainland, Jutland, and many low islands. The west coast of Jutland is low with sand dunes and sand bars while the slightly higher east coast is indented with fjords. Jutland's average elevation is low, only 30m (about 100ft) above sea level.

Denmark's climate is mild due to the warming influence of the Gulf Stream that flows northward along the western coast, and the prevailing wind from the west which brings warmth to the land, particularly in winter.

Best time: May to August.

June to August: Summer. Pleasantly warm. Afternoon temperatures average 22°C (70°F). Although rain falls year–round, expect 10 days of rain in each of June, July and August which are some of the wettest months. Seven to 8 hours of sunshine daily.
September to May: Light rain. December to February is cloudy. January and February are the coldest months with near freezing temperatures. Snowfalls occur from January to March on 6 to 9 days per month. September and May are mild months, 17°C (62°F) in the afternoons, with 5 and 8 hours of daily sunshine respectively.

Copenhagen, Denmark: Altitude 9m (30ft)

	Jan	Feb	Mar	Apr	May	Jun
Sunrise °C(°F)	−2(29)	−2(29)	0(32)	2(35)	7(44)	11(51)
Mid–afternoon °C(°F)	2(35)	2(35)	5(41)	10(50)	15(59)	19(66)
Days with precipitation	9	7	8	9	8	8
Precipitation mm	40	32	30	43	43	54
Precipitation inches	1.6	1.3	1.2	1.7	1.7	2.1
Daily hours of sunshine	1	2	4	6	8	8
Snow mm	152	126	75	25	0	0
Snow inches	6	5	3	1	0	0

	Jul	Aug	Sep	Oct	Nov	Dec
Sunrise °C(°F)	13(55)	13(55)	10(50)	7(44)	0(32)	0(32)
Mid–afternoon °C(°F)	21(69)	20(68)	17(62)	12(53)	7(44)	4(39)
Days with precipitation	9	12	8	9	10	11
Precipitation mm	55	80	47	53	55	53
Precipitation inches	2.2	3.2	1.9	2.1	2.2	2.1
Daily hours of sunshine	8	8	5	3	2	1
Snow mm	0	0	0	25	101	126
Snow inches	0	0	0	1	4	5

DJIBOUTI

Official Name: Republic of Djibouti

Capital: Djibouti
Languages: French, Arabic, Somali, Afar, Issa

This small country is comprised of a low–lying coastal plain and an inland region which rises beyond 600m (about 2000ft). Djibouti City is located on an inlet of the Gulf of Aden.

Weather, in general: Very hot and humid year–round, with little rain.

Best time to visit: November to March.

November to April: Sunny. Light, erratic rains. Cooler season, 30°C (86°F) in the afternoons.
May to October: Sunny. Dry and hot, reaching 40°C (104°F).

Djibouti City, Djibouti: Altitude 19m (62ft)

	Jan	Feb	Mar	Apr	May	Jun
Sunrise °C(°F)	22(72)	23(73)	24(75)	25(77)	27(80)	29(84)
Mid–afternoon °C(°F)	29(84)	29(84)	30(86)	32(89)	35(95)	39(102)
Days with precipitation	3	2	2	1	1	0
Precipitation mm	10	19	20	29	17	0
Precipitation inches	0.4	0.7	0.8	1.1	0.7	0
Daily hours of sunshine	8	8	8	9	10	9

	Jul	Aug	Sep	Oct	Nov	Dec
Sunrise °C(°F)	31(87)	31(87)	29(84)	26(78)	23(73)	22(72)
Mid–afternoon °C(°F)	42(107)	41(105)	37(98)	33(91)	31(87)	29(85)
Days with precipitation	1	1	1	1	2	2
Precipitation mm	6	6	3	20	22	11
Precipitation inches	0.2	0.2	0.1	0.8	0.9	0.4
Daily hours of sunshine	8	9	9	10	10	9

DOMINICA

Official Name: Commonwealth of Dominica
(Independent nation; formerly a British possession)
Dominica, pronounced dahm–in–ee'ka, should not be
confused with the Spanish–speaking Dominican Republic

Capital: Roseau
Languages: English, a French patois, Creole

Mountains dominate Dominica. Volcanic peaks rise
beyond 1220m (4000ft). The fertile land of luxuriant
vegetation is drained by short unnavigable rivers.

Best time: November to May and June.

Mid–November to May: Generally dry. However,
showers can occur during these months. Average
afternoon temperature is 30°C (86°F). Humidity is high.
June to mid–November: Usually the wettest season.
Afternoon average, 32°C (90°F).
Sunshine: Expect 8 hours of sunshine daily throughout
the year, even in the wet season as the rains are often late afternoon downpours.
Temperatures: Cooler in the mountains compared with Roseau at sea level.
Rain: Annual rainfall on the coast is about 2000mm (80 inches) but can be as much as 7500mm (300
inches) in the mountains.
Humidity: High throughout the year.

Note: See under Caribbean Islands for general weather information.

Roseau, Dominica: Altitude 18m (60ft)

	Jan	Feb	Mar	Apr	May	Jun
Sunrise ºC(ºF)	20(68)	19(67)	20(68)	21(69)	22(72)	23(73)
Mid–afternoon ºC(ºF)	29(84)	29(85)	31(87)	31(88)	32(90)	32(90)
Days with precipitation	16	10	13	10	11	15
Precipitation mm	132	74	74	61	97	196
Precipitation inches	5.2	2.9	2.9	2.4	3.8	7.7
Daily hours of sunshine	8	8	9	8	8	7

	Jul	Aug	Sep	Oct	Nov	Dec
Sunrise ºC(ºF)	22(72)	23(73)	23(73)	22(72)	22(72)	21(69)
Mid–afternoon ºC(ºF)	32(89)	32(89)	32(89)	32(89)	31(87)	30(86)
Days with precipitation	22	22	16	16	18	16
Precipitation mm	274	262	226	198	224	163
Precipitation inches	10.8	10.3	8.9	7.8	8.8	6.4
Daily hours of sunshine	8	8	8	7	8	8

DOMINICAN REPUBLIC

Official Name: Dominican Republic
The Dominican Republic should not be confused with
English–speaking Dominica

Capital: Santo Domingo
Language: Spanish

The country occupies the eastern two–thirds of
Hispaniola, the island it shares with Haiti. A series
of mountain ranges extends in a northwest–southeast
direction, covering 80 percent of the country. The highest
peak is Duarte, 3175m (10417ft). The land is fertile and is
drained by numerous small and large rivers.

Best time: January to April. December is also good.

January to April: Warm with average afternoon coastal temperature, 29°C (84°F). Light rains fall an
average of 6 days per month. Wetter and cooler in mountainous interior.
May to November: Wet season. Warm and humid. Afternoon average on south coast (Santo
Domingo), 31°C (87°F). Expect 11 rainy days per month on the south coast, but more on the north
coast.
Humidity: High in rainy season, medium in the drier season and in the mountains.
Hurricanes are possible July to November, but they rarely touch down.
Note: See under Caribbean Islands for general weather information.

Santo Domingo, Dominican Republic: Altitude 14m (46ft)

	Jan	Feb	Mar	Apr	May	Jun
Sunrise °C(°F)	20(68)	20(68)	20(68)	21(69)	22(72)	23(73)
Mid–afternoon °C(°F)	29(84)	29(84)	29(84)	30(86)	30(86)	31(87)
Days with precipitation	7	6	6	7	11	10
Precipitation mm	63	57	54	72	188	140
Precipitation inches	2.5	2.2	2.1	2.8	7.4	5.5
Daily hours of sunshine	7	8	8	8	8	8

	Jul	Aug	Sep	Oct	Nov	Dec
Sunrise °C(°F)	23(73)	23(73)	23(73)	22(72)	21(69)	20(68)
Mid–afternoon °C(°F)	31(87)	31(87)	31(87)	31(87)	31(87)	30(86)
Days with precipitation	11	12	11	13	9	9
Precipitation mm	145	177	181	187	100	84
Precipitation inches	5.7	7.0	7.1	7.4	3.9	3.3
Daily hours of sunshine	8	8	7	7	7	7

EASTER ISLAND

(External territory of Chile)
Spanish name: Isla de Pascua. Local name: Rapa Nui

Capital: Hanga Roa
Languages: Official is Spanish. Indigenous Polynesian
language is Rapa Nui. English is understood.

Located 3790km (2355 miles) from Chile, this triangular–
shaped island has a small extinct volcanic crater at each
corner. The land between them is of undulating grassland.

Being an isolated island there are no major temperature
variations. Rainfall occurs every month. The island is a
year–round destination.

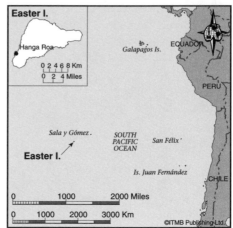

The best time to visit can be given as September to May but be aware that January and February are
the busiest months for tourism.

November to March are hot, wet months. January and February are the hottest, 26ºC (78ºF).
April to June are cool, wet months. Cool winds from Antarctica bring down the temperatures. May
and June are the wettest months. Light showers are common.
July to October is relatively dry and cool, but still warm. July and August are the coolest months,
21ºC (70ºF) in the afternoon. Mist and drizzle are common.

Hanga Roa, Easter Island: Altitude 47m (154ft)

	Jan	Feb	Mar	Apr	May	Jun
Sunrise ºC(ºF)	21(70)	21(70)	21(70)	19(67)	18(64)	17(62)
Mid–afternoon ºC(ºF)	26(78)	26(78)	26(78)	24(75)	23(73)	22(72)
Precipitation mm	111	83	113	114	118	129
Precipitation inches	4.4	3.3	4.4	4.4	4.6	5.1

	Jul	Aug	Sep	Oct	Nov	Dec
Sunrise ºC(ºF)	16(61)	16(61)	16(61)	17(62)	19(66)	20(68)
Mid–afternoon ºC(ºF)	21(70)	21(70)	21(70)	22(72)	24(75)	25(77)
Precipitation mm	92	90	76	70	112	127
Precipitation inches	3.6	3.6	3.0	2.8	4.4	5.0

EAST TIMOR
Official Name: Democratic Republic of East Timor

Capital: Dili
Languages: Tetum (also spelled Tetun) and other local languages

The country shares Timor Island with Indonesia. It is mountainous with peaks exceeding 2300m (7500ft).

Best time to visit: April to October.

April to October: Dry season. Humid. Expect 7 to 9 hours of sunshine daily. Afternoon temperatures are a fairly constant 30°C (86°F).
November to March: Rainy season. Humid. Rain falls as afternoon thunderstorms in the rainy season. Increased cloud reduces sunshine to 4 to 5 hours daily. Afternoon temperatures are the same throughout the year, a fairly constant, warm 30°C (86°F).

ECUADOR
Official Name: Republic of Ecuador

Capital: Quito
Languages: Spanish, Quechua
(Note: Galapagos Islands, part of Ecuador, is listed under **G)**

Along the coast is a narrow plain. Inland are two high mountain ranges that enclose a central plateau. In the east is part of the Amazon basin where a forested lowland covers half of the country.

Best time: Any time of year, but June to January is preferable.

There are three main regions, Andes, Coastal and Eastern lowlands (Amazon basin).
1. Andes region. (Includes Quito.)
November to May: Wet season. Most rain falls as afternoon thunderstorms. April is rainiest.
June to September: Dry season, or season of less rain.
Sunshine: Expect 5 hours per day in the wet season, and 7 in the dry season.
Temperature: Average afternoon year–round temperature, 22°C (72°F).

2. Coastal region.
The coast is divided into north and south.
The north: (Includes Esmeraldas.) Rainy throughout the year.
The south: (Includes Guayaquil.) Dry, June to December. Rainy, January to May.
Rain decreases as you travel south of Guayaquil; at the Peru border rainfall is zero.
Sunshine: Expect 4 hours per day throughout year along the coast.
Coastal temperature: Average afternoon year–round temperature, 31°C (87°F). Humid all year.

3. Eastern lowlands (Amazon basin).

Rain all year. Rainiest months are June to August; driest are September to December, the best months. Average afternoon temperature throughout year is 30 to 32ºC (86 to 90ºF).

Quito, Ecuador: Altitude 2879m (9446ft)

	Jan	Feb	Mar	Apr	May	Jun
Sunrise ºC(ºF)	8(46)	8(47)	8(47)	8(47)	8(47)	7(45)
Mid–afternoon ºC(ºF)	22(72)	22(72)	22(72)	21(70)	21(70)	22(72)
Days with precipitation	10	11	15	15	13	7
Precipitation mm	74	114	127	147	98	37
Precipitation inches	2.9	4.5	5.0	5.8	3.9	1.5
Daily hours of sunshine	5	5	4	5	5	6

	Jul	Aug	Sep	Oct	Nov	Dec
Sunrise ºC(ºF)	7(44)	7(44)	7(44)	8(46)	7(44)	8(46)
Mid–afternoon ºC(ºF)	22(72)	23(73)	23(73)	22(72)	22(72)	22(72)
Days with precipitation	5	5	11	14	11	11
Precipitation mm	26	32	79	115	79	83
Precipitation inches	1.0	1.3	3.1	4.5	3.1	3.3
Daily hours of sunshine	7	7	8	5	6	6

Guayaquil, Ecuador: Altitude 9m (29ft)

	Jan	Feb	Mar	Apr	May	Jun
Sunrise ºC(ºF)	21(70)	22(71)	22(72)	22(71)	20(68)	20(68)
Mid–afternoon ºC(ºF)	31(87)	31(87)	31(87)	32(89)	31(87)	31(87)
Days with precipitation	12	14	15	10	4	1
Precipitation mm	230	242	252	153	60	33
Precipitation inches	9.1	9.5	9.9	6.0	2.4	1.3
Daily hours of sunshine	3	4	5	5	5	4

	Jul	Aug	Sep	Oct	Nov	Dec
Sunrise ºC(ºF)	19(67)	18(65)	19(66)	20(68)	20(68)	21(70)
Mid–afternoon ºC(ºF)	29(84)	30(86)	31(87)	30(86)	31(87)	31(87)
Days with precipitation	0	0	0	1	0	2
Precipitation mm	10	1	2	3	6	34
Precipitation inches	0.4	0.04	0.08	0.1	0.2	1.3
Daily hours of sunshine	4	4	5	4	4	4

EGYPT
Official Name: Arab Republic of Egypt

Capital: Cairo
Language: Arabic

About 96 percent of Egypt consists of deserts with some oases. Most habitation and cultivation occur along the Nile River and its delta.
Weather is sunny all year. Evenings become cold when the sun goes down. Carry a sweater.

Best time to visit: October to February.

December to February: Winter. Warm sunny days, cool desert nights. Light rains fall in Alexandria. A rain shower is possible in Cairo. Rain decreases to zero as you head south to Luxor and Aswan. Temperatures increase from north to south. Afternoon temperatures are 19°C (65°F) in Alexandria, 20°C (68°F) in Cairo, and 24°C (75°F) in Aswan.
March to May: Spring. Dry, sunny, warm days. Cool nights. Khamsin winds, the hot, dry, dust–laden sandstorms from the Western Desert, blow intermittently in March, April and May. They can disrupt domestic flights.
June to August: Summer. Dry, sunny and hot with northerly winds. Temperatures increase from north to south, with afternoon temperatures averaging 31°C (87°F) in Alexandria, 36°C (96°F) in Cairo, and 42°C (107°F) in Aswan. Nights are cool in this desert climate.
September to November: Autumn. Dry, sunny and warm days. Cool nights. Light rains begin in the north, e.g. Alexandria. The rest of the country is dry.

Note: Sinai throughout the year has hot days which can rise above 45°C (113°F) and cold nights that could fall to freezing point, particularly in the mountains.

Cairo, Egypt: Altitude 74m (243ft)

	Jan	Feb	Mar	Apr	May	Jun
Sunrise ºC(ºF)	9(48)	10(50)	12(53)	15(59)	18(64)	20(68)
Mid–afternoon ºC(ºF)	19(66)	21(69)	23(73)	28(82)	32(89)	34(93)
Days with precipitation	1	1	0	0	0	0
Precipitation mm	7	4	4	2	0	0
Precipitation inches	0.3	0.1	0.1	0.08	0	0
Daily hours of sunshine	7	8	9	10	10	12

	Jul	Aug	Sep	Oct	Nov	Dec
Sunrise ºC(ºF)	22(72)	22(72)	20(68)	18(64)	14(58)	10(50)
Mid–afternoon ºC(ºF)	34(93)	34(93)	33(91)	30(86)	25(77)	20(68)
Days with precipitation	0	0	0	0	0	1
Precipitation mm	0	0	0	1	3	5
Precipitation inches	0	0	0	0.04	0.1	0.2
Daily hours of sunshine	12	11	10	9	8	6

EL SALVADOR

Official Name: Republic of El Salvador

Capital: San Salvador
Languages: Spanish, Nuhuatl

Two mountain ranges extend east–west across the country. Between them is a plateau about 600m (2000ft) above sea level. Along the Pacific coast extends a coastal plain about 20km (12 miles) wide.

Good time to visit: December to April. (Dry.)

Mid–November to mid–April: Dry season, although light rains may fall. Afternoon temperatures average about 32ºC (90ºF) with high humidity. Ten hours of sunshine daily.
Mid–May to mid–October: Wet season. Rain usually falls in late afternoons in cloudbursts, and falls 19 days per month during the wet season. Afternoon temperatures change little; they remain about 32ºC (90ºF). Expect 7 or 8 hours of sunshine daily.

The weeks between the dry and wet seasons receive light rains but the afternoon temperature changes little from the 32ºC (90ºF) average. The country is not affected by hurricanes.

San Salvador, El Salvador: Altitude 621m (2037ft)

	Jan	Feb	Mar	Apr	May	Jun
Sunrise ºC(ºF)	16(60)	17(62)	18(64)	19(66)	20(68)	20(68)
Mid–afternoon ºC(ºF)	30(86)	30(86)	32(90)	32(90)	31(87)	30(86)
Days with precipitation	1	1	1	4	13	19
Precipitation mm	5	2	9	36	152	292
Precipitation inches	0.2	0.08	0.4	1.4	6.0	11.5
Daily hours of sunshine	10	10	10	8	8	6

	Jul	Aug	Sep	Oct	Nov	Dec
Sunrise ºC(ºF)	19(66)	19(66)	19(66)	19(66)	18(64)	17(62)
Mid–afternoon ºC(ºF)	30(86)	30(86)	29(84)	29(84)	29(84)	30(86)
Days with precipitation	19	19	20	16	4	2
Precipitation mm	316	311	348	217	36	10
Precipitation inches	12.4	12.3	13.7	8.5	1.4	0.4
Daily hours of sunshine	8	8	6	7	9	10

EQUATORIAL GUINEA
Official Name: Republic of Equatorial Guinea

Capital: Malabo (on Bioko Island)
Languages: Spanish, French, Fang, Bubi, other African languages

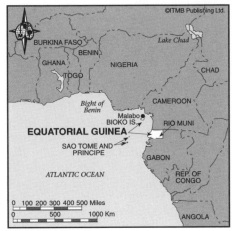

The country is in two parts, Bioko Island, a mountainous off–shore island, and Rio Muni, the enclave on the African mainland which has heavily wooded rolling terrain. They have different weather patterns but the average afternoon maximum temperature for both regions, year–round, is 30°C (86°F). Both regions experience cloud throughout the year which reduces the amount of sunshine to two to three hours daily in the wet season, and to five hours in the dry season. Humidity is high throughout the year.

Best time for Bioko Island: November to mid–March. (Dry.)
Best time for Rio Muni: Mid–November to mid–March (dry), **and June to August** (dry).

1. Bioko Island (formerly Fernando Po).
December to February: Dry season.
March to June: Heavy rains.
July and August: Lighter rains.
September to early November: Heavy rains.

2. Rio Muni, the mainland enclave.
December to February: Dry season.
March to mid–June: Heavy rains.
Mid–June to August: Dry.
September to November: Heavy rains.

Malabo, Bioko Island, Equatorial Guinea:

	Jan	Feb	Mar	Apr	May	Jun
Sunrise °C(°F)	19(67)	21(69)	21(69)	21(70)	22(71)	21(69)
Mid–afternoon °C(°F)	31(87)	32(89)	31(88)	32(89)	31(87)	29(85)
Days with precipitation	3	5	13	15	23	23
Precipitation mm	5	31	193	163	262	302
Precipitation inches	0.2	1.2	7.6	6.4	10.3	11.9
Daily hours of sunshine	4	5	3	4	4	3

	Jul	Aug	Sep	Oct	Nov	Dec
Sunrise °C(°F)	21(69)	21(69)	21(69)	21(70)	22(71)	21(70)
Mid–afternoon °C(°F)	29(84)	29(85)	30(86)	30(86)	30(86)	31(87)
Days with precipitation	17	14	24	23	12	4
Precipitation mm	160	114	201	231	117	20
Precipitation inches	6.3	4.5	7.9	9.1	4.6	0.8
Daily hours of sunshine	2	2	2	2	3	4

ERITREA
Official Name: State of Eritrea

Capital: Asmara
Languages: Arabic, English, Tigrinya and other indigenous languages.

Travellers to Eritrea usually confine themselves to the plateau region which has a moderate climate and which is where Asmara is located. Other climatic regions are the hot coastal plain along the Red Sea where Massawa is located, and the arid, sparsely populated western lowlands.

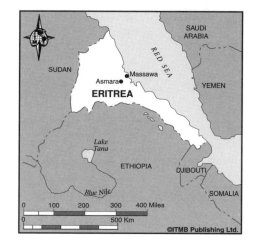

Best time to visit in general: October to February.

1. Plateau region. (Includes Asmara.)
Best time: October to February.

Mid–September to February: Dry season. Sunny and warm. Average daily maximum temperature, 24°C (76°F).
March and April: Light rains but mainly dry. Sunny and warm, 25°C (77°F).
Late June to early September: Main rainy season. Sunny and warm with the daily maximum ranging 21 to 24°C (70 to 76°F). July and August are the cooler months.

2. Coastal region. (Includes Massawa.)
Best time: December to February.

December to February: Light rains may fall, bringing cooler, pleasant temperatures although the coast is hot year–round.
Other months: Dry, steamy and uncomfortably hot, exceeding 32°C (89°F).

3. Western lowlands.
Year–round: Arid, hot. Temperatures can reach 40°C (104°F).

Asmara, inland Eritrea: Altitude 2325m (7628ft)

	Jan	Feb	Mar	Apr	May	Jun
Sunrise °C(°F)	4(39)	5(41)	8(46)	9(48)	10(50)	11(51)
Mid–afternoon °C(°F)	22(72)	24(75)	25(77)	25(77)	25(77)	25(77)
Days with precipitation	0	0	2	4	5	4
Precipitation mm	4	2	15	33	41	39
Precipitation inches	0.1	0.08	0.6	1.3	1.6	1.5
Daily hours of sunshine	9	9	9	9	8	7

	Jul	Aug	Sep	Oct	Nov	Dec
Sunrise °C(°F)	11(51)	11(51)	9(48)	8(46)	7(44)	5(41)
Mid–afternoon °C(°F)	22(72)	22(72)	23(73)	22(72)	22(72)	22(72)
Days with precipitation	13	12	2	2	2	1
Precipitation mm	175	156	16	15	20	3
Precipitation inches	6.9	6.1	0.6	0.6	0.8	0.1
Daily hours of sunshine	5	5	7	9	9	9

Massawa, coastal Eritrea: Altitude 10m (33ft)

	Jan	Feb	Mar	Apr	May	Jun
Sunrise °C(°F)	19(66)	19(66)	20(68)	22(72)	24(75)	26(78)
Mid–afternoon °C(°F)	29(85)	29(85)	32(89)	34(93)	37(98)	40(104)
Days with precipitation	3	2	2	1	1	0
Precipitation mm	35	22	10	4	8	0
Precipitation inches	1.4	0.9	0.4	0.1	0.3	0

	Jul	Aug	Sep	Oct	Nov	Dec
Sunrise °C(°F)	28(82)	28(82)	26(78)	23(73)	21(70)	20(68)
Mid–afternoon °C(°F)	41(105)	40(104)	39(102)	36(97)	33(92)	31(87)
Days with precipitation	1	1	0	2	1	3
Precipitation mm	8	8	3	22	24	40
Precipitation inches	0.3	0.3	0.1	0.9	0.9	1.6

ESTONIA

Official Name: Republic of Estonia

Capital: Tallinn
Languages: Estonian, Russian, Ukrainian

Gently undulating hills and low–lying plains with many rivers and lakes cover the country.

Best time to visit: May to September, but rainy July and August.

May to September: May, June and September are the preferred months of cooler, pleasant afternoon temperatures over 20°C (70°F), and less rain. July and August are wettest, warmest months with afternoon temperatures reaching 29°C (85°F). Sunny days can be quickly marred by overcast skies and short cloudbursts, especially late June, July and August. Summer evenings can be cool. The sun sets at 11pm around mid–summer.

October: Transitional month. Could be mild or cold. Afternoon temperature, 10°C (50°F).

November to March: Winter. Some fog. Cold with below freezing temperatures. Snow is on the ground permanently from December to April inland, and January to March in coastal areas.

April: Transitional month, varies from winter to spring–like conditions. Average afternoon temperature, 7°C (45°F).

Tallinn, Estonia: Altitude 34m (112ft)

	Jan	Feb	Mar	Apr	May	Jun
Sunrise ºC(ºF)	–9(16)	–8(18)	–4(25)	2(35)	7(44)	10(50)
Mid–afternoon ºC(ºF)	–3(27)	–2(29)	3(37)	10(50)	18(64)	21(69)
Days with precipitation	11	8	8	8	7	8
Precipitation mm	45	29	29	36	37	53
Precipitation inches	1.8	1.1	1.1	1.4	1.5	2.1
Daily hours of sunshine	1	2	4	5	7	10

	Jul	Aug	Sep	Oct	Nov	Dec
Sunrise ºC(ºF)	12(53)	11(51)	7(44)	3(37)	–1(30)	–6(21)
Mid–afternoon ºC(ºF)	22(72)	21(71)	16(60)	10(50)	4(39)	–1(30)
Days with precipitation	11	11	12	11	14	14
Precipitation mm	79	84	82	70	68	55
Precipitation inches	3.1	3.3	3.2	2.8	2.7	2.2
Daily hours of sunshine	9	7	5	3	1	0

ETHIOPIA

Official Name: Federal Democratic Republic of Ethiopia

Capital: Addis Ababa
Languages: Amharic, Orominya, Tigrinya, Arabic, English

In the centre of Ethiopia lies a mountainous plateau, also called the highlands, that occupies more than half the country. The plateau is bisected in a northeast–southwest direction by the Rift Valley which contains eight lakes. The plateau is partly surrounded by lowlands in the west and east.

The plateau region, 1800 to 2600m (5500 to 8000ft), has the bulk of attractions and receives most visitors. It includes Addis Ababa, Lake Tana, Tisisat Falls, Lalibela, Gondar, Axum, Simien Mountains, Harar, and Bale Mountains.

Weather in general: The plateau region and the Rift Valley have a pleasant climate. The lowlands in the west are hot and damp. The arid lowlands in the east which include the Ogaden and the Danikel desert are hot and dry with unreliable rainfall.

Best time to visit: October to February. March to May are also good months.

The plateau region weather is described below.
October to February: Dry season. Sunny, warm, about 23°C (73°F) in the afternoons. Eight to 9 hours of sunshine daily.
March to May: Light rains, sunny, warm, 24°C (75°F). Six to 7 hours of sunshine daily.
Mid–June to early October: Heavy rains which fall as sudden thunderstorms. July and August are the wettest months. Cloudy skies reduce sunshine to 4 to 5 hours daily.

Natural attractions:
1. Tisisat (or Blue Nile) Falls: Best time to visit the falls is September to November, after the rainy season. Mornings are better for photography.
2. Simien Mountains and 3. Bale Mountains: Some peaks rise beyond 4000m (13000ft). The best time for hiking, horse trekking and mule trekking is November to February, in the dry season. Daytime temperatures are warm but nighttime temperatures can drop to freezing.

Cultural event: Timkat (Feast of the Epiphany): January 18 and 19. Colourful processions with richly–robed priests. In Addis Ababa, Gondar, Lalibela and elsewhere.

Addis Ababa, Ethiopia: Altitude 2450m (8038ft)

	Jan	Feb	Mar	Apr	May	Jun
Sunrise ºC(ºF)	6(43)	8(47)	9(49)	10(50)	10(50)	9(49)
Mid–afternoon ºC(ºF)	24(75)	24(75)	25(77)	25(77)	25(77)	23(74)
Days with precipitation	2	5	8	10	10	20
Precipitation mm	13	38	66	86	86	137
Precipitation inches	0.5	1.5	2.6	3.4	3.4	5.4
Daily hours of sunshine	9	9	8	7	8	6

	Jul	Aug	Sep	Oct	Nov	Dec
Sunrise ºC(ºF)	10(50)	10(50)	9(49)	7(45)	6(43)	5(41)
Mid–afternoon ºC(ºF)	21(69)	21(69)	22(72)	24(75)	23(73)	23(73)
Days with precipitation	28	27	21	3	2	2
Precipitation mm	279	300	191	20	15	5
Precipitation inches	11.0	11.8	7.5	0.8	0.6	0.2
Daily hours of sunshine	3	3	5	8	9	9

FALKLAND ISLANDS

Official Name: Colony of the Falkland Islands
(Dependent Territory of the United Kingdom)
The islands are also claimed by Argentina which calls
them Islas Malvinas.

Capital: Stanley (on East Falkland)
Language: English

About 200 islands make up the Falklands. They are
windswept and almost devoid of trees. The larger islands
of East Falkland and West Falkland have low rolling
grazing pastures and hills rising to 700m (2300ft).

Best months: December to February.
Best months to view wildlife: October to March.

December to February: Summer. Afternoon temperatures reach a mild 13ºC (56ºF). Seven hours of
sunshine daily.
Other months: The exposed islands suffer frequent high winds, particularly in winter, June to August,
but can also experience them September to November. Snow falls in winter.
Rainfall: The weather is changeable year–round with cloud and rain. Rainfall averages 50mm (2in)
per month.

Natural attractions: Between October and March, penguins, seals, albatrosses, cormorants, geese
and ducks return to the islands.

Stanley, East Falkland: Altitude 2m (6ft)

	Jan	Feb	Mar	Apr	May	Jun
Sunrise ºC(ºF)	6(42)	5(41)	4(40)	3(37)	1(34)	–1(31)
Mid–afternoon ºC(ºF)	13(56)	13(56)	12(53)	9(49)	7(44)	5(41)
Days with precipitation	17	12	15	14	15	13
Precipitation mm	71	58	64	66	66	53
Precipitation inches	2.8	2.3	2.5	2.6	2.6	2.1
Daily hours of sunshine	7	6	5	3	2	2

	Jul	Aug	Sep	Oct	Nov	Dec
Sunrise ºC(ºF)	–1(31)	–1(31)	1(33)	2(35)	3(37)	4(39)
Mid–afternoon ºC(ºF)	4(40)	5(41)	7(45)	9(48)	11(52)	12(54)
Days with precipitation	13	13	12	11	12	15
Precipitation mm	51	51	38	41	51	71
Precipitation inches	2.0	2.0	1.5	1.6	2.0	2.8
Daily hours of sunshine	2	3	4	5	7	7

FAROE ISLANDS

Official Name: Faroe Islands
(Dependent Territory of Denmark)

Capital: Tórshavn (on island of Stremoy)
Languages: Faroese, Danish

Twenty–one islands which are largely treeless comprise the group. They have high escarpments and plateaus that are separated by deep rifts.

The climate of the Faroes is moderated by the warm waters of the Gulf Stream which flow north from the Atlantic Ocean.
Best time to visit: June to August.
June to August: Summer. Cool, cloudy and windy. Frequent rain falls as drizzle and also as heavy downpours. There is less rain May to August compared with September to April. At the same time on any day there can be rainstorms on some islands and sunshine on others. Afternoon temperatures hover around 13ºC (55ºF) and sunshine averages only 3 or 4 hours per day.
September to May: Cool, rainy, windy and mostly sunless days. The Gulf Stream keeps the temperatures mild, about 6ºC (43ºF) in mid–winter (January) afternoons.
Faroe Islands:

	Jan	Feb	Mar	Apr	May	Jun
Sunrise ºC(ºF)	2(35)	1(34)	2(36)	3(37)	5(41)	7(45)
Mid–afternoon ºC(ºF)	6(43)	6(43)	7(44)	8(46)	10(49)	12(53)
Days with precipitation	25	22	23	22	16	16
Precipitation mm	149	136	114	106	67	74
Precipitation inches	5.9	5.4	4.5	4.2	2.6	2.9
Daily hours of sunshine	1	1	2	4	5	5

Faroe Islands: (continued)

	Jul	Aug	Sep	Oct	Nov	Dec
Sunrise ºC(ºF)	9(48)	9(48)	8(46)	5(42)	4(39)	3(37)
Mid–afternoon ºC(ºF)	13(56)	14(56)	12(54)	10(50)	8(47)	7(45)
Days with precipitation	18	20	12	24	24	26
Precipitation mm	79	96	132	157	156	167
Precipitation inches	3.1	3.8	5.2	6.2	6.1	6.6
Daily hours of sunshine	4	3	3	2	1	0

FIJI

Official Name: Republic of the Fiji Islands

Capital: Suva
Languages: Fijian, English, Hindi

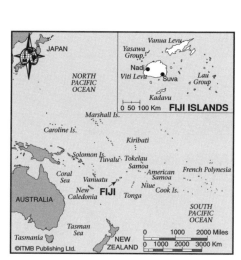

More than 800 islands and islets comprise Fiji. The two main islands of Viti Levu and Vanua Levu are volcanic in origin and have mountain ranges averaging 1300m (4000ft) above sea level. The main international airport is at Nadi (pronounced Nandi), on Viti Levu.

Good time to visit: April to November. Best months are June and July. (Cooler and less rain.)

April to November: Temperate season. Warm, humid, but tempered by cool southeast tradewinds. Average afternoon temperature, 27ºC (80ºF).
December to March: Wet season. Hot, humid. Cyclones may occur. Afternoon temperature, 29ºC (86ºF).
Sunshine throughout the year averages 7 hours per day.
Rain, when it occurs, usually comes late afternoon, and humidity increases.
Recreational activity: The season for yacht cruising is April to November.

Suva, Fiji: Altitude 6m (20ft)

	Jan	Feb	Mar	Apr	May	Jun
Sunrise ºC(ºF)	23(74)	23(74)	23(74)	23(73)	22(71)	21(69)
Mid–afternoon ºC(ºF)	30(86)	30(86)	30(86)	29(84)	28(82)	27(80)
Days with precipitation	18	18	21	19	16	13
Precipitation mm	314	299	386	343	280	177
Precipitation inches	12.4	11.8	15.2	13.5	11.0	7.0

	Jul	Aug	Sep	Oct	Nov	Dec
Sunrise ºC(ºF)	20(68)	20(68)	21(69)	21(70)	22(71)	23(74)
Mid–afternoon ºC(ºF)	26(79)	26(79)	27(80)	27(81)	28(83)	29(85)
Days with precipitation	14	15	16	15	15	18
Precipitation mm	148	200	212	218	268	313
Precipitation inches	5.8	7.8	8.3	8.6	10.6	12.3

FINLAND
Official Name: Republic of Finland

Capital: Helsinki
Languages: Finnish, Swedish (both official)

Most of Finland consists of tableland that ranges 120 to 180m (400 to 600ft) above sea level. It is largely covered with silver birch, spruce and pine and is dotted with numerous lakes.

Finland's weather is variable from day to day in all seasons. It is influenced by cold winds from the north, warm, humid winds from the south, rain–bearing winds and cloud from the west and dry winds from the east.

Best time: June to August. (May and September are reasonable months, but cooler.)

June to August: Summer. In the centre and south, temperatures are warm, 20°C (68°F), but there are spells of hotter weather, to 27°C (80°F), and colder spells to 10°C (50°F). Rainfall is low. Days are long in this period of midnight sun. Be prepared for mosquitoes which are out in force in the warm weather.

September to May: September and May are usually free of snow in the south, e.g. Helsinki, and are reasonable months to visit, although cool, 14°C (58°F). October to April are cold; most precipitation falls as snow.

Helsinki, Finland: Altitude 56m (184ft)

	Jan	Feb	Mar	Apr	May	Jun
Sunrise °C(°F)	−10(14)	−10(14)	−7(19)	−1(30)	4(39)	9(48)
Mid–afternoon °C(°F)	−4(25)	−4(25)	1(33)	7(44)	15(59)	20(68)
Days with precipitation	9	8	8	8	6	8
Precipitation mm	41	31	34	37	35	44
Precipitation inches	1.6	1.2	1.3	1.5	1.4	1.7
Daily hours of sunshine	1	3	4	6	9	10

	Jul	Aug	Sep	Oct	Nov	Dec
Sunrise °C(°F)	12(53)	11(51)	6(42)	2(35)	−3(27)	−7(19)
Mid–afternoon °C(°F)	21(70)	20(68)	14(57)	8(46)	2(35)	−2(29)
Days with precipitation	10	11	11	11	13	12
Precipitation mm	73	80	73	73	72	58
Precipitation inches	2.9	3.2	2.9	2.9	2.8	2.3
Daily hours of sunshine	9	7	4	3	1	1

FRANCE

Official Name: Republic of France

Capital: Paris
Language: French

In the north and west are vast rolling plains. In the east and south are mountain chains that form natural borders with neighbouring countries. In the south–central part of the country is a plateau, the Massif Central, with outcroppings of volcanic rock and, farther south, deeply eroded limestone tablelands.

Most of France has a temperate climate. Many parts of the country have micro–climates where weather can change quickly. Even towns that are near each other can have different weather on the same day.

Best time for the whole country: Late April to June. (Neither too hot, too wet or too crowded.) Also good is September to early October. Note: August is an extremely busy holiday time for the local people.

We have divided the weather into six regions. Refer to map for corresponding numbers.
1. North–central. (Includes Paris.)
April to June: Mild, 16 to 21°C (60 to 70°F), light rain.
July to August: Warm, 24°C (75°F). Summer rains with thunderstorms.
September and October: Extended autumn with crisp mornings and usually bright, clear skies by midday. Temperatures begin dropping from September's 20°C (68°F) to October's 15°C (59°F).
November to March: Cold and rainy with a chance of frost and snow.

Paris, north–central France: Altitude 65m (213ft)

	Jan	Feb	Mar	Apr	May	Jun
Sunrise °C(°F)	1(33)	1(33)	3(37)	5(41)	8(46)	11(51)
Mid–afternoon °C(°F)	6(42)	8(46)	11(51)	14(57)	18(64)	22(72)
Days with precipitation	11	10	11	9	11	8
Precipitation mm	54	46	54	47	63	58
Precipitation inches	2.1	1.8	2.1	1.9	2.5	2.3
Daily hours of sunshine	2	3	4	6	7	7

	Jul	Aug	Sep	Oct	Nov	Dec
Sunrise °C(°F)	13(55)	13(55)	11(51)	8(46)	4(39)	2(35)
Mid–afternoon °C(°F)	24(75)	24(75)	21(69)	16(60)	10(50)	7(44)
Days with precipitation	8	8	8	9	10	10
Precipitation mm	54	52	54	56	56	56
Precipitation inches	2.1	2.0	2.1	2.2	2.2	2.2
Daily hours of sunshine	8	7	6	4	3	2

2. Mountain regions. (Includes Vosges and Jura mountains and the French Alps which are all in the east, the mountainous Central Massif, and the Pyrenees along the border with Spain.)

April and May: Spring. June is a transitional month. Mild, rising from 15°C (59°F) in April to 20°C (68°F) in June. Rain falls in the mountains on 10 days per month. Eight hours of sunshine daily.

July and August: Summer. All mountain regions experience hot weather, 27°C (80°F), and summer rain. Expect 8 days with rain per month and an average of 9 hours of sunshine daily. Around midday, clouds may enshroud the mountain tops but leave the valleys clear.

September and October: Autumn. All mountain regions have mild temperatures, 19°C (66°F), and heavy rain. About 8 days with rain per month. Expect 8 hours of sunshine daily.

November to March: Long winter. Mountain regions experience harsh, cold, wet winters with much of the precipitation falling as snow. Expect 9 wet days per month. Mountain valleys may be obscured by cloud while the peaks are clear.

Recreational activities:
1. Skiing and snowboarding: Popular January to March in the French Alps at Chamonix–Mont Blanc, Courchevel, Megeve and Val d'Isere.
2. The spa season: People "take the waters" at Aix–les–Bains and Evian–les–Bains from July to September.

3. Mediterranean coast. (Includes Nice.)
The Mediterranean coast has France's driest climate.

March to May: Spring. Warm, 15 to 24°C (59 to 75°F). Occasional rain. Eight hours of sunshine daily.

June to August: Summer. Dry, hot, 28°C (82°F). The air is tempered by cool, gentle breezes. Although rain is rare, there could be occasional, brief thunderstorms. Days are sunny with a daily average of 11 hours.

September to November: Autumn. Warm, 25°C (77°F) in September to 15°C (59°F) in November. Occasional rain. Seven hours of sunshine daily.

December to February: Winter. Sunny, cool, wet with heavy thunderstorms which are brief and often fall in the middle of the day. The region is affected by the mistral, a cold, fierce, dry wind from the north that sweeps the Riviera and the lower Rhône River valley. It may blow for many days and generally appears in winter and spring, but it may blow at other times.

Cultural event: Festival of the Holy Maries (**Fête des Saintes Maries**) at Les Saintes Maries–de–la–Mer near Marseilles on May 24 and 25. Statues of saints including St Sarah, patron saint of gypsies, are carried in procession to be blessed and bathed in the sea. Hundreds of gypsies attend. This coincides with entertaining competitions of man versus bull by the French cowboys of the Camargue.

Nice, southeast France: Altitude 10m (33ft)

	Jan	Feb	Mar	Apr	May	Jun
Sunrise °C(°F)	5(41)	6(42)	7(44)	10(50)	13(55)	16(60)
Mid–afternoon °C(°F)	13(55)	13(55)	15(59)	17(62)	20(68)	23(74)
Days with precipitation	7	6	6	6	5	4
Precipitation mm	83	76	71	62	49	37
Precipitation inches	3.3	3.0	2.8	2.4	1.9	1.5
Daily hours of sunshine	5	5	7	8	9	10

Nice, southeast France: (continued)

	Jul	Aug	Sep	Oct	Nov	Dec
Sunrise ºC(ºF)	19(66)	19(66)	17(62)	13(55)	9(48)	6(42)
Mid–afternoon ºC(ºF)	26(78)	27(80)	24(75)	21(69)	16(60)	14(57)
Days with precipitation	2	3	4	6	7	6
Precipitation mm	16	31	54	108	104	78
Precipitation inches	0.6	1.2	2.1	4.3	4.1	3.1
Daily hours of sunshine	11	10	8	7	5	5

4. Southwest region. (Includes Bordeaux.)
Rainfall is distributed fairly evenly throughout the year but most falls in winter.
March to May: Spring. Mild to warm daytime temperatures range 15 to 20ºC (59 to 68ºF). Rainy.
June to August: Summer. Sunny, hot. Expect 8 hours of sunshine daily. July and August are the hottest months, 25ºC (77ºF). Rain often comes as heavy, brief, dramatic thunderstorms. Summers are wetter in the south towards the Pyrenees.
September to November: Autumn. Warm to mild. Temperatures begin dropping from 20ºC (68ºF) in September to 10ºC (50ºF) in November. Rain gets progressively heavier towards late autumn.
December to February: Winter. Mild temperatures remain at about 10ºC (50ºF) but there are occasional short–lived cold spells brought by chilly winds. Rain is heaviest in December and January.

Bordeaux, southwest France: Altitude 61m (200ft)

	Jan	Feb	Mar	Apr	May	Jun
Sunrise ºC(ºF)	2(35)	3(37)	4(39)	6(42)	10(50)	12(53)
Mid–afternoon ºC(ºF)	9(48)	11(51)	14(57)	16(60)	20(68)	23(73)
Days with precipitation	13	12	12	11	11	9
Precipitation mm	100	86	76	72	77	56
Precipitation inches	3.9	3.4	3.0	2.8	3.0	2.2
Daily hours of sunshine	3	4	5	6	7	8

	Jul	Aug	Sep	Oct	Nov	Dec
Sunrise ºC(ºF)	14(57)	14(57)	12(53)	9(48)	5(41)	3(37)
Mid–afternoon ºC(ºF)	26(78)	26(78)	24(75)	19(66)	13(55)	10(50)
Days with precipitation	7	8	9	10	12	12
Precipitation mm	47	54	74	88	94	99
Precipitation inches	1.9	2.1	2.9	3.5	3.7	3.9
Daily hours of sunshine	9	8	7	5	3	3

5. Northwest. (Includes Caen.)
Rain falls throughout the year, but mostly in winter.
March to May: Spring. Mild daytime temperatures rise from 10ºC (50ºF) in March to 15ºC (59ºF) in May. Light rains fall.
June to August: Summer. Mild, 19ºC (67ºF) and fairly dry.
September to November: Autumn. Mild to cool. Many drizzly days, particularly October to December.
December to February: Winter. Cool and rainy with little sunshine. There is occasional snow.

Caen, northwest France: Altitude 67m (220ft)

	Jan	Feb	Mar	Apr	May	Jun
Sunrise ºC(ºF)	2(35)	2(35)	3(37)	5(41)	8(46)	10(50)
Mid–afternoon ºC(ºF)	7(44)	8(46)	11(51)	13(55)	16(60)	19(66)
Days with precipitation	12	11	12	10	11	8
Precipitation mm	64	58	56	46	58	52
Precipitation inches	2.5	2.3	2.2	1.8	2.3	2.0
Daily hours of sunshine	2	3	4	6	7	7

	Jul	Aug	Sep	Oct	Nov	Dec
Sunrise ºC(ºF)	12(53)	12(53)	11(51)	8(46)	5(41)	3(37)
Mid–afternoon ºC(ºF)	22(72)	22(72)	20(68)	16(60)	11(51)	8(46)
Days with precipitation	7	8	9	10	14	12
Precipitation mm	48	47	61	68	85	69
Precipitation inches	1.9	1.9	2.4	2.7	3.4	2.7
Daily hours of sunshine	7	7	6	4	3	2

6. Corsica. (Includes Ajaccio.)
March to May: Spring. Cool, 15ºC (59ºF) to a mild 20ºC (68ºF) with negligible rain.
June to September: Long summer. Sunny, dry, hot, 28ºC (83ºF) on the coast. Some days are over 30ºC (86ºF). Sea temperatures remain above 25ºC (77ºF). Rain is rare.
October to November: Autumn. Mostly fine and mild, 20ºC (68ºF), but days of heavy rain with severe storms begin in October and continue through December.
December to February: Winter. Mild, 14ºC (57ºF) on the coast. This is the rainiest season. In the mountains, winter snowfall can be severe and snow may stay until April or May.

Ajaccio, Corsica, France: Altitude 9m (30ft)

	Jan	Feb	Mar	Apr	May	Jun
Sunrise ºC(ºF)	4(39)	4(39)	5(41)	7(44)	11(51)	14(57)
Mid–afternoon ºC(ºF)	13(55)	14(57)	15(59)	17(62)	21(70)	25(77)
Days with precipitation	9	9	8	7	6	3
Precipitation mm	74	70	58	52	40	19
Precipitation inches	2.9	2.8	2.3	2.0	1.6	0.7
Daily hours of sunshine	4	5	6	8	9	11

	Jul	Aug	Sep	Oct	Nov	Dec
Sunrise ºC(ºF)	16(60)	17(62)	14(57)	11(51)	8(46)	5(41)
Mid–afternoon ºC(ºF)	28(82)	28(82)	25(77)	22(72)	18(64)	14(57)
Days with precipitation	1	2	4	7	9	9
Precipitation mm	11	20	44	87	96	76
Precipitation inches	0.4	0.8	1.7	3.4	3.8	3.0
Daily hours of sunshine	12	11	9	7	5	4

FRENCH GUIANA

Official Name: Department of Guiana
(Overseas Department of France)

Capital: Cayenne
Language: French

The coastal region is marshy. The land rises to a broad
central plateau which is densely forested and continues
to rise to the mountain ranges in the extreme south.
Numerous rivers start in the mountains and empty into the
Atlantic Ocean.

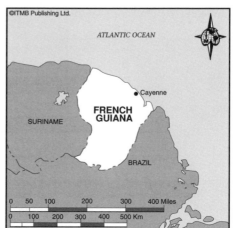

Best time: February and March. (Rain showers are
short, sometimes a drizzle.)
For trips into the jungle, the best time is the dry season, mid–July to early December.

Mid–November to mid–July: Main rainy season. There is a slackening of rain in February and
March, and a slight drop in the afternoon temperature to 29°C (85°F).
Mid–July to mid–November: Almost dry. This is the hottest time. September and October are the
hottest with afternoon temperatures sometimes exceeding 33°C (91°F).

Cayenne, French Guiana: Altitude 6m (20ft)

	Jan	Feb	Mar	Apr	May	Jun
Sunrise ºC(ºF)	23(73)	23(73)	23(73)	23(73)	23(73)	23(73)
Mid–afternoon ºC(ºF)	29(84)	29(84)	29(84)	30(86)	30(86)	30(86)
Days with precipitation	21	17	20	20	26	23
Precipitation mm	439	305	394	400	599	460
Precipitation inches	17.3	12.0	15.5	15.7	23.6	18.1
Daily hours of sunshine	4	4	4	5	5	5

	Jul	Aug	Sep	Oct	Nov	Dec
Sunrise ºC(ºF)	22(72)	22(72)	22(72)	22(72)	22(72)	23(73)
Mid–afternoon ºC(ºF)	30(86)	31(87)	32(89)	32(89)	31(87)	30(86)
Days with precipitation	19	10	4	4	10	19
Precipitation mm	244	165	74	82	154	359
Precipitation inches	9.6	6.5	2.9	3.2	6.1	14.1
Daily hours of sunshine	7	8	8	8	7	5

FRENCH POLYNESIA

Official Name: Territory of French Polynesia
(Overseas Territory of France)

Capital: Papeete (on Tahiti)
Languages: Local languages and French. English is
understood.

Various island groups make up this French overseas
territory. One is the Society Islands which comprises
Tahiti, Moorea, Bora Bora, Raiatea and Huahine. Other
island groups are Marquesas, Austral (or Tubuai),
Tuamotu and Gambier. The islands are volcanic in origin
with steep craggy peaks, deep valleys and waterfalls.

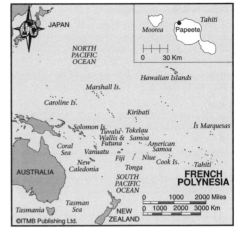

Best time to visit: April to November.

April to November: Season of less rain. Warm, humid, but tempered by pleasant southeast
tradewinds that sweep the South Pacific Ocean. Average afternoon temperature, 30°C (86°F).
December to March: Wet season. Hot, humid. Cyclones may occur occasionally. Afternoon
temperature, 31°C (87°F). Rain, when it occurs, usually comes late afternoon, and humidity increases.

Papeete, Tahiti: Altitude 2m (6ft)

	Jan	Feb	Mar	Apr	May	Jun
Sunrise °C(°F)	23(73)	24(75)	24(75)	24(75)	22(72)	21(69)
Mid–afternoon °C(°F)	30(86)	30(86)	31(87)	31(87)	30(86)	29(84)
Days with precipitation	16	16	17	10	10	8
Precipitation mm	315	233	195	141	92	60
Precipitation inches	12.4	9.2	7.7	5.6	3.6	2.4
Daily hours of sunshine	7	8	7	8	7	7

	Jul	Aug	Sep	Oct	Nov	Dec
Sunrise °C(°F)	21(70)	20(68)	21(69)	22(72)	23(73)	23(73)
Mid–afternoon °C(°F)	28(82)	28(82)	29(84)	29(84)	29(84)	30(86)
Days with precipitation	5	6	6	9	13	14
Precipitation mm	61	48	46	91	162	317
Precipitation inches	2.4	1.9	1.8	3.6	6.4	12.5
Daily hours of sunshine	8	8	8	7	7	6

GABON

Official Name: Gabonese Republic

Capital: Libreville
Languages: French, Fang, other Bantu languages

Along the coast are lowlands that vary in width from 30 to 200km (20 to 125 miles). Beyond this region are a plateau and mountains with numerous rivers. A dense rainforest covers most of the country.

Best time to visit: June to September. (Dry.)

June to September: Dry season. Humid. Comparatively cooler.
October to May: Rainy season. Hot, very high humidity, cloudy.

Libreville, coastal Gabon: Altitude 15m (49ft)

	Jan	Feb	Mar	Apr	May	Jun
Sunrise ºC(ºF)	24(75)	24(75)	24(75)	23(73)	24(75)	23(73)
Mid–afternoon ºC(ºF)	30(86)	30(86)	30(86)	30(86)	29(85)	28(82)
Days with precipitation	13	11	15	14	11	1
Precipitation mm	250	243	363	339	247	54
Precipitation inches	9.8	9.6	14.3	13.3	9.7	2.1
Daily hours of sunshine	6	6	6	6	5	4

	Jul	Aug	Sep	Oct	Nov	Dec
Sunrise ºC(ºF)	22(72)	22(72)	23(73)	23(73)	23(73)	23(73)
Mid–afternoon ºC(ºF)	26(78)	27(80)	28(82)	28(82)	28(82)	29(85)
Days with precipitation	0	1	11	19	20	14
Precipitation mm	7	14	104	427	490	303
Precipitation inches	0.3	0.6	4.1	16.8	19.3	11.9
Daily hours of sunshine	4	3	3	4	4	4

GALAPAGOS ISLANDS

Official name: Archipiélago de Colon
(Part of Ecuador)

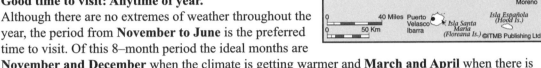

Fifteen major islands and many small islands comprise the group. The islands are volcanic in origin. In general, shorelines are broad aprons of lava and shell sand. Some islands are fringed with mangroves. The interiors are mountainous with high central craters, some of which rise beyond 1500m (5000ft).

Good time to visit: Anytime of year.
Although there are no extremes of weather throughout the year, the period from **November to June** is the preferred time to visit. Of this 8–month period the ideal months are **November and December** when the climate is getting warmer and **March and April** when there is less rain.

January to May: Hot season. Average afternoon temperature, 30°C (86°F). Expect clear skies, very bright sun, a warm water temperature of 26°C (79°F), calm seas, decreased winds, occasional showers particularly at higher elevations, moderate humidity and 8 hours of sunshine daily. The best months for underwater visibility are January to March. February and March are warmest and sunniest months. **June to December:** Cool season. Average afternoon temperature, 27°C (81°F). Overcast sky, fog can develop, misty rain falls on the mountains but scant rain falls on coastal areas. Wet days have only a trace of moisture. This is indicated in the weather table with extremely low precipitation figures. Strong winds blow and the sea can be rough, particularly July to September. Lowest temperatures are usually in August. Expect six hours of sunshine daily.

Notes: 1. Busy vacation times are Easter week (February or March), and June to August, and November and December. 2. Most species of birds nest year–round so the chances are good for observing courtship rituals, mating and hatching.

Galapagos Islands (Ecuador):

	Jan	Feb	Mar	Apr	May	Jun
Sunrise °C(°F)	22(72)	24(75)	24(75)	24(75)	23(73)	22(71)
Mid–afternoon °C(°F)	30(86)	30(86)	31(88)	31(87)	30(86)	28(83)
Days with precipitation	8	9	6	6	4	4
Precipitation mm	20	36	28	18	18	8
Precipitation inches	0.8	1.4	1.1	0.7	0.7	0.3

	Jul	Aug	Sep	Oct	Nov	Dec
Sunrise °C(°F)	21(69)	19(67)	19(67)	19(67)	20(68)	21(70)
Mid–afternoon °C(°F)	27(81)	27(81)	27(81)	27(81)	27(81)	28(83)
Days with precipitation	9	8	7	2	4	6
Precipitation mm	13	8	13	8	13	13
Precipitation inches	0.5	0.3	0.5	0.3	0.5	0.5

GAMBIA

Official Name: Republic of The Gambia

Capital: Banjul
Languages: English, Mandinka, Fulani, Wolof

From the Atlantic coast Gambia extends inland only 320km (200 miles) on both sides of the lower reaches of the Gambia River. Beyond the mangrove swamps which line the river are plains. This small country is no more than 30km (about 20 miles) wide.

Best time to visit: November to February. (Dry, relatively cool.) March to May are also good months, but temperatures are beginning to rise.

November to May: Sunny, dry season. December to March is a popular time for beach vacationers from Europe.
June to October: Rainy season. Rainfall usually lasts no more than a few hours and is not a major inconvenience. Often it falls at night. The wettest months are July to September.

Banjul, Gambia: Altitude 27m (89ft)

	Jan	Feb	Mar	Apr	May	Jun
Sunrise °C(°F)	15(59)	16(61)	17(63)	18(65)	19(67)	23(73)
Mid–afternoon °C(°F)	31(88)	32(90)	34(94)	33(91)	32(89)	32(89)
Days with precipitation	0	0	0	0	1	5
Precipitation mm	3	3	0	0	10	58
Precipitation inches	0.1	0.1	0	0	0.4	2.3
Daily hours of sunshine	9	10	10	10	10	9

	Jul	Aug	Sep	Oct	Nov	Dec
Sunrise °C(°F)	23(73)	23(73)	23(73)	22(72)	18(65)	16(61)
Mid–afternoon °C(°F)	30(86)	29(85)	31(87)	32(89)	32(89)	31(88)
Days with precipitation	16	19	19	8	1	0
Precipitation mm	282	500	310	109	18	3
Precipitation inches	11.1	19.7	12.2	4.3	0.7	0.1
Daily hours of sunshine	6	6	6	8	8	9

GEORGIA

Official Name: Republic of Georgia

Capital: T'bilisi
Languages: Georgian, Russian, Armenian

Georgia is a mountainous country with the subtropical lowlands and Black Sea to the west, and steppes to the east. Rain falls in the western region year–round.

Best time: May and June, and September to mid– October.

May and June: Warm and humid with light rain on the Black Sea coast. Mild in the mountains. These are T'bilisi's wettest months.

July and August: Hot, 24ºC (76ºF), humid and wet including torrential downpours in lower altitudes including the Black Sea coast. Mountain temperatures are mild.

September and October: Warm and humid with light rain on the Black Sea coast, and mild in the mountains. Foliage changes colour to golden hues at this time.

November to April: Cool, 5ºC (41ºF), and wet on the Black Sea coast. Cold in the mountains and valleys where snow can block roads.

T'bilisi, Georgia: Altitude 490m (1608ft)

	Jan	Feb	Mar	Apr	May	Jun
Sunrise ºC(ºF)	−1(30)	0(32)	3(38)	8(46)	12(54)	16(61)
Mid-afternoon ºC(ºF)	7(44)	9(48)	13(55)	17(62)	24(75)	28(82)
Days with precipitation	4	5	6	8	10	9
Precipitation mm	19	26	30	51	78	76
Precipitation inches	0.7	1.0	1.2	2.0	3.1	3.0
Daily hours of sunshine	3	4	5	6	7	8

	Jul	Aug	Sep	Oct	Nov	Dec
Sunrise ºC(ºF)	19(66)	19(66)	15(60)	10(50)	5(41)	1(34)
Mid-afternoon ºC(ºF)	31(87)	30(86)	26(78)	20(68)	14(57)	9(48)
Days with precipitation	6	6	5	6	4	4
Precipitation mm	45	48	36	38	30	21
Precipitation inches	1.8	1.9	1.4	1.5	1.2	0.8
Daily hours of sunshine	8	8	7	5	3	3

GERMANY

Official Name: Federal Republic of Germany

Capital: Berlin
Language: German

In the north is a lowland plain. In the centre is a region of uplands comprised of low mountains, river valleys and basins which lie between the latitude of Hannover and Berlin in the north, and Frankfurt in the south. Farther south is a mountainous region.

Germany's climate is influenced by air masses from Russia in the northeast, and winds from the Atlantic in the west. Seasons such as summers and winters can differ greatly from year to year, depending on which influence is dominant. The two influences cause weather that can change day to day.

Best time to visit: May to October.
We have split Germany's weather into two regions, the northern lowlands, and the central and southern hilly region. See weather tables: Northern lowlands include Hamburg and Berlin. Central includes Frankfurt. Southern hilly region includes Munich.

December to February: Winter. In the north, it is rainy with cold easterly winds that blow from Russia. In the south, winters are cold, particularly January, especially the southeast near the Bavarian Alps. Munich is the gateway for the Alps, a popular skiing area.
March to May: Spring. Can be wet or dry, cold or warm. In the south in the Alps region a warm, dry wind, the föhn, brings clear skies and rising temperatures to 20°C (68°F) and higher. This is the result of wind from the Mediterranean rising over the Alps and flowing down the northern slopes, warming quickly as it does so.
June to August: Summer. Moderately warm. Cool, rainy days are possible, even in July and August. Summers are rainier than winters; expect afternoon downpours. The Alps especially can be very wet. The sunniest areas are in the south such as Baden–Württemberg and Bavaria.
September to November: Autumn. Can be drizzly or dry, cold or warm. In the south in some years an Indian summer is experienced, in which warm temperatures extend into early winter. The föhn, wind from the south, can blow in autumn as it does in spring.

Event: Munich hosts the world's biggest beer festival, the Oktoberfest. It runs mid–September to early October.

Frankfurt, central Germany: Altitude 103m (338ft)

	Jan	Feb	Mar	Apr	May	Jun
Sunrise ºC(ºF)	−2(29)	−1(31)	2(35)	5(41)	8(48)	12(53)
Mid–afternoon ºC(ºF)	3(37)	6(42)	9(49)	14(58)	19(67)	22(72)
Days with precipitation	9	9	9	9	9	9
Precipitation mm	44	32	41	37	50	64
Precipitation inches	1.7	1.3	1.6	1.5	2.0	2.5
Daily hours of sunshine	1	2	4	5	7	8
Snow mm	179	125	52	0	0	0
Snow inches	7	5	2	0	0	0

	Jul	Aug	Sep	Oct	Nov	Dec
Sunrise ºC(ºF)	13(56)	13(56)	11(51)	6(43)	2(36)	−1(31)
Mid–afternoon ºC(ºF)	24(75)	23(74)	19(67)	13(56)	7(45)	4(39)
Days with precipitation	10	10	9	9	9	11
Precipitation mm	71	66	49	57	52	50
Precipitation inches	2.8	2.6	1.9	2.2	2.0	2.0
Daily hours of sunshine	7	7	5	3	1	1
Snow mm	0	0	0	0	152	279
Snow inches	0	0	0	0	6	11

Berlin, northern Germany: Altitude 58m (190ft)

	Jan	Feb	Mar	Apr	May	Jun
Sunrise ºC(ºF)	−3(27)	−2(29)	1(33)	4(39)	8(46)	11(51)
Mid–afternoon ºC(ºF)	2(35)	4(39)	8(46)	13(55)	19(66)	22(72)
Days with precipitation	10	9	8	9	10	10
Precipitation mm	43	37	38	42	55	71
Precipitation inches	1.7	1.5	1.5	1.6	2.2	2.8
Daily hours of sunshine	1	3	4	5	7	7
Snow mm	126	152	25	0	0	0
Snow inches	5	6	1	0	0	0

	Jul	Aug	Sep	Oct	Nov	Dec
Sunrise ºC(ºF)	13(55)	12(53)	9(48)	6(42)	2(35)	−1(30)
Mid–afternoon ºC(ºF)	23(73)	23(73)	19(66)	13(55)	7(44)	3(37)
Days with precipitation	9	9	9	8	10	11
Precipitation mm	53	65	46	36	50	55
Precipitation inches	2.1	2.6	1.8	1.4	2.0	2.2
Daily hours of sunshine	0	0	0	0	2	1
Snow mm	0	0	0	0	50	25
Snow inches	0	0	0	0	2	5

Hamburg, northern Germany: Altitude 15m (49ft)

	Jan	Feb	Mar	Apr	May	Jun
Sunrise ºC(ºF)	–2(29)	–2(29)	0(32)	3(37)	7(44)	10(50)
Mid–afternoon ºC(ºF)	3(37)	4(39)	7(44)	12(53)	17(62)	20(68)
Days with precipitation	12	9	11	10	10	11
Precipitation mm	61	41	56	51	57	74
Precipitation inches	2.4	1.6	2.2	2.0	2.2	2.9
Daily hours of sunshine	1	2	3	5	7	7

	Jul	Aug	Sep	Oct	Nov	Dec
Sunrise ºC(ºF)	12(53)	12(53)	9(48)	6(42)	3(37)	–1(30)
Mid–afternoon ºC(ºF)	21(70)	22(72)	18(64)	13(55)	8(46)	4(39)
Days with precipitation	12	11	11	10	12	12
Precipitation mm	82	70	70	63	71	72
Precipitation inches	3.2	2.8	2.8	2.5	2.8	2.8
Daily hours of sunshine	7	7	5	3	2	1

Munich, southern Germany: Altitude 447m (1467ft)

	Jan	Feb	Mar	Apr	May	Jun
Sunrise ºC(ºF)	–5(23)	–4(25)	–1(31)	3(37)	7(45)	11(51)
Mid–afternoon ºC(ºF)	1(33)	3(37)	8(46)	13(55)	18(64)	21(69)
Days with precipitation	10	9	9	10	11	12
Precipitation mm	45	42	47	55	88	109
Precipitation inches	1.8	1.6	1.9	2.2	3.5	4.3
Daily hours of sunshine	2	3	4	5	7	7
Snow mm	305	279	75	52	25	0
Snow inches	12	11	3	2	1	0

	Jul	Aug	Sep	Oct	Nov	Dec
Sunrise ºC(ºF)	12(53)	12(53)	9(48)	4(40)	–1(31)	–3(26)
Mid–afternoon ºC(ºF)	23(73)	23(73)	19(66)	14(57)	6(42)	2(36)
Days with precipitation	11	11	9	7	10	10
Precipitation mm	100	98	68	49	55	49
Precipitation inches	3.9	3.9	2.7	1.9	2.2	1.9
Daily hours of sunshine	7	7	6	4	2	2
Snow mm	0	0	0	51	77	253
Snow inches	0	0	0	2	3	10

GHANA
Official Name: Republic of Ghana

Capital: Accra
Languages: English, Akan, Mossi, Ewe, Ga

A plain extends along the coast. Inland are rainforests then, farther north, rolling grassy plains.

Best time for the whole country: November to April.
(Dry, lower humidity.) Late June to October is also a good time.

We have divided the weather into two regions.

1. Coastal region. (Includes Accra.)
December to April: Dry season. Accra experiences hottest temperatures from November to January, 31°C (88°F).
May and June: Main rainy season.
July and August: Dry.
September to November: Wet, light rain.

2. Northern region. (Includes Tamale.)
November to March: Dry season. The hot, dry, harmattan wind blows from the northeast, starting in late November and continuing to March. It brings dust from the Sahara which reduces visibility.
May to September: Wet season.

Natural attraction: Mole National Park, Ghana's largest game reserve, is in the northeast and is best visited October to March, in the dry season, when the animal viewing is easier because of low grass. However, the dust–laden harmattan winds can make the sky hazy.

Accra, Ghana: Altitude 27m (88ft)

	Jan	Feb	Mar	Apr	May	Jun
Sunrise ºC(ºF)	23(73)	24(75)	24(75)	24(75)	24(75)	23(74)
Mid–afternoon ºC(ºF)	31(87)	31(88)	31(88)	31(88)	31(87)	29(84)
Days with precipitation	1	2	4	6	9	10
Precipitation mm	15	33	56	81	142	178
Precipitation inches	0.6	1.3	2.2	3.2	5.6	7.0
Daily hours of sunshine	7	8	7	7	7	5

	Jul	Aug	Sep	Oct	Nov	Dec
Sunrise ºC(ºF)	23(73)	22(71)	23(73)	23(74)	24(75)	24(75)
Mid–afternoon ºC(ºF)	27(80)	27(80)	27(80)	29(85)	31(87)	31(87)
Days with precipitation	4	3	4	6	3	2
Precipitation mm	46	15	36	64	36	23
Precipitation inches	1.8	0.6	1.4	2.5	1.4	0.9
Daily hours of sunshine	5	5	6	7	8	8

GIBRALTAR

Official Name: Gibraltar
(Dependent Territory of United Kingdom)

Capital: Gibraltar
Language: English

The Rock of Gibraltar, formed of limestone, rises to 425m (1396ft) above sea level. It is connected to the Spanish mainland by a sandy isthmus.

Best time: May to mid–October.

June to August: Summer. Dry, warm, average afternoon temperature, 27°C (81°F). Winds keep the summers pleasant. The winds could be the dry westerlies or the humid easterlies. The moisture in the warm air of the easterlies is forced upwards by the cliffs and, as its temperature is lowered, condenses over the peak of the Rock to form a blanket of cloud.
September to November: Autumn. Mild, 21°C (70°F). Some rain.
December to February: Winter. Mild, 16°C (60°F) in the daytime. Rainy. December and January have the heaviest rains.
March to May: Spring. Mild. Temperatures begin to increase as summer approaches, and the rainstorms decrease.

Gibraltar: Altitude 2m (7ft)

	Jan	Feb	Mar	Apr	May	Jun
Sunrise °C(°F)	10(50)	11(51)	12(54)	13(56)	15(60)	18(64)
Mid–afternoon °C(°F)	16(60)	17(62)	18(65)	20(68)	23(73)	25(78)
Days with precipitation	10	7	10	6	4	1
Precipitation mm	152	98	106	59	25	4
Precipitation inches	6.0	3.9	4.2	2.3	1.0	0.2
Daily hours of sunshine	6	7	7	8	10	11

	Jul	Aug	Sep	Oct	Nov	Dec
Sunrise °C(°F)	20(68)	21(69)	19(67)	17(62)	14(57)	11(53)
Mid–afternoon °C(°F)	28(83)	29(83)	26(79)	23(73)	19(66)	17(62)
Days with precipitation	0	1	2	5	7	10
Precipitation mm	1	3	23	55	114	127
Precipitation inches	0	0.1	0.9	2.2	4.5	5.0
Daily hours of sunshine	11	11	9	7	6	6

GREECE
Official Name: Hellenic Republic

Capital: Athens
Languages: Greek, English, French

Greece is mountainous with valleys and plains between
the mountains. The north has the largest plains in the
Macedonian region. The islands in the Aegean Sea are
high and rocky.

Best time: Late May to early June, and September.
(Pleasantly warm and uncrowded.) Wildflowers are
blooming in May and June.

Late May to June: Throughout most of Greece it is pleasantly warm, 27°C (80°F) with little rain, if
any. The mountainous interior in the north remains cool.
July to August: Summer. Hot, humid, sunny and mainly dry.
In southern Greece, which includes Athens and the islands in the Aegean Sea, the weather is dry
and hot with daytime temperatures rising 30 to 35°C (85 to 95°F). They sometimes go beyond 40°C
(104°F).
Winds from the north, the meltemi, blow during summer, appreciably cooling the evenings on the
islands in the Aegean Sea and the eastern coast of mainland Greece, including Athens. They also
reduce humidity. These winds, however, can make the seas quite rough and upset ferry schedules.
The western coast and the islands in the Ionian Sea, which include Corfu, are not affected by the
meltemi.
In the mountainous interior of northern Greece, July, August and September are attractive to mountain
hikers because the snow has melted and the weather is pleasant and dry.
In the extreme south, on the island of Crete, swimming can be enjoyed from mid–April to November
because of the warm climate, lack of rain, and a sea temperature of about 25°C (77°F).
September: Pleasant, 25 to 30°C (77 to 86°F), with minimal rain.
October: Can be balmy. Rains start in mid–October in most regions and the temperature drops, but
there are sunny days. The changing colours of the trees are spectacular.
November to February: Winter. Generally cold and wet but crisp, sunny days with blue skies are
possible. In the south, including Athens, most precipitation occurs in winter. Snow occasionally falls
in Athens. It also falls in northern Greece which experiences harsh, freezing winters and it falls on the
mountains in Crete where it lies between November and April. Snow rarely falls on the other Greek
Islands.
March to May: These are transitional months when the temperatures increase gradually from 15 to
25°C (60 to 77°F) and the rains diminish. Days vary between mild and warm, wet and dry.

Athens, Greece: Altitude 107m (351ft)

	Jan	Feb	Mar	Apr	May	Jun
Sunrise ºC(ºF)	7(44)	7(44)	9(48)	12(53)	16(60)	20(68)
Mid–afternoon ºC(ºF)	13(55)	14(57)	16(60)	19(66)	24(75)	29(84)
Days with precipitation	5	6	6	4	2	1
Precipitation mm	45	48	44	25	14	6
Precipitation inches	1.8	1.9	1.7	1.0	0.6	0.2
Daily hours of sunshine	4	5	6	8	10	11

	Jul	Aug	Sep	Oct	Nov	Dec
Sunrise ºC(ºF)	23(73)	23(73)	20(68)	16(60)	12(53)	9(48)
Mid–afternoon ºC(ºF)	32(89)	31(87)	28(82)	23(73)	19(66)	15(59)
Days with precipitation	1	1	1	4	5	7
Precipitation mm	6	8	10	48	51	66
Precipitation inches	0.2	0.3	0.4	1.9	2.0	2.6
Daily hours of sunshine	12	11	9	7	5	4

Thessaloniki, northern Greece: Altitude 4m (13ft)

	Jan	Feb	Mar	Apr	May	Jun
Sunrise ºC(ºF)	1(33)	2(35)	4(39)	7(44)	12(53)	16(60)
Mid–afternoon ºC(ºF)	9(48)	11(51)	14(57)	19(66)	25(77)	29(84)
Days with precipitation	6	6	7	5	6	4
Precipitation mm	37	40	46	36	44	32
Precipitation inches	1.5	1.6	1.8	1.4	1.7	1.3
Daily hours of sunshine	3	4	5	7	8	10

	Jul	Aug	Sep	Oct	Nov	Dec
Sunrise ºC(ºF)	18(64)	18(64)	15(59)	11(51)	7(44)	3(37)
Mid–afternoon ºC(ºF)	31(87)	31(87)	27(80)	21(71)	15(59)	11(51)
Days with precipitation	3	3	3	5	7	7
Precipitation mm	26	21	26	41	58	53
Precipitation inches	1.0	0.8	1.0	1.6	2.3	2.1
Daily hours of sunshine	10	10	8	5	4	3

Heraklion, island of Crete, Greece: Altitude 39m (128ft)

	Jan	Feb	Mar	Apr	May	Jun
Sunrise ºC(ºF)	9(48)	9(48)	10(50)	12(53)	15(59)	19(66)
Mid–afternoon ºC(ºF)	15(59)	16(60)	17(62)	20(68)	24(75)	27(80)
Days with precipitation	10	9	7	3	2	1
Precipitation mm	92	77	57	30	15	3
Precipitation inches	3.6	3.0	2.2	1.2	0.6	0.1
Daily hours of sunshine	4	4	6	8	10	12

Heraklion, island of Crete, Greece: (continued)

	Jul	Aug	Sep	Oct	Nov	Dec
Sunrise ºC(ºF)	22(72)	22(72)	19(66)	17(62)	13(55)	11(51)
Mid–afternoon ºC(ºF)	29(84)	28(82)	26(78)	23(73)	20(68)	17(62)
Days with precipitation	0	0	1	5	6	9
Precipitation mm	1	1	20	69	59	77
Precipitation inches	0.04	0.04	0.8	2.7	2.3	3.0
Daily hours of sunshine	12	11	9	6	5	4

Rhodes, island of Rhodes, Greece: Altitude 11m (40ft)

	Jan	Feb	Mar	Apr	May	Jun
Sunrise ºC(ºF)	9(48)	9(48)	10(50)	13(55)	16(60)	20(68)
Mid–afternoon ºC(ºF)	15(59)	15(59)	17(62)	20(68)	24(75)	28(82)
Days with precipitation	12	9	7	3	2	1
Precipitation mm	148	118	75	24	14	3
Precipitation inches	5.8	4.6	3.0	0.9	0.6	0.1
Daily hours of sunshine	4	5	7	8	10	12

	Jul	Aug	Sep	Oct	Nov	Dec
Sunrise ºC(ºF)	22(72)	23(73)	20(68)	17(62)	13(55)	10(50)
Mid–afternoon ºC(ºF)	31(87)	31(87)	28(82)	24(76)	20(68)	17(62)
Days with precipitation	0	0	1	5	6	11
Precipitation mm	0	0	7	64	88	145
Precipitation inches	0	0	0.3	2.5	3.5	5.7
Daily hours of sunshine	13	13	11	7	5	4

GREENLAND

Official Name: Greenland (Grønland)
(Dependent Territory of Denmark)

Capital: Nuuk (formerly Godthab)
Languages: Greenlandic (East Inuit), Danish, English

The interior is a high plateau ranging in altitude from 1200 to 2700m (4000 to 9000ft) above sea level. Most of the land is covered by ice. Only about 15 percent is ice–free. The entire coast is lined with fjords.

Best time to visit: July and August. (Ice is minimal, wildflowers are in bloom, wildlife is active.)

Greenland has two weather regions, south and north.

1. South. (Includes Nuuk.)

June to August: Summer. Afternoon temperatures can climb above 15°C (59°F) but usually average about 10°C (50°F). The warmest days can be cool. Night temperatures often fall below 0°C (32°F). Weather is unpredictable; snow may fall in July or temperatures may rise to 20°C (68°F). Around the southern coast, morning fog is common but it will lift by noon to reveal a sunny day. Expect 5 or 6 hours of sunshine daily.

September to May: Long, severe winters with daytime temperatures dropping to –20°C (–4°F). Strong winds are characteristic of coastal winters but the coldest days are sometimes clear and windless. The northern lights, aurora borealis, are best seen in the southern region between mid–September and early November and between mid–February and early April.

2. North.

June to August: Summer. Afternoon temperatures range 5 to 8°C (41 to 46°F). Temperatures rise above freezing point for brief periods only. Night temperatures are often below 0°C (32°F). Wildflowers bloom from mid–July to mid–August.

September to May: Long, severe winter. Low temperatures of –40°C (–40°F) can last for many weeks.

Natural attraction: The multicoloured, flashing luminosity of the northern lights, aurora borealis, are best seen from the southern half of the country rather than in the northern regions which are too far north.

Nuuk (Godthab), Greenland: Altitude 70m (230ft)

	Jan	Feb	Mar	Apr	May	Jun
Sunrise ºC(ºF)	–10(14)	–11(13)	–11(13)	–6(21)	–2(29)	1(33)
Mid–afternoon ºC(ºF)	–5(23)	–5(23)	–5(23)	–1(30)	4(39)	8(46)
Days with precipitation	9	9	10	9	9	8
Precipitation mm	39	47	50	46	55	62
Precipitation inches	1.5	1.9	2.0	1.8	2.2	2.4
Daily hours of sunshine	1	3	5	7	6	6

	Jul	Aug	Sep	Oct	Nov	Dec
Sunrise ºC(ºF)	4(39)	4(39)	2(35)	–2(29)	–6(21)	–9(16)
Mid–afternoon ºC(ºF)	11(51)	10(50)	6(42)	2(35)	–1(30)	–3(27)
Days with precipitation	10	9	12	10	11	10
Precipitation mm	82	89	88	70	74	54
Precipitation inches	3.2	3.5	3.5	2.8	2.9	2.1
Daily hours of sunshine	6	4	3	2	1	0

GRENADA

Official Name: Grenada (pronounced Grenayda)
(Independent nation; formerly a British possession)

Capital: Saint George's
Languages: English, French patois

The island, volcanic in origin, is mountainous with fertile valleys. The highest point is 838m (2749ft).

Best time to visit: January to April.

January to May: Dry and mild. Pleasant tropical climate with average afternoon temperature, 30ºC (85ºF).
June to December: Wet season. Afternoon temperature, 31ºC (88ºF).
Rain rarely falls for more than one hour a day. The coastal plains and most valleys remain relatively dry. Rainfall is highest in the hilly regions of the island.
Sunshine: Expect 8 hours of sun per day throughout the year.
Humidity is extreme during the wet season.
Hurricane season is June to December but a touchdown is rare.

Note: See under Caribbean Islands for general weather information.

St George's, Grenada: Altitude: sea level

	Jan	Feb	Mar	Apr	May	Jun
Sunrise ºC(ºF)	23(73)	23(73)	23(74)	23(74)	24(76)	24(76)
Mid–afternoon ºC(ºF)	29(84)	30(85)	30(85)	30(86)	31(87)	31(87)
Days with precipitation	14	8	8	7	10	17

	Jul	Aug	Sep	Oct	Nov	Dec
Sunrise ºC(ºF)	24(76)	25(77)	25(77)	24(76)	24(76)	24(75)
Mid–afternoon ºC(ºF)	30(86)	31(87)	31(88)	31(88)	31(87)	30(85)
Days with precipitation	20	21	18	16	18	16

GUADELOUPE

Official Name: Department of Guadeloupe
(Dependency of France)

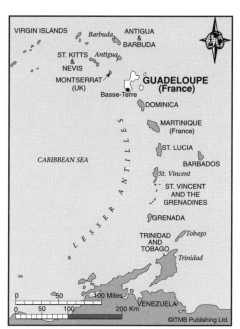

Capital: Basse–Terre
Languages: French and Creole. English is understood.

The terrain of Guadeloupe, pronounced gwad–eh–loop,
and the terrain of nearby islands it administers, are
described below.
- Guadeloupe consists of two volcanic islands, Grande–
  Terre and Basse–Terre, of which Basse–Terre is the
  most mountainous. Grande–Terre has popular beaches
  on the south coast.
- St Barthélemy (St Barts for short) with an arid climate
  has dry, hilly and rocky terrain with about 20 beaches
  in small bays and coves.
- Marie–Galante is flat and undulating.
- Désirade has low hills that rise to 273m (900ft). It has
  good beaches.
- Les Saintes, a group of 8 islands, has high rugged hills
  with good beaches on Terre–de–Bas and Terre–de–Haut.
- Saint–Martin is hilly in the interior. The flat coastal lowlands contain some saltponds, and there are
  coves with beaches of white sand.

The weather table for Saint–Martin/Sint Maarten represents coastal weather of these islands as well
as coastal Guadeloupe. The weather table for Point–a–Pitre represents the mountainous region of
Guadeloupe.

Best time to visit: December to May.

December to May: Drier season. Cooler, with average afternoon temperature, 26°C (78°F).
June to November: Wet season. Humid, warm, afternoon average, 28°C (82°F).
Tradewinds from the northeast temper the tropical climate but bring more rain to the mountainous
regions, compared with the coast.
Hurricanes are possible, August to October, but a touchdown is rare.

Note: See under Caribbean Islands for general weather information.

Point–a–Pitre, Guadeloupe: Altitude 533m (1750ft)

	Jan	Feb	Mar	Apr	May	Jun
Sunrise °C(°F)	18(64)	17(63)	17(63)	18(65)	19(67)	21(69)
Mid–afternoon °C(°F)	25(77)	24(76)	25(77)	26(79)	27(80)	27(80)
Days with precipitation	23	18	20	20	23	25
Precipitation mm	234	155	206	185	292	358
Precipitation inches	9.2	6.1	8.1	7.3	11.5	14.1
Daily hours of sunshine	7	8	8	8	7	8

Point–a–Pitre, Guadeloupe: (continued)

	Jul	Aug	Sep	Oct	Nov	Dec
Sunrise ºC(ºF)	20(68)	21(69)	21(69)	20(68)	19(67)	18(65)
Mid–afternoon ºC(ºF)	27(80)	28(82)	28(82)	27(80)	27(80)	26(78)
Days with precipitation	27	26	23	24	22	23
Precipitation mm	447	389	417	315	312	257
Precipitation inches	17.6	15.3	16.4	12.4	12.3	10.1
Daily hours of sunshine	7	7	7	7	7	7

Saint–Martin/Sint Maarten: Altitude 9m (30ft)

	Jan	Feb	Mar	Apr	May	Jun
Sunrise ºC(ºF)	23(75)	23(75)	23(75)	25(77)	25(78)	26(80)
Mid–afternoon ºC(ºF)	28(83)	28(83)	28(83)	28(84)	30(86)	31(88)
Days with precipitation	11	9	8	8	11	10
Precipitation mm	62	44	44	67	96	63
Precipitation inches	2.4	1.7	1.7	2.6	3.8	2.5
Daily hours of sunshine	8	8	9	9	8	8

	Jul	Aug	Sep	Oct	Nov	Dec
Sunrise ºC(ºF)	26(80)	26(80)	26(80)	26(80)	25(78)	24(76)
Mid–afternoon ºC(ºF)	31(88)	31(88)	31(88)	30(87)	29(85)	28(83)
Days with precipitation	12	14	13	14	14	13
Precipitation mm	76	99	131	109	130	86
Precipitation inches	3.0	3.9	5.2	4.3	5.1	3.4
Daily hours of sunshine	8	8	8	8	8	8

GUAM

Official Name: Territory of Guam
(Unincorporated Outlying Territory of the U.S.A.)

Capital: Hagatña (formerly Agaña)
Languages: English, Chamorro

Guam is of volcanic origin. The northern two–thirds is a flat plateau. The southern one–third is mountainous with jungle and waterfalls.

Best time: January to April.

January to April: Dry season. Average temperatures are slightly lower compared with other months. The northeast tradewinds bring cooling breezes. Humidity is also lower.
May to December: Rain increases month–by–month, peaking in September, then the rainfall decreases towards December. Most rain falls July to mid–November. Cyclones, with their strong winds and heavy rainstorms, are possible June to November.

Guam:

	Jan	Feb	Mar	Apr	May	Jun
Sunrise ºC(ºF)	24(75)	24(75)	24(75)	24(75)	24(75)	25(77)
Mid–afternoon ºC(ºF)	30(86)	32(89)	32(89)	32(89)	33(91)	33(91)
Days with precipitation	15	14	14	14	15	19
Precipitation mm	113	95	76	99	154	164
Precipitation inches	4.4	3.8	3.0	3.9	6.1	6.5
Daily hours of sunshine	6	6	7	7	7	6

	Jul	Aug	Sep	Oct	Nov	Dec
Sunrise ºC(ºF)	25(77)	25(77)	25(77)	25(77)	25(77)	24(76)
Mid–afternoon ºC(ºF)	34(93)	33(91)	32(89)	32(89)	32(89)	32(89)
Days with precipitation	23	22	22	22	22	19
Precipitation mm	268	349	343	307	208	137
Precipitation inches	10.6	13.8	13.5	12.1	8.2	5.4
Daily hours of sunshine	5	5	4	4	5	5

GUATEMALA
Official Name: Republic of Guatemala

Capital: Guatemala City
Languages: Spanish, Amerindian dialects

About two–thirds of the central and southern region is comprised of mountains of which many are volcanic. Most are extinct but some are active. The northern region is a low plain that supports forests and grazing lands.

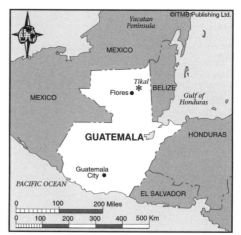

Best time for the whole country: December to April.
(Dry, warm. May to November is wet.)

There are two weather regions: highlands in the south and west, and lowlands in the north.
1. Highlands in south and west. (Includes Guatemala City.)
December to April: Dry. Warm days with average afternoon temperatures of about 25ºC (77ºF), but cool nights. The highest elevations may have snow at night. Lower levels can occasionally reach 32ºC (90ºF) in afternoons. Five hours of sunshine daily. Warmest months are March and April. On the Pacific and Caribbean coasts the dry season runs January to April.
May to November: Rainy. Wettest months are June to October which average 21 rainy days per month. Rain in the highlands usually falls in the afternoons. Days are warm and spring–like with average afternoon temperatures of about 26ºC (79ºF). Nights are cool. Two hours of sunshine daily. On the Pacific and Caribbean coasts the rainy season runs May to December.

2. Lowlands in north. (Includes Flores, and Tikal in the forest of Petén.)
Rain is year–round, but most falls May to September. Days and nights are warmer than the highlands. Afternoons average 30ºC (86ºF); nights are 20ºC (68ºF).

Archaeological site: For visiting **Tikal** in Petén, mid–November to April is the high season because of good weather and foreign visitors' vacation time. March and April are the driest months with warm days, cool nights. Rains start in May and continue into December, but August is often dry.

Guatemala City, Guatemala: Altitude 1480m (4855ft)

	Jan	Feb	Mar	Apr	May	Jun
Sunrise °C(°F)	12(53)	12(54)	14(57)	14(58)	16(60)	16(61)
Mid–afternoon °C(°F)	23(73)	25(77)	27(81)	28(82)	29(84)	27(81)
Days with precipitation	4	2	3	5	15	23
Precipitation mm	8	3	13	31	152	274
Precipitation inches	0.3	0.1	0.5	1.2	6.0	10.8
Daily hours of sunshine	5	5	5	4	3	1

	Jul	Aug	Sep	Oct	Nov	Dec
Sunrise °C(°F)	16(60)	16(60)	16(60)	16(60)	14(57)	13(55)
Mid–afternoon °C(°F)	26(78)	26(78)	26(78)	24(76)	23(74)	22(72)
Days with precipitation	21	21	22	18	7	4
Precipitation mm	203	198	231	173	23	8
Precipitation inches	8.0	7.8	9.1	6.8	0.9	0.3
Daily hours of sunshine	2	1	2	2	3	5

GUINEA

Official Name: Republic of Guinea

Capital: Conakry
Languages: French, African languages

From the shoreline a coastal plain extends about 50km (30 miles) inland then rises to a mountainous plateau. Farther east are grassy plains. In the extreme southeast are forested mountains.

Best time: November to mid–April.

November to mid–April: Dry season. Hot and humid. The period November to early December is ideal because the air is clear immediately after the rains. From mid–December to mid–April the air can be hazy.
May to October: Rainy season. It is heaviest along the coast in July and August. Rainfall is less farther inland.

Conakry, coastal Guinea: Altitude 26m (85ft)

	Jan	Feb	Mar	Apr	May	Jun
Sunrise ºC(ºF)	19(66)	20(68)	21(69)	22(72)	21(68)	20(68)
Mid–afternoon ºC(ºF)	32(89)	33(91)	33(91)	34(93)	33(91)	32(89)
Days with precipitation	0	0	0	2	9	18
Precipitation mm	1	1	2	22	137	396
Precipitation inches	0.04	0.04	0.1	0.9	5.4	15.6
Daily hours of sunshine	7	8	8	7	7	5

	Jul	Aug	Sep	Oct	Nov	Dec
Sunrise ºC(ºF)	20(68)	21(71)	21(71)	20(68)	21(71)	20(68)
Mid–afternoon ºC(ºF)	30(86)	30(86)	31(87)	31(87)	32(89)	32(89)
Days with precipitation	27	27	22	17	6	1
Precipitation mm	1130	1104	617	295	70	8
Precipitation inches	44.5	43.4	24.3	11.6	2.8	0.3
Daily hours of sunshine	4	3	5	6	7	7

GUINEA–BISSAU

Official Name: Republic of Guinea–Bissau

Capital: Bissau
Languages: Portuguese, Crioulo, African languages

The country includes about 60 islands adjacent to the mainland. The mainland consists of tropical rainforests and mangrove swamps.

Best time to travel: November to mid–April.

November to mid–April: Dry season. Hot, humid, average daily maximum is mostly 30ºC (86ºF) but it rises in March and April to 32ºC (90ºF).

May to October: Rainy season. July and August are the wettest months. Air is hot and humid.

GUYANA

Official Name: Co–operative Republic of Guyana
Capital: Georgetown
Languages: English, Amerindian dialects

Along the coast are lowlands. Inland, or southwards, is a thickly forested region that covers four–fifths of the country. The forest extends into the mountains. Beyond the mountains are grassy plains.

Weather in brief: The climate is hot and damp with high humidity year–round. Even in the dry season there is some rain, but Guyana escapes Caribbean hurricanes. Year round, the average afternoon temperature hovers around 29°C (84°F) along the coastal belt which includes Georgetown. The coast is fanned by daily sea breezes. In the uplands in the south, temperatures are slightly lower.

Best time for the whole country: December to April. (Cooler period, 29°C (84°F).

We have divided the weather into two regions, coastal and uplands.
1. Coastal. (Includes Georgetown.)
The coast has two dry seasons and two wet seasons.
Total rainfall in the coastal region is about 2300mm (90in) per year.
February to April: Dry.
May to August: Rainy.
Mid–August to October: Dry.
Mid–November to mid–January: Rainy.
2. Uplands.
The uplands in the southern interior have one long, dry season and a short, wet season.
Mid–August to mid–April: Dry season, but with occasional rain.
Mid–April to August: Rainy season. Rainfall is about 1500mm (60in) per year, less than the heavy rains that fall in the north.
Georgetown, Guyana: Altitude 2m (6ft)

	Jan	Feb	Mar	Apr	May	Jun
Sunrise ºC(ºF)	24(75)	24(75)	24(75)	24(75)	24(75)	24(75)
Mid–afternoon ºC(ºF)	29(84)	29(84)	29(84)	30(86)	29(85)	29(85)
Days with precipitation	16	10	10	12	19	23
Precipitation mm	185	89	111	141	286	328
Precipitation inches	7.3	3.5	4.4	5.6	11.3	12.9
Daily hours of sunshine	7	7	7	7	6	5

	Jul	Aug	Sep	Oct	Nov	Dec
Sunrise ºC(ºF)	24(75)	24(75)	24(75)	24(75)	24(75)	24(75)
Mid–afternoon ºC(ºF)	30(86)	31(87)	31(87)	31(87)	30(86)	29(85)
Days with precipitation	21	15	9	9	12	18
Precipitation mm	268	201	98	107	186	262
Precipitation inches	10.6	7.9	3.9	4.2	7.3	10.3
Daily hours of sunshine	6	8	8	8	7	6

HAITI
Official Name: Republic of Haiti

Capital: Port–au–Prince
Languages: French, Creole

Haiti is mountainous throughout. It occupies the
western third of Hispaniola, an island it shares with
the Dominican Republic.

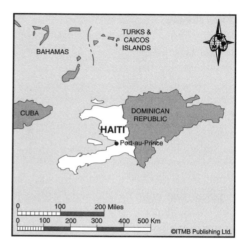

Best time to visit: December to March.

Port–au–Prince, the capital, has two wet seasons and two
dry seasons:
April to June: Wet.
July: Dry.
August to November: Wet.
December to March: Dry.
Hottest: June to September temperatures reach 34°C (93°F). Humidity is high.
Mildest: February to April, 32°C (89°F).
Hurricanes tend to miss Haiti by passing to the north and south of Hispaniola, the island Haiti shares
with the Dominican Republic.

Note: See under Caribbean islands for general Caribbean weather.

Port–au–Prince, Haiti: Altitude 37m (121ft)

	Jan	Feb	Mar	Apr	May	Jun
Sunrise °C(°F)	20(68)	20(68)	21(69)	22(71)	22(72)	23(73)
Mid–afternoon °C(°F)	31(87)	31(88)	32(89)	32(89)	32(90)	33(92)
Days with precipitation	3	5	7	11	13	8
Precipitation mm	33	58	86	160	231	102
Precipitation inches	1.3	2.3	3.4	6.3	9.1	4.0
Daily hours of sunshine	9	9	9	9	9	8

	Jul	Aug	Sep	Oct	Nov	Dec
Sunrise °C(°F)	23(73)	23(73)	23(73)	22(72)	22(71)	21(69)
Mid–afternoon °C(°F)	34(93)	34(93)	33(91)	32(90)	31(88)	31(87)
Days with precipitation	7	11	12	12	7	3
Precipitation mm	74	145	175	170	86	33
Precipitation inches	2.9	5.7	6.9	6.7	3.4	1.3
Daily hours of sunshine	9	9	8	8	7	7

HONDURAS

Official Name: Republic of Honduras

Capital: Tegucigalpa
Languages: Spanish, Amerindian dialects

Honduras is a plateau of broad plains, fertile pastures, deep valleys, extensive forests, and mountains that rise to 3000m (10000ft). There is an extensive lowland in the extreme east.

Best time to visit: November to April. (Mostly dry.)

There are two weather regions, firstly Central and Southern, and secondly the Caribbean coast and Bay Islands.

1. Central and Southern. (Includes Tegucigalpa.)
November to April: Dry. Average afternoon temperatures vary little throughout the season, rising from about 25°C (77°F) in December to 30°C (86°F) in April, the hottest month. Seven to 9 hours of sunshine daily. This hilly area is cooler than the coast.
May to October: Rainy, but with many dry days. The sun shines in the mornings. Rain falls mid–afternoon and early evening in brief cloudbursts. Six to 8 hours of sunshine daily. Average afternoon temperatures are around 28°C (82°F).

2. Caribbean coast and Bay Islands.
Throughout the year the coastal region is rainy but with 8 hours of sunshine daily. October and November are the rainiest months. Rain doesn't fall every day. Sea breezes cool the coastal region. Afternoon temperatures exceed 31°C (87°F), higher than the hilly interior.

Tegucigalpa, Honduras: Altitude 1007m (3304ft)

	Jan	Feb	Mar	Apr	May	Jun
Sunrise °C(°F)	14(57)	15(59)	16(61)	17(62)	18(64)	18(64)
Mid–afternoon °C(°F)	26(78)	27(80)	30(86)	30(86)	30(86)	29(84)
Days with precipitation	1	1	1	2	9	12
Precipitation mm	5	5	10	43	144	159
Precipitation inches	0.2	0.2	0.4	1.7	5.7	6.3
Daily hours of sunshine	7	8	9	8	7	6

	Jul	Aug	Sep	Oct	Nov	Dec
Sunrise °C(°F)	18(64)	18(64)	18(64)	17(62)	16(61)	15(59)
Mid–afternoon °C(°F)	28(82)	29(84)	29(84)	27(80)	26(78)	25(77)
Days with precipitation	9	9	13	10	4	2
Precipitation mm	82	89	177	109	40	10
Precipitation inches	3.2	3.5	7.0	4.3	1.6	0.4
Daily hours of sunshine	6	7	6	6	6	7

HONG KONG, see CHINA

HUNGARY
Official Name: Republic of Hungary

Capital: Budapest
Language: Hungarian

This landlocked country is mostly flat and is partly encircled in the west by the Alps, and in the north and east by the Carpathian Mountains.

Hungary has the long hot summers, the long cold winters and the brief springs and autumns peculiar to inland regions of the Continent.

Best time: June to September.

June to September: June to August is warm to hot, 27°C (80°F). Summer days are sunny but are often interspersed with brief rainstorms. By September, temperatures begin to decrease and less rain falls.

October to April: Temperatures decrease quickly; rains continue throughout these months. Snow falls November to March. The coldest daytime temperature, 2°C (35°F), and highest snowfalls, 126mm (5in), occur in January. Winter can be more severe when cold easterly winds blow from the Ukraine.

May: May is warm, 22°C (71°F), but has showers. Rain falls throughout the year, but May is usually the rainiest with thunderstorms.

Budapest, Hungary: Altitude 139m (456ft)

	Jan	Feb	Mar	Apr	May	Jun
Sunrise °C(°F)	−4(25)	−2(29)	2(35)	6(42)	11(52)	14(57)
Mid–afternoon °C(°F)	1(33)	5(41)	10(50)	16(60)	21(70)	24(75)
Days with precipitation	7	6	6	6	8	8
Precipitation mm	32	31	29	38	55	63
Precipitation inches	1.3	1.2	1.1	1.5	2.2	2.5
Daily hours of sunshine	2	3	4	6	7	8

	Jul	Aug	Sep	Oct	Nov	Dec
Sunrise °C(°F)	15(59)	15(59)	12(53)	7(44)	2(35)	−2(29)
Mid–afternoon °C(°F)	27(80)	26(78)	22(72)	16(60)	8(46)	3(37)
Days with precipitation	7	6	5	5	7	7
Precipitation mm	52	51	40	33	52	40
Precipitation inches	2.0	2.0	1.6	1.3	2.0	1.6
Daily hours of sunshine	9	8	7	5	2	1

ICELAND

Official Name: Republic of Iceland

Capital: Reykjavik
Language: Icelandic

Most of Iceland's surface consists of vast lava tablelands containing volcanoes, thermal springs, boiling mud lakes and geysers. In the southwest are the populated lowlands that occupy 25 percent of the country. Almost 15 percent of Iceland is covered by glaciers and snowfields.

Iceland's climate is moderated by the warm waters of the Gulf Stream, especially in the south and southwest. Reykjavik is in this region.

Best time to visit: June to August. (July and August are the most popular months, the "high season." September is good, but many hotels and campsites close about August 15, marking the end of the main tourist season.)

June to August: Summer. Cool, cloudy, frequent rain with mist and fog and occasional sunny days of pleasant weather. Average afternoon temperature, 14°C (57°F). July is the warmest month. Continuous daylight with as many as 20 hours.

September to November: Autumn. Frequent rain. The northern lights (aurora borealis) are often visible during autumn and early winter. Long twilights prevail in September and October. After September, afternoon temperatures begin dropping to about 1°C (34°F).

December to February: Winter. Much of the precipitation is snow. Violent windstorms occur. On the coast temperatures range 2 to –2°C (36 to 28°F). The interior is colder. Days are short with as few as 4 hours of light.

March to May: Spring. Frequent rain. Afternoon temperatures begin rising from 0°C (32°F) in March to 10°C (50°F) in May.

Rain occurs year–round but it is rainier in the south and southwest with an annual average of 2180mm (86in), less in the north, 300 to 560mm (12 to 22in), and 2000mm (79in) in the mountainous regions.

Winds: The island is in a cyclonic area subject to cold winds from the Arctic which can blow from December to May, and the prevailing warm winds from the south and southwest. In the interior desert area, violent winds can occur at any time of the year.

Snowstorms can occur in the highlands at any time of the year. Some high areas are snow–covered year–round.

Reykjavik, Iceland: Altitude 61m (200ft)

	Jan	Feb	Mar	Apr	May	Jun
Sunrise °C(°F)	–3(27)	–2(29)	–2(29)	0(32)	4(39)	7(44)
Mid–afternoon °C(°F)	2(35)	3(37)	3(37)	6(42)	9(48)	12(53)
Days with precipitation	13	13	14	12	10	11
Precipitation mm	76	72	82	58	44	50
Precipitation inches	3.0	2.8	3.2	2.3	1.7	2.0
Daily hours of sunshine	1	2	4	5	6	6

Reykjavik, Iceland: (continued)

	Jul	Aug	Sep	Oct	Nov	Dec
Sunrise ºC(ºF)	8(46)	8(46)	5(41)	2(35)	–1(30)	–3(27)
Mid–afternoon ºC(ºF)	13(55)	13(55)	10(50)	7(44)	3(37)	2(35)
Days with precipitation	10	12	12	15	13	14
Precipitation mm	52	62	67	86	73	79
Precipitation inches	2.0	2.4	2.6	3.4	2.9	3.1
Daily hours of sunshine	6	5	4	2	1	0

INDIA

Official Name: Republic of India

Capital: New Delhi
Languages: Hindi, English, 17 other major Indian languages

India's terrain has four main regions: the Himalaya mountains along its northwest and northeast borders; flat plains that stretch across the country south of and parallel to the Himalaya; the hilly, triangular shaped Deccan plateau south of the plains and lastly, the Eastern Ghats and Western Ghats – mountain ranges on the eastern and western edges of the Deccan plateau.

The best time to visit, in general, is October to March.

We have divided the weather into ten regions and have shown the best time to visit each region.
Refer to map for corresponding numbers.

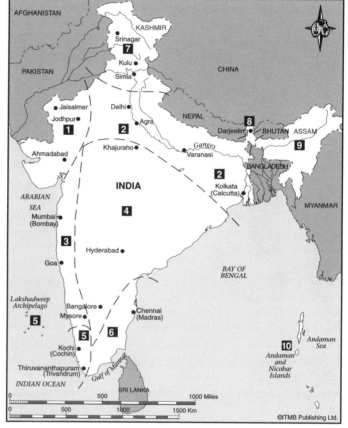

1. Western desert. (Includes Jaisalmer, Jodhpur, Ahmadabad.)
Best time to visit: October to March.

October to March: Dry, sunny, warm, 24 to 35ºC (75 to 95ºF) in the afternoons.
April: Dry and sunny. Temperatures start to exceed 35ºC (95ºF).
May to August: Dry and sunny with afternoon temperatures exceeding an uncomfortable 40ºC (104ºF). Light rain may fall in July and August.
September: Dry, sunny. Temperatures start decreasing to below 40ºC (approximately 100ºF).

Cultural event: Pushkar camel fair. At Pushkar during full moon of Karttika (around October–November) horses, donkeys, sheep, goats and thousands of camels are sold. Camel races are held.

Jaisalmer, India:

	Jan	Feb	Mar	Apr	May	Jun
Sunrise ºC(ºF)	8(46)	11(52)	17(63)	21(69)	26(79)	27(81)
Mid–afternoon ºC(ºF)	24(75)	28(83)	32(90)	38(100)	42(107)	41(105)
Precipitation mm	2	1	3	2	5	7
Precipitation inches	0.07	0.03	0.1	0.07	0.2	0.3

	Jul	Aug	Sep	Oct	Nov	Dec
Sunrise ºC(ºF)	27(81)	26(79)	25(77)	20(68)	13(55)	9(49)
Mid–afternoon ºC(ºF)	38(100)	36(97)	36(97)	36(97)	31(88)	26(79)
Precipitation mm	90	86	14	1	5	2
Precipitation inches	3.5	3.3	0.5	0.03	0.2	0.07

2. Northern plains. (Includes Delhi, Agra, Varanasi, Khajuraho, Kolkata, formerly Calcutta.)
Best time to visit: October to March.

October to May: Dry, warm, medium humidity, 8 to 9 hours of sunshine daily.
June to September: Rainy, particularly July and August. High humidity. Expect 5 to 6 hours of sunshine daily.

Cultural event: Jagannath Festival, also called **Rath Yatra**, at Puri in Orissa State during month of Sravana (July–August). In this colourful procession three tall chariots or carts containing images of gods are pulled by hundreds of people through the streets from one temple to another.

Delhi, India: Altitude 216m (709ft)

	Jan	Feb	Mar	Apr	May	Jun
Sunrise ºC(ºF)	8(46)	10(50)	15(59)	22(72)	26(78)	28(82)
Mid–afternoon ºC(ºF)	21(69)	23(73)	29(84)	36(96)	39(102)	39(102)
Days with precipitation	2	3	3	2	3	6
Precipitation mm	19	20	15	21	25	70
Precipitation inches	0.7	0.8	0.6	0.8	1.0	2.8
Daily hours of sunshine	7	8	8	9	8	7

	Jul	Aug	Sep	Oct	Nov	Dec
Sunrise ºC(ºF)	27(80)	26(78)	25(77)	20(68)	13(55)	8(46)
Mid–afternoon ºC(ºF)	35(95)	34(93)	34(93)	33(91)	28(82)	23(73)
Days with precipitation	12	12	6	2	1	2
Precipitation mm	237	235	113	17	9	9
Precipitation inches	9.3	9.3	4.4	0.7	0.4	0.4
Daily hours of sunshine	5	6	7	9	8	7

Kolkata (formerly Calcutta), India: Altitude 6m (20ft)

	Jan	Feb	Mar	Apr	May	Jun
Sunrise ºC(ºF)	14(57)	17(62)	22(72)	25(77)	26(78)	26(78)
Mid–afternoon ºC(ºF)	26(78)	29(84)	34(93)	35(95)	34(93)	34(93)
Days with precipitation	1	2	3	5	9	15
Precipitation mm	11	30	35	60	142	288
Precipitation inches	0.4	1.2	1.4	2.4	5.6	11.3
Daily hours of sunshine	7	7	7	8	7	4

	Jul	Aug	Sep	Oct	Nov	Dec
Sunrise ºC(ºF)	26(78)	26(78)	26(78)	24(76)	20(68)	15(59)
Mid–afternoon ºC(ºF)	32(89)	32(89)	32(89)	32(89)	30(86)	27(80)
Days with precipitation	21	20	16	8	2	1
Precipitation mm	411	349	288	143	26	17
Precipitation inches	16.2	13.8	11.3	5.6	1.0	0.7
Daily hours of sunshine	3	3	4	6	6	7

Varanasi, India:

	Jan	Feb	Mar	Apr	May	Jun
Sunrise ºC(ºF)	9(49)	11(52)	17(63)	22(72)	27(80)	28(83)
Mid–afternoon ºC(ºF)	23(73)	27(81)	33(91)	39(102)	41(105)	39(102)
Precipitation mm	23	8	14	1	8	102
Precipitation inches	0.9	0.3	0.5	0.03	0.3	4.0

	Jul	Aug	Sep	Oct	Nov	Dec
Sunrise ºC(ºF)	26(79)	26(79)	25(77)	21(70)	13(55)	9(49)
Mid–afternoon ºC(ºF)	33(91)	32(90)	32(90)	32(90)	29(84)	25(77)
Precipitation mm	346	240	261	38	15	2
Precipitation inches	13.6	9.4	10.3	1.5	0.6	0.07

3. West Coast. (Includes Goa and Mumbai, formerly Bombay.)
Best time: October to April.
October to May: Dry with clear skies. Expect 9 to 10 hours of sunshine daily.
June to September: Monsoon season of heavy rains. On some days it rains non–stop. On other days there will be a torrential rainstorm for a few hours and then the sun will shine warmly. Expect an average of 2 to 5 hours of sunshine daily.

Goa, India: Altitude 60m (197ft)

	Jan	Feb	Mar	Apr	May	Jun
Sunrise ºC(ºF)	20(68)	21(70)	23(73)	25(77)	26(78)	25(77)
Mid–afternoon ºC(ºF)	32(90)	32(90)	32(90)	33(91)	33(91)	30(86)
Days with precipitation	0	0	0	1	4	24
Precipitation mm	0	0	1	5	56	891
Precipitation inches	0	0	0.04	0.2	2.2	35.0
Daily hours of sunshine	10	10	9	10	10	4

Goa, India: (continued)

	Jul	Aug	Sep	Oct	Nov	Dec
Sunrise ºC(ºF)	24(75)	24(75)	24(75)	24(75)	22(72)	21(70)
Mid–afternoon ºC(ºF)	29(84)	29(84)	30(86)	32(89)	33(91)	33(91)
Days with precipitation	28	27	15	7	4	0
Precipitation mm	853	622	237	111	35	2
Precipitation inches	34.0	24.5	9.3	4.4	1.4	0.08
Daily hours of sunshine	3	4	6	8	9	10

Mumbai (Bombay), India: Altitude 11m (36ft)

	Jan	Feb	Mar	Apr	May	Jun
Sunrise ºC(ºF)	19(66)	20(68)	23(73)	25(77)	27(80)	26(78)
Mid–afternoon ºC(ºF)	30(86)	30(86)	31(87)	32(89)	33(91)	32(89)
Days with precipitation	0	0	0	0	1	17
Precipitation mm	0	0	0	2	12	592
Precipitation inches	0	0	0	0.08	0.5	23.0
Daily hours of sunshine	9	9	9	9	10	5

	Jul	Aug	Sep	Oct	Nov	Dec
Sunrise ºC(ºF)	25(77)	25(77)	25(77)	25(77)	23(73)	21(69)
Mid–afternoon ºC(ºF)	30(86)	30(86)	30(86)	32(89)	33(91)	32(89)
Days with precipitation	25	25	15	5	2	0
Precipitation mm	682	487	307	61	23	2
Precipitation inches	27.0	19.0	12.1	2.4	0.9	0.08
Daily hours of sunshine	2	2	5	8	8	8

4. Central India. (Includes Bangalore, Hyderabad, Mysore.)
Best time to visit: October to March.

October to March: Dry and warm, 9 to 10 hours of sunshine daily.
April and May: Dry with increasing temperatures, 9 hours of sunshine daily.
June to September: Monsoon rains. Humidity increases. Expect 6 to 7 hours of sunshine daily.

Mysore, India: Altitude 756m (2480ft)

	Jan	Feb	Mar	Apr	May	Jun
Sunrise ºC(ºF)	16(61)	18(65)	20(68)	21(69)	21(69)	20(68)
Mid–afternoon ºC(ºF)	28(83)	31(91)	34(93)	34(93)	33(91)	29(85)
Precipitation mm	3	6	12	68	156	61
Precipitation inches	0.1	0.2	0.4	2.6	6.1	2.4

	Jul	Aug	Sep	Oct	Nov	Dec
Sunrise ºC(ºF)	20(68)	20(68)	19(67)	20(68)	18(64)	17(63)
Mid–afternoon ºC(ºF)	27(81)	28(83)	29(85)	28(83)	27(81)	27(81)
Precipitation mm	72	80	116	180	67	15
Precipitation inches	2.8	3.4	4.5	7.0	2.6	0.6

Hyderabad, India: Altitude 545m (1788ft)

	Jan	Feb	Mar	Apr	May	Jun
Sunrise °C(°F)	16(60)	18(64)	21(69)	25(77)	26(78)	24(75)
Mid–afternoon °C(°F)	29(84)	32(89)	35(95)	38(100)	39(102)	34(93)
Days with precipitation	1	1	1	2	3	10
Precipitation mm	6	9	16	17	40	116
Precipitation inches	0.2	0.4	0.6	0.7	1.6	4.6
Daily hours of sunshine	9	10	8	9	9	6

	Jul	Aug	Sep	Oct	Nov	Dec
Sunrise °C(°F)	23(73)	22(72)	22(72)	21(69)	17(62)	15(59)
Mid–afternoon °C(°F)	31(87)	30(86)	31(87)	31(87)	29(84)	28(82)
Days with precipitation	12	14	10	6	3	1
Precipitation mm	155	163	152	97	29	3
Precipitation inches	6.1	6.4	6.0	3.8	1.1	0.1
Daily hours of sunshine	5	4	6	7	8	8

5. Southwest coast. (Includes Kochi, formerly Cochin, and Thiruvananthapuram, formerly Trivandrum, and Lakshadweep archipelago, formerly Laccadive Islands.)
Best time: Mid–November to Mid–April.

Mid–October to mid–April: Dry.
Mid–April to mid–October: Monsoon season of heavy rains. June is the wettest.

Kochi (formerly Cochin), India:

	Jan	Feb	Mar	Apr	May	Jun
Sunrise °C(°F)	23(73)	24(75)	26(79)	26(79)	26(79)	24(76)
Mid–afternoon °C(°F)	31(88)	31(88)	31(88)	31(88)	31(88)	29(85)
Precipitation mm	10	34	50	140	364	756
Precipitation inches	0.4	1.3	1.9	5.5	14.3	29.7

	Jul	Aug	Sep	Oct	Nov	Dec
Sunrise °C(°F)	24(76)	24(76)	24(76)	24(76)	24(76)	24(76)
Mid–afternoon °C(°F)	28(83)	28(83)	28(83)	29(84)	30(86)	30(86)
Precipitation mm	572	386	235	333	184	37
Precipitation inches	22.5	15.1	9.2	13.1	7.2	1.4

6. Southeast coast. (Includes Chennai, formerly Madras.)
Best time to visit: January to March.

January to March: Dry, warm, sunny.
April and May: Dry; temperatures rise. Sunny days.
June to September: Light rains. Temperatures and humidity increase. Expect 6 to 7 hours of sunshine daily.
October to end of December: Heavy monsoon rainfall. Humid. On some days it will rain non–stop but expect an average of 7 hours of sunshine daily.

Cultural event: Meenakshi Kalyanam. Held at full moon of Phalguna (in April) in Madurai, in the south–eastern state of Tamil Nadu. There are processions through the streets with chariots carrying the Meenakshi temple images dressed in special robes.

Chennai (formerly Madras), India: Altitude 16m (52ft)

	Jan	Feb	Mar	Apr	May	Jun
Sunrise ºC(ºF)	20(68)	22(72)	23(73)	26(78)	28(82)	27(80)
Mid–afternoon ºC(ºF)	29(84)	31(87)	33(91)	36(96)	38(101)	37(98)
Days with precipitation	2	1	0	1	2	8
Precipitation mm	27	34	4	12	39	71
Precipitation inches	1.1	1.3	0.1	0.5	1.5	2.8
Daily hours of sunshine	9	10	9	10	9	7

	Jul	Aug	Sep	Oct	Nov	Dec
Sunrise ºC(ºF)	26(78)	26(78)	25(77)	24(75)	23(73)	21(69)
Mid–afternoon ºC(ºF)	35(95)	35(95)	34(93)	31(87)	29(85)	29(85)
Days with precipitation	10	11	10	12	12	7
Precipitation mm	121	138	161	373	409	152
Precipitation inches	4.8	5.4	6.3	14.7	16.1	6.0
Daily hours of sunshine	6	6	7	6	6	7

7. Himalaya mountains on western side of India. (Includes Kashmir.)

Best time: April to mid–October.

Good trekking months are mid–May to mid–October. Expect 8 hours per day of sunshine and a temperature range of 22 to 31°C (71 to 88°F).

June: Snow is still on some higher passes.

July and August: Sunny. Light rains. Wildflowers are plentiful. Longer treks are popular at this time.

September and October: Clear and usually dry.

Mid–October to April: Heavy snowfalls. Not conducive to trekking.

Monsoons: Kashmir is in the part of the Indian Himalayas that does not experience the Indian monsoons.

Recreational activity: The trekking season for Leh, Kulu Valley and Simla is mid–May to mid–October.

Srinagar, Kashmir, India: Altitude 1587m (5207ft)

	Jan	Feb	Mar	Apr	May	Jun
Sunrise ºC(ºF)	–2(29)	0(32)	3(37)	8(46)	11(51)	15(59)
Mid–afternoon ºC(ºF)	7(44)	8(46)	14(57)	20(68)	24(75)	30(86)
Days with precipitation	7	7	10	9	8	6
Precipitation mm	48	68	121	85	68	39
Precipitation inches	1.9	2.7	4.8	3.4	2.7	1.5

	Jul	Aug	Sep	Oct	Nov	Dec
Sunrise ºC(ºF)	18(64)	17(62)	12(53)	6(42)	1(33)	–2(29)
Mid–afternoon ºC(ºF)	30(86)	30(86)	27(80)	22(72)	15(59)	8(46)
Days with precipitation	8	7	4	3	3	5
Precipitation mm	62	76	28	33	28	54
Precipitation inches	2.4	3.0	1.1	1.3	1.1	2.1

8. Himalaya mountains on eastern side of India. (Includes Darjeeling and State of Sikkim.)

Best time for mountain views: First choice: Mid–September to mid–December, but December gets very cold. Second choice: Mid–March to mid–June.

Mid–September to mid–December: Cool, dry. Best time to visit.
December to February: Cold, dry. Clear mountain views.
Mid–March to mid–June: Cool. Good time to visit, but May and June are rainy.
Mid–June to mid–September: Monsoon season. Heaviest rains in July. Clouds obscure the mountains.

Recreational activity: Trekking seasons for Darjeeling and Sikkim are March to May, and mid–September to December.

Darjeeling, India: Altitude 2265m (7431ft)

	Jan	Feb	Mar	Apr	May	Jun
Sunrise ºC(ºF)	2(35)	2(35)	6(42)	9(49)	12(53)	13(56)
Mid–afternoon ºC(ºF)	8(47)	9(48)	14(57)	17(62)	18(64)	18(64)
Days with precipitation	1	3	4	7	14	21
Precipitation mm	13	28	43	104	216	589
Precipitation inches	0.5	1.1	1.7	4.1	8.5	23.2

	Jul	Aug	Sep	Oct	Nov	Dec
Sunrise ºC(ºF)	14(57)	14(57)	13(55)	10(50)	6(42)	3(37)
Mid–afternoon ºC(ºF)	19(66)	18(64)	18(64)	16(61)	12(54)	9(49)
Days with precipitation	26	24	17	5	1	1
Precipitation mm	798	638	447	130	23	8
Precipitation inches	31.4	25.1	17.6	5.1	0.9	0.3

9. Northeast region. (Includes Assam.)
Best time: November to February. March is also a good month.

November to February: Dry. Average afternoon temperatures, 17ºC (62ºF) in the mountains and 25ºC (77ºF) in the lowlands.
March to May: Light rains. Afternoon average temperatures, 22ºC (72ºF) in the mountains and 30ºC (86ºF) in the lowlands.
June to October: Monsoon season of heavy rains. Humid, warm. Afternoon average temperature in the mountains, 22ºC (72ºF), and in the lowlands, 30ºC (86ºF).

10. Andaman and Nicobar Islands.
Best time to visit: Mid–November to mid–April.

Mid–November to mid–April: Relatively dry but there are rains from the northeast monsoon from November to January. December and January are busy tourist months.
Mid–May to October: Monsoon rains from the southwest.

Note: Because of year–round sea breezes, the temperatures vary little, staying in the range of 23 to 32ºC (73 to 90ºF), and the humidity averages 80% all year.

INDONESIA
Official Name: Republic of Indonesia

Capital: Jakarta
Languages: Bahasa Indonesia,
English, Dutch, Javanese and other
local dialects

Most islands are mountainous, many
with live or extinct volcanoes that
rise above 3000m (10000ft). The
larger islands have coastal plains.

**Best time to visit, in general, is
May to September.**

Temperatures vary little from month
to month in Indonesia. The average
afternoon temperature throughout the
country is 30°C (86°F). It is always
hot and humid.
Rainfall often comes as

thunderstorms in the afternoon. If your travels take you into a wet season you will find that you can do
your sightseeing from first light to 3:30pm.
Sunshine in the rainy season averages only 4 to 5 hours daily because there is more cloud. In the dry
season, 7 to 9 hours per day can be expected.

We have divided Indonesia into ten weather regions.
Refer to map for corresponding numbers.

1. Java (includes Jakarta), **Sumatra** (includes Medan and Padang), and **South Kalimantan** on island
of Borneo.
Best season: May to September.

May to November: Dry season. (Coolest and driest, July to September.)
November to March: Wet season.

Jakarta, Java, Indonesia: Altitude 8m (26ft)

	Jan	Feb	Mar	Apr	May	Jun
Sunrise °C(°F)	23(74)	23(74)	23(74)	24(75)	24(75)	23(74)
Mid–afternoon °C(°F)	29(84)	29(84)	30(86)	31(87)	31(87)	31(87)
Days with precipitation	18	17	15	11	9	7
Precipitation mm	300	300	211	147	114	97
Precipitation inches	11.8	11.8	8.3	5.8	4.5	3.8
Daily hours of sunshine	5	5	6	7	7	7

Jakarta, Java, Indonesia: (continued)

	Jul	Aug	Sep	Oct	Nov	Dec
Sunrise ºC(ºF)	23(73)	23(73)	23(73)	23(73)	23(73)	23(73)
Mid–afternoon ºC(ºF)	31(87)	31(87)	31(87)	31(87)	30(86)	29(85)
Days with precipitation	5	4	5	8	12	14
Precipitation mm	64	43	66	112	142	203
Precipitation inches	2.5	1.7	2.6	4.4	5.6	8.0
Daily hours of sunshine	7	8	8	7	6	5

Medan, northeast Sumatra, Indonesia: Altitude 24m (79ft)

	Jan	Feb	Mar	Apr	May	Jun
Sunrise ºC(ºF)	22(71)	22(71)	22(71)	23(73)	23(73)	22(71)
Mid–afternoon ºC(ºF)	29(85)	31(87)	31(87)	32(89)	32(89)	32(89)
Days with precipitation	11	7	8	10	12	9
Precipitation mm	137	91	104	132	175	132
Precipitation inches	5.4	3.6	4.1	5.2	6.9	5.2
Daily hours of sunshine	4	3	4	5	8	5

	Jul	Aug	Sep	Oct	Nov	Dec
Sunrise ºC(ºF)	22(72)	22(72)	22(72)	22(72)	22(72)	22(72)
Mid–afternoon ºC(ºF)	32(89)	32(89)	31(88)	30(86)	30(86)	29(85)
Days with precipitation	9	13	14	17	17	15
Precipitation mm	135	178	211	259	246	229
Precipitation inches	5.3	7.0	8.3	10.2	9.7	9.0
Daily hours of sunshine	6	6	7	9	8	5

Padang, western Sumatra, Indonesia: Altitude 7m (23ft)

	Jan	Feb	Mar	Apr	May	Jun
Sunrise ºC(ºF)	23(74)	23(74)	23(74)	24(75)	24(75)	23(74)
Mid–afternoon ºC(ºF)	31(87)	31(87)	31(87)	31(87)	31(87)	31(87)
Days with precipitation	16	13	15	17	14	12
Precipitation mm	351	259	307	363	315	307
Precipitation inches	13.8	10.2	12.1	14.3	12.4	12.1
Daily hours of sunshine	7	8	7	8	8	8

	Jul	Aug	Sep	Oct	Nov	Dec
Sunrise ºC(ºF)	23(74)	23(74)	23(74)	23(74)	23(74)	23(74)
Mid–afternoon ºC(ºF)	31(87)	31(87)	30(86)	30(86)	30(86)	30(86)
Days with precipitation	12	14	16	20	21	20
Precipitation mm	277	348	152	495	518	480
Precipitation inches	10.9	13.7	6.0	19.5	20.4	18.9
Daily hours of sunshine	7	7	7	7	6	6

2. East Kalimantan. (Includes Balikpapan on island of Borneo.)
Best season: September and October. (Months of lowest rainfall.)
Rain falls throughout the year.

Balikpapan, Kalimantan, Indonesia: Altitude 7m (23ft)

	Jan	Feb	Mar	Apr	May	Jun
Sunrise ºC(ºF)	23(73)	23(73)	23(73)	23(73)	23(73)	23(73)
Mid–afternoon ºC(ºF)	29(85)	30(86)	30(86)	29(85)	29(85)	29(85)
Days with precipitation	14	13	15	13	13	12
Precipitation mm	201	175	231	208	231	193
Precipitation inches	7.9	6.9	9.1	8.2	9.1	7.6

	Jul	Aug	Sep	Oct	Nov	Dec
Sunrise ºC(ºF)	23(73)	23(73)	23(73)	23(73)	23(73)	23(73)
Mid–afternoon ºC(ºF)	28(83)	29(84)	29(84)	29(85)	29(85)	29(85)
Days with precipitation	11	11	9	9	12	15
Precipitation mm	180	163	140	132	168	206
Precipitation inches	7.1	6.4	5.5	5.2	6.6	8.1

3. Bali.
Best season: May to October.

April to October: Dry season. Driest, May to September.
Weather is warm and humid throughout the year.
November to March: Wet season. Heaviest, December and January.

Denpasar, Bali, Indonesia: Altitude 5m (16ft)

	Jan	Feb	Mar	Apr	May	Jun
Sunrise ºC(ºF)	23(73)	23(73)	23(73)	22(72)	22(72)	21(70)
Mid–afternoon ºC(ºF)	32(89)	32(89)	32(89)	33(91)	32(89)	31(88)
Days with precipitation	19	19	16	12	10	8
Precipitation mm	403	213	205	126	40	50
Precipitation inches	15.9	8.4	8.1	5.0	1.6	2.0

	Jul	Aug	Sep	Oct	Nov	Dec
Sunrise ºC(ºF)	20(68)	21(71)	21(71)	21(71)	22(72)	21(71)
Mid–afternoon ºC(ºF)	31(87)	30(86)	31(88)	32(89)	33(91)	32(89)
Days with precipitation	6	3	5	6	14	21
Precipitation mm	85	37	9	121	200	373
Precipitation inches	3.4	1.5	0.4	4.8	7.9	14.7

4. West Nusa Tenggara. (Includes Lombok and Sumbawa.)
Best season: April to September.

April to September: Dry season. Driest, May to July.
October to March: Wet, hot season.

5. East Nusa Tenggara. (Includes Flores, Komodo, Sumba.)
Best season: April to September. (Peak tourist months are July to September.)

June to September: Dry season.
October to May: Wet season.

6. South Sulawesi. (Includes Ujung Pandang.)
Best season: August and September. (Less rain.)

April to September: Dry season.
October to March: Wet season.

Ujung Pandang, Sulawesi, Indonesia: Altitude 2m (6ft)

	Jan	Feb	Mar	Apr	May	Jun
Sunrise ºC(ºF)	23(74)	24(75)	23(74)	23(74)	23(74)	22(72)
Mid–afternoon ºC(ºF)	29(84)	29(84)	29(84)	30(86)	31(87)	30(86)
Days with precipitation	25	20	18	10	8	6
Precipitation mm	686	536	424	150	89	74
Precipitation inches	27.0	21.1	16.7	5.9	3.5	2.9
Daily hours of sunshine	5	6	6	8	8	8

	Jul	Aug	Sep	Oct	Nov	Dec
Sunrise ºC(ºF)	21(70)	21(69)	21(70)	22(72)	23(74)	23(74)
Mid–afternoon ºC(ºF)	30(86)	31(87)	31(87)	31(87)	30(86)	29(84)
Days with precipitation	4	2	2	5	11	22
Precipitation mm	36	10	15	43	178	610
Precipitation inches	1.4	0.4	0.6	1.7	7.0	24.0
Daily hours of sunshine	9	10	10	10	9	5

7. North Sulawesi.
Best season: June to August.

May to October: Dry season.
November to April: Wet season.

8. Halmahera. (In northern Maluku.)
Best season: August and September. (Less rain.)
There is no clear distinction between wet and dry seasons. Rain falls throughout the year.

9. Central Maluku. (Includes Ambon.)
Best season: October to April.

September to March: Dry season.
May to August: Wet season.

Ambon, Maluku, Indonesia: Altitude 4m (14ft)

	Jan	Feb	Mar	Apr	May	Jun
Sunrise ºC(ºF)	24(76)	24(76)	24(76)	24(76)	24(76)	23(74)
Mid–afternoon ºC(ºF)	31(88)	31(88)	31(88)	30(86)	29(84)	28(82)
Days with precipitation	13	13	15	19	22	24
Precipitation mm	127	119	135	279	516	638
Precipitation inches	5.0	4.7	5.3	11.0	20.3	25.1
Daily hours of sunshine	6	7	7	6	5	4

	Jul	Aug	Sep	Oct	Nov	Dec
Sunrise ºC(ºF)	23(74)	23(74)	23(74)	23(74)	24(75)	24(75)
Mid–afternoon ºC(ºF)	27(81)	27(81)	28(83)	29(85)	31(88)	31(88)
Days with precipitation	23	20	15	13	11	13
Precipitation mm	602	401	241	155	114	132
Precipitation inches	23.7	15.8	9.5	6.1	4.5	5.2
Daily hours of sunshine	4	4	5	6	7	7

10. Irian Jaya.
Best season: July to September.
There is no clear distinction between wet and dry seasons. Rain falls throughout the year.

IRAN
Official Name: Islamic Republic of Iran

Capital: Tehran
Language: Farsi (Persian), Turkic, Kurdish, Luri

Iran is an expansive plateau which is arid desert and steppe in the central, southern and eastern parts. The plateau is bordered by the Elburz mountains in the north and the Zagros mountains in the west and southwest. Most of Iran is on this plateau which is 1000 – 1500m (3300 – 5000ft) above sea level. Two small areas, the Caspian Sea coast and the Persian Gulf coast, have different weather which is described separately.

Best time to visit: March to May, and mid–September to mid–November.

We have divided the weather into three regions. Refer to map for corresponding numbers.
1. Plateau. (Includes Tehran.)
Best times: March to May, and mid–September to mid–November.

March to May: Spring. Moderate temperature. Light rains.
June to August: Summer. Hot and dry, long summer. Almost continuous sunshine. High temperatures, 35ºC (95ºF) but humidity is pleasantly low. The high elevation on which most of Iran is situated accounts for moderate heat, but makes for cold winters.
September to November: Autumn. Moderate temperatures. Dry.

December to February: Winter. Cold and mainly dry. Light rains fall. Cold air from the north, from Siberia, can bring snow and frost.

2. Caspian Sea coast, and the inner arc of the northern slopes of the Elburz range.
Best times to visit are May to early June, and late August to September when temperatures are a moderate 30°C (86°F).

July and August: Mid–Summer. Can top 40°C (104°F) with humidity at an uncomfortable 98%.
January to February: Winter. Can be cold, 0°C (32°F).
Rain can be expected year–round, but most rain falls between August and January.

3. Persian Gulf coast.
Best time to visit: December to March.

December to March: Winter. Mild, 20°C (68°F) and light rain.
April and May, and September to November are hot months, 30 to 40°C (86 to 104°F), with high humidity and little or no rain.
June to August: Summer. Temperatures can top 40°C (104°F) accompanied by high humidity. Summer is without rain.

Tehran, north central Iran: Altitude 1191m (3907ft)

	Jan	Feb	Mar	Apr	May	Jun
Sunrise ºC(ºF)	–1(30)	1(33)	6(42)	12(53)	17(62)	22(72)
Mid–afternoon ºC(ºF)	7(44)	10(50)	15(59)	22(72)	28(82)	34(93)
Days with precipitation	6	5	6	5	4	1
Precipitation mm	37	34	37	28	15	3
Precipitation inches	1.5	1.3	1.5	1.1	0.6	0.1
Daily hours of sunshine	6	6	7	7	9	12

	Jul	Aug	Sep	Oct	Nov	Dec
Sunrise ºC(ºF)	24(75)	21(69)	17(62)	11(51)	4(39)	0(32)
Mid–afternoon ºC(ºF)	37(98)	35(95)	31(87)	24(75)	16(60)	10(50)
Days with precipitation	1	0	0	3	3	6
Precipitation mm	3	1	1	14	21	36
Precipitation inches	0.1	0.04	0.04	0.6	0.8	1.4
Daily hours of sunshine	11	11	10	8	7	5

IRAQ
Official Name: Republic of Iraq

Capital: Baghdad
Languages: Arabic, Kurdish (official in Kurdish region), Assyrian, Armenian

The north and northeast are mountainous but the rest of Iraq is mainly flat. The centre has a plain drained by the Tigris and Euphrates rivers. The west is desert and the extreme southeast is marshland.

Best times: Late September to November, and March to early May.

October to November: Autumn. Mild. Light rains start in November.
December to February: Winter. Mild. Light rains fall except in the northeast where rains are heavier. Snow falls in the mountains in the northeast.
March to April: Spring. Mild with light rains.
May to September: Summer. Sunny, dry but extremely hot throughout the country, except in the mountainous northeast where it is cooler.

Baghdad, Iraq: Altitude 34m (111ft)

	Jan	Feb	Mar	Apr	May	Jun
Sunrise ºC(ºF)	4(39)	6(42)	9(48)	14(57)	19(67)	23(73)
Mid–afternoon ºC(ºF)	16(60)	18(64)	22(71)	29(85)	36(97)	41(105)
Days with precipitation	4	3	4	3	1	0
Precipitation mm	23	25	28	13	3	0
Precipitation inches	0.9	1.0	1.1	0.5	0.1	0
Daily hours of sunshine	6	7	8	9	10	12

	Jul	Aug	Sep	Oct	Nov	Dec
Sunrise ºC(ºF)	24(76)	24(76)	21(70)	16(61)	11(51)	6(42)
Mid–afternoon ºC(ºF)	43(110)	43(110)	40(104)	33(92)	25(77)	18(64)
Days with precipitation	0	0	0	1	3	5
Precipitation mm	0	0	0	3	20	25
Precipitation inches	0	0	0	0.1	0.8	1.0
Daily hours of sunshine	11	11	11	9	7	6

IRELAND

Official Name: Republic of Ireland. (Also called Eire, it shares the island with Northern Ireland, part of the United Kingdom.)
Capital: Dublin
Languages: English, Irish (Gaelic)

In the centre and east of the centre is a large plain with lakes and bogs. Mountain ranges encircle the island. Ireland's climate is warmer than its latitude would suggest because of the moderating influence of the Gulf Stream, the warm ocean current which comes from the warmer south.

Best time: April to September.

April to June: This is the driest time of the year. May is often a sunny month with daytime temperatures a mild 16°C (60°F). However, the weather is changeable between sun and rain, warmth and coldness. Travelling is easier because of less crowds.
July and August: Mid–summer. These are the warmest months, 18 to 20°C (65 to 68°F). Occasionally the thermometer climbs above 20°C (68°F). These are extremely crowded months but the benefit is longer daylight. It is light until 11pm. Expect some rain.
September: Mild, 17°C (62°F). Changeable with sunshine one day, drizzle the next. The benefit of September is the lack of crowds.
October to March: Cold and rainy. Most rain falls in these months. Daytime temperatures drop to 5 to 10°C (40 to 50°F) in January and February, the coldest months. Snow is rare. From December to February it gets dark at about 4pm.
Rain falls all year round, with most in October to March. Rain is brought by the prevailing southwest winds which carry moisture from the Atlantic Ocean. The first high ground in the path of the moisture–laden clouds are the scenic mountains in Kerry in southwest Ireland. This is the rainiest area of Ireland. Rain often falls as drizzle. The driest area, and also the sunniest, are the counties of Waterford and Wexford in the southeast.

Dublin, Ireland: Altitude 85m (279ft)

	Jan	Feb	Mar	Apr	May	Jun
Sunrise °C(°F)	3(37)	3(37)	3(37)	4(39)	7(44)	10(50)
Mid–afternoon °C(°F)	8(46)	8(46)	10(50)	11(51)	14(57)	17(62)
Days with precipitation	13	10	11	10	12	10
Precipitation mm	69	50	53	51	55	56
Precipitation inches	2.7	2.0	2.1	2.0	2.2	2.2
Daily hours of sunshine	2	3	4	5	6	6

	Jul	Aug	Sep	Oct	Nov	Dec
Sunrise °C(°F)	11(51)	11(51)	10(50)	8(46)	4(39)	3(37)
Mid–afternoon °C(°F)	19(66)	19(66)	17(62)	14(57)	10(50)	8(46)
Days with precipitation	9	11	10	11	11	12
Precipitation mm	50	71	66	70	64	76
Precipitation inches	2.0	2.8	2.6	2.8	2.5	3.0
Daily hours of sunshine	5	5	4	3	2	2

ISRAEL
Official Name: State of Israel

Capital: Jerusalem
Languages: Hebrew, Arabic, English

The northern half consists of hills and plains. The southern half, south of Beersheba, consists of the Negev desert. The weather descriptions encompass the West Bank and Gaza, claimed and occupied by Israel.

Good time: April to October. Dry. The most comfortable times, weatherwise, are April to May, and September to October when it is cooler.
An exception is Eilat, where it is pleasant to visit November to March.

Israel has two main geographical divisions: The northern half and the southern half.
April to May: Spring. Dry. The weather is pleasant, 26°C (80°F), in the north and 32°C (90°F) in the south. Expect 10 hours of sunshine daily throughout the country. Strong, unpleasant dry winds, the khamsin, can blow in from the east, raising temperatures to over 32°C (90°F) in the north and 38°C (100°F) in the south.
June to October: Long summer. Dry, hot. Mid–summer, July and August, can be almost unbearably hot in the south, e.g. Eilat, 40°C (104°F) in the afternoons, and in the north e.g. Dead Sea and Jerusalem, 31°C (87°F) in the afternoons, but nights are mild. Heat on the Mediterranean coast in July and August can be humid and oppressive, 32°C (90°F), but it is tempered by sea breezes. June, September and October are a more comfortable 2°C (4°F) cooler. Expect 10 to 13 hours of sunshine daily between June and October. In September and October the khamsin, the hot, dry, unpleasant easterly winds can raise temperatures.
November to March: Winter. Wet, cool. Inland (e.g. Jerusalem) daytime temperatures can be a cool 4°C (40°F) in the morning, rising to 13°C (55°F) in the afternoon. Inland is rainy, and snow may fall. Eilat (in the south) has pleasant mid–winter (January) temperatures of 21°C (70°F) in the afternoon, blue skies and negligible rain. This is a good time to visit Eilat. On the Mediterranean coast winter is mild with short, heavy rainfalls interspersed with long periods of sunshine. Six to 8 hours of sunshine daily can be expected throughout the country.

Eilat, southern Israel: Altitude 12m (39ft)

	Jan	Feb	Mar	Apr	May	Jun
Sunrise °C(°F)	9(48)	11(51)	14(57)	18(64)	21(69)	24(75)
Mid–afternoon °C(°F)	21(69)	23(73)	26(79)	31(87)	35(95)	38(100)
Days with precipitation	1	1	1	1	0	0
Precipitation mm	5	5	4	3	1	0
Precipitation inches	0.2	0.2	0.1	0.1	0.04	0
Daily hours of sunshine	7	8	8	9	10	11

Eilat, southern Israel: (continued)

	Jul	Aug	Sep	Oct	Nov	Dec
Sunrise ºC(ºF)	25(77)	25(77)	24(75)	20(68)	15(59)	11(52)
Mid–afternoon ºC(ºF)	40(104)	39(102)	37(98)	33(91)	27(80)	22(72)
Days with precipitation	0	0	0	0	1	1
Precipitation mm	0	0	0	3	4	6
Precipitation inches	0	0	0	0.1	0.1	0.2
Daily hours of sunshine	11	11	10	9	8	7

Jerusalem, inland Israel: Altitude 757m (2484ft)

	Jan	Feb	Mar	Apr	May	Jun
Sunrise ºC(ºF)	4(39)	5(41)	6(42)	10(50)	12(53)	15(59)
Mid–afternoon ºC(ºF)	12(53)	13(55)	16(60)	21(70)	25(77)	28(82)
Days with precipitation	10	8	7	3	1	0
Precipitation mm	143	113	98	32	2	0
Precipitation inches	5.6	4.4	3.9	1.3	0.08	0
Daily hours of sunshine	6	9	7	9	11	13

	Jul	Aug	Sep	Oct	Nov	Dec
Sunrise ºC(ºF)	17(62)	17(62)	16(60)	14(57)	10(50)	6(42)
Mid–afternoon ºC(ºF)	29(84)	29(84)	28(82)	25(77)	19(66)	14(57)
Days with precipitation	0	0	0	2	5	8
Precipitation mm	0	0	0	24	68	110
Precipitation inches	0	0	0	0.9	2.7	4.3
Daily hours of sunshine	12	12	10	9	8	6

ITALY

Official Name: Italian Republic

Capital: Rome
Languages: Italian, German, French

Alps encircle northern Italy in a wide arc, forming the northern borders. A vast fertile plain stretches between Turin and Venice. Along both sides of peninsula Italy are coastal lowlands. Extending along the middle of the peninsula is a backbone of mountains, the Appenines. Both Sicily and Sardinia are mountainous.

Best time for the whole country: Late April to June, and September to mid–October. These months avoid the summer crowds of July and August.

We have divided the weather into three regions. Refer to map for corresponding numbers.
1. Alpine region. (Includes Italian Alps.)
March to May: Spring. Mild with occasional thunderstorms.

June to August: Summer. Warm, 21°C (70°F). This is the rainiest time with frequent storms.
September to November: Autumn. Mild with occasional thunderstorms.
December to February: Winter. Severe winters with temperatures below freezing. Rain and snow fall in the northern mountains.

2. Northern plain and valleys. (Includes Venice.)
March to May: Spring. Mild with temperatures increasing from 10°C (50°F) to 24°C (75°F). Rainy.
June to August: Summer. Warm, 27°C (80°F). Rainy.
September to November: Autumn. Mild, decreasing temperatures from 27°C (80°F) to 10°C (50°F). Rainy.
December to February: Winter. Severe winters with snow, frosts, fog and temperatures below freezing.
Rain is fairly evenly distributed throughout the year but the region around Venice is the wettest.

3. The Peninsula, (includes Rome), **Sicily** (includes Palermo), and **Sardinia.**
March to May: Spring. Mild temperatures, increasing from 16°C (60°F) to 24°C (75°F). Light rains fall over the peninsula and the islands of Sicily and Sardinia.
June to August: Summer. Dry and warm. Temperatures are in the high 20s°C (in the 80s°F). July and August are the hottest months, and muggy. Hot summer days are tempered by cooling sea breezes. The east coast temperatures are often lower because of the cool prevailing winds from the northeast. Rain is minimal. The dry summer season extends as you go south.
September to November: Autumn. Mild temperatures, decreasing from 27°C (80°F) to 16°C (60°F). Heavy rains are brought by westerly winds. Rainfall is heavier in the north. The heaviest rains in Italy occur in autumn and winter.
December to February: Winter. Mild, with a variety of sunny, cloudy, wet and dry days but the rains are endless. Heaviest falls are in the north.
Temperatures: In any given season there is little variation of temperature along the coasts from north to south.
Rainfall on the islands, Sicily and Sardinia, is irregular, but generally falls October to March.

Rome, central Italy: Altitude 24m (79ft)

	Jan	Feb	Mar	Apr	May	Jun
Sunrise °C(°F)	3(37)	4(39)	5(41)	8(46)	11(51)	15(59)
Mid–afternoon °C(°F)	12(53)	13(55)	15(59)	18(64)	23(73)	27(80)
Days with precipitation	9	9	9	9	6	4
Precipitation mm	103	99	68	65	48	34
Precipitation inches	4.1	3.9	2.7	2.6	1.9	1.3
Daily hours of sunshine	4	5	5	7	8	10

	Jul	Aug	Sep	Oct	Nov	Dec
Sunrise °C(°F)	17(62)	18(64)	15(59)	11(51)	7(44)	4(39)
Mid–afternoon °C(°F)	30(86)	30(86)	27(80)	22(72)	16(60)	13(55)
Days with precipitation	2	3	6	8	11	10
Precipitation mm	23	33	68	94	130	111
Precipitation inches	0.9	1.3	2.7	3.7	5.1	4.4
Daily hours of sunshine	11	10	8	6	4	4

Venice, northern Italy: Altitude 6m (20ft)

	Jan	Feb	Mar	Apr	May	Jun
Sunrise ºC(ºF)	−1(30)	1(33)	4(39)	8(46)	12(53)	16(60)
Mid–afternoon ºC(ºF)	6(42)	8(46)	12(53)	16(60)	21(69)	25(77)
Days with precipitation	7	6	7	8	8	9
Precipitation mm	58	54	57	64	69	76
Precipitation inches	2.3	2.1	2.2	2.5	2.7	3.0
Daily hours of sunshine	3	4	5	6	7	8

	Jul	Aug	Sep	Oct	Nov	Dec
Sunrise ºC(ºF)	18(64)	17(62)	14(57)	9(48)	4(39)	0(32)
Mid–afternoon ºC(ºF)	28(82)	27(80)	24(75)	18(64)	12(53)	7(44)
Days with precipitation	6	7	5	6	8	6
Precipitation mm	63	83	66	69	87	54
Precipitation inches	2.5	3.3	2.6	2.7	3.4	2.1
Daily hours of sunshine	9	8	7	5	3	2

Palermo, island of Sicily, Italy: Altitude 21m (69ft)

	Jan	Feb	Mar	Apr	May	Jun
Sunrise ºC(ºF)	10(50)	10(50)	11(51)	13(55)	16(60)	20(68)
Mid–afternoon ºC(ºF)	15(59)	15(59)	16(61)	18(65)	22(72)	25(77)
Days with precipitation	10	10	9	6	3	2
Precipitation mm	72	65	60	44	26	12
Precipitation inches	2.8	2.6	2.4	1.7	1.0	0.5
Daily hours of sunshine	4	5	6	7	8	9

	Jul	Aug	Sep	Oct	Nov	Dec
Sunrise ºC(ºF)	23(73)	24(75)	22(72)	18(65)	14(57)	12(53)
Mid–afternoon ºC(ºF)	28(82)	29(85)	27(81)	23(74)	19(67)	16(60)
Days with precipitation	1	2	4	8	9	11
Precipitation mm	5	13	42	98	94	80
Precipitation inches	0.2	0.5	1.6	3.9	3.7	3.2
Daily hours of sunshine	10	9	8	7	6	4

IVORY COAST, see COTE D'IVOIRE

JAMAICA
Official Name: Jamaica
(Independent nation; formerly a British possession.)

Capital: Kingston
Languages: English, Creole

The island is extremely mountainous; the highest peaks
are in the east. The south has some lowland areas.

Best time to visit: December to April. (Cool, dry.)
The mountainous interior is wetter and cooler than the
coast.

May and June: Rainy.
July and August: Dry. Hottest months. Afternoon temperatures of 32ºC (90ºF) on the coast.
September to November: Rainy.
December to April: Dry. Coolest months on the coast are January and February, 30ºC (86ºF).
Hurricanes are possible, late August to November.

Note: See under Caribbean Islands for general Caribbean weather.

Kingston, Jamaica: Altitude 34m (110ft)

	Jan	Feb	Mar	Apr	May	Jun
Sunrise ºC(ºF)	19(67)	19(67)	20(68)	21(70)	22(72)	23(74)
Mid–afternoon ºC(ºF)	30(86)	30(86)	30(86)	31(87)	31(87)	32(89)
Days with precipitation	3	3	2	3	4	5
Precipitation mm	23	15	23	31	102	89
Precipitation inches	0.9	0.6	0.9	1.2	4.0	3.5
Daily hours of sunshine	8	9	9	9	8	8

	Jul	Aug	Sep	Oct	Nov	Dec
Sunrise ºC(ºF)	23(73)	23(73)	23(73)	23(73)	22(71)	21(69)
Mid–afternoon ºC(ºF)	32(90)	32(90)	32(90)	31(88)	31(87)	31(87)
Days with precipitation	4	7	6	9	5	4
Precipitation mm	89	91	99	180	74	36
Precipitation inches	3.5	3.6	3.9	7.1	2.9	1.4
Daily hours of sunshine	9	8	8	7	8	8

JAPAN
Official Name: Japan

Capital: Tokyo
Language: Japanese

The islands of Japan, part of a huge, high mountain range, are rugged with deep valleys, short rivers and small plains. There are dormant and active volcanoes and numerous thermal springs.

Best months, from north to south:
1. Northern Japan (Hokkaido and northern Honshu): **June.**
2. Eastern Japan (includes Tokyo): **May.**
3. Western Japan: May.
4. Southern Japan (southern Honshu, Kyushu and Shikoku): **May.**
5. Southwest islands (includes Okinawa): **November to April.**

We have divided the weather into 5 regions. Refer to map for corresponding numbers.

1. Northern Japan. (Includes Sapporo on Hokkaido, and northern Honshu.)
Best month: June. (In the short summer.)

December to February: Winter. Hokkaido is the coldest part of Japan where daily afternoon temperatures remain below freezing. Sunshine averages 2 to 3 hours daily. Skiing is possible, December to April.
March to May: Spring. Rain decreases. Average afternoon temperatures rise from 4°C (40°F) in March to 16°C (60°F) in May.
June to mid–July: Early summer. Weather becomes hot and sultry. Light rains which occur in early July reach their maximum in September.
Mid–July to August: Late summer. A short wet summer with the possibility of cool winds blowing from the northeast. Sunshine averages 5 or 6 hours per day. Average afternoon temperature is 25°C (77°F).
September to November: Autumn. Variable weather (cloudy, wet, sunny) starts early October and moves south. Northeastern Honshu, particularly the Pacific coast, receives heavy rain.

Sapporo, Hokkaido Island, Japan: Altitude 19m (62ft)

	Jan	Feb	Mar	Apr	May	Jun
Sunrise ºC(ºF)	–8(18)	–8(18)	–4(25)	2(35)	7(44)	12(53)
Mid–afternoon ºC(ºF)	–1(30)	–1(30)	4(39)	11(51)	17(62)	21(69)
Days with precipitation	17	15	14	9	8	8
Precipitation mm	108	94	82	62	55	66
Precipitation inches	4.3	3.7	3.2	2.4	2.2	2.6
Daily hours of sunshine	3	4	5	6	7	6

	Jul	Aug	Sep	Oct	Nov	Dec
Sunrise ºC(ºF)	17(62)	18(64)	13(55)	6(42)	0(32)	–5(23)
Mid–afternoon ºC(ºF)	25(77)	26(78)	22(72)	16(60)	8(46)	2(35)
Days with precipitation	8	10	10	12	13	15
Precipitation mm	69	142	138	116	99	100
Precipitation inches	2.7	5.6	5.4	4.6	3.9	3.9
Daily hours of sunshine	6	5	6	5	3	3

2. Eastern Japan. (Includes Tokyo.)
Best month: May. (Before the rains start and when it is pleasantly warm.)

December to February: Winter. Dry, relatively warm. Average afternoon temperature is 10ºC (50ºF). Five hours of sunshine daily. Light snow in late winter (February) and early spring (March). Little or no snow in Tokyo. In December temperatures fall, and rain decreases. The severity of winter declines from north to south.
March to May: Spring. Rainfall increases. Average afternoon temperatures rise from 10ºC (50ºF) in March to 22ºC (72ºF) in May. Cherry blossom season in Tokyo is April. See note below under Natural attractions.
June to mid–July: Early summer. Weather becomes hot and sultry. Heavy, intense rain starts falling in Tokyo and environs in mid–June and stops by the end of July. This is the first of the two rainy periods. The second is September and October.
Mid–July to August: Late summer. Variable weather of fine, dry periods and thunderstorms. Temperatures can be oppressively hot, 35ºC (95ºF), with high humidity. Expect 6 to 7 hours of sunshine daily.
September to November: Autumn. This is the second rainy period. By mid–October all of Japan has variable weather of cloud, rain and sun. By November, temperatures have decreased.

Tokyo, Honshu Island, Japan: Altitude 36m (118ft)

	Jan	Feb	Mar	Apr	May	Jun
Sunrise ºC(ºF)	1(33)	2(35)	4(39)	10(50)	15(59)	19(66)
Mid–afternoon ºC(ºF)	10(50)	10(50)	13(55)	18(64)	23(73)	25(77)
Days with precipitation	4	6	9	10	10	12
Precipitation mm	45	60	100	125	138	185
Precipitation inches	1.8	2.4	3.9	4.9	5.4	7.3
Daily hours of sunshine	6	5	5	5	6	5

	Jul	Aug	Sep	Oct	Nov	Dec
Sunrise ºC(ºF)	22(72)	24(75)	20(68)	14(57)	9(48)	4(39)
Mid–afternoon ºC(ºF)	29(84)	31(87)	27(80)	21(69)	17(62)	12(53)
Days with precipitation	10	8	11	9	6	4
Precipitation mm	126	148	180	164	89	46
Precipitation inches	5.0	5.8	7.1	6.5	3.5	1.8
Daily hours of sunshine	6	7	5	4	5	5

3. Western Japan.
Best month: May.

December to February: Winter. Cloudy with heavy snow, as much as 3m (10ft), particularly in the mountains facing west towards the Sea of Japan. Snow can fall daily. Temperatures fall in December to an afternoon average of 3ºC (37ºF), but begin to rise in mid–February to 4ºC (40ºF).
March to May: Spring. Cloudy with rain and some snow but also sunny. Temperatures begin to rise.
June to mid–July: Early summer. Weather becomes hot and sultry. This is the first of the two rainy periods. The second is September and October.
Mid–July to August: Late summer. Variable weather of fine, dry periods and thunderstorms. Temperatures can be oppressively hot, 35ºC (95ºF), with high humidity. Expect 6 to 7 hours of sunshine daily, but longer periods of sunshine on the western coast.
September to November: Autumn. This is the second rainy period. By mid–October all of Japan has variable weather of cloud, rain and sun. By November, temperatures have decreased and snow falls on the mountain slopes of western Japan.

4. Southern Japan. (Includes southern Honshu, Kyushu and Shikoku.)
Best month: May. (Before the rains start and when it is pleasantly warm.)

December to February: Winter. Mild, light rain, negligible snow. Average afternoon temperature, 12ºC (53ºF). Five hours of sunshine daily.
March to May: Spring. Cloudy with rain but also sunny. Average afternoon temperatures begin to rise from 13ºC (55ºF) in March to 21ºC (70ºF) in May. Sunshine averages 6 hours daily.
June to mid–July: Early summer. Weather becomes hot and sultry. This is the first of the two rainy periods. The second is September and October.
Mid–July to August: Late summer. Variable weather of fine, dry periods and thunderstorms. Temperatures can be oppressively hot, 35ºC (95ºF), with high humidity. Expect 6 to 7 hours of sunshine daily.

September to November: Autumn. This is the second rainy period. By mid–October all of Japan has variable weather of cloud, rain and sun. In southern Japan (e.g. Kyushu) temperatures drop, rainfall decreases, and warm, pleasant days extend into November.

Nagasaki, Kyushu Island, Japan: Altitude 35m (115ft)

	Jan	Feb	Mar	Apr	May	Jun
Sunrise ºC(ºF)	3(37)	4(39)	6(42)	11(51)	15(59)	19(66)
Mid–afternoon ºC(ºF)	10(50)	11(51)	14(57)	19(66)	23(73)	26(78)
Days with precipitation	10	9	10	11	11	13
Precipitation mm	78	86	116	174	193	332
Precipitation inches	3.1	3.4	4.6	6.9	7.6	13.1
Daily hours of sunshine	3	4	5	5	6	5

	Jul	Aug	Sep	Oct	Nov	Dec
Sunrise ºC(ºF)	24(75)	25(77)	21(70)	15(59)	10(50)	5(41)
Mid–afternoon ºC(ºF)	30(86)	31(87)	28(82)	23(73)	18(64)	13(55)
Days with precipitation	11	8	9	6	8	9
Precipitation mm	334	187	190	104	85	66
Precipitation inches	13.1	7.4	7.5	4.1	3.4	2.6
Daily hours of sunshine	6	7	6	6	5	3

5. Southwest islands. (Includes Okinawa.)
Best months: November to April.

November to April: Cooler. Visibility under water is best for divers.
May and June: Rainy.
July and August: Hot season, 30ºC (87ºF) in afternoon. This is a busy season.
September and October: Typhoon season.
Typhoons from the Pacific Ocean approach Japan from July to October bringing heavy rains, mainly to the Pacific coast. Generally late August and September is the peak time for typhoons. There may be 3 or 4 major typhoons per year.

Natural attractions:
1) Autumn colours: October is the month to see the vivid colours of the changing autumn foliage.
2) Cherry blossoms: The "cherry blossom front" starts in the south in late March. Temperatures become warmer as it heads north. April is cherry blossom time in Tokyo. By the end of April it is cherry blossom time in northern Honshu. The season ends in early May in the north.
3) Mt Fuji: Climbing season is July and August.

JORDAN

Official Name: Hashemite Kingdom of Jordan

Capital: Amman
Languages: Arabic, English is understood

The Jordan River flows southward into the Dead Sea, the lowest place on earth. To the east of the river is an expansive arid plateau. About 90 percent of Jordan is desert, but the northwest is hilly where some summits reach 1200m (4000ft).

Best time: April or October. Avoid hot summer months, especially June to August. However, with fine weather year round, virtually any month is good.

May to September: Summer. Dry, sunny, hot. Afternoon temperatures reach 32°C (90°F) and higher. Evenings are pleasantly cool. Humidity in the desert is low. Expect 12 to 13 hours of sunshine daily. Jordan valley, 400m (1300ft) below sea level is extremely hot, 38°C (100°F), in summer. In May and September, hot, dry, khamsin winds from Arabia arrive, sometimes as dust storms. They can last one or two days each time.

October to November: Dry. Gradual decrease in afternoon temperature from 27°C (81°F) in October to 20°C (68°F) in November.

December to March: Winter. Damp, cool. January is coolest; temperatures can fall to 4°C (39°F). Snow falls in the hills. Jordan valley, 400m (1300ft) below sea level is pleasantly warm in winter. Six to 7 hours of sunshine daily throughout the country. Rain falls November to March with most in December and January. It comes as cloudbursts then will clear up and be followed by a long, dry period. Most rain falls in the hilly northwest, but it is minimal.

April to May: Dry. Gradual increase in afternoon temperature from 23°C (73°F) in April to 28°C (82°F) in May.

Amman, Jordan: Altitude 768m (2520ft)

	Jan	Feb	Mar	Apr	May	Jun
Sunrise °C(°F)	3(37)	4(39)	6(43)	9(48)	13(55)	17(62)
Mid-afternoon °C(°F)	12(53)	14(57)	17(62)	23(73)	27(80)	31(87)
Days with precipitation	7	7	5	3	1	0
Precipitation mm	62	54	51	17	3	0
Precipitation inches	2.4	2.1	2.0	0.7	0.1	0
Daily hours of sunshine	6	7	7	9	11	12

	Jul	Aug	Sep	Oct	Nov	Dec
Sunrise °C(°F)	18(64)	18(64)	16(60)	13(55)	9(48)	5(41)
Mid-afternoon °C(°F)	32(89)	32(89)	31(87)	27(80)	20(68)	14(57)
Days with precipitation	0	0	0	1	3	5
Precipitation mm	0	0	0	8	25	51
Precipitation inches	0	0	0	0.3	1.0	2.0
Daily hours of sunshine	12	12	10	9	8	6

KAZAKHSTAN
Official Name: Republic of Kazakhstan

Capital: Astana
Languages: Kazakh, Russian

The country largely consists of semi–arid plains and expansive deserts. The eastern border region is mountainous.

Good time to visit: May to September. (Especially May and September.)

May: Dry, warm. Sunrise temperature is 10°C (50°F); afternoon temperature, 20°C (68°F). Eight hours of sunshine daily.

June to August: Summer. Dry, hot. Possibility of hot winds and dust–laden storms. Temperatures can reach 30 to 35°C (86 to 95°F). Ten hours of sunshine daily.

September: Dry, warm. Average afternoon temperature, 22°C (71°F). Eight hours of sunshine daily.

October to November: By November it is cold everywhere.

December to February: Daytime temperatures are below freezing and snow stays on the ground.

March to April: Rainy months. Cool. 4 to 10°C (40 to 50°F).

Almaty, Kazakhstan: Altitude 775m (2543ft)

	Jan	Feb	Mar	Apr	May	Jun
Sunrise °C(°F)	–14(7)	–13(8)	–6(21)	3(37)	10(50)	14(57)
Mid–afternoon °C(°F)	–5(23)	–3(27)	4(39)	13(55)	20(68)	24(76)
Days with precipitation	6	6	10	10	10	7
Precipitation mm	32	37	71	104	107	64
Precipitation inches	1.3	1.5	2.8	4.1	4.2	2.5
Daily hours of sunshine	4	4	5	7	8	9

	Jul	Aug	Sep	Oct	Nov	Dec
Sunrise °C(°F)	16(60)	14(57)	8(46)	2(35)	–5(23)	–9(16)
Mid–afternoon °C(°F)	27(81)	27(81)	22(72)	13(55)	4(39)	–2(29)
Days with precipitation	5	4	4	7	7	6
Precipitation mm	32	26	30	62	55	33
Precipitation inches	1.3	1.0	1.2	2.4	2.2	1.3
Daily hours of sunshine	10	10	8	6	4	3

KENYA

Official Name: Republic of Kenya

Capital: Nairobi
Languages: English, Swahili, other African languages

There is a low coastal strip along the Indian Ocean. From it the land rises to extensive arid plateaus on which are mountains, including the permanently snowcapped Mt Kenya.

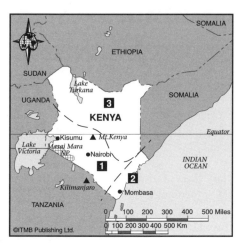

Good time: December to March.
The main tourist season is January and February (hot, dry). This coincides with vacation time in Europe and North America. Another good choice is June to September (hot, dry). Local Kenyans often prefer September, and into October.
Wet seasons are March to May, and October and November. But rain can occur in all months, often at night or early morning.

See Natural attractions below for information on wildlife viewing.

We have divided the weather into three regions. Refer to map for corresponding numbers.

1. Central Highlands Region. (Includes Nairobi and Kisumu.)
December to March: Season of negligible rain, sunniest time, not too hot. Afternoon, 23 to 26°C (74 to 79°F). Eight to 9 hours of sunshine daily.
March to May: "Long rains." These rains come as intermittent downpours. Most rain falls in April. Afternoon average temperature is 24°C (75°F). Eight hours of sunshine daily.
June to September: Season of negligible rain. July has the lowest precipitation. Cloudy period (sky can be a sheet of white cloud). Rain is a light drizzle. Highlands can be chilly. Frost may occur. Mornings range 10 to 14°C (50 to 57°F). Afternoon average is 21°C (70°F). Five to 6 hours of sunshine daily. Nairobi is cool and cloudy, 21°C (70°F).
October to November and into December: "Short rains." Afternoon temperature, 23°C (74°F). Seven hours of sunshine daily.

Note: Kisumu, near Lake Victoria, is influenced by this large body of water and so receives a higher rainfall than other parts of the plateau.

Nairobi, Kenya: Altitude 1798m (5899ft)

	Jan	Feb	Mar	Apr	May	Jun
Sunrise °C(°F)	11(51)	11(51)	12(53)	13(55)	12(53)	10(50)
Mid–afternoon °C(°F)	26(78)	27(80)	27(80)	25(77)	24(75)	23(73)
Days with precipitation	6	6	11	16	17	9
Precipitation mm	58	50	92	242	190	39
Precipitation inches	2.3	2.0	3.6	9.5	7.5	1.5
Daily hours of sunshine	9	10	9	7	6	5

Nairobi, Kenya: (continued)

	Jul	Aug	Sep	Oct	Nov	Dec
Sunrise ºC(ºF)	9(48)	9(48)	10(50)	11(51)	13(55)	12(53)
Mid–afternoon ºC(ºF)	22(72)	23(73)	25(77)	26(78)	24(75)	24(75)
Days with precipitation	6	6	7	8	15	11
Precipitation mm	18	24	31	61	150	108
Precipitation inches	0.7	0.9	1.2	2.4	5.9	4.3
Daily hours of sunshine	4	4	6	7	7	8

2. Coastal Region. (Includes Mombasa.)
December to March: Low rainfall, the "dry season." February is the driest month. Humidity is high; afternoon temperatures average 31ºC (87ºF).
March to June: "Long rains." April is very wet but May is the wettest with as many as 20 rainy days per month. Afternoons are humid and hot, 29ºC (85ºF).
June to September: Low rainfall. Good months to visit. Afternoon temperature, 27ºC (81ºF).
October to November: "Short rains." Rains 10 days per month. Temperatures rise above 30ºC (86ºF) in the afternoons.

Note: The coast is hot and humid year–round but is tempered by daytime sea breezes. Seven to 9 hours of sunshine can be expected for all months.

Mombasa, Kenyan coast: Altitude 55m (180ft)

	Jan	Feb	Mar	Apr	May	Jun
Sunrise ºC(ºF)	22(72)	23(73)	23(73)	23(73)	22(72)	20(68)
Mid–afternoon ºC(ºF)	33(91)	34(93)	34(93)	33(91)	31(87)	29(84)
Days with precipitation	3	1	5	10	14	10
Precipitation mm	34	14	56	154	236	88
Precipitation inches	1.3	0.6	2.2	6.1	9.3	3.5
Daily hours of sunshine	9	9	9	8	7	7

	Jul	Aug	Sep	Oct	Nov	Dec
Sunrise ºC(ºF)	19(66)	19(66)	20(68)	21(70)	22(72)	22(72)
Mid–afternoon ºC(ºF)	29(84)	29(84)	30(86)	31(87)	32(89)	33(91)
Days with precipitation	10	8	9	9	8	7
Precipitation mm	72	68	67	103	105	76
Precipitation inches	2.8	2.7	2.6	4.1	4.1	3.0
Daily hours of sunshine	7	8	8	9	9	8

3. Northern Region.
Throughout the year afternoon temperatures exceed 35ºC (95ºF). Nightly lows can drop to 20ºC (68ºF). Rainfall is sparse and comes as violent thunderstorms. November is the wettest month; July is the driest.

Natural attractions:
1. Wildlife viewing.
January and February are ideal months. Compared with other months there is more bird life on Rift Valley lakes and animals can be spotted easily near streams. Kenya, straddling the equator, has daylight year–round from 6am to 7pm. Best times to view wildlife are 6:30am to 9:30am, and 3:30pm to 6:30pm, when they are active.
June to September is popular (dry season), particularly July, August and September when the spectacular migration of wildebeest and zebras takes place in the Masai Mara. The herds of wildebeest and zebras leave Masai Mara in October and/or November to head south into the Serengeti, in Tanzania, and leave there in May and/or June to return to the Masai Mara where they arrive back in July or August. (See **Tanzania** for information and a migration map showing the annual migration routes of wildebeest and zebras.)
2. Trekking.
Mt Kenya, 5199m (17057ft). Best times to climb/trek Mt Kenya are in the dry seasons, mid–January to late February, and late August to September.

KIRIBATI

Official Name: Republic of Kiribati (pronounced Kir–ih–bahss)

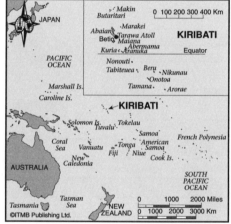

Capital: Tarawa
Languages: English (official), Kiribati

The country consists of more than 30 palm–studded islands made up of the Gilbert Islands, Phoenix Islands, Line Islands and Banaba.

Best time to visit: March to October.

April to October: Season of less rain. Sunny, hot, humid. Sea breezes temper the humid climate. Expect 6 days with rain per month. Average afternoon temperature, 32°C (89°F).
November to March: Wet season. Hot, humid, gales. Expect 13 rainy days per month. Rain, when it occurs, usually comes late afternoon, and humidity increases. Continuous sea breezes throughout the year temper the hot and humid climate. Afternoon temperature, 32°C (89°F).
Sunshine throughout the year averages 6 hours per day.

KOREA (North)

Official Name: Democratic People's Republic of Korea

Capital: P'yongyang
Language: Korean

The country is mountainous with deep, narrow valleys. The coastal plains are wide in the west, with occasional plains in the east.

Best time to visit: September to October. (Dry, and the foliage is changing to reds, browns and golds.) April, May and June, before the rains, are also excellent months.

April to June: Spring. Warm but changeable with frequent light showers. Afternoon maximum temperatures rise from 16°C (60°F) in April to 26°C (79°F) in June.

Mid–July to mid–September: Summer. Hot with occasional thunderstorms, with humidity of 75 to 80%. Temperatures rise to 35°C (95°F) but coastal areas are tempered by sea breezes. August is the hottest month. Heavy rains start in late June or early July. The moisture is carried by warm winds blowing northeast from near the Philippines in the South China Sea. Up to two–thirds of the annual rainfall falls mid–July to early August. It is not continuous; a few rainy days will be followed by sunny days with blue skies. The air becomes heavy and muggy immediately after the rains. From late July to early September typhoons are possible but they usually peter out before hitting the Korean peninsula.

Mid–September to mid–November: Autumn. Mainly a dry period with clear blue skies but with occasional light rain. Humidity is lower compared with summer.

Mid–November to March: Winter. Cold to bitterly cold. Cold northwest winds blow out of Siberia. Rivers can freeze and remain so up to 4 months. Snow falls between December and March. P'yongyang can expect more than 30 snowy days. At higher elevations the snow starts in late October and stays through May. Temperatures in January and February are the coldest.

P'yongyang, North Korea: Altitude 38m (125ft)

	Jan	Feb	Mar	Apr	May	Jun
Sunrise °C(°F)	−12(11)	−10(14)	−4(25)	3(37)	9(48)	15(59)
Mid–afternoon °C(°F)	−3(27)	1(33)	7(44)	15(59)	22(72)	26(80)
Days with precipitation	3	3	4	5	7	7
Precipitation mm	15	11	25	46	67	76
Precipitation inches	0.6	0.4	1.0	1.8	2.6	3.0
Daily hours of sunshine	6	7	7	8	8	7

	Jul	Aug	Sep	Oct	Nov	Dec
Sunrise °C(°F)	19(66)	20(68)	14(57)	6(42)	−2(29)	−10(14)
Mid–afternoon °C(°F)	28(82)	29(84)	24(75)	18(64)	9(48)	0(32)
Days with precipitation	13	11	7	6	7	4
Precipitation mm	237	228	112	45	41	21
Precipitation inches	9.3	9.0	4.4	1.8	1.6	0.8
Daily hours of sunshine	6	7	7	8	6	6

KOREA (South)

Official Name: Republic of Korea
Capital: Seoul
Languages: Korean, English
Mountains predominate the peninsula except in the southwest where there are low hills and valleys.

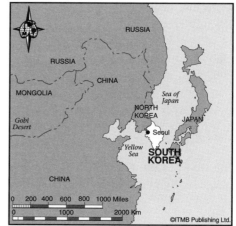

Best time to visit: September and October. (After the rains.) April, May and June, before the rains, are also excellent months.
April to June: Spring. Warm, but changeable with frequent light showers. Afternoon maximum temperatures rise from 17°C (62°F) in April to 27°C (81°F) in June.
Mid–July to mid–September: Summer. Hot with occasional thunderstorms, and with humidity 80 to 85%.
Temperatures rise to 37°C (98°F) but coastal areas are tempered by sea breezes. August is the hottest month. Heavy rains start in late June or early July. The moisture is carried by warm winds blowing northeast from near the Philippines in the South China Sea. Up to two–thirds of the annual rainfall falls mid–July to early August. It is not continuous; a few rainy days will be followed by sunny days with blue skies. The air becomes heavy and muggy immediately after the rains. From late July to early September typhoons are possible but they usually peter out before hitting the Korean peninsula.
Mid–September to mid–November: Autumn. Mainly a dry period with clear blue skies but with occasional light rain. Humidity is lower compared with summer.
Mid–November to March: Winter. Cold to bitterly cold. Cold northwest winds blow out of Siberia. Snow falls between December and March but at higher elevations it starts in late October and stays through May. Temperatures in January and February, the coldest months, fall to –12°C to 2°C (10 to 35°F) in the interior. The coastal temperatures stay just above freezing. The southern island of Cheju–do stays above 7°C (45°F). In the mountains temperatures drop to –15°C (5°F) at night. A characteristic of winter is its fairly consistent seven–day cycle of three cold days followed by four warmer ones.
Natural attraction: Foliage is colourful. The tree leaves change to browns, reds and golds. The colour change begins in the north of the country in early October and progresses southward until the changes are complete by early November.

Seoul, South Korea: Altitude 87m (285ft)

	Jan	Feb	Mar	Apr	May	Jun
Sunrise °C(°F)	–7(19)	–5(23)	0(32)	7(44)	13(55)	17(62)
Mid–afternoon °C(°F)	1(33)	3(37)	10(50)	17(62)	23(73)	27(80)
Days with precipitation	8	6	7	8	10	10
Precipitation mm	23	25	47	94	92	134
Precipitation inches	0.9	1.0	1.9	3.7	3.6	5.3
Daily hours of sunshine	5	6	7	7	7	6

	Jul	Aug	Sep	Oct	Nov	Dec
Sunrise °C(°F)	22(72)	22(72)	17(62)	10(50)	3(37)	–4(25)
Mid–afternoon °C(°F)	29(84)	30(86)	26(78)	20(68)	11(51)	4(39)
Days with precipitation	16	13	9	7	9	9
Precipitation mm	369	294	169	50	53	21
Precipitation inches	14.5	11.6	6.7	2.0	2.1	0.8
Daily hours of sunshine	4	5	6	7	5	5

KUWAIT

Official Name: State of Kuwait

Capital: Kuwait City (Al Kuwait)
Languages: Arabic, English

The independent State of Kuwait is on the northwest coast
of the Persian Gulf. The terrain consists of low–lying
barren desert.

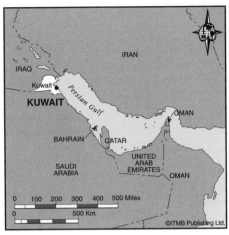

Best time: November to April.

December to February: Winter. Mild, warm days,
mostly dry. Occasional rain can come as thunderstorms
but the rainfall is light. When cool winds blow from the
northwest, night temperatures can drop to freezing point. Winds that blow from the southeast bring
warm spells.

March to May: Spring. Pleasantly warm days, cool nights, mostly dry. Winds carry warm air from
the south which is cooled by occasional rains, particularly in March. Sandstorms are fairly prevalent
in spring.

June to September: Summer. Hot days, cool nights. Humidity increases when warm breezes blow
from the sea. July and August are the hottest months when afternoon temperatures can reach the high
40s°C (beyond 100°F), especially when hot winds, sometimes as sand and dust storms, blow from the
deserts of Saudi Arabia.

October and November: Autumn. October days are warm to hot, but November is mild to cool. Light
rains fall in November.

Kuwait City, Kuwait: Altitude 55m (180ft)

	Jan	Feb	Mar	Apr	May	Jun
Sunrise °C(°F)	7(44)	9(48)	13(55)	18(64)	24(75)	28(82)
Mid–afternoon °C(°F)	18(64)	21(69)	26(78)	32(89)	39(102)	44(111)
Days with precipitation	2	2	2	1	0	0
Precipitation mm	26	16	13	15	4	0
Precipitation inches	1.0	0.6	0.5	0.6	0.1	0
Daily hours of sunshine	6	8	7	8	9	10

	Jul	Aug	Sep	Oct	Nov	Dec
Sunrise °C(°F)	29(84)	29(84)	25(77)	20(68)	13(55)	9(48)
Mid–afternoon °C(°F)	44(111)	45(112)	42(108)	35(95)	27(80)	20(68)
Days with precipitation	0	0	0	0	1	3
Precipitation mm	0	0	0	3	14	17
Precipitation inches	0	0	0	0.1	0.6	0.7
Daily hours of sunshine	10	10	10	8	7	6

KYRGYZSTAN

Official Name: Kyrgyz Republic

Capital: Bishkek
Languages: Kirghiz, Russian (both official)

Most of the country is mountainous with year–round snow–covered peaks.

Good time to visit: May to September. (Particularly May and September.)

Mid–May to mid–June: Pleasant and mainly dry although rain may fall intermittently. Seven to 8 hours of sunshine daily. Afternoons are warm, 22°C (72°F).

End of June to mid–August: Dry, sunny. Afternoon temperatures exceed 30°C (86°F). August is the hottest month. The mountain valleys are cooler.

September: Pleasant. Light rain. Eight hours of sunshine daily. Warm, 21°C (71°F).

October to April: Occasional sunshine. Cool weather starts in October. Winter arrives with cold winds blowing from the polar regions. Snow falls in Bishkek, December to February. January is the coldest month with below freezing daytime temperatures. Mountain nights can be below freezing between October and April. Light rain can be expected in March and April. Bishkek can experience foggy, hazy days but the mountainsides beyond the city can be clear.

Bishkek, Kyrgyzstan: Altitude 760m (2493ft)

	Jan	Feb	Mar	Apr	May	Jun
Sunrise °C(°F)	−10(14)	−8(18)	−3(27)	5(41)	10(50)	11(51)
Mid–afternoon °C(°F)	−1(30)	1(33)	7(44)	16(60)	20(68)	23(73)
Days with precipitation	6	6	9	9	8	5
Precipitation mm	26	31	50	77	64	35
Precipitation inches	1.0	1.2	2.0	3.0	2.5	1.4
Daily hours of sunshine	4	4	5	7	9	10

	Jul	Aug	Sep	Oct	Nov	Dec
Sunrise °C(°F)	16(60)	14(57)	9(48)	3(37)	−1(30)	−7(19)
Mid–afternoon °C(°F)	27(80)	27(80)	23(73)	13(55)	10(50)	3(37)
Days with precipitation	3	2	3	6	7	6
Precipitation mm	16	12	16	44	44	28
Precipitation inches	0.6	0.5	0.6	1.7	1.7	1.1
Daily hours of sunshine	11	11	9	7	5	4

LAOS
Official Name: Lao People's Democratic Republic

Capital: Vientiane
Languages: Lao, French, English, ethnic languages

Ninety percent of Laos is mountainous with forests. In the extreme south and southwest there is a small lowland area.

Best time: November to February. (Cool, dry.)

November to mid–February: Dry period. Afternoon temperatures keep to a relatively cool 29°C (85°F) due to cool breezes brought by the dry monsoon winds from the northeast. The lowest temperatures occur in December and January when morning temperatures can be 15°C (59°F). At the higher elevations, for example, in the mountains northeast of Vientiane, morning temperatures can drop to freezing point.

Mid–February to May: Dry period. Temperatures increase to 34°C (93°F) after the cooling affect of the northeast monsoon has run its course. March and April have the highest temperatures which can reach 38°C (100°F).

May to October: Period of heavy rains brought by the southwest monsoon. Most rain falls in July and August. Daytime temperatures reach 31°C (88°F) in the lowlands but the mountains are cooler, 25°C (77°F).

Vientiane, Laos: Altitude 171m (561ft)

	Jan	Feb	Mar	Apr	May	Jun
Sunrise °C(°F)	17(62)	19(66)	22(72)	24(76)	25(77)	25(77)
Mid–afternoon °C(°F)	23(73)	24(76)	27(80)	29(84)	29(84)	28(82)
Days with precipitation	1	2	4	7	15	17
Precipitation mm	6	12	36	85	255	273
Precipitation inches	0.2	0.5	1.4	3.4	10.0	10.7
Daily hours of sunshine	8	8	7	7	7	5

	Jul	Aug	Sep	Oct	Nov	Dec
Sunrise °C(°F)	25(77)	25(77)	24(75)	23(73)	19(66)	17(62)
Mid–afternoon °C(°F)	28(82)	28(82)	28(82)	27(80)	24(75)	22(72)
Days with precipitation	18	19	16	7	1	1
Precipitation mm	266	323	295	87	10	3
Precipitation inches	10.5	12.7	11.6	3.4	0.4	0.1
Daily hours of sunshine	5	5	5	8	8	8

LATVIA

Official Name: Republic of Latvia

Capital: Riga
Languages: Latvian, Lithuanian

Most of Latvia is a lakestrewn low–lying plain with many rivers, peat bogs and marshes.

Best time to visit: May to September, but rainy July and August.

May to September: May, June and September are the preferred months of cooler, pleasant afternoon temperatures over 20°C (70°F), and less rain. July and August are the wettest, warmest months with afternoon temperatures reaching 29°C (85°F). Sunny days can be quickly marred by overcast skies and short cloudbursts, especially late June, July and August. Summer evenings can be cool. The sun sets at 11pm around mid–summer.
October: Transitional month. Could be mild or cold. Afternoon temperature, 11°C (52°F).
November to March: Winter. Some fog. Cold with below freezing temperatures. Snow is on the ground permanently December to April inland, and January to March in coastal areas.
April: Transitional month, varies from winter to spring–like conditions. Afternoon temperature, 10°C (50°F).

Riga, Latvia: Altitude 7m (23ft)

	Jan	Feb	Mar	Apr	May	Jun
Sunrise °C(°F)	−10(14)	−10(14)	−6(21)	1(33)	6(42)	10(50)
Mid–afternoon °C(°F)	−4(25)	−3(27)	2(35)	10(50)	18(64)	21(70)
Days with precipitation	9	7	8	8	8	9
Precipitation mm	33	25	31	39	43	61
Precipitation inches	1.3	1.0	1.2	1.5	1.7	2.4
Daily hours of sunshine	1	2	4	6	9	10

	Jul	Aug	Sep	Oct	Nov	Dec
Sunrise °C(°F)	12(53)	11(51)	7(44)	3(37)	−1(30)	−7(19)
Mid–afternoon °C(°F)	22(72)	22(72)	16(60)	10(50)	3(37)	−1(30)
Days with precipitation	11	11	12	12	13	12
Precipitation mm	79	79	76	60	61	49
Precipitation inches	3.1	3.1	3.0	2.4	2.4	1.9
Daily hours of sunshine	9	7	5	3	1	1

LEBANON
Official Name: Lebanese Republic

Capital: Beirut
Languages: Arabic, French, English

Lebanon is a narrow country that runs north–south whose
geographical features run in the same direction. They
are the coastal plain, the Lebanon Mountains, the Bekaa
Valley, and the Anti–Lebanon Mountains. The latter form
the border with Syria.

**Best time: April and May, and late September,
October and November.** However, note that skiing is
possible in winter, and that mountain weather in summer
is pleasant, which makes Lebanon attractive year–round.

March to May: Spring. On the coast, some rain falls in early March. March and April are pleasantly
warm, 21°C (70°F). May is the start of the dry, warmer period. In the Bekaa Valley, weather is sunny
and cool – a good time to visit.

Late May to mid–September: Summer.
- **On the coast:** Dry with little or no rain, (70% humidity in July) and hot, sometimes over 40°C
  (over 100°F). Westerly winds help cool the temperature in the late afternoons and evenings but the
  nights can still be balmy. July and August are the hottest and most humid months.
- **In the mountains:** Mountain temperatures are sometimes as high as the coastal temperatures
  but there is less humidity in the mountains. This has led to the popularity of numerous mountain
  resorts. Days are sunny. Mountain breezes cool the air. Nights can be chilly, even in July and
  August.
- **In the Bekaa Valley:** Dry and hot, over 40°C (over 100°F). Being shielded by the Lebanon
  Mountains, there is less rain and lower humidity than on the coast.
  Dry, hot, khamsin winds sometimes blow from Saudia Arabia, raising temperatures.
  September to November: The coast, mountains and valley are sunny, dry and pleasantly warm – a
  good time to visit. Rain arrives at the end of November.

Mid–November to mid–March: Winter.
- **On the coast:** Cold, 13°C (55°F) but the warming effect of the Mediterranean Sea stops the
  temperature from becoming chilly. Rainy from mid–November to early March. Westerly winds
  capture moisture from the Mediterranean Sea and unload it on the western slopes of the Lebanon
  Mountains.
- **In the mountains:** Snow falls and lies at high elevations as late as mid–June. Ski season runs
  mid–December to mid–April.
- **In the Bekaa Valley:** Freezing winds. Generally dry with a little rain. December to February is
  when the majority of rain falls in the valley, but it is minimal.

Beirut, Lebanon: Altitude 19m (62ft)

	Jan	Feb	Mar	Apr	May	Jun
Sunrise ºC(ºF)	11(51)	11(51)	12(53)	14(57)	18(64)	21(69)
Mid–afternoon ºC(ºF)	17(62)	17(62)	19(66)	22(72)	26(78)	28(82)
Days with precipitation	15	11	9	5	2	0
Precipitation mm	191	133	111	46	15	2
Precipitation inches	7.5	5.2	4.4	1.8	0.6	0.08
Daily hours of sunshine	5	5	6	8	10	12

	Jul	Aug	Sep	Oct	Nov	Dec
Sunrise ºC(ºF)	23(73)	23(73)	23(73)	21(69)	16(60)	13(55)
Mid–afternoon ºC(ºF)	31(87)	32(89)	30(86)	27(81)	23(73)	18(64)
Days with precipitation	0	0	1	5	8	12
Precipitation mm	0	0	2	60	101	164
Precipitation inches	0	0	0.08	2.4	4.0	6.5
Daily hours of sunshine	12	12	10	8	7	5

LESOTHO

Official Name: Kingdom of Lesotho (pronounced le–soo–too)

Capital: Maseru
Languages: Sesotho, English

All of this small country lies above 1000m (about 3300ft). The highest peaks reach 3300m (about 11000ft).

Best time: October and April. (These months are the beginning and end of summer when temperatures are mild and rainfall is moderate.) However, Lesotho is a year–round destination.

October to April: Summer. Sunny, but rain is frequent, often as thunderstorms. Daytime temperatures are a moderate 22 to 28°C (72 to 82°F) but can drop to freezing at high elevations.
May to September: Sunny and cold. Frost, mist and light rain prevails. Snow falls on high peaks. At lower levels, daytime temperatures are mild, 16 to 22 °C (60 to 72°F) but nights can be freezing.

LIBERIA

Official Name: Republic of Liberia

Capital: Monrovia
Languages: English, African languages

Along the coast is a flat plain which averages 80km (50 miles) wide. From it the land rises to a forested plateau with intermittent mountains.

Best time to travel: November to April. (Dry.)

November to April: Dry season. Hot, 30°C (86°F) in the afternoons on the coast, but a little higher inland. Humidity is uncomfortably high. Skies may be hazy from mid–December to April as a result of the dust–laden harmattan winds blowing from the Sahara.
May to October: Rainy season. Rain is heaviest on the coast where Monrovia is situated, averaging 25mm (1in) per day. The rainfall decreases progressively inland. Coastal temperatures average 27°C (80°F) in the afternoons, but slightly higher inland. Humidity increases in the rainy season.

Monrovia, Liberia: Altitude 23m (75ft)

	Jan	Feb	Mar	Apr	May	Jun
Sunrise ºC(ºF)	23(73)	23(73)	23(73)	23(73)	22(72)	23(73)
Mid–afternoon ºC(ºF)	30(86)	29(85)	31(87)	31(87)	30(86)	27(80)
Days with precipitation	5	5	10	17	21	26
Precipitation mm	31	56	97	216	516	973
Precipitation inches	1.2	2.2	3.8	8.5	20.3	38.3
Daily hours of sunshine	6	6	7	6	5	4

	Jul	Aug	Sep	Oct	Nov	Dec
Sunrise ºC(ºF)	22(72)	23(73)	22(72)	22(72)	23(73)	23(73)
Mid–afternoon ºC(ºF)	27(80)	27(80)	27(80)	28(83)	29(85)	30(86)
Days with precipitation	24	20	26	22	19	12
Precipitation mm	996	373	744	772	236	130
Precipitation inches	39.2	14.7	29.3	30.4	9.3	5.1
Daily hours of sunshine	3	3	4	4	6	5

LIBYA

Official Name: Socialist People's Libyan Arab Jamahiriya

Capital: Tripoli
Languages: Arabic, English, Italian

About 95 percent of the country is comprised of barren, rock–strewn plains and seas of sand. In the inland region, days are hot, nights are cold and rain is irregular. Very little rain falls inland. The coastal climate of Libya is described below.

Best time: February to May. October to January is also good, although light rains fall on the coast.

March to May: Spring. Sunny, warm days, about 24°C (76°F). The heat can be intensified by hot, dry, dusty winds, locally called ghibli, that blow occasionally from the Sahara Desert. Rainfall is negligible.

June to August: Summer. Sunny. Daily temperatures reach 30°C (86°F) but can exceed 40°C (over 100°F) when the ghibli blow from the desert. Summers are rainless.

September to November: Autumn. Sunny, warm days and cold nights. Negligible rain.

December to February: Winter. Generally sunny with some light rain and cloud. Warm days, cold nights. December and January are the coldest months with a chance of snow on the coast.

Tripoli, Libya: Altitude 22m (72ft)

	Jan	Feb	Mar	Apr	May	Jun
Sunrise °C(°F)	8(47)	9(49)	11(52)	14(57)	16(61)	19(67)
Mid–afternoon °C(°F)	16(61)	17(63)	19(67)	22(72)	24(76)	27(81)
Days with precipitation	11	7	5	2	3	1
Precipitation mm	81	46	28	10	5	3
Precipitation inches	3.2	1.8	1.1	0.4	0.2	0.1
Daily hours of sunshine	5	6	6	7	8	10

	Jul	Aug	Sep	Oct	Nov	Dec
Sunrise °C(°F)	22(71)	22(71)	22(71)	18(65)	14(57)	9(49)
Mid–afternoon °C(°F)	29(85)	30(86)	29(85)	27(80)	23(73)	18(64)
Days with precipitation	0	0	2	5	7	11
Precipitation mm	0	0	10	41	66	94
Precipitation inches	0	0	0.4	1.6	2.6	3.7
Daily hours of sunshine	11	11	8	7	5	5

LIECHTENSTEIN

Official Name: Principality of Liechtenstein

Capital: Vaduz
Languages: German, Alemannic dialect

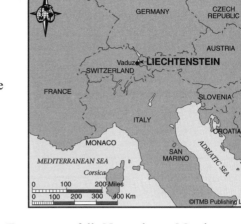

The country is mountainous except for the valley of the Rhine River in the west.

Best time: May to September.

May to September: Sunny, warm, 20 to 25°C (68 to 77°F). Rain falls mainly in June, July and August and often comes as brief downpours.
October to April: Cool to cold with freezing temperatures brought by cold winds from the northeast. Expect snowfalls November to March.
Rain falls year–round, caused by humid winds from the Adriatic Sea condensing their vapour when they reach the mountains.

LITHUANIA

Official Name: Republic of Lithuania

Capital: Vilnius
Languages: Lithuanian, Polish, Russian

Lithuania consists of a low–lying plain with numerous lakes and rivers. In the southeast and southwest are low hills.

Best time to visit: May to September, but rainy July and August.

May to September: May, June and September are the preferred months of cooler, pleasant afternoon temperatures over 20°C (68°F), and less rain. July and August are wettest, warmest months with afternoon temperatures reaching 29°C (85°F). Sunny days can be quickly marred by overcast skies and short cloudbursts, especially late June, July and August. Summer evenings can be cool. The sun sets at 11pm around mid–summer.
October: Transitional month. Could be mild or cold. Afternoon temperature, 11°C (52°F).
November to March: Winter. Some fog. Cold with below freezing temperatures. Snow is on the ground permanently December to April inland, and January to March in coastal areas.
April: Transitional month, varies from winter to spring–like conditions. Afternoon temperature, 12°C (54°F).

Vilnius, Lithuania: Altitude 156m (512ft)

	Jan	Feb	Mar	Apr	May	Jun
Sunrise ºC(ºF)	–9(16)	–8(18)	–4(25)	2(35)	8(46)	11(51)
Mid–afternoon ºC(ºF)	–4(25)	–2(29)	3(37)	11(51)	18(64)	21(70)
Days with precipitation	10	9	9	10	9	10
Precipitation mm	41	38	39	46	62	77
Precipitation inches	1.6	1.5	1.5	1.8	2.4	3.0
Daily hours of sunshine	1	2	4	5	8	8

	Jul	Aug	Sep	Oct	Nov	Dec
Sunrise ºC(ºF)	12(53)	12(53)	8(46)	3(37)	–1(30)	–5(23)
Mid–afternoon ºC(ºF)	22(72)	22(72)	16(60)	10(50)	4(39)	–1(30)
Days with precipitation	11	10	11	9	12	12
Precipitation mm	78	72	65	53	57	55
Precipitation inches	3.1	2.8	2.6	2.1	2.2	2.2
Daily hours of sunshine	7	7	5	3	1	1

LUXEMBOURG

Official Name: Grand Duchy of Luxembourg
Capital: Luxembourg
Languages: Official are French, German and
Luxembourgeois (related to German)
The northern one–third of the country is a tree–covered
mountainous region; the southern two–thirds is made up
of tablelands and ridges. There is a marked difference in
climatic conditions between north and south.

Best time: May to August. (April may also have mild,
sunny weather.)
May to August: These are the sunniest months. In the
north in mid–summer, July, it is 21ºC (70ºF). In the south
where the city of Luxembourg is located, it is slightly
warmer, 23ºC (73ºF). There is rain every month but the south is drier.
October to March: The north is cold and harsh, –3 to 0ºC (26 to 32ºF) in January. Temperatures are
known to go lower and snow is common in winter. The south's temperature in mid–winter, January,
ranges 1 to 4ºC (33 to 39ºF). Rain falls monthly throughout the country, spread fairly evenly over the
year.

Luxembourg: Altitude 379m (1243ft)

	Jan	Feb	Mar	Apr	May	Jun
Sunrise ºC(ºF)	–2(29)	–2(29)	1(33)	3(37)	7(44)	10(50)
Mid–afternoon ºC(ºF)	2(35)	4(39)	8(46)	12(53)	17(62)	20(68)
Days with precipitation	20	16	15	14	15	15
Precipitation mm	71	62	70	61	81	82
Precipitation inches	2.8	2.4	2.8	2.4	3.2	3.2
Daily hours of sunshine	1	3	4	5	7	7

Luxembourg: (continued)

	Jul	Aug	Sep	Oct	Nov	Dec
Sunrise ºC(ºF)	12(53)	12(53)	9(48)	6(42)	1(33)	–1(30)
Mid–afternoon ºC(ºF)	22(72)	21(71)	18(65)	13(55)	7(44)	3(37)
Days with precipitation	14	15	15	15	19	20
Precipitation mm	68	72	70	75	83	80
Precipitation inches	2.7	2.8	2.8	3.0	3.3	3.2
Daily hours of sunshine	8	7	5	3	2	1

MACEDONIA

Official Name: Republic of Macedonia. Also known as Former Yugoslav Republic of Macedonia (FYROM)

Capital: Skopje
Languages: Macedonian, Albanian

Most of the country is on a wide plateau averaging 600 to 900m (2000 to 3000ft) above sea level. The terrain is mountainous with deep valleys and basins.

Best time: June to September.

June to September: Mainly dry, but light rains fall. Hot, 30ºC (86ºF), in daytime.
October to May: Wet, mild to cold. In winter months, December to February, warm winds from the Aegean Sea blow along the Vardar Valley, bringing mild temperatures. The main snowfalls in the mountains usually occur in January and February. It remains all year in high, sheltered places.

Skopje, Macedonia: Altitude 240m (787ft)

	Jan	Feb	Mar	Apr	May	Jun
Sunrise ºC(ºF)	–3(27)	–1(30)	2(35)	5(41)	10(50)	13(55)
Mid–afternoon ºC(ºF)	4(39)	8(46)	14(57)	19(66)	24(75)	28(82)
Days with precipitation	6	6	6	7	9	6
Precipitation mm	34	37	36	40	62	46
Precipitation inches	1.3	1.5	1.4	1.6	2.4	1.8
Daily hours of sunshine	2	3	4	6	7	9

	Jul	Aug	Sep	Oct	Nov	Dec
Sunrise ºC(ºF)	15(59)	15(59)	11(51)	6(42)	1(33)	–2(29)
Mid–afternoon ºC(ºF)	30(86)	30(86)	26(79)	19(66)	10(50)	5(41)
Days with precipitation	5	5	5	6	7	7
Precipitation mm	34	31	41	44	56	46
Precipitation inches	1.3	1.2	1.6	1.7	2.2	1.8
Daily hours of sunshine	9	9	7	5	3	2

MADAGASCAR

Official Name: Democratic Republic of Madagascar

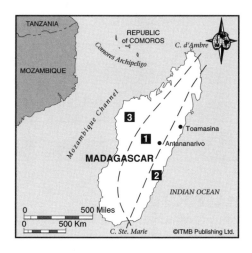

Capital: Antananarivo (called Tana for short)
Languages: French, Malagasy

In the centre of the island, mountains extend along its length. The east coast has narrow lowlands and the west coast has a wide coastal plain.

Best time: May to November. (Cool, dry.) Preferred months are October and November (less rain on east coast).

We have divided the weather into three regions. Refer to the map for corresponding numbers.
1. Central plateau. (The highlands where Antananarivo is located.)
Best months: May to November.

May to September: Winter. Dry season. Mild, pleasant. Afternoon temperatures range 20 to 23°C (68 to 74°F). Seven to 8 hours of sunshine daily. At high elevations temperatures can fall below freezing and snowfalls are possible. June is the coldest month.
October to April: Summer. Wet season. The main rains start at the end of November. February and March comprise the cyclone season of heavy rain. December to March can have 20 rainy days per month. Average afternoon temperature is around 26°C (79°F). Expect 7 to 8 hours of sunshine daily.

2. East coast. (Lowlands.)
Best travel months are May to November. October and November are preferred because of less rain – only 12 days per month. April and December are also good. Afternoon temperatures are hot, 24 to 30°C (75 to 86°F), and humid. Expect 6 to 8 hours of daily sunshine throughout the year.

Rain falls throughout the year, especially January, February and March (cyclonic rains).

3. West coast. (Wide plain.)
May to October: Dry season.
November to April: Wet season.
In general, weather is hot (hotter that the east coast) and sunny throughout the year with the rainfall decreasing from north to south. The southwest is the driest part of the country.

Natural attraction: Orchids. Main flowering season is January, February and March. February is best.

Antananarivo, on central plateau, Madagascar: Altitude 1276m (4186ft)

	Jan	Feb	Mar	Apr	May	Jun
Sunrise ºC(ºF)	17(62)	17(62)	16(60)	15(59)	12(53)	10(50)
Mid–afternoon ºC(ºF)	26(78)	27(80)	26(78)	25(77)	23(73)	21(70)
Days with precipitation	15	15	12	5	2	2
Precipitation mm	274	279	204	65	23	8
Precipitation inches	10.8	11.0	8.0	2.6	0.9	0.3
Daily hours of sunshine	7	6	6	7	7	7

	Jul	Aug	Sep	Oct	Nov	Dec
Sunrise ºC(ºF)	10(50)	10(50)	11(52)	13(55)	15(59)	16(60)
Mid–afternoon ºC(ºF)	20(68)	21(70)	24(75)	26(78)	27(80)	26(78)
Days with precipitation	2	1	1	6	12	17
Precipitation mm	11	10	11	76	188	310
Precipitation inches	0.4	0.4	0.4	3.0	7.4	12.2
Daily hours of sunshine	7	8	8	8	8	6

Toamasina (Tamatave), on east coast, Madagascar: Altitude 6m (20ft)

	Jan	Feb	Mar	Apr	May	Jun
Sunrise ºC(ºF)	23(73)	23(73)	22(72)	21(70)	20(68)	18(64)
Mid–afternoon ºC(ºF)	30(86)	30(86)	30(86)	29(84)	27(80)	26(78)
Days with precipitation	19	17	21	18	17	18
Precipitation mm	410	382	478	323	228	259
Precipitation inches	16.1	15.0	18.8	12.7	9.0	10.2
Daily hours of sunshine	7	7	6	7	6	6

	Jul	Aug	Sep	Oct	Nov	Dec
Sunrise ºC(ºF)	17(62)	17(62)	17(62)	19(66)	20(68)	22(72)
Mid–afternoon ºC(ºF)	25(77)	25(77)	26(78)	27(80)	28(82)	29(84)
Days with precipitation	22	20	15	13	14	17
Precipitation mm	289	218	121	133	170	357
Precipitation inches	11.4	8.6	4.8	5.2	6.7	14.1
Daily hours of sunshine	5	5	6	7	8	7

MADEIRA
(A Territory of Portugal)

Capital: Funchal
Language: Portuguese

Madeira consists of several small islands of which two are inhabited. The terrain is mountainous. Being surrounded by ocean, there are no extremes of temperature.

Best time: May to September, although the islands are sunny throughout the year.

May to September: Dry season. Sunny and warm, 23°C (73°F).
October to April: Mild, 20°C (68°F). This is the rainy season with an average of 7 rainy days per month. Days are generally sunny but some are cloudy.

Funchal, Madeira: Altitude 56m (184ft)

	Jan	Feb	Mar	Apr	May	Jun
Sunrise °C(°F)	13(55)	13(55)	13(55)	13(55)	15(59)	17(62)
Mid–afternoon °C(°F)	19(66)	19(66)	20(68)	20(68)	21(70)	22(72)
Days with precipitation	8	9	7	5	3	2
Precipitation mm	103	87	64	39	19	12
Precipitation inches	4.1	3.4	2.5	1.5	0.7	0.5
Daily hours of sunshine	5	5	6	6	7	7

	Jul	Aug	Sep	Oct	Nov	Dec
Sunrise °C(°F)	18(64)	19(66)	19(66)	18(64)	16(60)	14(57)
Mid–afternoon °C(°F)	24(75)	26(78)	26(78)	24(75)	22(72)	20(68)
Days with precipitation	0	1	3	6	8	9
Precipitation mm	2	3	37	75	101	100
Precipitation inches	0.08	0.1	1.5	3.0	4.0	3.9
Daily hours of sunshine	7	8	7	6	5	5

MALAWI

Official Name: Republic of Malawi

Capital: Lilongwe
Languages: Chichewa, English, African languages

The Great Rift Valley extends north–south through
Malawi. It contains lakes including Lake Malawi. To the
east and west of the Valley the land rises to form plateaus.

Good time to visit: April to November. Dry season. May
to August is the most pleasant time (warm, dry). In most
parts of the country the year–round temperatures range
20 to 27°C (68 to 80°F). The variations in temperature
are influenced by altitude. The lowland region, below
500m (1640ft), of Lake Malawi and the Shire Valley, is slightly warmer than the above–mentioned
temperatures. The upland areas (e.g. Lilongwe, Mulanje, Zomba) are slightly cooler.

May to August: Dry and warm. Afternoon temperature, 24°C (75°F). Eight hours of sunshine daily.
September and October: Dry, low humidity, very hot. Sometimes over 30°C (86°F) in the afternoons.
Nine hours of sunshine daily.
November to April: Wet, humid and hot. Afternoon temperatures average 27°C (75°F). Eight hours of
sunshine daily.

Note: Lilongwe. October is the hottest month, 29°C (84°F) in the afternoon. The rest of the year
averages 25°C (77°F).
Note: Salima. This town is 15km (9 miles) from the popular beach on Lake Malawi.

Salima, near Lake Malawi: Altitude 513m (1683ft)

	Jan	Feb	Mar	Apr	May	Jun
Sunrise °C(°F)	22(72)	22(72)	22(72)	21(71)	20(68)	18(64)
Mid–afternoon °C(°F)	29(84)	29(84)	30(86)	29(84)	28(82)	26(78)
Days with precipitation	19	17	17	6	1	0
Precipitation mm	339	266	254	93	11	2
Precipitation inches	13.3	10.5	10.0	3.7	0.4	0.08
Daily hours of sunshine	5	5	6	8	8	8

	Jul	Aug	Sep	Oct	Nov	Dec
Sunrise °C(°F)	17(62)	18(64)	19(66)	22(72)	23(73)	22(72)
Mid–afternoon °C(°F)	26(79)	28(82)	31(87)	33(91)	32(89)	30(86)
Days with precipitation	0	0	0	0	7	15
Precipitation mm	0	0	0	6	44	250
Precipitation inches	0	0	0	0.2	1.7	9.8
Daily hours of sunshine	8	8	9	9	8	6

MALAYSIA

Official Name: Malaysia

Capital: Kuala Lumpur
Languages: Malay, English, Chinese

Malaysia comprises West Malaysia and East Malaysia. West Malaysia consists of a peninsula with a backbone of mountains. In the north they exceed 2100m (about 7000ft) but their height diminishes to the level of the wide plains in the south. Wide plains also run parallel to the mountains along both coasts of the peninsula. East Malaysia consists of two states, Sabah and Sarawak, on the island of Borneo. Both have coastal lowlands and high interior mountains.

Best time to visit:
1. West coast of West Malaysia: October to March. (Less rain, but all other months are good for travel.)
2. East coast of West Malaysia: March to September. (Less rain.)
3. Sabah and Sarawak: March to October. (Less rain.)

We have divided the weather into three regions. Refer to map for corresponding numbers.
1. West coast of West Malaysia. (Includes Kuala Lumpur and Pinang, formerly Penang.)
Rain falls throughout the year and is distributed fairly evenly.
Best time: October to March.

October to March: Intermittent light rains. Six to 8 hours of sunshine daily. Hot and humid. Lowland temperatures range 23ºC (73ºF) in the mornings to 32ºC (89ºF) in the afternoons. Highland areas, e.g. Cameron Highlands, morning temperature is 14ºC (57ºF), daily maximum is 21ºC (70ºF).
April to October: Rain arrives with the southwest monsoon from the Indian Ocean. Most rain falls as thunderstorms April and May, and in September and October. These short, heavy showers clear up quickly. Six to 7 hours of sunshine daily. Hot and humid. Lowland temperatures range 23ºC (73ºF) in the mornings to 32ºC (89ºF) in the afternoons. Highland areas range 14ºC (57ºF) in the mornings to 23ºC (73ºF) in the afternoons.

Cultural event: Thaipusam. January or February in Pinang and Kuala Lumpur. Devotees walk in procession, their flesh pierced with hooks and skewers as a sign of penance.

Kuala Lumpur, inland of West Malaysia: Altitude 22m (72ft)

	Jan	Feb	Mar	Apr	May	Jun
Sunrise °C(°F)	22(72)	22(72)	23(73)	23(73)	23(73)	23(73)
Mid–afternoon °C(°F)	32(89)	33(91)	33(91)	33(91)	33(91)	33(91)
Days with precipitation	10	11	14	16	13	9
Precipitation mm	163	145	218	285	184	127
Precipitation inches	6.4	5.7	8.6	11.2	7.2	5.0
Daily hours of sunshine	6	7	7	7	7	6

	Jul	Aug	Sep	Oct	Nov	Dec
Sunrise °C(°F)	23(73)	23(73)	23(73)	23(73)	23(73)	23(73)
Mid–afternoon °C(°F)	32(89)	32(89)	32(89)	32(89)	31(87)	32(89)
Days with precipitation	10	11	13	17	18	15
Precipitation mm	129	146	192	272	275	230
Precipitation inches	5.1	5.7	7.6	10.7	10.8	9.1
Daily hours of sunshine	6	6	5	5	5	5

Pinang, west coast of West Malaysia: Altitude 5m (17ft)

	Jan	Feb	Mar	Apr	May	Jun
Sunrise °C(°F)	23(73)	24(75)	24(75)	24(75)	24(75)	24(75)
Mid–afternoon °C(°F)	32(89)	32(89)	32(89)	32(89)	32(89)	31(87)
Days with precipitation	5	6	9	14	14	11
Precipitation mm	69	72	146	221	203	178
Precipitation inches	2.7	2.8	5.7	8.7	8.0	7.0
Daily hours of sunshine	8	8	8	7	7	7

	Jul	Aug	Sep	Oct	Nov	Dec
Sunrise °C(°F)	23(73)	23(73)	23(73)	23(73)	23(73)	23(73)
Mid–afternoon °C(°F)	31(87)	31(87)	31(87)	30(86)	30(86)	31(87)
Days with precipitation	12	14	18	19	15	9
Precipitation mm	192	242	356	383	232	114
Precipitation inches	7.6	9.5	14.0	15.1	9.1	4.5
Daily hours of sunshine	7	6	5	5	6	7

2. East coast of West Malaysia. (Includes Kuantan.)
Best time: March to September.

March to September: Light rains. Six to 8 hours of sunshine daily. Hot and humid.
November to February: Rain. Northeast monsoon from the South China Sea brings strong winds and heavy rains, often causing floods which affect roads, bridges and boat services. The west coast is not affected by these rains. Hot and humid.

Kuantan, east coast of West Malaysia: Altitude 16m (52ft)

	Jan	Feb	Mar	Apr	May	Jun
Sunrise ºC(ºF)	22(72)	22(72)	22(72)	23(73)	23(73)	23(73)
Mid–afternoon ºC(ºF)	29(84)	30(86)	31(87)	32(89)	33(91)	33(91)
Days with precipitation	12	9	9	13	12	9
Precipitation mm	296	142	178	164	203	160
Precipitation inches	11.7	5.6	7.0	6.5	8.0	6.3
Daily hours of sunshine	5	7	7	7	7	6

	Jul	Aug	Sep	Oct	Nov	Dec
Sunrise ºC(ºF)	23(73)	23(73)	23(73)	23(73)	22(72)	22(72)
Mid–afternoon ºC(ºF)	32(89)	32(89)	32(89)	32(89)	30(86)	29(84)
Days with precipitation	11	11	14	16	19	18
Precipitation mm	173	174	233	272	344	564
Precipitation inches	6.8	6.9	9.2	10.7	13.6	22.2
Daily hours of sunshine	7	6	6	5	4	4

3. Sabah and Sarawak (on the island of Borneo shared with Brunei and Indonesia)
Best time: March to October.

May to September: Light rains. Six hours of sunshine daily. Hot and humid.
October to April: Heaviest rainfall occurs, brought by the northeast monsoon winds. Travel can be difficult, particularly November to February. Four to 5 hours of sunshine daily. Hot and humid.

Kota Kinabalu, Sabah, East Malaysia: On the coast

	Jan	Feb	Mar	Apr	May	Jun
Sunrise ºC(ºF)	23(74)	23(74)	23(74)	24(75)	24(75)	24(75)
Mid–afternoon ºC(ºF)	30(86)	30(86)	31(87)	32(89)	32(89)	31(87)
Days with precipitation	10	7	6	8	13	13
Precipitation mm	129	64	61	112	226	291
Precipitation inches	5.1	2.5	2.4	4.4	8.9	11.5
Daily hours of sunshine	6	7	8	8	7	7

	Jul	Aug	Sep	Oct	Nov	Dec
Sunrise ºC(ºF)	24(75)	24(75)	24(75)	23(73)	23(73)	23(73)
Mid–afternoon ºC(ºF)	31(87)	31(87)	31(87)	31(87)	31(87)	30(86)
Days with precipitation	13	13	15	16	16	13
Precipitation mm	255	260	285	336	298	230
Precipitation inches	10.0	10.2	11.2	13.2	11.7	9.1
Daily hours of sunshine	7	6	6	6	6	6

Kuching, Sarawak, East Malaysia: Altitude 26m (85ft)

	Jan	Feb	Mar	Apr	May	Jun
Sunrise °C(°F)	23(73)	23(73)	23(73)	23(73)	23(73)	23(73)
Mid–afternoon °C(°F)	30(86)	30(86)	31(87)	32(89)	33(91)	32(90)
Days with precipitation	23	18	17	17	15	14
Precipitation mm	692	537	362	265	238	202
Precipitation inches	27.2	21.1	14.3	10.4	9.4	8.0
Daily hours of sunshine	4	4	4	5	6	6

	Jul	Aug	Sep	Oct	Nov	Dec
Sunrise °C(°F)	23(73)	23(73)	22(72)	23(73)	23(73)	23(73)
Mid–afternoon °C(°F)	32(89)	32(89)	32(89)	32(89)	31(87)	31(87)
Days with precipitation	13	15	16	19	22	23
Precipitation mm	185	211	274	343	367	479
Precipitation inches	7.3	8.3	10.8	13.5	14.5	18.8
Daily hours of sunshine	6	6	5	5	5	4

MALDIVES
Official Name: Republic of Maldives

Capital: Malé
Languages: Dhivehi, English

Maldives consists of hundreds of low–lying coral islands with white sandy beaches. About 200 islands are inhabited. The ocean temperature remains between 20 and 30°C (68 and 86°F) but the waters of the lagoons often exceed 30°C (86°F).

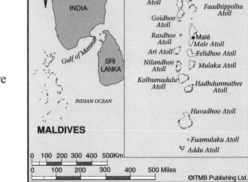

Best time: December to March. November is also a good month.

December to March: Dry, humid and warm, 30°C (86°F) in the afternoon. The comparatively dry northeast monsoon blows from the Asian land mass. The sky is blue and the sun shines an average of 9 hours daily. Seas are calm from November to May.

April to October: Rainy, humid and warm, 30°C (86°F) in the afternoon. The rainy southwest monsoon blows from the Indian Ocean where it picks up moisture and brings torrential downpours to the islands and causes the sea to be rough. April and May are transitional months and often have blue skies, little rain and calm seas.

Recreational activities: Snorkeling and scuba diving are best November to May. Many resorts stay open year–round.

Malé, Maldives: Altitude 2m (6ft)

	Jan	Feb	Mar	Apr	May	Jun
Sunrise ºC(ºF)	25(77)	26(78)	26(78)	26(78)	26(78)	26(78)
Mid–afternoon ºC(ºF)	30(86)	30(86)	31(87)	32(89)	31(87)	31(87)
Days with precipitation	5	4	6	9	14	13
Precipitation mm	75	50	73	132	216	172
Precipitation inches	3.0	2.0	2.9	5.2	8.5	6.8
Daily hours of sunshine	8	9	9	8	7	7

	Jul	Aug	Sep	Oct	Nov	Dec
Sunrise ºC(ºF)	26(78)	26(78)	25(77)	25(77)	25(77)	25(77)
Mid–afternoon ºC(ºF)	30(86)	30(86)	30(86)	30(86)	30(86)	30(86)
Days with precipitation	12	13	16	15	13	12
Precipitation mm	147	188	243	222	201	232
Precipitation inches	5.8	7.4	9.6	8.7	7.9	9.1
Daily hours of sunshine	7	7	7	8	8	7

MALI

Official Name: Republic of Mali

Capital: Bamako
Languages: French, African languages

Mali consists of broad, low plains with occasional outcroppings of hills.

Best time to visit: November to February. (The dry season.)

November to May: Dry, low humidity. Hot, dry, dusty harmattan winds blow from the Sahara and cause a haze, particularly mid–December to February.
March to May is the hottest season when temperatures can exceed 40ºC (104ºF).
June to October: Rainy season. Most rain falls in July and August as thunderstorms in the afternoons and evenings. More rain falls in the south of the country compared with the north.

River travel: Best time for the steamer on the Niger River from Koulikoro or Mopti to Timbuktu is August to November when the water is high enough.

Bamako, southern Mali: Altitude 381m (1250ft)

	Jan	Feb	Mar	Apr	May	Jun
Sunrise ºC(ºF)	17(62)	20(68)	23(73)	25(77)	25(77)	23(73)
Mid–afternoon ºC(ºF)	33(91)	36(96)	38(100)	39(102)	38(100)	35(95)
Days with precipitation	0	0	1	2	5	10
Precipitation mm	0	0	2	25	46	121
Precipitation inches	0	0	0.08	1.0	1.8	4.8
Daily hours of sunshine	9	9	9	8	8	8

	Jul	Aug	Sep	Oct	Nov	Dec
Sunrise ºC(ºF)	22(72)	22(72)	22(72)	22(72)	19(66)	17(62)
Mid–afternoon ºC(ºF)	32(89)	31(87)	32(89)	34(93)	35(95)	33(91)
Days with precipitation	16	17	12	6	1	0
Precipitation mm	218	234	165	65	2	0
Precipitation inches	8.6	9.2	6.5	2.6	0.08	0
Daily hours of sunshine	7	7	7	8	9	9

Timbuktu, central Mali: Altitude 264m (866ft)

	Jan	Feb	Mar	Apr	May	Jun
Sunrise ºC(ºF)	13(55)	15(59)	18(65)	22(72)	26(78)	27(80)
Mid–afternoon ºC(ºF)	30(86)	33(91)	36(96)	39(102)	42(107)	41(105)
Days with precipitation	0	0	1	0	2	5
Precipitation mm	0	0	0	1	4	15
Precipitation inches	0	0	0	0.04	0.1	0.6
Daily hours of sunshine	8	9	9	8	9	8

	Jul	Aug	Sep	Oct	Nov	Dec
Sunrise ºC(ºF)	26(78)	25(77)	25(77)	22(72)	17(62)	13(55)
Mid–afternoon ºC(ºF)	39(102)	37(98)	38(100)	38(100)	35(95)	30(86)
Days with precipitation	9	9	5	2	0	0
Precipitation mm	45	64	27	2	1	0
Precipitation inches	1.8	2.5	1.1	0.08	0.04	0
Daily hours of sunshine	8	8	8	9	9	8

MALTA
Official Name: Republic of Malta

Capital: Valletta
Languages: Maltese, English (both official)

The terrain of Malta, the main island, is low–lying with
gentle, arid hills. The smaller island of Gozo is thickly
vegetated with flat–topped hills and craggy cliffs.

Best time: April to June and September to October.
July and August are good, but just hotter.

April to October: Sunny, warm, dry. Cool, daytime sea
breezes can moderate the heat. Mid–summer temperatures
of July and August can top 30ºC (86ºF). The sirocco, the hot, dry wind from Africa can raise
temperatures even higher.
November to March: Mild. Daytime temperatures range around 16ºC (60ºF). This is the wet period
with most rain falling in December and January. Cool spells can occur when cold winds from central
Europe reach the islands, but these are rare.

Cultural event: Carnival. Five days of pre–Lenten festivities. Parade of floats with brass bands and
participants wearing grotesque masks.

Valletta, Malta: Altitude 70m (230ft)

	Jan	Feb	Mar	Apr	May	Jun
Sunrise ºC(ºF)	9(48)	9(48)	10(50)	12(53)	15(59)	18(64)
Mid–afternoon ºC(ºF)	15(59)	15(60)	17(62)	19(66)	23(73)	28(82)
Days with precipitation	14	11	9	6	3	1
Precipitation mm	89	61	41	23	7	3
Precipitation inches	3.5	2.4	1.6	0.9	0.3	0.1
Daily hours of sunshine	5	6	7	9	10	11

	Jul	Aug	Sep	Oct	Nov	Dec
Sunrise ºC(ºF)	21(69)	22(72)	20(68)	17(62)	14(57)	11(51)
Mid–afternoon ºC(ºF)	31(88)	31(88)	28(82)	24(75)	20(68)	17(62)
Days with precipitation	0	1	4	10	11	14
Precipitation mm	0	7	40	90	80	112
Precipitation inches	0	0.3	1.6	3.6	3.2	4.4
Daily hours of sunshine	12	11	9	7	6	5

MARSHALL ISLANDS
Official Name: Republic of the Marshall Islands

Capital: Majuro
Languages: English, Japanese, local dialects

The archipelago consists of atolls and coral reefs in the central Pacific Ocean.

Best time to visit: January to March.

January to March: Less rain. Sunny, humid and a degree or two cooler than other months. Rain showers are usually brief.

April to December: Rainy, sunny, hot, humid. September to November are the wettest months with heavy downpours. Cyclones are possible but they are rare.

Temperatures remain fairly constant throughout the year. Afternoons are about 30°C (86°F). It is always humid but sea breezes temper the humidity.

Majuro, Marshall Islands: Altitude 3m (10ft)

	Jan	Feb	Mar	Apr	May	Jun
Sunrise °C(°F)	25(77)	25(77)	25(77)	25(77)	25(77)	25(77)
Mid–afternoon °C(°F)	30(86)	30(86)	30(86)	30(86)	30(86)	30(86)
Days with precipitation	14	12	15	17	20	21
Precipitation mm	214	156	210	261	284	294
Precipitation inches	8.4	6.1	8.3	10.3	11.2	11.6
Daily hours of sunshine	7	8	8	7	7	7

	Jul	Aug	Sep	Oct	Nov	Dec
Sunrise °C(°F)	25(77)	25(77)	25(77)	25(77)	25(77)	25(77)
Mid–afternoon °C(°F)	30(86)	30(86)	30(86)	30(86)	30(86)	30(86)
Days with precipitation	21	21	20	21	20	19
Precipitation mm	330	293	316	352	325	301
Precipitation inches	13.0	11.5	12.4	13.9	12.8	11.9
Daily hours of sunshine	7	7	7	7	6	6

MARTINIQUE

Official Name: Department of Martinique
(Overseas Department of France)

Capital: Fort–de–France
Languages: French and Creole. English is widely
understood.

This mountainous island is volcanic in origin with some
peaks still active.

Best time to visit: December to May.

December to May: Dry season. Cooler, with average
afternoon temperature of 29°C (84°F). Light rains.
June to November: Wet season. Humid, warm, afternoon
temperature of 31°C (87°F).
Tradewinds from the northeast temper the tropical
climate.
Hurricanes are possible, August to October, but a
touchdown is rare.

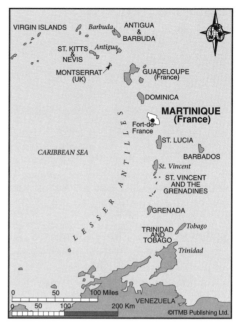

Note: See under Caribbean Islands for general weather information.

Fort–de–France, Martinique: Altitude 4m (13ft)

	Jan	Feb	Mar	Apr	May	Jun
Sunrise ºC(ºF)	21(69)	21(69)	21(69)	22(71)	23(73)	23(73)
Mid–afternoon ºC(ºF)	28(83)	29(84)	29(84)	30(86)	31(87)	30(86)
Days with precipitation	19	15	15	13	18	21
Precipitation mm	119	109	74	99	119	188
Precipitation inches	4.7	4.3	2.9	3.9	4.7	7.4
Daily hours of sunshine	8	8	9	8	8	7

	Jul	Aug	Sep	Oct	Nov	Dec
Sunrise ºC(ºF)	23(74)	23(74)	23(74)	23(73)	22(72)	22(71)
Mid–afternoon ºC(ºF)	30(86)	31(87)	31(87)	31(87)	30(86)	29(84)
Days with precipitation	22	22	29	19	20	19
Precipitation mm	239	262	236	246	201	150
Precipitation inches	9.4	10.3	9.3	9.7	7.9	5.9
Daily hours of sunshine	8	8	8	7	8	8

MAURITANIA

Official Name: Islamic Republic of Mauritania

Capital: Nouakchott
Languages: Arabic, French and African languages

Most of this arid country lies in the Sahara Desert where plant life is negligible. The exception is in the extreme south where the Senegal River flows.

Best time to visit: November to April. (Dry, comparatively cool.)

There are two weather regions, Coastal and Saharan.
1. Coastal. (Includes Nouakchott.)
November to April: Sunny, dry and comparatively less humid and cooler than June to October. Expect 30°C (86°F) in the afternoons. During March and April hot dusty winds may blow throughout the country.
June to October: Sunny, high humidity, hot, 32°C (90°F). Some rain may fall.

2. Saharan region.
December to February: Winter. Temperatures range from 0°C (32°F) at night to 37°C (98°F) in the day. Virtually rainless.
June to September: Summer. Temperatures range 15°C (59°F) at night to 48°C (118°F) in the day. Virtually rainless.

Nouakchott, Mauritania: Altitude 21m (69ft)

	Jan	Feb	Mar	Apr	May	Jun
Sunrise °C(°F)	14(57)	15(59)	17(63)	18(64)	21(69)	23(73)
Mid–afternoon °C(°F)	29(85)	31(87)	32(89)	32(89)	34(93)	33(92)
Days with precipitation	0	0	0	0	0	0
Precipitation mm	0	3	0	0	0	3
Precipitation inches	0	0.1	0	0	0	0.1
Daily hours of sunshine	8	8	10	10	10	10

	Jul	Aug	Sep	Oct	Nov	Dec
Sunrise °C(°F)	23(73)	24(75)	24(75)	22(71)	18(65)	13(56)
Mid–afternoon °C(°F)	32(89)	32(90)	34(93)	33(91)	32(89)	28(83)
Days with precipitation	1	3	3	1	0	0
Precipitation mm	13	104	23	10	3	0
Precipitation inches	0.5	4.1	0.9	0.4	0.1	0
Daily hours of sunshine	9	9	9	9	9	8

MAURITIUS

Official Name: Republic of Mauritius

Capital: Port Louis
Languages: English, French, Creole (based on French, African and Asian languages), Bhojpari, Hindi

This volcanic island with peaks over 750m (2500ft) is encircled by a coastal plain. There are no extremes of temperature; the coast is always warm. Some rain falls year–round. Inland regions are rainier, but cooler.

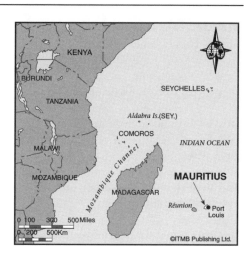

Good season to visit: May to November. (Drier.)

May to November: Drier season. Cooler. Afternoon maximum is 24°C (75°F). June to September is the popular vacation season for overseas visitors.
December to April: Wettest season with a chance of a cyclone. Temperatures are hotter, 29°C (85°F), in the afternoons, and humidity is higher.

Port Louis, Mauritius: Altitude 55m (181ft)

	Jan	Feb	Mar	Apr	May	Jun
Sunrise °C(°F)	23(73)	23(73)	22(72)	21(70)	19(66)	17(63)
Mid–afternoon °C(°F)	30(86)	29(85)	29(84)	28(82)	26(79)	24(76)
Days with precipitation	12	11	11	9	7	6
Precipitation mm	216	198	221	127	97	66
Precipitation inches	8.5	7.8	8.7	5.0	3.8	2.6
Daily hours of sunshine	8	8	7	8	8	7

	Jul	Aug	Sep	Oct	Nov	Dec
Sunrise °C(°F)	17(62)	17(62)	17(62)	18(64)	19(67)	22(71)
Mid–afternoon °C(°F)	24(75)	24(75)	25(77)	27(80)	28(83)	29(85)
Days with precipitation	6	6	4	4	4	7
Precipitation mm	58	64	36	41	46	117
Precipitation inches	2.3	2.5	1.4	1.6	1.8	4.6
Daily hours of sunshine	7	7	8	9	9	9

MEXICO

Official Name: United Mexican States

Capital: Mexico City
Languages: Spanish, Maya, regional indigenous languages

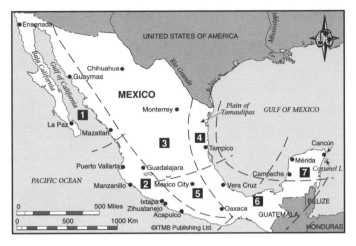

A broad elevated plateau extends through the centre of Mexico, flanked by mountain ranges. These mountains descend abruptly to the eastern and western shorelines, providing narrow, flat and sandy coastal plains. The Baja California peninsula has a mountain range running along it. The Yucatan peninsula is flat and low, averaging only 30m (100ft) above sea level.

The best time to visit in general is October to May.
Mexico has two seasons: Dry (November to May) and rainy (June to September or October).

We have divided the weather into 7 regions. Refer to map for corresponding numbers.
1. Northwest, and peninsula of Baja California. (Includes Guaymas, Cabo San Lucas, La Paz, Mazatlan.)
Good time to visit: Year–round (minimal rain). Best months are the mild months, March to May, and September to November.

March to May: Spring. Sunny, dry. 30ºC (86ºF).
June to August: Summer. Sunny. Days can be very hot, 35ºC (95ºF). Temperatures along the Sea of Cortes can reach 40ºC (104ºF). The Pacific Coast is a few degrees less. Desert areas are cold at night. Light rains may fall. In some years between July and October violent, gusting storms called chubascos bring heavy rains.
September to November: Autumn. Sunny. Days begin to cool from September, 35ºC (95ºF), to 28ºC (82ºF) in November. Rains are light, but the unpredictable chubascos may occur between July and October in some years.
December to February: Winter. Sunny with some cloud. Mild, 24ºC (75ºF). Minimal rain.

Guaymas, northwest Mexico: Altitude 8m (26ft)

	Jan	Feb	Mar	Apr	May	Jun
Sunrise ºC(ºF)	13(55)	14(57)	16(60)	18(64)	21(69)	24(76)
Mid–afternoon ºC(ºF)	23(73)	24(75)	26(79)	29(84)	31(88)	34(93)
Days with precipitation	2	1	2	1	1	1
Precipitation mm	5	0	8	5	5	3
Precipitation inches	0.2	0	0.3	0.2	0.2	0.1
Daily hours of sunshine	7	7	8	9	10	10

Guaymas, northwest Mexico: (continued)

	Jul	Aug	Sep	Oct	Nov	Dec
Sunrise ºC(ºF)	27(80)	27(80)	27(78)	22(72)	18(64)	13(56)
Mid–afternoon ºC(ºF)	34(94)	35(95)	35(95)	31(88)	28(82)	23(74)
Days with precipitation	7	8	6	2	3	5
Precipitation mm	43	91	61	10	15	38
Precipitation inches	1.7	3.6	2.4	0.4	0.6	1.5
Daily hours of sunshine	9	8	8	9	8	6

La Paz, Mexico's Baja California: Altitude 26m (86ft)

	Jan	Feb	Mar	Apr	May	Jun
Sunrise ºC(ºF)	12(54)	13(55)	13(56)	14(58)	16(61)	19(66)
Mid–afternoon ºC(ºF)	23(74)	25(77)	27(81)	30(86)	32(89)	34(94)
Days with precipitation	2	2	0	0	0	0
Precipitation mm	6	27	0	0	0	5
Precipitation inches	0.2	1.1	0	0	0	0.2

	Jul	Aug	Sep	Oct	Nov	Dec
Sunrise ºC(ºF)	23(73)	24(75)	24(75)	20(68)	17(63)	14(58)
Mid–afternoon ºC(ºF)	36(96)	35(95)	34(94)	32(90)	28(83)	25(77)
Days with precipitation	0	2	3	2	2	2
Precipitation mm	9	30	35	16	12	27
Precipitation inches	0.4	1.2	1.4	0.6	0.5	1.1

Mazatlan, northwest Mexico: On the coast

	Jan	Feb	Mar	Apr	May	Jun
Sunrise ºC(ºF)	15(59)	15(59)	15(59)	17(62)	20(68)	24(75)
Mid–afternoon ºC(ºF)	25(77)	25(77)	25(77)	27(80)	29(84)	31(87)
Days with precipitation	1	1	0	0	0	4
Precipitation mm	28	4	2	3	2	26
Precipitation inches	1.1	0.1	0.08	0.1	0.08	1.0
Daily hours of sunshine	7	8	8	9	10	9

	Jul	Aug	Sep	Oct	Nov	Dec
Sunrise ºC(ºF)	25(77)	25(77)	25(77)	23(73)	19(66)	16(60)
Mid–afternoon ºC(ºF)	32(89)	32(89)	32(89)	32(89)	29(85)	26(78)
Days with precipitation	14	15	14	4	2	2
Precipitation mm	212	216	217	95	23	25
Precipitation inches	8.3	8.5	8.5	3.8	0.9	1.0
Daily hours of sunshine	8	8	7	8	8	7

2. Pacific Coast. (Includes Puerto Vallarta, Manzanillo, Ixtapa, Ziahuatenejo, Acapulco.)

Good time to visit: November to early June. The best months are the driest months, March and April.

March to May: Spring. Sunny and warm, 31°C (88°F). Good beach weather. Balmy evenings. Driest months of the year along the Pacific coast are March and April. Rain starts in May and reaches a peak in September.

June to October: Summer. Sunny and very hot. Temperatures can top 33°C (92°F). Rain falls from June to September. September receives the most, with as many as 20 rainy days. Humidity is high. Early mornings are often clear and sunny, then by mid–morning clouds form. By the afternoon a storm has brewed which will bring heavy rains lasting 2 to 3 hours. The rains cool the air, making the evenings "jacket wearing" weather.

November to February: Winter. Lots of sun. Good beach weather. Warm, 30°C (86°F). Balmy evenings. Could be completely rainless but there is often a 2–week period of unsettled weather with a little rain in late December or early January.

Note: Busiest tourist months are December to February. To avoid crowds, visit in October and April or May.

Acapulco, Pacific coast, Mexico: Altitude 3m (10ft)

	Jan	Feb	Mar	Apr	May	Jun
Sunrise °C(°F)	21(71)	21(71)	21(71)	22(72)	23(73)	24(75)
Mid–afternoon °C(°F)	31(87)	31(87)	31(87)	32(89)	32(89)	33(92)
Days with precipitation	1	0	0	0	2	13
Precipitation mm	9	1	2	5	28	271
Precipitation inches	0.4	0.04	0.08	0.2	1.1	10.7
Daily hours of sunshine	9	9	9	9	8	7

	Jul	Aug	Sep	Oct	Nov	Dec
Sunrise °C(°F)	24(75)	24(75)	24(75)	24(75)	23(73)	22(72)
Mid–afternoon °C(°F)	33(91)	33(91)	32(89)	32(89)	32(89)	32(89)
Days with precipitation	13	14	16	9	2	1
Precipitation mm	209	312	341	145	50	14
Precipitation inches	8.2	12.3	13.4	5.7	2.0	0.6
Daily hours of sunshine	7	7	6	8	9	8

Puerto Vallarta, Pacific coast, Mexico:

	Jan	Feb	Mar	Apr	May	Jun
Sunrise °C(°F)	20(68)	19(67)	19(67)	19(67)	21(71)	24(76)
Mid–afternoon °C(°F)	30(86)	30(86)	30(86)	31(87)	32(89)	33(91)
Days with precipitation	2	2	1	0	1	10
Precipitation mm	3	5	0	0	3	119
Precipitation inches	0.1	0.2	0	0	0.1	4.7

	Jul	Aug	Sep	Oct	Nov	Dec
Sunrise °C(°F)	24(76)	24(76)	24(76)	24(76)	23(73)	21(70)
Mid–afternoon °C(°F)	34(93)	34(93)	32(90)	33(91)	32(89)	31(87)
Days with precipitation	11	12	20	8	3	3
Precipitation mm	144	163	367	129	23	45
Precipitation inches	5.7	6.4	14.5	5.1	0.9	1.8

3. Central Plateau. (Includes Chihuahua, Monterrey, Guadalajara.)

Good time to visit: All year round. (However, there is some rain June to October.)

November to May: Warm days. Rain is negligible.
June to October: Hot days. Rainy season.

Guadalajara, Mexican interior: Altitude 1525m (5003ft)

	Jan	Feb	Mar	Apr	May	Jun
Sunrise °C(°F)	7(44)	7(44)	9(49)	12(53)	14(57)	17(62)
Mid–afternoon °C(°F)	24(75)	26(78)	28(82)	30(86)	32(89)	30(86)
Days with precipitation	3	2	1	1	3	14
Precipitation mm	17	5	3	0	17	192
Precipitation inches	0.7	0.2	0.1	0	0.7	7.6

	Jul	Aug	Sep	Oct	Nov	Dec
Sunrise °C(°F)	17(62)	17(62)	16(61)	13(56)	9(48)	7(45)
Mid–afternoon °C(°F)	27(80)	27(80)	27(80)	27(80)	26(79)	24(76)
Days with precipitation	20	17	12	6	2	2
Precipitation mm	253	200	177	53	20	20
Precipitation inches	10.0	7.9	7.0	2.1	0.8	0.8

Monterrey, Mexico: Altitude 528m (1732ft)

	Jan	Feb	Mar	Apr	May	Jun
Sunrise °C(°F)	9(48)	11(52)	14(57)	17(62)	20(68)	22(71)
Mid–afternoon °C(°F)	20(68)	22(72)	24(76)	29(84)	31(87)	33(91)
Days with precipitation	6	5	7	7	9	8
Precipitation mm	15	18	20	33	33	76
Precipitation inches	0.6	0.7	0.8	1.3	1.3	3.0
Daily hours of sunshine	5	5	6	5	6	8

	Jul	Aug	Sep	Oct	Nov	Dec
Sunrise °C(°F)	22(71)	22(71)	21(70)	18(64)	13(55)	10(50)
Mid–afternoon °C(°F)	32(90)	33(92)	30(86)	27(80)	22(71)	18(65)
Days with precipitation	8	7	10	9	8	6
Precipitation mm	58	61	132	76	38	20
Precipitation inches	2.3	2.4	5.2	3.0	1.5	0.8
Daily hours of sunshine	7	6	6	6	5	4

4. Eastern coast. (Includes Tampico, and coastal plain of Tamaulipas.)
Good time to visit: November to June.

November to June: Warm days, 28°C (83°F). Dry season; only one or two rainy days per month.
July to October: Hot days, 32°C (89°F). Rainy season with 12 rainy days per month.

Note: The area south of Tampico is wetter and is often affected by nortes, the brisk northerly winds that bring a cool drizzle, particularly from September to March.

5. Inland triangle. (Includes Mexico City and Oaxaca.)
Because of the high elevation of Mexico City and Oaxaca, they experience mild temperatures. Mexico City is 2309m (7575ft); Oaxaca is 1546m (5070ft).
Good time to visit: November to April.
Best months are March and April, and October to December.
January and February are dry, but cool.

March to May: Sunny. Mild, 25°C (77°F). Rain begins in April and continues through to September.
June to August: Summer. Warm, 23°C (73°F). Rain falls daily in Mexico City in mid–summer, July and August, usually as 2–hour showers in the afternoons. July and August are the wettest months.
September: Warm and wet with 23 rainy days per month.
October to November: Mild, 20°C (68°F) but reasonably dry.
December to February: Winter. Mild, 19°C (66°F). At the high elevations of Mexico City and Oaxaca there are cool to cold spells; the coolest month is January. Cool winds blow in February and March.

Mexico City, inland Mexico: Altitude 2309m (7575ft)

	Jan	Feb	Mar	Apr	May	Jun
Sunrise °C(°F)	7(44)	7(44)	10(50)	11(51)	12(53)	13(55)
Mid–afternoon °C(°F)	21(69)	23(73)	25(77)	27(80)	27(80)	25(77)
Days with precipitation	4	5	9	14	17	22
Precipitation mm	9	9	13	27	58	157
Precipitation inches	0.4	0.4	0.5	1.1	2.3	6.2
Daily hours of sunshine	7	8	7	7	6	5

	Jul	Aug	Sep	Oct	Nov	Dec
Sunrise °C(°F)	12(53)	12(53)	12(53)	10(50)	8(46)	7(44)
Mid–afternoon °C(°F)	23(73)	23(73)	23(73)	23(73)	22(72)	21(69)
Days with precipitation	27	26	23	13	5	4
Precipitation mm	183	173	144	61	6	8
Precipitation inches	7.2	6.8	5.7	2.4	0.2	0.3
Daily hours of sunshine	5	5	5	6	7	6

6. States of Vera Cruz, Tabasco and Chiapas.
Good time to visit: December to May.

December to May: Warm days. December to March, 27°C (80°F); April and May, 31°C (88°F). Rain falls year–round, but is less rainy December to May. December has 10 rainy days; January to May have 5 rainy days per month.
June to October: Hot with afternoons averaging 32°C (89°F). Rainy with 15 days of rain per month.

7. Yucatan peninsula. (Includes Cancun, Cozumel, Merida and Campeche.)
Best time: November to May.

November to May: Mostly dry, sunny and mild, 27°C (81°F). Yucatan is affected by nortes, cold winds from the north that bring cool drizzle. Nights can be cold. December to April is an ideal time to visit.

June to October: Rainy season. High humidity. Hot, 29°C (84°F). Some days are cloudy but expect six hours of sunshine daily. Jungle in the interior is extremely hot and humid but the coasts of the Gulf of Mexico and the Caribbean are comfortably cool because of the tradewinds. Hurricanes can occur September to November. The risk is higher in September and October.

Cancun, Caribbean coast, Mexico: Altitude 5m (16ft)

	Jan	Feb	Mar	Apr	May	Jun
Sunrise ºC(ºF)	19(67)	20(68)	21(71)	23(73)	25(77)	26(78)
Mid–afternoon ºC(ºF)	27(81)	28(82)	29(84)	29(84)	31(88)	32(89)
Days with precipitation	5	4	3	2	4	6
Precipitation mm	2	32	25	25	63	88
Precipitation inches	0.8	1.3	1.0	1.0	2.5	3.5

	Jul	Aug	Sep	Oct ·	Nov	Dec
Sunrise ºC(ºF)	26(78)	25(77)	24(76)	23(74)	22(72)	21(69)
Mid–afternoon ºC(ºF)	32(90)	32(90)	32(90)	31(87)	29(84)	28(82)
Days with precipitation	4	4	7	8	5	6
Precipitation mm	63	70	114	177	177	32
Precipitation inches	2.5	2.8	4.5	7.0	7.0	1.3

Cozumel, Caribbean coast, Mexico: Altitude 5m (15ft)

	Jan	Feb	Mar	Apr	May	Jun
Sunrise ºC(ºF)	20(68)	20(68)	20(68)	22(72)	23(73)	23(73)
Mid–afternoon ºC(ºF)	28(82)	29(84)	29(84)	31(87)	30(86)	31(87)
Days with precipitation	10	14	5	10	13	19
Precipitation mm	95	121	50	172	207	378
Precipitation inches	3.8	4.8	2.0	6.8	8.2	14.9

	Jul	Aug	Sep	Oct	Nov	Dec
Sunrise ºC(ºF)	23(73)	23(73)	23(73)	23(73)	21(71)	20(68)
Mid–afternoon ºC(ºF)	31(87)	32(89)	36(97)	36(97)	34(93)	28(82)
Days with precipitation	11	10	20	6	5	5
Precipitation mm	144	121	360	93	88	63
Precipitation inches	5.7	4.8	14.2	3.7	3.5	2.5

Merida, northern Yucatan, Mexico: Altitude 22m (72ft)

	Jan	Feb	Mar	Apr	May	Jun
Sunrise ºC(ºF)	18(64)	18(64)	20(68)	21(70)	23(73)	23(73)
Mid-afternoon ºC(ºF)	29(84)	30(86)	33(91)	35(95)	36(96)	35(95)
Days with precipitation	8	8	8	8	10	18
Precipitation mm	26	26	24	23	63	144
Precipitation inches	1.1	1.2	0.9	0.9	2.5	5.7
Daily hours of sunshine	7	7	8	8	9	8

	Jul	Aug	Sep	Oct	Nov	Dec
Sunrise ºC(ºF)	23(73)	23(73)	23(73)	21(69)	19(66)	18(64)
Mid-afternoon ºC(ºF)	34(93)	34(93)	33(91)	32(89)	30(86)	30(86)
Days with precipitation	21	21	21	17	11	8
Precipitation mm	162	163	180	94	42	34
Precipitation inches	6.4	6.4	7.1	3.7	1.6	1.3
Daily hours of sunshine	8	8	7	7	7	6

Events throughout Mexico:
1. **Semana Santa.** Easter week in March or April (the date varies) is Mexico's biggest holiday season. Passion plays, music and dance are held in the town squares.
2. **Pre–Lenten Carnival** in February or March (the date varies) includes fireworks, music and dance in towns, notably Acapulco, Ensenada, La Paz, Mazatlan, Merida and Vera Cruz.

MICRONESIA

Official Name: Federated States of Micronesia
Consists of states of Chuuk (formerly Truk), Pohnpei (formerly Ponape), Kosrae and Yap.

Capital: Palikir (on Pohnpei Island)
Languages: English and indigenous languages of each of the island states: Chuukese, Pohnpeian, Yapese, Kosraean.

Chuuk, Pohnpei and Kosrae are high volcanic islands. Yap is a raised section of the Asian continental shelf.

Weather in general: Temperatures remain fairly steady year–round; morning temperatures average 24°C (75°F) and afternoon temperatures, 31°C (88°F). The drier, cooler months of January to March are a degree or two cooler. From December to April the northeast tradewinds blow. There are cool breezes and less rain than other months. From July to September warm prevailing winds blow from the southeast, bringing humidity and heavier rainfalls. Cyclones can occur during the rainy season, April to November, but they are extremely rare because the islands lie outside the cyclone zone.

Best time to visit: January to March. (Drier, cooler but the islands are a year–round destination.) Following are each island's wet and dry seasons.

- **Chuuk** (pronounced Chuke)
  January to March: Drier and cooler.
  April to December: Wet season.
- **Pohnpei** (pronounced Pon–pay)
  January to March: Drier and cooler.
  April to December: Wet season. April and May are the wettest.
- **Kosrae** (pronounced Ko–shrye)
  January to March: Drier.
  April to June: Wet.
  July to October: Drier.
  November to December: Wet.
- **Yap**
  February to April: Drier and cooler.
  May to January: Wet.

Pohnpei, Micronesia: Altitude 46m (151ft)

	Jan	Feb	Mar	Apr	May	Jun
Sunrise ºC(ºF)	24(75)	24(75)	24(75)	24(75)	24(75)	23(73)
Mid–afternoon ºC(ºF)	30(86)	30(86)	31(88)	31(88)	31(88)	31(88)
Days with precipitation	18	17	19	22	24	25
Precipitation mm	307	274	344	418	486	435
Precipitation inches	12.1	10.8	13.6	16.5	19.1	17.1
Daily hours of sunshine	5	5	6	5	5	5

	Jul	Aug	Sep	Oct	Nov	Dec
Sunrise ºC(ºF)	23(74)	23(74)	23(74)	23(74)	23(74)	24(75)
Mid–afternoon ºC(ºF)	31(87)	31(87)	31(87)	31(87)	31(87)	31(87)
Days with precipitation	24	23	21	23	22	22
Precipitation mm	467	420	408	424	400	387
Precipitation inches	18.4	16.5	16.1	16.7	15.7	15.2
Daily hours of sunshine	5	6	6	5	5	4

MOLDOVA

Official Name: Republic of Moldova

Capital: Chisinau
Languages: Romanian, Moldovan, Russian

Moldova is largely a hilly plain.

Best time: May to September. (April and October are also mild and pleasant for travel.)

May to September: Temperatures exceed 20°C (68°F) most days. The hottest months are July and August. Rain falls year–round; the wettest months in Chisinau are June and July.

October to April: Both October and April are mild, about 16°C (60°F). Winter is December to March. January and February stay below freezing point in the capital. Cold winds from Russia blow during winter.

Chisinau, Moldova: Altitude 173m (567ft)

	Jan	Feb	Mar	Apr	May	Jun
Sunrise ºC(ºF)	–8(18)	–5(23)	–1(30)	5(41)	11(51)	14(57)
Mid–afternoon ºC(ºF)	–1(30)	–1(30)	6(42)	16(60)	23(73)	26(78)
Days with precipitation	6	7	6	7	8	9
Precipitation mm	40	38	35	42	51	75
Precipitation inches	1.6	1.5	1.4	1.6	2.0	3.0
Daily hours of sunshine	2	3	4	6	8	9

	Jul	Aug	Sep	Oct	Nov	Dec
Sunrise ºC(ºF)	16(60)	15(59)	11(51)	7(44)	3(37)	–4(25)
Mid–afternoon ºC(ºF)	27(80)	27(80)	23(73)	17(62)	10(50)	2(35)
Days with precipitation	8	6	5	4	6	7
Precipitation mm	69	45	48	27	39	38
Precipitation inches	2.7	1.8	1.9	1.1	1.5	1.5
Daily hours of sunshine	10	10	8	6	2	2

MONACO
Official Name: Principality of Monaco

Capital: Monaco–ville
Languages: French, English, Italian

The principality is on a rocky promontory facing the
Mediterranean Sea and is bordered by France.

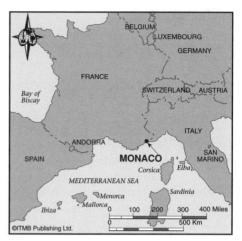

Best time: Late April to early October.

March to May: Spring. Mild to warm. Occasional rain.
June to August: Summer. Dry, hot. Rain is negligible but
there could be sudden thunderstorms.
September to November: Autumn. Warm with afternoon
temperatures decreasing in November. Expect daytime rainstorms, especially in October and
November.
December to February: Winter. Mild and wet, with daytime rainstorms, particularly in December.

Monte Carlo, Monaco: Altitude 55m (180ft)

	Jan	Feb	Mar	Apr	May	Jun
Sunrise ºC(ºF)	8(47)	8(47)	10(50)	12(54)	15(59)	19(66)
Mid–afternoon ºC(ºF)	12(54)	13(55)	14(57)	16(61)	19(66)	23(73)
Days with precipitation	5	5	7	5	5	4
Precipitation mm	61	58	71	65	64	33
Precipitation inches	2.4	2.3	2.8	2.6	2.5	1.3
Daily hours of sunshine	5	5	5	6	7	8

	Jul	Aug	Sep	Oct	Nov	Dec
Sunrise ºC(ºF)	22(71)	22(71)	20(67)	16(61)	12(54)	10(49)
Mid–afternoon ºC(ºF)	26(78)	26(78)	24(74)	20(68)	16(61)	14(56)
Days with precipitation	1	2	4	7	7	6
Precipitation mm	21	22	66	113	123	99
Precipitation inches	0.8	0.9	2.6	4.5	4.8	3.9
Daily hours of sunshine	9	9	7	6	5	4

MONGOLIA
Official Name: Mongolian People's Republic

Capital: Ulaanbaatar (also spelled Ulan Bator)
Languages: Khalkha Mongol, Russian, Chinese, Turkic

Two–thirds of the country consists of steppes and mountains; the remaining one–third is the Gobi Desert.

Best time to visit in general: Mid–June to mid–August.
May and September are also good. The best time for the Gobi Desert is September and October (cooler days).

Mid–June to mid–August: Short summer. Sunny.
Temperatures on the steppes are mild, 7°C (45°F), at sunrise, and 22°C (72°F) in the afternoon. Rainfall is low everywhere; it falls mainly in July and August. Annual rainfall in the mountains totals 500mm (20in). On the steppes it is 200mm (8in), and in the desert 100mm (4in) or less.
September: Frosts begin.
October to May: Long winter. Dry and cold, often with blue, sunny skies. Cold winds from the Arctic reduce temperatures on the steppes to below freezing, to –40°C (–40°F). Occasional light snow is possible on the steppes. Snow is heavier in the mountains.
Humidity: Because of Mongolia's high altitude and its long distance from oceans, humidity is low year–round.

Cultural event: The **Naadam**, a festival of traditional sports of horse riding, wrestling and archery is held in Ulaanbaatar annually, July 7 to 11.

Ulaanbaatar (Ulan Bator), Mongolia: Altitude 1306m (4285ft)

	Jan	Feb	Mar	Apr	May	Jun
Sunrise °C(°F)	–27(–16)	–24(–12)	–15(5)	–6(21)	3(37)	8(46)
Mid–afternoon °C(°F)	–15(5)	–11(13)	–2(29)	8(46)	17(62)	22(72)
Days with precipitation	0	1	1	2	3	10
Precipitation mm	1	2	3	8	13	42
Precipitation inches	0.04	0.08	0.1	0.3	0.5	1.6
Daily hours of sunshine	6	7	9	9	10	9

	Jul	Aug	Sep	Oct	Nov	Dec
Sunrise °C(°F)	11(51)	9(48)	2(35)	–6(21)	–16(3)	–24(–11)
Mid–afternoon °C(°F)	23(73)	22(72)	16(60)	7(44)	–4(25)	–14(7)
Days with precipitation	11	14	5	2	1	2
Precipitation mm	58	52	26	6	3	3
Precipitation inches	2.3	2.0	1.0	0.2	0.1	0.1
Daily hours of sunshine	8	8	8	7	6	5

MONTSERRAT

Official Name: Montserrat
(Dependent Territory of the United Kingdom)

Capital: Plymouth (subject to change)
Language: English

The island is mountainous with the highest point being the volcanic peak, Soufrière, 915m (3002ft).

Best time to visit: January to May. (However, weather is generally pleasant all year with low to medium humidity.)

January to April: Winter, reasonably dry.
May to December: Wet. Higher humidity.
Hurricane season: June to October. A touchdown is rare.

Note: See under Caribbean Islands for general Caribbean weather.

Plymouth, Montserrat: Altitude 40m (130ft)

	Jan	Feb	Mar	Apr	May	Jun
Sunrise ºC(ºF)	21(70)	21(70)	21(70)	22(72)	23(74)	24(75)
Mid–afternoon ºC(ºF)	28(82)	28(82)	29(84)	30(86)	31(87)	31(87)
Days with precipitation	12	9	9	8	10	13
Precipitation mm	122	86	112	89	97	112
Precipitation inches	4.8	3.4	4.4	3.5	3.8	4.4
Daily hours of sunshine	7	7	7	8	8	7

	Jul	Aug	Sep	Oct	Nov	Dec
Sunrise ºC(ºF)	24(75)	24(75)	23(73)	23(73)	23(73)	22(72)
Mid–afternoon ºC(ºF)	31(87)	31(87)	32(89)	31(87)	29(84)	28(82)
Days with precipitation	14	16	13	14	16	13
Precipitation mm	155	183	168	196	180	140
Precipitation inches	6.1	7.2	6.6	7.7	7.1	5.5
Daily hours of sunshine	8	8	7	8	7	7

MOROCCO

Official Name: Kingdom of Morocco

Capital: Rabat
Languages: Arabic is official, Berber, French

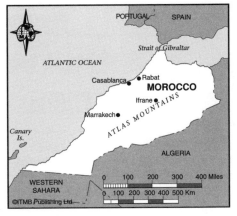

The Rif Mountains run parallel to the Mediterranean coast while the Atlas Mountains traverse the country in a northeast–southwest direction. A wide plain extends along the Atlantic Ocean and a narrow plain follows the Mediterranean coastline. South of the Atlas Mountains are valleys and plains that merge with the Sahara Desert in the southeast.

Best time: April to May, and September to October.
Many people prefer April to May, being springtime when flowers and fruits are blossoming.

April to May: Spring. Mild to warm. The waters along the Atlantic and Mediterranean coasts are warm enough for swimming. Light rains fall on the northern coasts and in the mountains. Occasionally, winds blow off the mountains, bringing cool days. Rainfall decreases as you travel from north to south.
June to August: Summer. Dry. Days have low humidity and are pleasantly hot, about 28°C (82°F), along the Mediterranean and Atlantic coasts. Along the Atlantic coast the cool Canaries current keeps the coastal temperature pleasant but occasionally this cool offshore water produces fog and cloud when it combines with warm air from the inland regions. Inland desert regions are extremely hot, but the mountains can be pleasant. Daytime temperatures in the coastal lowlands can be raised beyond 40°C (104°F) when hot winds, the sirocco, or chergui, blow from the Sahara Desert.
September to October: Autumn. Light rains fall throughout the country and temperatures are a pleasant 27 to 32°C (80 to 90°F).
November: Transitional month with warm temperatures, 21°C (70°F), and light rain.
December to February: Winter. Chilly and damp in the north, e.g. Tangiers. Sunny and mild, 18°C (64°F), along the coastal lowlands, including Agadir in the south. Marrakech, in the foothills of the Atlas Mountains, can be a pleasant 20°C (68°F) in the daytime but nights are cold. Snow falls in the mountains where temperatures are sub–zero. Snow does not fall along the Atlantic coast. Winds blowing off the central mountain ranges can cause chilly days. Snow skiing is possible at Ifrane, Oukaimeden and in the High Atlas near Marrakech.
March: Transitional month with warm temperatures, 21°C (70°F), and light rain.

Cultural event:
1. Camel festival at Goulimine. Usually July. Thousands of Tuaregs gather to buy and sell camels and other products.
2. Rose Festival. Parade of floats. Traditional music. Folk–dancing competitions between Berber clans. At El Kelāa, April or May.

Casablanca, coastal Morocco: Altitude 62m (203ft)

	Jan	Feb	Mar	Apr	May	Jun
Sunrise °C(°F)	8(46)	9(48)	10(50)	12(53)	14(57)	17(62)
Mid–afternoon °C(°F)	17(62)	18(64)	18(64)	20(68)	21(69)	23(73)
Days with precipitation	9	8	8	7	5	1
Precipitation mm	62	59	51	40	19	6
Precipitation inches	2.4	2.3	2.0	1.6	0.7	0.2
Daily hours of sunshine	6	7	8	9	9	10

	Jul	Aug	Sep	Oct	Nov	Dec
Sunrise °C(°F)	19(66)	20(68)	18(64)	15(59)	12(53)	9(48)
Mid–afternoon °C(°F)	25(77)	26(78)	25(77)	23(73)	20(68)	18(64)
Days with precipitation	0	0	1	4	8	9
Precipitation mm	1	0	5	31	74	78
Precipitation inches	0.04	0	0.2	1.2	2.9	3.1
Daily hours of sunshine	10	9	8	7	6	6

Marrakech, inland Morocco: Altitude 466m (1529ft)

	Jan	Feb	Mar	Apr	May	Jun
Sunrise °C(°F)	6(42)	8(46)	9(48)	11(51)	14(57)	16(60)
Mid–afternoon °C(°F)	18(64)	20(68)	22(72)	24(75)	28(82)	31(87)
Days with precipitation	6	6	6	6	2	1
Precipitation mm	32	38	38	39	24	5
Precipitation inches	1.3	1.5	1.5	1.5	0.9	0.2
Daily hours of sunshine	7	7	8	8	9	10

	Jul	Aug	Sep	Oct	Nov	Dec
Sunrise °C(°F)	20(68)	20(68)	18(64)	15(59)	10(50)	7(44)
Mid–afternoon °C(°F)	37(98)	37(98)	33(92)	28(83)	22(72)	19(67)
Days with precipitation	0	0	1	4	4	6
Precipitation mm	1	3	6	24	41	31
Precipitation inches	0.04	0.1	0.2	0.9	1.6	1.2
Daily hours of sunshine	11	10	9	8	7	7

MOZAMBIQUE

Official Name: People's Republic of Mozambique

Capital: Maputo (pronounced Ma–poo–too)
Languages: Portuguese, African languages

Along the coast are lowlands. The land rises from the coast to scattered plateaus with small mountain ranges which are found mainly in the west and northwest.

Best time to visit: May and June. (April, July, August and September are also good months.)

April to September: Dry, cooler season, 24 to 27°C (75 to 80°F) in the afternoons. Sunny and pleasantly warm on the coast.

October to April: Wet, humid, hot, 30°C (86°F) in the afternoons. Most rain falls January to March. Cyclones are possible. Flooding can result from the strong winds and heavy rain.

Maputo, Mozambique: Altitude 59m (194ft)

	Jan	Feb	Mar	Apr	May	Jun
Sunrise °C(°F)	22(71)	22(71)	21(69)	19(66)	16(60)	13(55)
Mid–afternoon °C(°F)	30(86)	31(87)	29(85)	28(83)	27(80)	25(77)
Days with precipitation	9	8	9	5	3	2
Precipitation mm	130	125	125	53	28	20
Precipitation inches	5.1	4.9	4.9	2.1	1.1	0.8
Daily hours of sunshine	8	8	8	8	8	8

	Jul	Aug	Sep	Oct	Nov	Dec
Sunrise °C(°F)	13(55)	14(57)	16(61)	18(64)	19(67)	21(69)
Mid–afternoon °C(°F)	24(76)	26(78)	27(80)	28(82)	28(82)	29(85)
Days with precipitation	2	2	3	5	7	9
Precipitation mm	13	13	28	48	81	97
Precipitation inches	0.5	0.5	1.1	1.9	3.2	3.8
Daily hours of sunshine	8	8	8	7	7	7

MYANMAR

Official Name: Union of Myanmar (Was formerly Union of Burma)

Capital: Yangon (formerly Rangoon)
Languages: Myanmar (Burmese), minority ethnic languages

The north, northwest and east are mountainous. Also in the east is the vast Shan plateau at an elevation of 900m (3000ft). Central Myanmar has a narrow, elongated plain watered by the Ayeyarwadi (formerly Irrawaddy) and Sittang Rivers which flow from north to south.

Best months: November to February. (Dry, "cool"). March and April are also good. (Dry but hotter.)

November to April: Dry over the whole country. The dry northeast monsoon winds from China's Yunnan plateau bring a long, dry period. Temperatures vary little in this season, or even throughout the year, but November to the end of February is cooler when days average 21 to 28°C (70 to 82°F). This is preferable to March and April when days can average 32°C (90°F). Humidity is high.
May to October: Rainy, cloudy. July is usually the rainiest. Most rain falls in the afternoons. The southwest monsoon brings rain from the Bay of Bengal. Central Myanmar, where Mandalay and Bagan (Pagan) are located, is shielded by mountain ranges and receives only one–third of Yangon's rainfall. Mandalay receives 915mm (36in) annually; Yangon receives 2617mm (103in).

Yangon (formerly Rangoon), Myanmar: Altitude 15m (49ft)

	Jan	Feb	Mar	Apr	May	Jun
Sunrise °C(°F)	18(64)	19(66)	22(72)	24(75)	25(77)	24(75)
Mid–afternoon °C(°F)	32(89)	35(95)	36(96)	37(98)	33(91)	30(86)
Days with precipitation	0	0	1	2	14	23
Precipitation mm	5	2	7	15	303	547
Precipitation inches	0.2	0.08	0.3	0.6	11.9	21.5
Daily hours of sunshine	10	10	10	10	7	4

	Jul	Aug	Sep	Oct	Nov	Dec
Sunrise °C(°F)	24(75)	24(75)	24(75)	24(75)	22(72)	19(66)
Mid–afternoon °C(°F)	30(86)	30(86)	30(86)	32(89)	32(89)	32(89)
Days with precipitation	25	26	20	10	3	1
Precipitation mm	559	602	368	206	60	7
Precipitation inches	22.0	23.7	14.5	8.1	2.4	0.3
Daily hours of sunshine	3	3	5	6	6	8

Mandalay, central Myanmar: Altitude 77m (252ft)

	Jan	Feb	Mar	Apr	May	Jun
Sunrise ºC(ºF)	13(55)	15(59)	20(68)	24(75)	26(78)	26(78)
Mid–afternoon ºC(ºF)	29(84)	32(89)	36(96)	38(100)	37(98)	34(93)
Days with precipitation	0	0	0	2	8	7
Precipitation mm	4	2	1	38	144	129
Precipitation inches	0.1	0.08	0.04	1.5	5.7	5.1
Daily hours of sunshine	9	9	9	9	8	6

	Jul	Aug	Sep	Oct	Nov	Dec
Sunrise ºC(ºF)	25(77)	25(77)	25(77)	23(73)	20(68)	15(59)
Mid–afternoon ºC(ºF)	34(93)	33(91)	33(91)	32(89)	30(86)	28(82)
Days with precipitation	7	8	9	8	3	1
Precipitation mm	78	133	156	185	38	7
Precipitation inches	3.1	5.2	6.1	7.3	1.5	0.3
Daily hours of sunshine	5	4	6	7	8	9

NAMIBIA

Official Name: Republic of Namibia
Capital: Windhoek
Languages: Afrikaans, English, German, African languages

Along the barren coast is the Namib Desert with a width of 100 to 160km (60 to 100 miles). Inland is a semi–desert plateau at an elevation of 1000 to 1200m (3000 to 4000ft) above sea level.

Best time in general: April to October.

May to September: Sunny, clear skies. Pleasantly warm with afternoon temperatures reaching 25°C (77°F). Nights are cold, often with below freezing temperatures.

October to April: Summer. From October to December the "little rains" fall in northeastern Namibia, then from December to March the main rains fall, coming as short showers and thunderstorms. The desert of coastal Namibia has little rain, and in some years none. December to March is the hottest season on the coast and inland. Afternoon temperatures can reach an unpleasant 38°C (100°F).

Fog along the coast is frequent. It forms when the hot air that blows out of the desert meets the cold air above the cold Benguela current that sweeps north from the south polar regions. The fog can reduce sunshine as far as 60km inland (about 35 miles).

Natural attraction: Etosha National Park, a wildlife habitat consisting of a vast salt pan surrounded by grassland, woodland and scrub. The **best time** for game viewing is from **July to late October**, in the dry season, when animals congregate at waterholes near the roads.

Rains fall from November to March or April. During and after the rainy season the vegetation grows lush, tempting the animals away from the roadside waterholes into the bush. November to June is not a premium time to spot game.

Windhoek, Namibia: Altitude 1728m (5669ft)

	Jan	Feb	Mar	Apr	May	Jun
Sunrise ºC(ºF)	17(63)	16(61)	15(59)	13(55)	9(48)	7(44)
Mid–afternoon ºC(ºF)	29(85)	28(83)	27(80)	25(77)	22(72)	20(68)
Days with precipitation	8	8	8	4	1	0
Precipitation mm	76	74	79	41	8	0
Precipitation inches	3.0	2.9	3.1	1.6	0.3	0
Daily hours of sunshine	9	9	8	9	10	10

	Jul	Aug	Sep	Oct	Nov	Dec
Sunrise ºC(ºF)	6(43)	8(47)	12(53)	15(59)	15(59)	17(62)
Mid–afternoon ºC(ºF)	20(68)	23(73)	25(77)	29(84)	29(84)	30(86)
Days with precipitation	0	0	0	2	3	6
Precipitation mm	0	0	3	10	23	48
Precipitation inches	0	0	0.1	0.4	0.9	1.9
Daily hours of sunshine	10	11	10	10	10	10

NAURU

Official Name: Republic of Nauru
Capital: Yaren District (no capital city)
Languages: Nauruan, English

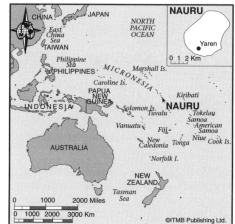

This small island has a fertile coastal strip around its 20km (12 miles) circumference. The interior consists of a plateau of phosphate of lime that rises to 30m (100ft).

Best time to visit: March to November.

March to November: Season of less rain. Sunny, hot, humid. Average afternoon temperature, 32ºC (90ºF).
December to March: Wet season. Hot, humid. Rain, when it occurs, usually comes late afternoon, and humidity increases. Afternoon temperature, 31ºC (88ºF).
Rain: In some years there is no rain. In other years it is torrential, exceeding the average by as much as ten times. The following table shows average rainfall over past years, and is not indicative of any particular year.

Yaren District, Nauru: Altitude 27m (87ft)

	Jan	Feb	Mar	Apr	May	Jun
Sunrise ºC(ºF)	23(74)	24(75)	24(75)	24(75)	23(74)	23(74)
Mid–afternoon ºC(ºF)	31(87)	31(87)	32(89)	32(89)	32(89)	32(89)
Days with precipitation	15	11	9	6	5	8
Precipitation mm	315	206	180	94	53	99
Precipitation inches	12.4	8.1	7.1	3.7	2.1	3.9
Daily hours of sunshine	6	5	5	6	7	6

Yaren District, Nauru: (continued)

	Jul	Aug	Sep	Oct	Nov	Dec
Sunrise °C(°F)	23(74)	23(74)	23(74)	23(74)	23(74)	23(74)
Mid–afternoon °C(°F)	32(89)	32(89)	32(89)	32(89)	32(89)	32(89)
Days with precipitation	11	10	6	5	7	13
Precipitation mm	155	193	122	99	152	239
Precipitation inches	6.1	7.6	4.8	3.9	6.0	9.4
Daily hours of sunshine	6	5	7	6	6	6

NEPAL

Official Name: Kingdom of Nepal

Capital: Kathmandu
Languages: Nepali, 20 other languages

Nepal is a kingdom wedged between China and India. The three geographical areas favoured by tourists are the oval–shaped Kathmandu Valley, the Himalaya mountains for trekking, and the Terai plains for wildlife viewing.

Best time to visit in general: October to May.

The three geographical areas are discussed separately, below.

1. Kathmandu Valley.
Best months are October to May, but pleasant weather is experienced most of the year.

October to March: Cool mornings with mist, then sunny and warm until mid–afternoon. Overnight temperatures can drop to freezing point. Frosts occur but snow is rare.
April to May: Temperatures gradually increase to 30°C (86°F). Rainstorms are common, often in the afternoons.
Mid–June to September: Monsoon rains fall mainly at night but they are not as heavy as the monsoon rains experienced on the Terai plains in the south.

Cultural events:
1. Bisket Jatra (New Year festival) in Bhaktapur, near Kathmandu. Always in mid–April. Devotees pull a chariot with images of gods through the streets.
2. Indra Jatra in Kathmandu, September to October. An 8–day festival with dancers and chariots during which The Living Goddess is brought from her palace.
3. Sweta (White) Machhendranath and
4. Rato (Red) Machhendranath. These two festivals include the pulling of a large chariot or wagon through the streets which contains an image of the god of rain, a god worshipped by both Buddhists and Hindus. The White is held in Kathmandu in March or April; the Red is held in Patan, near Kathmandu, in April or May.

Kathmandu, Nepal: Altitude 1338m (4388ft)

	Jan	Feb	Mar	Apr	May	Jun
Sunrise ºC(ºF)	2(35)	4(39)	7(45)	12(53)	16(61)	19(67)
Mid–afternoon ºC(ºF)	18(65)	19(67)	25(77)	28(83)	30(86)	29(85)
Days with precipitation	1	5	2	6	10	15
Precipitation mm	15	41	23	58	122	246
Precipitation inches	0.6	1.6	0.9	2.3	4.8	9.7
Daily hours of sunshine	6	6	8	6	5	2

	Jul	Aug	Sep	Oct	Nov	Dec
Sunrise ºC(ºF)	20(68)	20(68)	19(66)	13(56)	7(45)	3(37)
Mid–afternoon ºC(ºF)	29(84)	28(83)	28(83)	27(80)	23(74)	19(67)
Days with precipitation	21	20	12	4	1	0
Precipitation mm	373	345	155	38	8	3
Precipitation inches	14.7	13.6	6.1	1.5	0.3	0.1
Daily hours of sunshine	2	3	5	10	10	9

2. The Himalayas.

Trekking is popular, particularly October to May, because of clear days.

October and November: Clear skies, good mountain views. These are the peak months for trekking, just after the monsoons which have greened the land.
December and January: Coldest months. Good for lowland and middle valley treks such as Ghandrung and Ghorapani treks out of Pokhara; and the lower Everest region. High passes can be snowbound but if properly prepared it is still a good period for trekking.
February and March: Spring in Nepal, warmer weather. Rhododendrons are in bloom. Langtang valley (north of Kathmandu) and Kali Gandaki valley (in Annapurna region) are good trekking areas at this time.
April and May: The high passes open. Treks around Annapurna and to the Everest Base Camp are ideal although mountain views may not be as clear as in October, November and December.
June to September: Monsoon rains make it difficult if not impossible for good trekking. Leeches can attach themselves to you. Flowers are colourful at this time. This season is reserved for keen, accomplished trekkers.

3. The Terai. (Plains in southern Nepal.)

Wildlife viewing by elephant safari to see rhinos, crocodiles, tigers and bird life are possible in the Chitwan National Park in the Terai. The altitude varies from 200 to 700 metres (650 to 2300ft) above sea level.
Best time is October to February. Cool, dry season. March is also a good month.

October to February: Cool mornings, dry, humid, warm days, 26ºC (78ºF).
March: Transitional month. In Chitwan National Park game viewing is still reasonably good because the grass is low. It has been cut by local villagers who have the right to cut grass in February for roof thatch.
April: Occasional rainstorms begin.
May to August: Temperatures rise to the 30sºC (90sºF). Monsoon rains prevail, making roads impassable. In Chitwan National Park most wildlife lodges are closed.
September: Some wildlife lodges reopen, but muddy ground makes transportation difficult.

Chitwan National Park, Nepal:

	Jan	Feb	Mar	Apr	May	Jun
Sunrise ºC(ºF)	7(44)	8(46)	12(53)	18(64)	20(68)	23(73)
Mid–afternoon ºC(ºF)	24(75)	26(78)	33(91)	35(95)	35(95)	35(95)

	Jul	Aug	Sep	Oct	Nov	Dec
Sunrise ºC(ºF)	24(76)	24(75)	22(72)	18(64)	12(53)	8(46)
Mid–afternoon ºC(ºF)	33(92)	33(91)	32(89)	31(87)	29(84)	24(75)

Other recreational activities: Rafting and kayaking.
**Best time for rafting and kayaking: First choice, mid–October to beginning of December.
Second choice, March to beginning of June.**

Mid–October to early December: Weather is pleasant and river levels allow for challenging rapids.
December to February: Water is cold.
March to early June: This is also a popular time on the rivers although, with lower water levels
before the rainy season, the rapids are not as challenging as in October and November. Rivers,
however, begin rising in May as a result of melting snow and May rains.
June to August: Monsoon rains cause rivers to rise, and possibly to flood, making them dangerous.

NETHERLANDS
Official Name: Kingdom of the Netherlands
It is sometimes called Holland, after the provinces of
North Holland and South Holland.

Capital: Amsterdam. The Hague is the seat of
government.
Languages: Dutch, or Nederlands

The country lies on a flat plain of which more than 25
percent is below sea level.

General weather: Sunniest months are May to August;
warmest are June to September. Rain is evenly distributed
throughout the year, mostly coming as light showers.
Cloudy days are common. Windy at all times of the year. Seasons may vary year to year, and day to
day weather is changeable.

Best time to visit: May to August.
June is an ideal month for warm temperatures, little chance of rain, and long days. September is also a
reasonable month.

June to August: Summer. Afternoon temperatures reach 21ºC (70ºF) but nights are cool. Westerly
winds keep the temperature mild; it rarely goes above 27ºC (80ºF). Rain in June is light. July and
August are the wettest months with thunderstorms bringing heavy showers. It can rain two to three
times per week. Summers are variable year to year. There could be a cool, unsettled summer or a long,
warm summer.
September to November: Autumn. Temperatures start becoming unpleasantly cool, and stormy
winds are common along the coast.

December to February: Winter. Rainy. Westerly winds moderate the cold of winter, keeping daytime temperatures above freezing point. However, in some years, rivers and canals may freeze. Winter gales sometimes pound the coast.

March to May: Spring. Temperatures begin to increase. There is less chance of rain. Daffodils start blooming in April, and tulips in May.

Amsterdam, Netherlands: Altitude 2m (6ft)

	Jan	Feb	Mar	Apr	May	Jun
Sunrise ºC(ºF)	1(33)	1(33)	3(37)	5(41)	9(48)	12(53)
Mid–afternoon ºC(ºF)	5(41)	5(41)	8(46)	11(51)	15(59)	18(64)
Days with precipitation	19	15	13	14	12	12
Precipitation mm	50	36	32	41	45	46
Precipitation inches	2.0	1.4	1.3	1.6	1.8	1.8
Daily hours of sunshine	2	3	4	5	6	7
Snow mm	101	102	76	26	0	0
Snow inches	4	4	3	1	0	0

	Jul	Aug	Sep	Oct	Nov	Dec
Sunrise ºC(ºF)	14(57)	14(57)	13(55)	10(50)	5(41)	3(37)
Mid–afternoon ºC(ºF)	20(68)	21(71)	18(64)	14(57)	9(48)	6(42)
Days with precipitation	14	14	15	18	19	19
Precipitation mm	68	68	71	70	65	55
Precipitation inches	2.7	2.7	2.8	2.8	2.6	2.2
Daily hours of sunshine	7	6	5	3	2	1
Snow mm	0	0	0	0	25	101
Snow inches	0	0	0	0	1	4

NETHERLANDS ANTILLES

Official Name: Netherlands Antilles
(Dependent Territory of the Netherlands)

Capital: Willemstad (on Curaçao island)
Languages: Papiamento (Dutch–Spanish–Portuguese language with English and African traces), Dutch, English

Two island groups comprise Netherlands Antilles:
1. Islands of St Eustatius, Saba and Sint Maarten (Sint Maarten is the southern part of an island shared with French Antilles. The French call their part Saint Martin.)
2. Islands of Bonaire and Curaçao.

Terrain of the islands:
- St Eustatius (pronounced you–stay–shus), called Statia for short (pronounced stay–sha) consists of an extinct volcano, hills, a plain, steep shoreline cliffs but few beaches.
- Saba, pronounced Say–bah, is the peak of an extinct volcano. The coastline consists of steep cliffs without beaches.

- St Maarten has a hilly interior, flat coastal lowlands and coves with white–sand beaches.
- Bonaire and Curaçao are tops of submerged mountains linked with the Andes. They are rather flat and rocky with scant vegetation. Bonaire's coastline is stark. Curaçao has small white–sand beaches.

1. St Eustatius, Saba, Sint Maarten. (Located east of Puerto Rico.)
Language: Dutch. English is widely spoken.
Best time: January to May.

January to March: Dry season. Winter. Average afternoon temperature, 27°C (81°F).
April to December: Wet season. Light rains.
Hurricanes are possible, June to October, but a touchdown is rare.

Note: See under Caribbean Islands for general weather information.

St Martin/St Maarten: Altitude 9m (30ft)

	Jan	Feb	Mar	Apr	May	Jun
Sunrise °C(°F)	23(75)	23(75)	23(75)	25(77)	25(78)	26(80)
Mid–afternoon °C(°F)	28(83)	28(83)	28(83)	28(84)	30(86)	31(88)
Days with precipitation	11	9	8	8	11	10
Precipitation mm	62	44	44	67	96	63
Precipitation inches	2.4	1.7	1.7	2.6	3.8	2.5
Daily hours of sunshine	8	8	9	9	8	8

	Jul	Aug	Sep	Oct	Nov	Dec
Sunrise °C(°F)	26(80)	26(80)	26(80)	26(80)	25(78)	24(76)
Mid–afternoon °C(°F)	31(88)	31(88)	31(88)	30(87)	29(85)	28(83)
Days with precipitation	12	14	13	14	14	13
Precipitation mm	76	99	131	109	130	86
Precipitation inches	3.0	3.9	5.2	4.3	5.1	3.4
Daily hours of sunshine	8	8	8	8	8	8

2. Bonaire and Curaçao.
These islands are located off Venezuela's north coast. Aruba, an adjacent island, seceded from Netherlands Antilles to become a separate entity within the Kingdom of Netherlands. For weather, see Aruba.

Best time: All year round. (However, the drier months of February to October are preferable.)

February to October: Drier season. Driest are usually April and May. Warmest are August and September.
November to January: Wet season.
Winds: Pleasant tradewinds blow all year, including during hot summers, July to September.
Hurricanes: These islands are outside the hurricane belt.

Willemstad, Curaçao, Netherlands Antilles: Altitude 23m (75ft)

	Jan	Feb	Mar	Apr	May	Jun
Sunrise °C(°F)	24(75)	23(73)	24(75)	24(75)	25(77)	26(79)
Mid–afternoon °C(°F)	28(82)	28(82)	29(84)	30(86)	30(86)	31(87)
Days with precipitation	8	5	3	3	3	3
Precipitation mm	46	28	15	19	25	21
Precipitation inches	1.8	1.1	0.6	0.7	1.0	0.8
Daily hours of sunshine	8	9	9	8	8	9

	Jul	Aug	Sep	Oct	Nov	Dec
Sunrise °C(°F)	26(78)	26(78)	26(78)	26(78)	25(77)	24(75)
Mid–afternoon °C(°F)	31(87)	31(87)	32(89)	31(87)	30(86)	28(82)
Days with precipitation	6	5	5	8	10	12
Precipitation mm	34	41	45	83	96	99
Precipitation inches	1.3	1.6	1.8	3.3	3.8	3.9
Daily hours of sunshine	9	9	8	8	8	8

NEW CALEDONIA

Official Name: Territory of New Caledonia and
Dependencies (Overseas Territory of France)
Capital: Nouméa
Language: French

The main island, Grande Terre, is mountainous and is
400km (250 miles) long and 50km (30 miles) wide.

Best time to visit: April to November.

April to November: Temperate season. Sunny, warm,
humid, but kept cool by the refreshing southeast
tradewinds, particularly June to September.
December to March: Wet season. Hot, humid, rainy.
Cyclones may occur. Afternoon temperature, 29°C (86°F).
Rain, when it occurs, usually comes late afternoon, and humidity increases. The northeast coast of
the main island, Grande Terre, can receive 3000mm (120in) a year, while the southwest coast where
Nouméa is located receives only 800 to 1200mm (30 to 50in) because it is in a rain shadow.

Nouméa, New Caledonia: Altitude 72m (236ft)

	Jan	Feb	Mar	Apr	May	Jun
Sunrise °C(°F)	23(73)	23(73)	22(72)	21(70)	19(66)	18(64)
Mid–afternoon °C(°F)	29(84)	29(85)	29(85)	28(83)	25(77)	24(75)
Days with precipitation	9	10	12	10	10	11
Precipitation mm	113	123	135	111	91	129
Precipitation inches	4.4	4.8	5.3	4.4	3.6	5.1
Daily hours of sunshine	8	7	6	7	6	5

Nouméa, New Caledonia: (continued)

	Jul	Aug	Sep	Oct	Nov	Dec
Sunrise ºC(ºF)	17(62)	17(62)	18(64)	19(66)	21(71)	22(72)
Mid–afternoon ºC(ºF)	23(73)	23(73)	24(75)	26(78)	27(80)	28(82)
Days with precipitation	10	8	5	6	6	6
Precipitation mm	73	70	39	53	63	73
Precipitation inches	2.9	2.8	1.5	2.1	2.5	2.9
Daily hours of sunshine	6	6	7	8	8	8

NEW ZEALAND
Official Name: New Zealand

Capital: Wellington
Languages: English, Maori

The terrain consists of mountains and large plains.

New Zealand's two main islands are the North Island and the South Island which are separated by Cook Strait. The North Island is warmer than the South.

For general touring the warmer months of December to March are usually the best months but they are also the busiest. The New Zealand schools' summer holidays, from about December 20 to the end of January, are in this time period. Pre–booking of transport and accommodation is suggested. Crowds can be avoided by travelling in October and November, or March and April.

The northern part of the North Island can be enjoyed year–round. It does not snow, and the temperature rarely drops below 10°C (50°F).

Good months to travel: October to April for general touring; **June to September** for winter sports.

We have divided the weather into two regions, North and South. Refer to map for corresponding numbers.
1. North. (Includes North Island and the northern part of South Island.)
December to February: Summer. Generally sunny, dry and warm with average daily maximum of 21°C (70°F). Best months for beach weather are January and February, the warmest months.
March to May: Autumn. Mild with light rain. Winds are calm in autumn.
June to August: Winter. Mild, 14°C (58°F) but rainy. Most rain falls in winter and is distributed evenly throughout the North Island and the northern part of the South Island. An exception is the volcanoes of the North Island. They are wetter on their western sides because moisture–laden winds blow from the west. Snow falls in the plateau area around Tongariro National Park but is extremely rare in the far north.
September to November: Spring. Mild with light rain. Spring is the windy season. Starting in November, temperatures begin to climb by a few degrees.

2. South. (Includes most of the South Island.)

December to February: Summer. Mild, 20°C (68°F). Prevailing westerly winds drop their moisture on the western side of the Southern Alps. Rainfall is heavy. After losing their moisture the winds become hot and dry as they blow down the eastern slopes. The winds melt snow and warm the Canterbury Plains, the driest part of the country, near Christchurch. This warming effect can last for a few hours or a day or so. January and February are the warmest months.

March to May: Autumn. Mild. Rain, especially on the western side of the Southern Alps. Winds are at their calmest in autumn. March is usually warm while April is the beginning of the cooler season.

June to August: Winter. Cold in the mountains. Mild at lower altitudes. Rainy on the western slopes of the Southern Alps. Snow falls on the peaks of the Alps and sometimes at sea level, especially in the far south. Westerly winds, after they have dropped their moisture on the western slopes of the Alps, rise over the peaks and descend the eastern slopes as warm, dry winds, melting snow in the process and raising temperatures on the plains for a few hours or a day or so.

September to November: Spring. Mild and rainy, especially on the windward (western) slopes of the Alps. These are the windiest months. November is the start of the warmer months that run to February.

General weather information applicable to North, and South:

Rain: The North Island and the northern part of the South Island receive most of their rain in winter (June to August) but all months have rain mixed with fine sunny weather. The west coast of the South Island has heavy rains all year, about twenty times the amount that falls on the eastern side of the island. The eastern side has showers with intermittent sunny periods.

Winds: Winds throughout the year blow west to east, sometimes lightly but also strongly. They are stronger in winter, June to August. These are moisture–laden warm winds. Winds also blow from the south, from Antarctica, which bring cold weather. Winds can bring fast changes to weather conditions on any given day.

Temperatures: Because of the moderating influence of the surrounding ocean there are no extreme fluctuations of temperature. The North Island is a few degrees warmer than the South.

Recreational activities:

Hiking (called tramping in New Zealand): The Milford and the Routeburn Tracks in the South Island are two of the most popular trails for overseas visitors. The busiest time is December and January. Note that many trails are closed due to snow from the end of April to early September.

Cycling: Best time for less crowded roads is February to April. This is also a drier period with less wind. Another time for uncrowded roads is October to early December, but it is windier.

Auckland, North Island, New Zealand: Altitude 26m (85ft)

	Jan	Feb	Mar	Apr	May	Jun
Sunrise °C(°F)	17(62)	17(62)	16(60)	14(57)	11(51)	9(48)
Mid–afternoon °C(°F)	23(74)	23(74)	22(72)	20(68)	17(62)	15(59)
Days with precipitation	10	10	11	14	19	19
Precipitation mm	76	70	89	93	101	116
Precipitation inches	3.0	2.8	3.5	3.7	4.0	4.6
Daily hours of sunshine	7	7	6	5	4	4

Auckland, North Island, New Zealand: (continued)

	Jul	Aug	Sep	Oct	Nov	Dec
Sunrise °C(°F)	8(46)	9(48)	10(50)	12(53)	13(55)	15(59)
Mid–afternoon °C(°F)	14(57)	15(59)	16(60)	17(62)	19(66)	21(69)
Days with precipitation	20	19	17	16	14	11
Precipitation mm	119	114	92	80	84	86
Precipitation inches	4.7	4.5	3.6	3.2	3.3	3.4
Daily hours of sunshine	4	5	6	6	7	7

Christchurch, South Island, New Zealand: Altitude 10m (32ft)

	Jan	Feb	Mar	Apr	May	Jun
Sunrise °C(°F)	12(53)	12(53)	11(51)	8(46)	4(39)	2(35)
Mid–afternoon °C(°F)	23(73)	22(72)	20(68)	18(64)	14(57)	12(53)
Days with precipitation	10	9	10	10	11	12
Precipitation mm	46	40	57	59	61	56
Precipitation inches	1.8	1.6	2.2	2.3	2.4	2.2
Daily hours of sunshine	7	7	6	5	4	4

	Jul	Aug	Sep	Oct	Nov	Dec
Sunrise °C(°F)	2(35)	3(37)	5(41)	7(44)	9(48)	11(51)
Mid–afternoon °C(°F)	11(51)	13(55)	15(59)	18(64)	19(66)	21(70)
Days with precipitation	13	11	10	10	10	10
Precipitation mm	76	63	41	49	49	47
Precipitation inches	3.0	2.5	1.6	1.9	1.9	1.9
Daily hours of sunshine	4	5	5	6	7	7

Wellington, North Island, New Zealand: Altitude 127m (415ft)

	Jan	Feb	Mar	Apr	May	Jun
Sunrise °C(°F)	14(57)	14(57)	14(57)	11(51)	9(48)	7(44)
Mid–afternoon °C(°F)	21(69)	21(69)	20(68)	17(62)	15(59)	13(55)
Days with precipitation	10	9	11	13	15	17
Precipitation mm	67	48	76	87	99	113
Precipitation inches	2.6	1.9	3.0	3.4	3.9	4.4
Daily hours of sunshine	8	7	6	5	4	4

	Jul	Aug	Sep	Oct	Nov	Dec
Sunrise °C(°F)	6(42)	7(44)	8(46)	10(50)	11(51)	13(55)
Mid–afternoon °C(°F)	12(53)	13(55)	14(57)	16(60)	18(64)	20(68)
Days with precipitation	17	16	14	14	13	12
Precipitation mm	111	106	82	81	74	74
Precipitation inches	4.4	4.2	3.2	3.2	2.9	2.9
Daily hours of sunshine	4	4	5	6	7	7

NICARAGUA

Official Name: Republic of Nicaragua
Capital: Managua
Languages: Spanish, English, Amerindian dialects

Nicaragua has a Pacific seaboard, a Caribbean seaboard and central mountains. The main variations of weather are between the Pacific and Caribbean coasts. Central mountains separate the two coasts.

Best time to visit the whole country: November to April. December and January are the most pleasant months in the Pacific region.

We have divided the weather into three regions. Refer to map for corresponding numbers.

1. Pacific region. (Includes Managua.)

November to April: Dry season. Temperatures usually stay in the range 27 to 32ºF (80 to 90ºF), but 38ºC (100ºF) is not uncommon in the hottest months of March to May.

May to October: Wet season. Temperatures range 30 to 35ºC (86 to 95ºF). The rainfalls are usually short, lasting about an hour, but clouds may persist, obliterating blue skies. The wettest months are usually June to October.

2. Caribbean region.

Rain falls through the year, brought by prevailing moisture–laden northeast winds. Humidity varies from 90% to 100%. Most rain falls between May and December on an average of 15 days per month. October receives the heaviest falls. The total for the year is 2500 to 3750mm (100 to 150in). After raining, the temperature drops. The temperature range on the Caribbean lowlands is 27 to 32ºC (80 to 90ºF).

3. Central mountains.

The central mountains are cooler because of their elevation; they rise beyond 2000m (6500ft). The western part of the mountains is drier than the eastern part. The eastern part is humid and wetter because of the higher rainfall on the mountainsides facing the Caribbean Sea.

Managua, Nicaragua: Altitude 56m (184ft)

	Jan	Feb	Mar	Apr	May	Jun
Sunrise ºC(ºF)	20(68)	20(68)	21(69)	23(73)	23(73)	23(73)
Mid–afternoon ºC(ºF)	32(90)	33(91)	34(93)	35(95)	34(93)	32(90)
Days with precipitation	1	1	1	1	8	15
Precipitation mm	4	2	3	6	131	196
Precipitation inches	0.1	0.08	0.1	0.2	5.2	7.7
Daily hours of sunshine	8	8	9	8	7	5

	Jul	Aug	Sep	Oct	Nov	Dec
Sunrise ºC(ºF)	23(73)	23(73)	23(73)	22(72)	20(68)	20(68)
Mid–afternoon ºC(ºF)	31(87)	32(89)	31(87)	31(87)	31(87)	31(87)
Days with precipitation	14	14	16	15	6	2
Precipitation mm	144	151	210	197	54	11
Precipitation inches	5.7	5.9	8.3	7.8	2.1	0.4
Daily hours of sunshine	6	6	6	6	7	8

NIGER

Official Name: Republic of Niger

Capital: Niamey
Languages: French, Hausa, Djerma

The northern half of Niger is desert while the central region is lightly wooded. The southern region has a belt of desert scrub and savanna.

Best time: November to February.

October to February: Sunny, dry, warm. Desert temperatures at night can fall to near freezing. Dry, northeasterly harmattan winds from the Sahara often carry dust, causing a hazy sky.
March to May: Sunny with low humidity. Hottest time of the year when temperatures can reach 45°C (113°F).
June to September: Rain in the southern region brings cooler temperatures, 32°C (89°F). Most rain falls in August. Rain in the northern region is sparse and unreliable. Sunshine is mixed with cloud.

Niamey, Niger: Altitude 216m (709ft)

	Jan	Feb	Mar	Apr	May	Jun
Sunrise ºC(ºF)	14(58)	18(65)	22(71)	25(77)	27(80)	25(77)
Mid–afternoon ºC(ºF)	34(93)	37(98)	41(105)	42(108)	41(106)	38(101)
Days with precipitation	0	0	0	1	4	6
Precipitation mm	0	0	5	8	33	81
Precipitation inches	0	0	0.2	0.3	1.3	3.2
Daily hours of sunshine	9	9	9	8	9	9

	Jul	Aug	Sep	Oct	Nov	Dec
Sunrise ºC(ºF)	23(73)	23(73)	23(73)	23(73)	18(65)	15(59)
Mid–afternoon ºC(ºF)	34(94)	32(89)	34(93)	38(101)	38(101)	34(94)
Days with precipitation	9	12	7	1	0	0
Precipitation mm	132	188	94	13	0	0
Precipitation inches	5.2	7.4	3.7	0.5	0	0
Daily hours of sunshine	8	7	8	9	10	9

NIGERIA

Official Name: Federal Republic of Nigeria

Capital: Abuja
Languages: English, Hausa, Iso, Yoruba

Along the coastal lowlands are mangrove forests and swamps. Inland are tropical rainforests. The land then rises to open woodland then to grasslands on a plateau which covers most of northern Nigeria. The extreme north is desert.

Best time for the whole country: November to February. (Mostly dry.)
There are two weather regions, northern and coastal.
1. Northern. (Includes Kano.)
October to April: Dry season. Warm to hot; low humidity. The hot, dry harmattan wind blows from the Sahara, carrying dust. March to May are extremely hot with afternoon temperatures reaching 40°C (104°F).
June to September: Rainy season.

Kano, northern Nigeria: Altitude 467m (1533ft)

	Jan	Feb	Mar	Apr	May	Jun
Sunrise °C(°F)	13(55)	16(60)	20(68)	24(75)	25(77)	23(74)
Mid–afternoon °C(°F)	30(86)	33(91)	37(98)	38(101)	37(99)	34(94)
Days with precipitation	0	0	0	1	4	8
Precipitation mm	0	0	2	12	50	118
Precipitation inches	0	0	0.08	0.5	2.0	4.6
Daily hours of sunshine	8	8	8	8	8	9

	Jul	Aug	Sep	Oct	Nov	Dec
Sunrise °C(°F)	21(70)	21(70)	21(70)	20(68)	17(62)	14(57)
Mid–afternoon °C(°F)	31(88)	29(85)	31(88)	34(94)	33(92)	31(87)
Days with precipitation	13	14	8	1	0	0
Precipitation mm	174	228	103	10	0	0
Precipitation inches	6.9	9.0	4.1	0.4	0	0
Daily hours of sunshine	7	7	8	9	9	8

2. Coastal. (Includes Lagos.)
On the coast, every month has some rain although there are two dry seasons and two wet seasons. Afternoon temperatures are constantly high, 28 to 31°C (82 to 88°F), and humidity is high, making for uncomfortable weather year–round.
December to February: Main dry season.
April to July: Main wet season.
August: Short dry season.
September and October: Short wet season.

Lagos, coastal Nigeria: Altitude 38m (125ft)

	Jan	Feb	Mar	Apr	May	Jun
Sunrise ºC(ºF)	22(72)	24(75)	24(75)	24(75)	23(73)	22(72)
Mid–afternoon ºC(ºF)	32(89)	33(91)	33(91)	32(89)	31(87)	29(84)
Days with precipitation	2	3	7	9	13	16
Precipitation mm	13	41	84	146	202	316
Precipitation inches	0.5	1.6	3.3	5.7	8.0	12.4
Daily hours of sunshine	5	6	6	6	6	4

	Jul	Aug	Sep	Oct	Nov	Dec
Sunrise ºC(ºF)	22(72)	22(72)	22(72)	22(72)	23(73)	23(73)
Mid–afternoon ºC(ºF)	28(82)	28(82)	29(84)	30(86)	31(87)	32(89)
Days with precipitation	13	12	13	11	5	2
Precipitation mm	243	122	160	125	40	15
Precipitation inches	9.6	4.8	6.3	4.9	1.6	0.6
Daily hours of sunshine	3	3	4	5	6	6

NIUE

Official Name: Niue (pronounced nee–oo'ay)
(Self governing Territory in free association with New Zealand)

Capital: Alofi
Language: English

This small island, with a circumference of 65km (40 miles), is an elevated atoll with a central plateau that rises to 60m (200ft).

Best time to visit: April to November.

April to November: Season of less rain. Hot, humid.
December to March: Wet season. Hot, humid. Cyclones may occur.
Rain, when it occurs, usually comes late afternoon, and humidity increases.
Sunshine throughout year averages 7 hours per day.

Note: Refer to weather table for Apia, Samoa, which has a similar climate.

NORTH KOREA, see KOREA, (North)

NORTHERN MARIANAS

Official Name: The Commonwealth of the Northern
Mariana Islands
(Outlying Territory of the U.S.A.)

Capital: Saipan
Languages: English, Chamorro, Carolinian

The chain of 14 islands are the tips of a submerged
mountain range. The northern islands are volcanic. The
southern islands are limestone with fringing reefs. The
largest town is Garapan, on Saipan.

Best time: December to May. (Particularly January to
March. Cool, dry.)

December to May: Winter. Dry season. Sunny. Northeast tradewinds bring cooling breezes which
also lower the humidity.
June: Hottest month, 29°C (84°F) in afternoons. Light rains.
July to October: Wet season of heavy rains. High humidity. A cyclone is possible between August
and December.
November: Transitional month when afternoon temperatures decrease slightly to 27°C (80°F). Light
rains.

Saipan, Northern Marianas: Altitude 206m (676ft)

	Jan	Feb	Mar	Apr	May	Jun
Sunrise °C(°F)	22(72)	22(72)	23(73)	23(73)	23(73)	24(75)
Mid–afternoon °C(°F)	27(81)	27(81)	28(82)	28(83)	29(84)	29(84)
Days with precipitation	12	11	13	14	13	17
Precipitation mm	69	91	97	71	94	130
Precipitation inches	2.7	3.6	3.8	2.8	3.7	5.1
Daily hours of sunshine	6	7	8	9	9	9

	Jul	Aug	Sep	Oct	Nov	Dec
Sunrise °C(°F)	23(73)	24(75)	23(73)	24(75)	24(75)	23(73)
Mid–afternoon °C(°F)	28(83)	29(84)	28(82)	28(82)	28(82)	28(82)
Days with precipitation	23	23	22	22	19	19
Precipitation mm	254	333	338	290	188	137
Precipitation inches	10.0	13.1	13.3	11.4	7.4	5.4
Daily hours of sunshine	6	7	6	6	7	7

NORWAY

Official Name: Kingdom of Norway
Capital: Oslo
Language: Norwegian

Almost 75 percent of the country consists of wastelands, lakes and barren mountains but there are large forested regions and there is a large lowland area around Oslo. Along the west coast are numerous fjords.

Best time: May to September.

May to September: Sunny and mild to warm, 20°C (68°F), but expect rain. Rain falls year–round. Although much of Norway lies within the Arctic Circle the coastal regions are mild, 20°C (68°F), in the south and 10°C (50°F) or lower in the north. These mild temperatures are a result of the warm waters of the Gulf Stream that come from the south. The mountainous west coast receives heavy rains throughout the year, brought by winds from the southwest. Bergen, on the west coast, is the rainiest city. The lowlands in the southeast, which include Oslo, are left relatively dry, sunny and warm, 20°C (68°F). Daylight hours get longer. At midsummer, Oslo has 19 hours of daylight. In the Arctic Circle at midsummer, daylight is continuous.

October to April: In the interior mountains and plateaus, frosty, snowy conditions and strong winds occur, particularly from November to March. On the west coast, temperatures remain cool to mild because of the Gulf Stream. The fjords are subject to receiving strong, cold winds blowing in from the snow–covered mountains and plateaus. In the southeast, which includes Oslo, expect light rain and mild to cold temperatures that can drop to freezing point. Winter sports are popular January to April.

Bergen, Norway: Altitude 36m (118ft)

	Jan	Feb	Mar	Apr	May	Jun
Sunrise °C(°F)	−1(30)	−1(30)	0(32)	3(37)	7(44)	10(50)
Mid–afternoon °C(°F)	3(37)	3(37)	6(42)	9(48)	14(57)	16(60)
Days with precipitation	20	15	17	13	14	11
Precipitation mm	190	152	170	114	106	132
Precipitation inches	7.5	6.0	6.7	4.5	4.2	5.2
Daily hours of sunshine	1	2	3	5	6	6
Snow mm	304	304	152	25	0	0
Snow inches	12	12	6	1	0	0

	Jul	Aug	Sep	Oct	Nov	Dec
Sunrise °C(°F)	12(53)	12(53)	10(50)	6(42)	3(37)	1(33)
Mid–afternoon °C(°F)	19(66)	19(66)	15(59)	11(51)	8(46)	5(41)
Days with precipitation	15	17	20	22	17	21
Precipitation mm	148	190	283	271	259	235
Precipitation inches	5.8	7.5	11.1	10.7	10.2	9.3
Daily hours of sunshine	5	5	3	2	1	0
Snow mm	0	0	0	25	152	202
Snow inches	0	0	0	1	6	8

Oslo, Norway: Altitude 94m (308ft)

	Jan	Feb	Mar	Apr	May	Jun
Sunrise ºC(ºF)	–7(19)	–7(19)	–4(25)	1(33)	6(42)	10(50)
Mid–afternoon ºC(ºF)	–2(29)	–1(30)	4(39)	10(50)	16(60)	20(68)
Days with precipitation	9	8	8	7	8	10
Precipitation mm	49	36	47	41	53	65
Precipitation inches	1.9	1.4	1.9	1.6	2.1	2.6
Daily hours of sunshine	1	3	4	6	7	8
Snow mm	329	228	101	25	0	0
Snow inches	13	9	4	1	0	0

	Jul	Aug	Sep	Oct	Nov	Dec
Sunrise ºC(ºF)	13(55)	12(53)	8(46)	3(37)	–1(30)	–4(25)
Mid–afternoon ºC(ºF)	22(72)	21(69)	16(60)	9(48)	3(37)	0(32)
Days with precipitation	11	11	11	11	10	9
Precipitation mm	81	89	90	84	73	55
Precipitation inches	3.2	3.5	3.6	3.3	2.9	2.2
Daily hours of sunshine	8	7	5	3	2	1
Snow mm	0	0	0	50	228	431
Snow inches	0	0	0	2	9	17

OMAN

Official Name: Sultanate of Oman

Capital: Muscat
Languages: Arabic, English, Baluchi, Urdu

Oman consists of two sections. The larger section consists of a coastal plain, an interior plateau, and mountains that exceed 2700m (9000ft) above sea level. The smaller section is a rocky promontory, the Musandam Peninsula, that juts into the Strait of Hormuz.

Best time: Mid–October to mid–March. (Warm, dry.)

We have divided the weather of the larger section of Oman into two regions, Northern and Southern.
1. Northern region. (Where Muscat is located.)
October to March: Sunny and pleasantly warm in Muscat. Light rain.
Mid–March to October: Hot and very humid in Muscat. May to September are the hottest, 38ºC (100ºF), and most uncomfortable months. Although rare, there could be some light rain.

2. Southern region. (Where Salalah, the second largest city, is located.)
Throughout the year temperatures are hot and humid. June to September is cloudy with monsoon rains.

Muscat, Oman: Altitude 5m (15ft)

	Jan	Feb	Mar	Apr	May	Jun
Sunrise ºC(ºF)	19(66)	19(66)	22(72)	26(78)	30(86)	31(88)
Mid–afternoon ºC(ºF)	25(77)	25(77)	28(83)	32(90)	37(98)	38(100)
Days with precipitation	2	1	1	1	0	0
Precipitation mm	28	18	10	10	0	3
Precipitation inches	1.1	0.7	0.4	0.4	0	0.1
Daily hours of sunshine	9	10	9	11	12	12

	Jul	Aug	Sep	Oct	Nov	Dec
Sunrise ºC(ºF)	31(87)	29(84)	28(83)	27(80)	23(73)	20(68)
Mid–afternoon ºC(ºF)	36(97)	33(92)	34(93)	34(93)	30(86)	26(79)
Days with precipitation	0	0	0	0	1	2
Precipitation mm	0	0	0	3	10	18
Precipitation inches	0	0	0	0.1	0.4	0.7
Daily hours of sunshine	9	10	11	10	10	9

PAKISTAN
Official Name: Islamic Republic of Pakistan

Capital: Islamabad
Languages: Urdu, English, Punjabi, Sindhi

The Indus River flows through dry regions of Pakistan from the northeast to the south. Along its eastern side lies the Indus Plain. On the western side are mountain plateaus that are offshoots of the high mountain ranges in northern Pakistan.

Best months are October to May for the plains and plateaus. These months apply to all of the country except the northern mountains.
Best months for the northern mountains, for trekking, are late April to October.
Best months to travel along the Karakoram Highway from Islamabad or Rawalpindi to Kashi (China) are May and June.

We have divided the weather into two regions. Refer to map for corresponding numbers.
1. Plains and plateaus. (Includes Islamabad and Karachi.)
October to May: Warm and mainly dry with 8 hours of sunshine daily. Temperatures increase progressively from north to south.
June to September: In July and August, Punjab and the northern region between Peshawar and Lahore receive heavy downpours of the southwest monsoon, accompanied by high humidity and cloudy skies. Even so, expect 6 to 7 hours of sunshine daily. The south which includes Sindh and Baluchistan is sunny, hot and humid but has little rain. Expect 7 hours of sunshine daily. June and July are the hottest months on the plains and plateaus when afternoon temperatures can reach the 40sºC (over 100ºF).

2. Northern mountains. (Hindu Kush and Karakoram ranges.)
May to October, especially June to September, has pleasant cool to warm trekking weather. The mountains are not affected by monsoon rains. Flowers are in bloom. The Khunjerab Pass on the Karakoram Highway is open May 1 to mid–November.
From November to February high mountains have cold days and nights with drizzle or snowfalls. Some roads and high mountain passes are blocked by snow.

Islamabad, northeastern Pakistan: Altitude 508m (1667ft)

	Jan	Feb	Mar	Apr	May	Jun
Sunrise ºC(ºF)	3(37)	5(41)	10(50)	15(59)	20(68)	24(75)
Mid–afternoon ºC(ºF)	18(64)	19(66)	24(75)	30(86)	35(95)	39(102)
Days with precipitation	7	6	7	6	4	7
Precipitation mm	56	74	90	62	39	62
Precipitation inches	2.2	2.9	3.6	2.4	1.5	2.4
Daily hours of sunshine	6	7	7	8	10	10

	Jul	Aug	Sep	Oct	Nov	Dec
Sunrise ºC(ºF)	24(75)	24(75)	21(70)	14(57)	8(46)	3(37)
Mid–afternoon ºC(ºF)	35(95)	33(91)	34(93)	31(87)	25(77)	20(68)
Days with precipitation	13	10	5	2	1	3
Precipitation mm	267	310	98	29	18	37
Precipitation inches	10.5	12.2	3.9	1.1	0.7	1.5
Daily hours of sunshine	9	9	9	9	8	6

Karachi, coastal Pakistan: Altitude 4m (13ft)

	Jan	Feb	Mar	Apr	May	Jun
Sunrise ºC(ºF)	10(50)	13(55)	18(64)	22(72)	26(78)	28(82)
Mid–afternoon ºC(ºF)	26(78)	28(82)	32(89)	34(93)	35(95)	35(95)
Days with precipitation	1	1	1	1	0	1
Precipitation mm	6	10	12	4	0	6
Precipitation inches	0.2	0.4	0.5	0.1	0	0.2
Daily hours of sunshine	9	9	9	9	10	7

	Jul	Aug	Sep	Oct	Nov	Dec
Sunrise ºC(ºF)	27(80)	26(78)	25(77)	21(70)	16(60)	12(53)
Mid–afternoon ºC(ºF)	33(91)	32(90)	33(91)	35(95)	32(89)	27(80)
Days with precipitation	2	2	1	0	0	1
Precipitation mm	86	67	20	1	2	4
Precipitation inches	3.4	2.6	0.8	0.04	0.08	0.1
Daily hours of sunshine	5	5	7	9	9	9

PALAU

Official Name: Republic of Palau
(also called Belau)

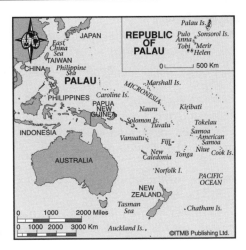

Capital: Koror
Languages: English, Palauan

Located in the western Caroline Islands, the republic contains 343 small islands, many of which are clothed in jungle. Only 9 are inhabited.

Best time to visit: February to April.

February to April: Dry season, but light rain is possible. Sunny, humid, hot, 30°C (86°F) in the afternoons.
May to January: Wet season. Sunny, humid, hot, 31°C (87°F) in the afternoons. June to August are the wettest months. Cyclones can occur July to November but Palau is normally outside the cyclone belt.
Humidity: It is always humid, 80%, but sea breezes tend to moderate the humidity.

Koror, Palau: Altitude 33m (108ft)

	Jan	Feb	Mar	Apr	May	Jun
Sunrise °C(°F)	24(75)	24(75)	24(75)	24(75)	24(75)	24(75)
Mid–afternoon °C(°F)	31(87)	31(87)	31(87)	31(87)	31(87)	31(87)
Days with precipitation	19	16	17	15	20	22
Precipitation mm	272	232	208	220	305	439
Precipitation inches	10.7	9.1	8.2	8.7	12.0	17.3
Daily hours of sunshine	6	7	8	8	7	6

	Jul	Aug	Sep	Oct	Nov	Dec
Sunrise °C(°F)	24(75)	24(75)	25(77)	24(75)	24(75)	24(75)
Mid–afternoon °C(°F)	31(87)	31(87)	31(87)	31(87)	31(87)	31(87)
Days with precipitation	21	20	17	20	19	20
Precipitation mm	458	380	301	352	288	304
Precipitation inches	18.0	15.0	11.9	13.9	11.3	12.0
Daily hours of sunshine	6	6	7	6	6	6

PANAMA

Official Name: Republic of Panama
Capital: Panama City
Languages: Spanish, English

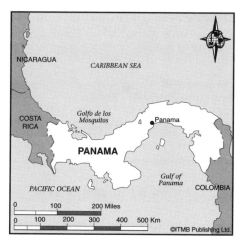

Panama is on a narrow isthmus along which runs a mountain chain. The oceans on both sides have a strong influence on weather, providing abundant moisture which is captured by the mountains.

Best time for the whole country: December to mid–April. (Drier season.)
We have divided the weather into two regions, the Pacific coast and the Caribbean coast.

1. Pacific coast. (Includes Panama City.)
December to April: Sunny, humid, 32°C (90°F). Dry season. February is driest month.
May to November: Cloud and intermittent sunshine, humid, hot, 30°C (86°F). Wet season. November is the wettest month.
2. Caribbean coast.
January to March: Short dry season, humid, hot, 32°C (90°F). Although it is the "dry" season rain can fall daily.
April to December: Long wet season, hot and humid. Daily downpours are heavy but brief. June to November is the hurricane season in the Caribbean but hurricanes are rare along Panama's Caribbean coast.
General weather notes:
Rain: There is twice as much rain on the Caribbean coast compared with the Pacific coast.
Wind: Tradewinds from the north and northeast prevail year–round, dumping rain on the eastern slopes of the central mountains.
Temperatures are high at low altitudes but decrease the higher you go into the mountains.
Humidity on the coast is high all year but is moderated by sea breezes.

Panama City, Panama: Altitude 33m (108ft)

	Jan	Feb	Mar	Apr	May	Jun
Sunrise °C(°F)	22(72)	22(72)	22(72)	23(73)	23(73)	23(73)
Mid–afternoon °C(°F)	31(88)	32(89)	32(89)	31(87)	30(86)	31(87)
Days with precipitation	4	2	1	6	15	16
Precipitation mm	25	10	18	74	203	213
Precipitation inches	1.0	0.4	0.7	2.9	8.0	8.4
Daily hours of sunshine	10	9	8	7	5	4

	Jul	Aug	Sep	Oct	Nov	Dec
Sunrise °C(°F)	23(73)	23(73)	23(73)	23(73)	23(73)	23(73)
Mid–afternoon °C(°F)	31(87)	30(86)	29(85)	29(85)	29(85)	31(87)
Days with precipitation	15	15	16	18	18	12
Precipitation mm	180	201	208	257	259	122
Precipitation inches	7.1	7.9	8.2	10.1	10.2	4.8
Daily hours of sunshine	5	5	5	5	5	7

PAPUA NEW GUINEA

Official Name: Independent State of Papua New Guinea

Capital: Port Moresby
Languages: English and 715 indigenous languages

The main island has a central mountain range running east–west which rises to over 4000m (13000ft). In addition there are numerous islands.

Weather is hot and damp year–round. Humidity is high, 70 to 85%. Lowland temperatures range 22 to 32°C (73 to 90°F) throughout the year. Highland towns are temperate with days of 20°C (70°F) and cool, comfortable nights. Rainfall is heavy year–round, although some months are wetter than others. The northwest monsoon brings rain from December to March. This is the wet season. The southeast tradewinds bring lighter rains from May to October, the "dry" season. Throughout the country, when the skies are blue there are always clouds, and overcast skies are common.

Best time to visit is in the dry season May to November. The exception is Daru in the Western and Gulf region where it is best from November to April.

We have listed the main towns and regions and their wet and dry seasons.
Any months not mentioned are transitional months which could be either wet or relatively dry. Refer to map for location of towns and regions.

- **Port Moresby.**
  Best time: May to November.
  May to October: Dry and sometimes dusty. Minimal rain.
  December to March: Wet. Rainfall is comparatively light, only 1000mm (40in) per year, because the city is in the rain shadow of the nearby Owen Stanley range.

- **Lae.** (Pronounced Lay.)
  Best time: May to November.
  May to October: Drier season, but Lae receives heavy rain from June to August. The rain tends to lower the temperatures.
  December to March: Wet season. Hot and humid.

- **Highlands.** (Includes towns of Mount Hagen and Goroka.)
  Best time: May to November.
  When compared with the coast, highland daytime temperatures are cooler, 20°C (68°F), and the nights and mornings are chilly.
  May to October: Although this is not the main wet season, rain falls during these months.
  November to April: Wet season.

- **Sepik River region.** (Includes Wewak.)
  Best time: June to November.
  July to November: Drier season.
  December to April: Wet season.

- **Madang.**
  Best time: June to October.
  June to October: Drier season.
  November to May: Wet season.

- **Milne Bay region.**
  Best time is in a dry season.
  February to March: Dry.
  April to August: Wet.
  September to October: Dry.
  November to January: Wet.

- **Islands: New Britain** (includes Rabaul), **Manus, New Ireland, and Bougainville.**
  Best time: May to October.
  May to October: Drier season.
  November to April: Wet season.

- **Western and Gulf region.** (Includes Daru.)
  Best time: November to April.
  Note that the seasons are reversed.
  May to October: Wet season of heaviest rains.
  November to April: Less rain.

Cultural events: Highland Shows, or Sing–Sings. Thousands of warriors in traditional dress gather for chanting, dancing and drumming. Held in Mt Hagen in August, and Goroka in September.

Port Moresby, Papua New Guinea: Altitude 38m (126ft)

	Jan	Feb	Mar	Apr	May	Jun
Sunrise ºC(ºF)	24(75)	24(75)	24(75)	24(75)	24(75)	23(73)
Mid–afternoon ºC(ºF)	32(89)	31(87)	31(87)	31(87)	30(86)	29(84)
Days with precipitation	8	7	9	5	2	3
Precipitation mm	178	193	170	107	64	33
Precipitation inches	7.0	7.6	6.7	4.2	2.5	1.3
Daily hours of sunshine	6	5	6	7	7	7

	Jul	Aug	Sep	Oct	Nov	Dec
Sunrise ºC(ºF)	23(73)	23(73)	23(73)	24(75)	24(75)	24(75)
Mid–afternoon ºC(ºF)	28(83)	28(83)	29(84)	30(86)	31(87)	32(90)
Days with precipitation	2	2	2	2	3	6
Precipitation mm	28	18	25	36	48	112
Precipitation inches	1.1	0.7	1.0	1.4	1.9	4.4
Daily hours of sunshine	7	7	7	7	8	7

PARAGUAY
Official Name: Republic of Paraguay

Capital: Asunción
Languages: Spanish, Guarani

Most of Paraguay consists of lowlands with grassy plains
and scrub forests.

Best time: May to September. (Dry, warm.)

May to September: Dry season. In eastern Paraguay
(includes Asunción) light rains may fall on one day in five
and temperatures are pleasantly warm with afternoons
ranging 25 to 28°C (77 to 83°F). In mid–winter, July and
August, nighttime temperatures can go down to 5°C (41°F). Temperatures below freezing are rare. It
never snows. Six to 7 hours of sunshine daily from May to September. In Western Paraguay (includes
Gran Chaco plain), rainfall is less and temperatures higher.
October to April: Hot, rainy. Eastern Paraguay has maximum temperatures in summer (December to
February) of 35°C (95°F) and heavy rains falling every one day out of four. Humidity is high. Western
Paraguay has highs over 40°C (104°F) in summer, but less rain.

Asunción, Paraguay: Altitude 101m (331ft)

	Jan	Feb	Mar	Apr	May	Jun
Sunrise °C(°F)	23(73)	22(72)	21(70)	19(66)	16(60)	14(57)
Mid–afternoon °C(°F)	33(91)	33(91)	32(89)	28(82)	25(77)	23(73)
Days with precipitation	5	5	5	5	4	4
Precipitation mm	158	122	115	157	110	72
Precipitation inches	6.2	4.8	4.5	6.2	4.3	2.8
Daily hours of sunshine	8	6	6	8	6	5

	Jul	Aug	Sep	Oct	Nov	Dec
Sunrise °C(°F)	14(57)	14(57)	16(60)	18(64)	20(68)	22(72)
Mid–afternoon °C(°F)	23(73)	24(75)	26(78)	29(84)	31(88)	32(89)
Days with precipitation	3	4	3	5	5	5
Precipitation mm	42	77	79	116	153	132
Precipitation inches	1.6	3.0	3.1	4.6	6.0	5.2
Daily hours of sunshine	5	5	6	7	8	7

PERU

Official Name: Republic of Peru

Capital: Lima
Languages: Spanish, Quecha (both official), Aymara (unofficial)

There are three topographical regions. Along the coast is a narrow plain of sand dunes and gravel 60 to 160km (40 to 100 miles) wide. Parallel to the coastal plain are the Andes Mountains. In the northeast are the dense forests of the Amazon basin.

Best months for touring: March to May (autumn) and **September to November** (spring).
Good trekking months: May to September.

Note: Peru's varied attractions tend to override the importance of requiring the best weather.

We have divided Peru into three weather regions.
1. Coastal desert. (Includes Lima.)
Good touring months: September to May.

October to May: Sunny, dry days. December to March are hottest, 28°C (83°F). Beach weather for the people of Lima is December to April and is the best time to visit Lima. Sunny and clear, hot and humid with 5 to 7 hours of sunshine daily.
June to October: A fine mist or fog hangs over the coast, including Lima, giving only one hour of sunshine daily.

Lima, Peru: Altitude 13m (43ft)

	Jan	Feb	Mar	Apr	May	Jun
Sunrise ºC(ºF)	19(66)	19(66)	19(66)	17(63)	16(60)	14(57)
Mid–afternoon ºC(ºF)	28(82)	28(83)	28(83)	27(80)	23(74)	20(68)
Days with precipitation	1	0	0	0	1	1
Precipitation mm	3	0	0	0	5	5
Precipitation inches	0.1	0	0	0	0.2	0.2
Daily hours of sunshine	6	7	7	7	4	1

	Jul	Aug	Sep	Oct	Nov	Dec
Sunrise ºC(ºF)	14(57)	13(56)	14(57)	14(57)	16(60)	17(62)
Mid–afternoon ºC(ºF)	19(66)	19(66)	20(68)	22(71)	23(74)	26(78)
Days with precipitation	1	2	1	1	1	0
Precipitation mm	8	8	8	3	3	0
Precipitation inches	0.3	0.3	0.3	0.1	0.1	0
Daily hours of sunshine	1	1	1	3	4	5

2. Andes mountains. (Includes Cuzco.)
Best time: May to September.
Good trekking months: May to September. June is usually ideal; dry, but cold.

May to September: Dry with 8 hours of sunshine daily.
October to April: Rainy season, heaviest in January. Expect 5 to 6 hours of sunshine daily.

Cultural event: Inti Raymi Fiesta. June 24 in Cuzco. Mock sacrifice to the sun. Week–long celebration and dances.

Cuzco, Peru: Altitude 3249m (10659ft)

	Jan	Feb	Mar	Apr	May	Jun
Sunrise ºC(ºF)	7(44)	7(44)	7(44)	4(40)	2(35)	1(33)
Mid–afternoon ºC(ºF)	20(68)	21(69)	21(70)	22(71)	21(70)	21(69)
Days with precipitation	18	13	11	8	3	2
Precipitation mm	163	150	109	51	15	5
Precipitation inches	6.4	5.9	4.3	2.0	0.6	0.2
Daily hours of sunshine	5	4	5	7	8	8

	Jul	Aug	Sep	Oct	Nov	Dec
Sunrise ºC(ºF)	–1(31)	1(34)	4(40)	6(43)	6(43)	7(44)
Mid–afternoon ºC(ºF)	21(70)	21(70)	22(71)	22(72)	23(73)	22(71)
Days with precipitation	2	2	7	8	12	16
Precipitation mm	5	10	25	66	76	137
Precipitation inches	0.2	0.4	1.0	2.6	3.0	5.4
Daily hours of sunshine	8	8	7	6	7	5

3. Amazon basin.
Good time for the Amazon basin: May to October.

May to October: Dry season.
November to April: Rainy season. The wettest months are January to April. The rain often falls once a day, coming as a downpour usually in the late afternoon or overnight. River levels begin to rise.
June, July and August are excellent months for travelling the Amazon due to it being the dry season, and the river level being high after the rains. All other months are bearable for travel despite the rain. The authors of this weather guide have travelled on local cargo boats on the Amazon in Peru in November and December during the rainy season, and found the rains not to be a deterrent.

The Amazon River in Peru
The Amazon River at Iquitos rises by 10m (30ft) in the rainy season. This high water level remains from April to June before it starts to subside. From September to December it is low again.

Cargo/passenger boats ply between Pucallpa and Iquitos but from July to November the tributary, the Ucayali River, may be too low for boats. There is never a low–water problem between Iquitos and Belem at the mouth of the Amazon in Brazil. Ocean going ships travel this section year–round. To view wildlife you need to go on a tour along a tributary. These are available at Iquitos (Peru), and Manaus (Brazil). Photography tip: For better pictures in the shade of the jungle use a flash or high speed film.

PHILIPPINES
Official Name: Republic of The Philippines

Capital: Manila
Languages: Tagalog, English (both official)

The country is comprised of more than 7000 islands, all of them mountainous. They are tips of a submerged mountain range, volcanic in origin. Some are still active. The larger mountainous islands such as Luzon and Mindanao have fertile valleys and broad plains.

Good months to visit: November to May. (Dry, warm, sunny days.)
Best month is January. (Dry, cooler.) November and December can have rain. March to May are dry but hotter. The weather is warm and humid throughout the year. Dry season is December to May. Wet season is June to November.

November and December: Warm days. 30ºC (86ºF) in afternoons with a chance of rain. Six hours of sunshine daily.
January and February: Dry, "cool" period, 31ºC (87ºF) in afternoons. Pleasant sea breezes on the coast. Seven hours of sunshine daily.
March to May: Dry, hot period, 34ºC (93ºF) in afternoons. May is hottest. Seven hours of sunshine daily.
June to October: Rainy season. Humid, cloudy. Four to 5 hours of sunshine daily. Rains almost daily, July to September. July and August are the rainiest.
Typhoon season is June to November. It sometimes starts in May. Peak months for typhoons are August to November. There could be more than a dozen annually. The northern half of the Philippines is more susceptible to typhoons than the southern half such as Mindanao and the Visayas.

Manila, Luzon Island, Philippines: Altitude 14m (47ft)

	Jan	Feb	Mar	Apr	May	Jun
Sunrise ºC(ºF)	21(70)	21(70)	23(73)	24(75)	25(77)	24(75)
Mid–afternoon ºC(ºF)	30(86)	31(87)	33(91)	34(93)	34(93)	32(89)
Days with precipitation	5	3	4	5	12	17
Precipitation mm	6	3	7	9	113	273
Precipitation inches	0.2	0.1	0.3	0.4	4.4	10.7
Daily hours of sunshine	6	7	7	8	7	5

	Jul	Aug	Sep	Oct	Nov	Dec
Sunrise ºC(ºF)	24(75)	24(75)	24(75)	24(75)	23(73)	22(72)
Mid–afternoon ºC(ºF)	31(87)	32(89)	31(87)	31(87)	31(87)	30(86)
Days with precipitation	24	23	22	19	14	11
Precipitation mm	341	398	326	230	120	49
Precipitation inches	13.4	15.7	12.8	9.1	4.7	1.9
Daily hours of sunshine	4	4	4	5	5	5

PITCAIRN ISLANDS

Official Name: Pitcairn, Henderson, Ducie and Oeno
Islands
(Dependent Territory of the United Kingdom)

Capital: Adamstown (on Pitcairn)
Language: English

The dependency consists of four islands: Pitcairn,
Henderson, Ducie and Oeno. They are located midway
between Tahiti and Easter Island and are administered by
the British Consulate–General in Auckland, New Zealand.
Pitcairn, the only inhabited island, has an area of 5 sq. km
(2 sq. miles). Steep cliffs of volcanic rock rise from the
sea. On the top, 160m (525ft) above sea level, is a fertile
plain.

Visit any time of year. Although there is little difference in rainfall over the months, July and August
are the driest and November the wettest. Temperatures are mild, 19 to 24°C (66 to 76°F), with June to
August being the coolest and December to February being the warmest time.

POLAND

Official Name: Republic of Poland

Capital: Warsaw
Language: Polish

Most of Poland consists of low–lying undulating plains
but in the extreme south there are mountains.

Best time: May to September.
To avoid the crowds during the peak tourist season of July
and August, choose mid–May to June, or September.

May to September: May has warm days, chilly nights.
From June to August, temperatures in most places are a
warm 23°C (73°F), but in the northern region near the Baltic coast temperatures are lower by about
3°C (7°F). Throughout Poland extremely hot days are unusual. Summer has frequent thunderstorms,
making it the wettest season. June and July are the rainiest months. September is pleasantly warm. The
prevailing winds during these months come from the west.
October and November: Transitional months with cooling temperatures and some rain. Snow starts
falling, especially in the southern mountains.
December to February: Winter. Bitterly cold, especially when strong, cold winds blow in from the
Russian plains. The northern lowland region near the Baltic Sea is not as cold as eastern Poland and
the southern mountains. Snow falls from November to March. Most precipitation in winter arrives
as snow. It is heaviest in the southern mountains where it lingers until April or May; it does not stay
all year. Winter sports are popular in the Carpathian mountains in the south. The main ski resort is at
Zakopane in the Tatras, the highest range in the Carpathians, 100km (60 miles) south of Krakow.
March to April: Transitional months with warming temperatures and light rainfall.

Warsaw, central Poland: Altitude 106m (348ft)

	Jan	Feb	Mar	Apr	May	Jun
Sunrise ºC(ºF)	–6(21)	–5(23)	–2(29)	3(37)	8(46)	11(51)
Mid–afternoon ºC(ºF)	–1(30)	1(33)	6(42)	13(55)	19(66)	22(72)
Days with precipitation	6	6	7	7	9	9
Precipitation mm	22	21	26	33	58	71
Precipitation inches	0.9	0.8	1.0	1.3	2.3	2.8
Daily hours of sunshine	1	2	3	5	7	8

	Jul	Aug	Sep	Oct	Nov	Dec
Sunrise ºC(ºF)	13(55)	12(53)	9(48)	5(41)	1(33)	–3(27)
Mid–afternoon ºC(ºF)	23(73)	23(73)	18(65)	13(56)	6(42)	1(33)
Days with precipitation	9	8	8	7	9	8
Precipitation mm	69	62	43	37	41	32
Precipitation inches	2.7	2.4	1.7	1.5	1.6	1.3
Daily hours of sunshine	8	7	5	3	1	1

PORTUGAL

Official Name: Portuguese Republic

Capital: Lisbon
Language: Portuguese

The northern half of Portugal is mountainous and the southern half is flat except for the extreme south, the Algarve, where it is hilly.
(Azores and Madeira which belong to Portugal are listed separately under A and M.)

Best time:
For the centre and north: May to September. (June is a good month, before the crowds.)
For the south, the Algarve: March to November. (The Algarve's busiest season is June to September.)

May to September: Summer. Sunny. Weather starts warming up in May and stays hot until September. July and August are the driest and hottest, 28ºC (82ºF). The Algarve on the southern coast is popular longer, from March to November, because it is dry, sunny and warm, 31ºC (88ºF), and the sea temperature is higher than the western coast.
October: Sunny, mild, 21ºC (70ºF), and light rain.
November to March: Winter. Temperatures start dropping everywhere. This is the wet season. The north and centre are rainier than the south. The rainfalls can be heavy or light. In the northern mountains, Serra de Estrela, snow falls. Waters off the western coast are a cool, uninviting 16ºC (61ºF). The south–facing Algarve has sunny days in winter, but the air temperatures are a cool to mild 10 to 15ºC (50 to 60ºF).
April: Changeable month with a mix of sunny and rainy days. Rain is heavier in the north. The south has little rain.

Lisbon, Portugal: Altitude 95m (312ft)

	Jan	Feb	Mar	Apr	May	Jun
Sunrise ºC(ºF)	8(47)	9(48)	10(50)	11(51)	13(55)	16(60)
Mid–afternoon ºC(ºF)	15(59)	15(60)	18(64)	19(66)	22(72)	25(77)
Days with precipitation	11	11	8	8	6	3
Precipitation mm	110	111	69	64	39	21
Precipitation inches	4.3	4.4	2.7	2.5	1.5	0.8
Daily hours of sunshine	5	5	7	8	9	10

	Jul	Aug	Sep	Oct	Nov	Dec
Sunrise ºC(ºF)	17(62)	18(64)	17(62)	15(59)	11(51)	9(48)
Mid–afternoon ºC(ºF)	27(80)	28(82)	26(78)	22(72)	18(64)	15(59)
Days with precipitation	1	1	4	8	10	10
Precipitation mm	5	6	26	80	114	108
Precipitation inches	0.2	0.2	1.0	3.2	4.5	4.3
Daily hours of sunshine	11	11	9	7	5	5

PUERTO RICO

Official Name: Commonwealth of Puerto Rico
(Commonwealth associated with the U.S.A.)

Capital: San Juan
Languages: Spanish, English widely understood.

Broad level plains follow the coastline. Mountain ranges
extend east–west along the centre of the island.

Best time to visit: Any time of year. Preferred months
are January to May. (Slightly cooler and less humidity.)

January to May: Cooler season. Average afternoon
temperature, 27ºC (80ºF).
June to December: Warmer season. Afternoon average, 29ºC (84ºF).
Sunshine: Sunny and warm almost every day of the year in this tropical climate. Expect 8 hours per
day of sunshine despite the many rainy days.
Rain: There is no dry season. Northwest tradewinds bring heavy rain to the north coast where San
Juan is located, and to the mountainous interior. The south side of the island, protected by mountains,
receives less rain.
Humidity is high throughout the year although slightly less between January and May.
Hurricanes are a possibility between June and November, but are not likely to occur.

San Juan, Puerto Rico: Altitude 25m (82ft)

	Jan	Feb	Mar	Apr	May	Jun
Sunrise ºC(ºF)	21(69)	21(69)	21(69)	22(72)	23(73)	24(75)
Mid–afternoon ºC(ºF)	27(80)	27(80)	27(80)	28(82)	29(84)	29(84)
Days with precipitation	20	15	15	14	16	17
Precipitation mm	109	69	74	104	150	137
Precipitation inches	4.3	2.7	2.9	4.1	5.9	5.4
Daily hours of sunshine	7	8	9	9	8	8

	Jul	Aug	Sep	Oct	Nov	Dec
Sunrise ºC(ºF)	24(75)	24(76)	24(75)	24(75)	23(73)	22(72)
Mid–afternoon ºC(ºF)	29(84)	29(84)	30(86)	29(85)	29(84)	27(81)
Days with precipitation	19	20	18	18	19	21
Precipitation mm	145	160	158	142	160	137
Precipitation inches	5.7	6.3	6.2	5.6	6.3	5.4
Daily hours of sunshine	8	9	7	8	7	7

QATAR

Official Name: State of Qatar

Capital: Doha
Languages: Arabic, English

The independent State of Qatar occupies the Qatar
Peninsula in the Persian Gulf. The land is low–lying,
stony and barren.

Best time: October to April.

November to February: Winter. Sunny with pleasant,
mild to warm days and cool evenings. Occasional showers
in December and January.

May to September: Summer. Dry. Extremely hot days which can exceed 40ºC (104ºF). Humidity can
reach an uncomfortable 90%.

Sand and dust storms can blow throughout the year, but mainly occur in springtime, March to May.

Doha, Qatar: Altitude 10m (33ft)

	Jan	Feb	Mar	Apr	May	Jun
Sunrise ºC(ºF)	13(55)	14(57)	17(62)	21(70)	25(77)	28(82)
Mid–afternoon ºC(ºF)	22(72)	23(73)	27(80)	32(89)	38(100)	41(105)
Days with precipitation	2	2	2	1	0	0
Precipitation mm	13	17	16	9	4	0
Precipitation inches	0.5	0.7	0.6	0.4	0.1	0
Daily hours of sunshine	8	8	8	9	10	11

Doha, Qatar: (continued)

	Jul	Aug	Sep	Oct	Nov	Dec
Sunrise ºC(ºF)	29(84)	29(84)	27(80)	23(73)	20(68)	15(59)
Mid–afternoon ºC(ºF)	42(107)	41(105)	39(102)	35(95)	30(86)	24(75)
Days with precipitation	0	0	0	0	0	1
Precipitation mm	0	0	0	1	3	12
Precipitation inches	0	0	0	0.04	0.1	0.5
Daily hours of sunshine	10	11	10	10	9	8

REUNION

Official Name: Department of Réunion
(Overseas Department of France)

Capital: Saint–Denis
Language: French

This Indian Ocean volcanic island reaches over 3000m
(10000ft). There are no extremes of temperature. Some
rain falls year–round. Refer to the weather table under
Mauritius for an example of similar weather.

Best time: May to November. (Drier.)

May to November: Drier season. Cooler. Afternoon
maximum is 24ºC (75ºF). Humidity is moderate.
December to April: Wet season. Rain is heavier at higher elevations. Cyclones sometimes occur. This
is the more humid and hotter season with an average daily maximum of 29ºC (85ºF).

ROMANIA

Official Name: Romania

Capital: Bucharest
Languages: Romanian, Hungarian, German

The northern half of Romania comprises a hilly basin
surrounded by the Carpathian Mountains in the north and
the Transylvanian Alps that extend across the centre of the
country. The southern half consists largely of plains.

Best time: Late June to early September.

June to September: Warm and wet. Warmest months are
June and July, about 30ºC (85ºF) in the afternoons, but
temperatures can rise to over 38ºC (100ºF). Winds from the southwest can raise temperatures. Most
rain falls May and June, often as thunderstorms.

October to May: Cold, less rain. Coldest months are January and February, about freezing point. Snow is frequent; most winter precipitation is snow. Dry, icy winds from the Russian steppes sometimes blow from the northeast. The mildest area in winter, December to February, is the Black Sea coast with an afternoon average of 4°C (40°F).

Bucharest, Romania: Altitude 92m (302ft)

	Jan	Feb	Mar	Apr	May	Jun
Sunrise °C(°F)	–6(21)	–3(27)	0(32)	6(42)	11(51)	14(57)
Mid–afternoon °C(°F)	2(35)	4(39)	11(51)	18(64)	23(73)	27(80)
Days with precipitation	6	6	6	7	6	6
Precipitation mm	40	36	38	46	70	77
Precipitation inches	1.6	1.4	1.5	1.8	2.8	3.0
Daily hours of sunshine	2	3	4	6	8	9

	Jul	Aug	Sep	Oct	Nov	Dec
Sunrise °C(°F)	16(60)	15(59)	11(51)	6(42)	2(35)	–3(27)
Mid–afternoon °C(°F)	29(84)	29(84)	25(77)	18(64)	10(50)	4(39)
Days with precipitation	7	6	5	5	6	6
Precipitation mm	64	58	42	32	49	43
Precipitation inches	2.5	2.3	1.6	1.3	1.9	1.7
Daily hours of sunshine	9	9	7	6	3	2

Constanta, on Black Sea coast, Romania: Altitude 14m (46ft)

	Jan	Feb	Mar	Apr	May	Jun
Sunrise °C(°F)	–2(29)	–1(30)	2(35)	7(44)	12(53)	16(60)
Mid–afternoon °C(°F)	4(39)	5(41)	8(46)	14(57)	19(66)	24(75)
Days with precipitation	5	5	5	5	6	6
Precipitation mm	30	29	26	30	38	40
Precipitation inches	1.2	1.1	1.0	1.2	1.5	1.6
Daily hours of sunshine	3	3	4	6	9	9

	Jul	Aug	Sep	Oct	Nov	Dec
Sunrise °C(°F)	18(64)	18(64)	15(59)	10(50)	5(41)	1(33)
Mid–afternoon °C(°F)	26(78)	26(78)	22(72)	17(62)	12(53)	6(42)
Days with precipitation	5	3	3	4	6	6
Precipitation mm	30	33	29	31	42	38
Precipitation inches	1.2	1.3	1.1	1.2	1.6	1.5
Daily hours of sunshine	10	10	8	6	3	2

RUSSIA
Official Name: Russian Federation

Capital: Moscow
Language: Russian

Russia's enormous area consists of vast level plains or steppes that are divided into two parts by the Ural Mountains.
They are the European Region and Siberian Region and will be described separately.

1. European Region. (West of Ural Mountains. Includes Moscow, St Petersburg.)
Good months to visit: May to September.

April and May: Spring. Snow melts. Cool. Light rains.
June to August: Short hot summer. These are the wettest months.
September: Cool. Light rains.
October to March: Long cold winter. Snow flurries begin in October. First frost occurs at end of October. Sunshine is negligible, from zero to 3 hours per day.

Note: Trans–Siberian Railway journey: Good travel months are May to September.

Moscow, Russia: Altitude 156m (512ft)

	Jan	Feb	Mar	Apr	May	Jun
Sunrise °C(°F)	−16(3)	−14(8)	−8(18)	1(34)	8(46)	11(51)
Mid–afternoon °C(°F)	−9(15)	−6(22)	0(32)	10(50)	19(66)	21(70)
Days with precipitation	18	15	15	13	13	12
Precipitation mm	39	38	36	37	53	58
Precipitation inches	1.5	1.5	1.4	1.5	2.1	2.3
Daily hours of sunshine	1	3	4	5	8	9

	Jul	Aug	Sep	Oct	Nov	Dec
Sunrise °C(°F)	13(55)	12(53)	7(45)	3(37)	−3(26)	−10(15)
Mid–afternoon °C(°F)	23(73)	22(72)	16(61)	9(48)	2(35)	−5(24)
Days with precipitation	15	14	13	15	15	23
Precipitation mm	88	71	58	45	47	54
Precipitation inches	3.5	2.8	2.3	1.8	1.9	2.1
Daily hours of sunshine	9	8	6	3	1	0

St Petersburg, Russia: Altitude 6m (20ft)

	Jan	Feb	Mar	Apr	May	Jun
Sunrise °C(°F)	−13(8)	−12(11)	−8(18)	0(33)	6(42)	11(51)
Mid–afternoon °C(°F)	−7(19)	−5(22)	0(32)	8(46)	15(59)	20(68)
Days with precipitation	21	17	14	12	13	12
Precipitation mm	35	30	31	36	45	50
Precipitation inches	1.4	1.2	1.2	1.4	1.8	2.0
Daily hours of sunshine	0	2	4	5	8	10

	Jul	Aug	Sep	Oct	Nov	Dec
Sunrise °C(°F)	13(55)	13(55)	9(47)	4(39)	−2(28)	−8(18)
Mid–afternoon °C(°F)	21(70)	20(69)	15(60)	9(48)	2(35)	−3(26)
Days with precipitation	13	14	17	18	18	22
Precipitation mm	72	78	64	76	46	40
Precipitation inches	2.8	3.1	2.5	3.0	1.8	1.6
Daily hours of sunshine	9	8	5	2	1	0

2. Siberian Region. (East of Ural Mountains. Includes Novosibirsk, Irkutsk, Lake Baikal, Vladivostok.)
The weather of two representative cities, Irkutsk and Vladivostok, will be described.
Irkutsk. (Near Lake Baikal.)
Good months to visit: June to early September.

June to August: Short warm summer with average afternoon temperatures of 20°C (68°F). This is the wettest season.
September: The month becomes progressively cooler with afternoon temperatures dropping from 18°C (65°F) at beginning of September to 7°C (45°F) at the end. Light rains.
October to April: Cold winter conditions with snowfalls, particularly November to March. Very little rain.

May: Gradual warming with average afternoon temperatures rising from 7°C (45°F) in early May to 18°C (65°F) in late May. Light rains.

Irkutsk, Russia: Altitude 469m (1539ft)

	Jan	Feb	Mar	Apr	May	Jun
Sunrise °C(°F)	−26(−15)	−25(−13)	−17(2)	−7(20)	1(33)	7(44)
Mid–afternoon °C(°F)	−16(3)	−12(10)	−4(25)	6(42)	13(56)	20(68)
Days with precipitation	3	3	2	4	8	7
Precipitation mm	13	10	8	15	33	56
Precipitation inches	0.5	0.4	0.3	0.6	1.3	2.2
Daily hours of sunshine	3	5	7	7	8	8

	Jul	Aug	Sep	Oct	Nov	Dec
Sunrise °C(°F)	10(50)	9(48)	2(35)	−6(21)	−17(2)	−24(−12)
Mid–afternoon °C(°F)	21(70)	20(68)	14(57)	5(41)	−7(20)	−16(4)
Days with precipitation	9	11	8	6	4	4
Precipitation mm	79	71	43	18	15	15
Precipitation inches	3.1	2.8	1.7	0.7	0.6	0.6
Daily hours of sunshine	8	7	6	5	3	2

Vladivostok. (On Pacific coast.)
Good months to visit: June to early September.

June to August: Hot summer with afternoon temperatures varying from 16°C (60°F) in June to 24°C (75°F) in August. Humidity increases due to warm moist air from the Pacific Ocean being carried by monsoon winds. This is the wettest season.
September: Cool. Afternoon temperatures range from 21°C (70°F) at the beginning of the month to 16°C (60°F) at the end. Rains continue but the wet season tapers off.
October to April: Cold winter months with snowfalls, particularly December to February. Little rain.

Vladivostok, Russia: Altitude 183m (600ft)

	Jan	Feb	Mar	Apr	May	Jun
Sunrise °C(°F)	−18(0)	−14(6)	−7(19)	1(34)	6(43)	11(52)
Mid–afternoon °C(°F)	−11(13)	−6(22)	1(33)	8(46)	13(55)	17(63)
Days with precipitation	2	2	4	5	8	10
Precipitation mm	8	10	18	31	53	74
Precipitation inches	0.3	0.4	0.7	1.2	2.1	2.9
Daily hours of sunshine	6	7	7	6	6	5

	Jul	Aug	Sep	Oct	Nov	Dec
Sunrise °C(°F)	16(60)	18(64)	13(55)	5(41)	−4(24)	−13(8)
Mid–afternoon °C(°F)	22(71)	24(75)	20(68)	13(55)	2(36)	−7(20)
Days with precipitation	10	9	7	5	4	3
Precipitation mm	84	119	109	48	31	15
Precipitation inches	3.3	4.7	4.3	1.9	1.2	0.6
Daily hours of sunshine	4	5	7	7	6	6

RWANDA

Official Name: Republic of Rwanda

Capital: Kigali
Languages: Kinyarwanda, French, English, (all official),
Kiswahili (Swahili)

This small mountainous country has cool to pleasantly
warm temperatures. Afternoon maximum temperatures
range 24 to 27°C (75 to 81°F) and humidity is moderate.
There are two dry seasons and two wet seasons although
some rain may fall every month.

Best time to visit: June to mid–September. (Dry.)

June to September: Long dry season.
October to December: Short rainy season.
January to February: Short dry season but sometimes these months are also wet.
March to May: Long rainy season.

Kigali, Rwanda: Altitude 150m (492ft)

	Jan	Feb	Mar	Apr	May	Jun
Sunrise ºC(ºF)	14(57)	14(57)	14(57)	14(57)	13(55)	12(53)
Mid–afternoon ºC(ºF)	25(77)	25(77)	25(77)	25(77)	24(75)	24(75)
Days with precipitation	14	15	18	22	18	4
Precipitation mm	69	100	106	183	92	20
Precipitation inches	2.7	3.9	4.2	7.2	3.6	0.8

	Jul	Aug	Sep	Oct	Nov	Dec
Sunrise ºC(ºF)	14(57)	14(57)	14(57)	14(57)	14(57)	14(57)
Mid–afternoon ºC(ºF)	26(79)	27(80)	27(80)	26(78)	25(77)	25(77)
Days with precipitation	2	5	11	16	20	17
Precipitation mm	9	34	86	102	127	100
Precipitation inches	0.4	1.3	3.4	4.0	5.0	3.9

ST HELENA
Official Name: St Helena
(Dependent Territory of the United Kingdom)

Capital: Jamestown
Language: English

St Helena, a remote island in the South Atlantic Ocean is small, 122 sq. km (47 sq. miles), and hilly. The highest point is 818m (2685ft).

Best time: Any time of year.
It is in the tropics but the temperature is modified by the cool Benguela current from Antarctic waters that passes by the island. The climate is warm and damp without major extremes of temperature. Fog or mist occurs for short durations on about 130 days of the year. The prevailing winds are the southeast trades that bring heavy rainfall to the south coast and higher elevations. Jamestown, on the north coast on the leeside of the hills, receives a low annual rainfall that ranges from 100 to 180mm (4 to 7in).

Jamestown, St Helena: Altitude 12m (40ft)

	Jan	Feb	Mar	Apr	May	Jun
Sunrise ºC(ºF)	21(69)	21(70)	22(71)	21(70)	19(67)	18(65)
Mid–afternoon ºC(ºF)	27(80)	27(81)	28(82)	27(81)	24(76)	23(74)
Days with precipitation	4	4	5	3	4	6
Precipitation mm	8	10	20	10	18	18
Precipitation inches	0.3	0.4	0.8	0.4	0.7	0.7
Daily hours of sunshine	5	5	4	4	5	4

	Jul	Aug	Sep	Oct	Nov	Dec
Sunrise ºC(ºF)	17(63)	17(63)	17(63)	18(64)	18(64)	19(66)
Mid–afternoon ºC(ºF)	22(72)	22(72)	22(72)	23(73)	23(73)	24(75)
Days with precipitation	8	3	2	1	0	1
Precipitation mm	8	10	5	3	0	3
Precipitation inches	0.3	0.4	0.2	0.1	0	0.1
Daily hours of sunshine	4	3	2	2	2	2

ST KITTS and NEVIS

Official Name: Federation of St Christopher and Nevis
(Nevis is pronounced Neevis)
(Independent nation; formerly a British possession)

Capital: Basseterre (on St Kitts)
Language: English

Both islands are hilly. St Kitts, also called St Christopher, has a mountain range which is forested on the upper slopes and carpeted with canefields on the lower slopes and on the lowlands. Nevis is dominated by a volcanic peak in the middle of the island.

Best time to visit: January to May. (Weather is pleasant most of the year.)

January to May: Cooler season. Average afternoon temperature, 28°C (82°F). Rain falls throughout the year, but there is less rain January to May.
June to November: Warmer season. Afternoon average, 30°C (86°F).
Winds: Cool breezes, the northeast trades, blow most of the year and reduce the humidity.
Hurricanes can occur August to October, but touchdowns are infrequent.

Note: See under Caribbean Islands for general weather information.

Basseterre, St Kitts: Altitude 48m (157ft)

	Jan	Feb	Mar	Apr	May	Jun
Sunrise °C(°F)	22(71)	21(70)	22(71)	23(73)	24(75)	24(76)
Mid–afternoon °C(°F)	27(80)	27(81)	28(82)	28(83)	29(84)	29(85)
Days with precipitation	17	11	11	10	12	12

	Jul	Aug	Sep	Oct	Nov	Dec
Sunrise °C(°F)	24(76)	24(76)	24(76)	24(76)	23(74)	23(74)
Mid–afternoon °C(°F)	30(86)	30(86)	30(86)	29(85)	29(85)	28(82)
Days with precipitation	16	16	16	16	16	16

ST LUCIA

Official Name: St Lucia (Lucia is pronounced Loosha.)
(Independent nation; formerly a British possession)

Capital: Castries
Languages: English, French patois

The island has a mountainous interior with deep valleys and has a coastline of sandy coves.

Best time to visit: January to May.

January to April: Dry season. Average afternoon temperature, 29°C (84°F). Sunny and not too hot. Rain also falls during the dry season.
May to November: Rainy season. August is the wettest month. Average afternoon temperature, 31°C (87°F).
Humidity is high throughout the year but is less in the dry season, January to April.
Hurricane season is July to November but a touchdown is rare.

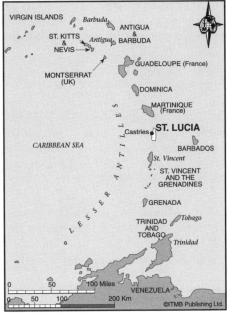

Note: See Caribbean Islands for general weather information.

Castries, St Lucia: Altitude 3m (10ft)

	Jan	Feb	Mar	Apr	May	Jun
Sunrise °C(°F)	21(69)	21(69)	21(69)	22(71)	23(73)	23(73)
Mid–afternoon °C(°F)	28(82)	28(82)	29(84)	31(87)	31(87)	31(87)
Days with precipitation	18	13	13	10	16	21
Precipitation mm	135	91	97	86	150	218
Precipitation inches	5.3	3.6	3.8	3.4	5.9	8.6

	Jul	Aug	Sep	Oct	Nov	Dec
Sunrise °C(°F)	23(74)	23(74)	23(73)	22(72)	22(72)	21(71)
Mid–afternoon °C(°F)	31(87)	31(87)	31(87)	31(87)	29(85)	28(83)
Days with precipitation	23	22	21	19	20	19
Precipitation mm	236	269	252	236	231	198
Precipitation inches	9.3	10.6	9.9	9.3	9.1	7.8

ST VINCENT and the GRENADINES

Official Name: St Vincent and the Grenadines.
(Independent nation; formerly a British possession)

Capital: Kingstown
Language: English, French patois

The Grenadines, islands south of St Vincent, consist of
Bequia, Mustique, Canouan, Mayreau, Tobago Cays,
Union Island, Palm Island, and Petit St Vincent.
Pronunciations are Beckway, Musteek, Can–oo–ahn,
May–ro, Toe–bay–go Keys.

St Vincent has an interior of high volcanic mountains with
deep valleys and luxuriant vegetation. The highest point
is 1234m (4049ft). The 30 or so Grenadines are low–lying
islands with coral reefs and sandy beaches.

**Best time to visit: Year–round is good with January to
May, the best.**

December to April: Dry season.
July to November: Wet season.
Sunshine: Sunny all year.
Hurricane season: July to November, but a touchdown is rare.

Note: See Caribbean Islands for general weather information

Kingstown, St Vincent: Altitude sea level

	Jan	Feb	Mar	Apr	May	Jun
Sunrise ºC(ºF)	23(73)	23(73)	23(74)	23(74)	24(76)	24(76)
Mid–afternoon ºC(ºF)	29(84)	29(85)	29(85)	30(86)	31(87)	31(87)
Days with precipitation	1	2	0	0	0	0

	Jul	Aug	Sep	Oct	Nov	Dec
Sunrise ºC(ºF)	24(76)	25(77)	25(77)	24(76)	24(76)	24(75)
Mid–afternoon ºC(ºF)	31(87)	31(87)	31(88)	31(88)	31(87)	29(85)
Days with precipitation	2	5	3	3	1	2

SAMOA

Official Name: Independent State of Samoa
(Was formerly Western Samoa)

Capital: Apia
Languages: Samoan (Polynesian), English

The islands (4 inhabited, 5 uninhabited) are volcanic.
Upolu island, where Apia is located, has rugged hills and
broad plains.

Best time to visit: April to November.

April to November: Season of less rain. Hot, humid.
December to March: Wet season. Hot, humid. Cyclones
may occur occasionally.
Rain, when it occurs, usually comes late afternoon, and humidity increases.

Apia, Samoa: Altitude 2m (7ft)

	Jan	Feb	Mar	Apr	May	Jun
Sunrise ºC(ºF)	24(75)	24(75)	23(74)	23(74)	23(74)	23(74)
Mid–afternoon ºC(ºF)	30(86)	30(86)	30(86)	30(86)	29(84)	29(84)
Days with precipitation	22	19	19	14	12	7
Precipitation mm	455	386	358	254	160	130
Precipitation inches	17.9	15.2	14.1	10.0	6.3	5.1
Daily hours of sunshine	6	6	6	6	7	7

	Jul	Aug	Sep	Oct	Nov	Dec
Sunrise ºC(ºF)	23(74)	23(74)	23(74)	23(74)	23(74)	23(74)
Mid–afternoon ºC(ºF)	29(85)	29(85)	29(85)	29(85)	29(85)	29(85)
Days with precipitation	9	9	11	14	16	19
Precipitation mm	81	89	132	170	267	371
Precipitation inches	3.2	3.5	5.2	6.7	10.5	14.6
Daily hours of sunshine	7	7	8	6	6	6

SAN MARINO

Official Name: Republic of San Marino

Capital: San Marino
Language: Italian

The dominant feature is Mt Titano, 743m (2437ft) above sea level. The capital city is on its slopes.

Best time: Late April to June, and September to mid–October. (These months avoid the summer crowds of July and August.)

March to May: Spring. Mild afternoon temperatures increase from 14°C (56°F) in March to 22°C (71°F) in May. Light rains fall.
June to August: Summer. Mainly dry and warm with an average daily maximum of 28°C (82°F).
September to February: Autumn and winter. Rainfall increases, with most falling in November. Afternoons are cool, often falling below 10°C (50°F) in winter, December to February.

SÃO TOMÉ and PRÍNCIPE

Official Name: Democratic Republic of São Tomé and Príncipe

Capital: São Tomé
Languages: Portuguese, local language

The islands are mountainous, of volcanic origin, and are densely forested.

Best time to visit: June to September. (Dry, cooler.)

June to September: Dry and humid with cloud.
October to May: Heavy rains, humid, cloudy.

São Tomé island: Altitude 5m (16ft)

	Jan	Feb	Mar	Apr	May	Jun
Sunrise °C(°F)	23(73)	23(73)	23(73)	23(73)	23(73)	22(71)
Mid–afternoon °C(°F)	30(86)	30(86)	31(87)	30(86)	29(85)	28(83)
Days with precipitation	6	8	9	10	8	2
Precipitation mm	81	107	150	127	135	28
Precipitation inches	3.2	4.2	5.9	5.0	5.3	1.1
Daily hours of sunshine	5	5	5	5	5	5

São Tomé island: (continued)

	Jul	Aug	Sep	Oct	Nov	Dec
Sunrise °C(°F)	21(69)	21(69)	21(69)	22(71)	22(71)	22(71)
Mid–afternoon °C(°F)	28(83)	28(83)	29(84)	29(84)	29(84)	29(84)
Days with precipitation	0	0	3	9	9	7
Precipitation mm	0	0	23	109	117	89
Precipitation inches	0	0	0.9	4.3	4.6	3.5
Daily hours of sunshine	5	5	4	4	5	5

SAUDI ARABIA
Official Name: Kingdom of Saudi Arabia

Capital: Riyadh
Language: Arabic

Saudi Arabia is a kingdom occupying the greater part of the Arabian Peninsula. The country is on a plateau, more than half of which is desert. Running parallel to the Red Sea coast is a mountain range. Its peaks exceed 3000m (10000ft) in the well–watered Asir province in the southwest, near Yemen. In the northeast near Oman are mountains that also rise above 3000m (10000ft). Along the coasts of the Red Sea and Persian Gulf are narrow plains. The climate is one of the world's hottest, and with low rainfall. Sand and dust storms can blow at any time of the year.

Best time for the whole country: November to February. (Mild.)

We have divided the weather into 3 regions: Inland, Red Sea coast and Persian Gulf coast.
1. Inland. (Includes Riyadh.)
November to February: Day temperatures range 20 to 30°C (68 to 86°F) and night temperatures can drop to a chilly 7°C (45°F), particularly in winter, December to January. Humidity is low.
April to October: Summers are hot and dry. From mid–April to October temperatures throughout the country can reach 40°C (104°F) in the daytime particularly in the summer months, May to September.

2. Red Sea coast: (Includes Jeddah.)
November to February: Day temperatures reach a moderate 30°C (86°F), and nights are mild, less than 20°C (68°F). Humidity is high. Nights can be unpleasantly warm.
April to October: Hot with high humidity. From mid–April to October temperatures can reach 40°C (104°F) in the daytime particularly in the summer months, May to September.

3. Persian Gulf coast: (Includes Dhahran.)
November to February: The climate is moderate, 20 to 30°C (68 to 86°F), with cold nights, 7°C (45°F), and light rain.
April to October: Hot with high humidity. From mid–April to October temperatures can reach 40°C (104°F) in the daytime particularly in the summer months, May to September.

Natural attraction: For visiting the mountainous Asir National Park in the southwest, March and April, and September and October are the preferred times.

Riyadh, Saudi Arabia: Altitude 620m (2034ft)

	Jan	Feb	Mar	Apr	May	Jun
Sunrise °C(°F)	8(46)	10(50)	14(57)	19(66)	24(75)	26(78)
Mid–afternoon °C(°F)	20(68)	23(73)	28(82)	32(89)	39(102)	42(107)
Days with precipitation	1	1	3	4	1	0
Precipitation mm	11	10	24	29	8	0
Precipitation inches	0.4	0.4	0.9	1.1	0.3	0
Daily hours of sunshine	7	8	8	8	9	11

	Jul	Aug	Sep	Oct	Nov	Dec
Sunrise °C(°F)	27(80)	27(80)	24(75)	19(66)	14(57)	9(48)
Mid–afternoon °C(°F)	43(109)	43(109)	40(104)	35(95)	27(80)	22(72)
Days with precipitation	0	0	0	0	1	1
Precipitation mm	0	1	0	1	6	11
Precipitation inches	0	0.04	0	0.04	0.2	0.4
Daily hours of sunshine	11	10	10	10	9	7

SENEGAL
Official Name: Republic of Senegal

Capital: Dakar
Languages: French, African languages

The country consists of an undulating plain with desert conditions in the centre, and savanna grasslands and tropical river forests in the north and south.

Best time to visit: November to February. (Dry, relatively cool.) March to May are also good months, but temperatures are beginning to rise.

November to May: Sunny, dry season. About 27°C (80°F) in the afternoons on the coast but the temperature is slightly higher inland. December to March is a popular time for beach vacationers from Europe. During December to February a hot, dry, northeasterly wind, the harmattan, blows from the Sahara often carrying dust which causes the sky to be hazy. The hot wind reduces humidity.

June to October: Rainy season. Rainfall usually lasts no more than a few hours and is not a major inconvenience. Often it falls at night. The amount of rainfall increases progressively from north to south. In the rainy season northern Senegal receives 300mm (12in), central Senegal, which includes Dakar, about 550mm (22in) and the southern half of the country from 1000 to 1500mm (40 to 60in). Rainfall decreases progressively from the coast to the inland regions. Temperatures are higher in the rainy season when daily maximums average 31°C (87°F); humidity is uncomfortably high.

Dakar, coastal Senegal: Altitude 24m (79ft)

	Jan	Feb	Mar	Apr	May	Jun
Sunrise °C(°F)	18(64)	18(64)	18(64)	18(64)	20(68)	23(73)
Mid–afternoon °C(°F)	26(78)	27(80)	27(80)	27(80)	29(84)	31(87)
Days with precipitation	0	0	0	0	0	2
Precipitation mm	2	1	0	0	0	10
Precipitation inches	0.08	0.04	0	0	0	0.4
Daily hours of sunshine	8	9	9	10	9	8

	Jul	Aug	Sep	Oct	Nov	Dec
Sunrise °C(°F)	24(75)	24(75)	24(75)	24(75)	23(73)	19(66)
Mid–afternoon °C(°F)	31(87)	31(87)	31(87)	32(89)	30(86)	27(80)
Days with precipitation	6	12	10	3	1	0
Precipitation mm	61	165	134	37	1	0
Precipitation inches	2.4	6.5	5.3	1.5	0.04	0
Daily hours of sunshine	7	7	7	8	8	8

SERBIA AND MONTENEGRO
(Previously was part of Yugoslavia)
Capital: Belgrade (Serbia), Podgorica (Montenegro)
Language: Serbo–Croat

Serbia, which is inland, has large, low–lying fertile plains in the north, hills in the centre and mountains in the south. Montenegro has a coastline along the Adriatic Sea. Beyond the coast are mountains which extend into the interior.

Best time: June to September.

We have divided the weather into 2 regions, Inland and Coast.

1. Inland. (Includes Belgrade.)
Best time: June to September.
June to September: Sunny and warm, 28°C (83°F) in daytime. Wettest season. June has the most rain.
October to November: Autumn. Transitional months with temperatures decreasing, October to November, from 20 to 10°C (68 to 50°F), and light rains.
December to February: Winter. Cold with temperature dropping to below freezing point. Cold winter winds from the north often blow through Belgrade. Expect light rains. Snow falls in the mountains and can stay for many weeks in high, sheltered places.
March to May: Spring. Transitional months with temperatures rising from 10°C (50°F) in March to 25°C (77°F) in May. Light rains fall.

Belgrade, Serbia: Altitude 132m (433ft)

	Jan	Feb	Mar	Apr	May	Jun
Sunrise °C(°F)	−2(29)	0(32)	3(37)	8(46)	12(53)	15(59)
Mid–afternoon °C(°F)	4(39)	6(42)	12(53)	18(64)	23(73)	25(77)
Days with precipitation	8	7	8	9	10	10
Precipitation mm	49	44	50	59	71	90
Precipitation inches	1.9	1.7	2.0	2.3	2.8	3.6
Daily hours of sunshine	2	3	5	6	7	8

	Jul	Aug	Sep	Oct	Nov	Dec
Sunrise °C(°F)	16(60)	16(60)	13(55)	8(46)	4(39)	0(32)
Mid–afternoon °C(°F)	27(80)	27(80)	24(75)	18(64)	11(51)	5(41)
Days with precipitation	7	6	6	6	9	9
Precipitation mm	66	51	51	40	54	58
Precipitation inches	2.6	2.0	2.0	1.6	2.1	2.3
Daily hours of sunshine	9	9	7	5	3	2

2. Coast. (Refer to weather table for Dubrovnik, Croatia, for similar weather.)
Best time: June to September.
June to September: Summer. Sunny and warm, 28°C (83°F). Mostly dry, but occasionally rain comes as heavy rainstorms.
October to November: Autumn. Temperature decrease from 20 to 15°C (68 to 59°F), but rains are heavy.

December to February: Winter. Mild and wet with daytime temperatures reaching 13°C (55°F), but cold, northerly winds are common. Rainfall is heavy, caused by clouds condensing on the coastal mountains.

March to May: Spring. Temperatures rise from a cool 15°C (59°F) in March to a mild 22°C (72°F) in May. Heavy rains fall.

SEYCHELLES

Official Name: Republic of Seychelles
Capital: Victoria
Languages: French, English and a Creole patois based on French and African languages

About 90 islands and islets comprise the republic. The main islands are mountainous. The highest point on Mahé, the largest island, is 912m (2993ft).

Weather in general is pleasant. There are no extremes of temperature. The variation throughout the year is only about 3°C (6°F). Throughout the year humidity is high, averaging almost 80% each day. The high temperatures and high humidity are tempered by sea breezes. As the islands are outside the cyclonic belt, strong winds and thunderstorms are rare.

Best time to visit: May to October.

May to October: Cooler, drier season. The southeast tradewinds blow over the islands bringing overcast skies, lowering temperatures slightly and causing seas to be rough.

November to April: Hot and humid. This is the rainy season. November to March are the rainiest months. More rain falls at higher elevations. The highest peak on Mahé, the main island, rises beyond 900m (almost 3000ft).

Victoria, Mahé island, Seychelles: Altitude 3m (10ft)

	Jan	Feb	Mar	Apr	May	Jun
Sunrise °C(°F)	24(75)	25(77)	25(77)	25(77)	25(77)	25(77)
Mid–afternoon °C(°F)	30(86)	30(86)	31(87)	31(87)	31(87)	29(85)
Days with precipitation	17	11	11	14	11	10
Precipitation mm	379	262	167	177	124	63
Precipitation inches	14.9	10.3	6.6	7.0	4.9	2.5
Daily hours of sunshine	5	6	7	8	8	8

	Jul	Aug	Sep	Oct	Nov	Dec
Sunrise °C(°F)	24(75)	24(75)	24(75)	24(75)	24(75)	24(75)
Mid–afternoon °C(°F)	28(82)	28(82)	29(84)	30(86)	30(86)	30(86)
Days with precipitation	10	10	11	12	14	18
Precipitation mm	80	97	121	206	215	281
Precipitation inches	3.2	3.8	4.8	8.1	8.5	11.1
Daily hours of sunshine	7	7	7	7	7	5

SIERRA LEONE
Official Name: Republic of Sierra Leone

Capital: Freetown
Languages: English, Krio, Mende, Temne

A wide well–forested coastal plain extends 120km (75 miles) inland. The land then rises gradually to a high rocky plateau and mountains on the Guinea border.

Best time to travel: November to April. (Dry.)

November to April: Dry season. Hot, 30°C (86°F) in the afternoons on the coast, but a little higher inland. Humidity is uncomfortably high. Skies may be hazy from mid–December to April as a result of the dust–laden harmattan winds blowing from the Sahara.
May to October: Rainy season. Rain is heaviest on the coast where Freetown is situated, averaging 25mm (1in) per day in July and August. The rainfall decreases progressively inland. Coastal temperatures average 28°C (82°F) in the afternoons, but slightly higher inland. Humidity increases in the rainy season.

Freetown, coastal Sierra Leone: Altitude 11m (37ft)

	Jan	Feb	Mar	Apr	May	Jun
Sunrise °C(°F)	24(76)	24(76)	24(76)	25(77)	24(76)	24(76)
Mid–afternoon °C(°F)	30(86)	30(86)	31(87)	31(87)	31(87)	30(86)
Days with precipitation	1	1	2	6	15	23
Precipitation mm	3	4	13	47	177	323
Precipitation inches	0.1	0.1	0.5	1.9	7.0	12.7
Daily hours of sunshine	7	7	7	7	6	5

	Jul	Aug	Sep	Oct	Nov	Dec
Sunrise °C(°F)	23(73)	23(73)	23(73)	23(73)	24(75)	24(75)
Mid–afternoon °C(°F)	29(84)	28(82)	29(84)	30(86)	30(86)	30(86)
Days with precipitation	26	27	24	22	10	3
Precipitation mm	734	791	484	266	88	16
Precipitation inches	28.9	31.1	19.0	10.5	3.5	0.6
Daily hours of sunshine	3	3	4	6	7	5

SINGAPORE

Official Name: Republic of Singapore

Capital: Singapore
Languages: Chinese, Malay, Tamil, English

The island republic consists of low–lying undulating terrain with Singapore City sited in the southeast corner. With adjacent islands, the area is 581 sq. km. (234 sq. miles).

It is hot, humid and wet year–round. Some months are wetter than others but the difference is small. Rainfall should not be a main factor in deciding when to go because it rains every month.

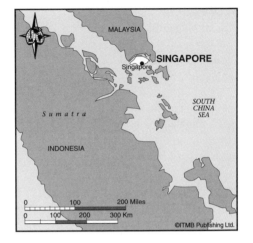

Best months: Good all year round.

November to January: Heaviest rainfalls.
March: Winds are extremely light compared with other months, making the heat harder to bear.
May to August: Less rain falls.
September: Winds are extremely light compared with other months, making the heat harder to bear.
Humidity hovers between 75 and 80%.
Daylight averages 12 hours daily because Singapore is near the equator.

Cultural event: Thaipusam. Held in January or February. Devotees walk in procession, their flesh pierced with hooks and skewers as a sign of penance.

Singapore City, Singapore: Altitude 10m (33ft)

	Jan	Feb	Mar	Apr	May	Jun
Sunrise ºC(ºF)	23(73)	24(75)	24(75)	24(75)	25(77)	25(77)
Mid–afternoon ºC(ºF)	30(86)	31(87)	31(87)	32(89)	32(89)	31(87)
Days with precipitation	12	10	13	14	14	13
Precipitation mm	198	154	171	141	158	140
Precipitation inches	7.8	6.1	6.7	5.6	6.2	5.5
Daily hours of sunshine	5	7	6	6	6	6

	Jul	Aug	Sep	Oct	Nov	Dec
Sunrise ºC(ºF)	24(75)	24(75)	24(75)	24(75)	23(73)	24(75)
Mid–afternoon ºC(ºF)	31(87)	31(87)	31(87)	31(87)	31(87)	30(86)
Days with precipitation	14	13	14	15	19	19
Precipitation mm	145	143	177	167	252	304
Precipitation inches	5.7	5.6	7.0	6.6	9.9	12.0
Daily hours of sunshine	6	6	5	5	4	4

SLOVAKIA
Official Name: Slovak Republic

Capital: Bratislava
Languages: Slovak, Hungarian

The north–central region is mountainous. The western region has flat, treeless plains except for the Low Tatra mountains in the extreme west. The east has rolling hills and is largely forested.

Best time to visit: April to end of September. (Note: rainiest months are June to August.)

April and May: Pleasant, mild temperatures in the daytime, cooler at night, frequent light rains, blue skies are common.
June to August: Summer. Thunderstorms bring heavy rain, especially from late June and into August. However, expect 8 hours of sunshine daily.
September: Occasional light rain, blue skies.
October to March: Cold with light rains. In winter, December, January and February, skies are often overcast and temperatures are at freezing point. Low temperatures may stay for several days if easterly winds from Russia prevail. Snow falls in the lowlands and in the mountains where there are ski resorts.

Bratislava, Slovakia: Altitude 153m (502ft)

	Jan	Feb	Mar	Apr	May	Jun
Sunrise ºC(ºF)	–5(23)	–3(27)	1(33)	5(41)	10(50)	13(55)
Mid–afternoon ºC(ºF)	2(35)	5(41)	11(51)	17(62)	22(72)	25(77)
Days with precipitation	7	6	6	6	8	8
Precipitation mm	34	34	27	39	55	61
Precipitation inches	1.3	1.3	1.1	1.5	2.2	2.4
Daily hours of sunshine	2	3	4	6	7	8

	Jul	Aug	Sep	Oct	Nov	Dec
Sunrise ºC(ºF)	14(57)	14(57)	10(50)	5(41)	1(33)	–3(27)
Mid–afternoon ºC(ºF)	27(80)	26(79)	22(72)	16(61)	8(46)	3(37)
Days with precipitation	7	7	6	5	8	8
Precipitation mm	51	57	39	32	54	40
Precipitation inches	2.0	2.2	1.5	1.3	2.1	1.6
Daily hours of sunshine	8	8	6	5	2	1

SLOVENIA
Official Name: Republic of Slovenia

Capital: Ljubljana
Languages: Slovene, Serbo–Croat

Forested mountains cover much of Slovenia. The peaks of the Julian Alps are snow–capped year–round.

Best time: Late April to September.
To visit outside the main summer season of July and August, consider September which still has summer warmth.

May to September: Temperatures on the coast start to become warmer in May, 21°C (70°F), and climb to 28°C (83°F) by July. Inland is a degree or two cooler. Days on the coast are sunny with 11 hours; inland has 7 hours. Rain on the coast is light with occasional thunderstorms; inland is much wetter.

October to April: Winter on the coast is mild, 14°C (56°F), while inland temperatures in the hilly interior fall below freezing, particularly January and February. Cold northerlies sometimes blow from eastern and central Europe. Snow falls in the mountains and can stay until late May. From October into December excessive amounts of rain fall in the coastal region, caused by clouds condensing on the coastal mountains.

Ljubljana, inland Slovenia: Altitude 316m (1037ft)

	Jan	Feb	Mar	Apr	May	Jun
Sunrise ºC(ºF)	–4(25)	–2(29)	1(33)	5(41)	9(48)	12(53)
Mid–afternoon ºC(ºF)	2(35)	6(42)	10(50)	15(59)	20(68)	24(75)
Days with precipitation	9	8	9	11	12	12
Precipitation mm	82	80	98	109	122	155
Precipitation inches	3.2	3.2	3.9	4.3	4.8	6.1
Daily hours of sunshine	1	3	4	5	7	7

	Jul	Aug	Sep	Oct	Nov	Dec
Sunrise ºC(ºF)	14(57)	14(57)	11(51)	7(44)	2(35)	–2(29)
Mid–afternoon ºC(ºF)	26(78)	25(77)	22(72)	16(60)	8(46)	3(37)
Days with precipitation	10	10	8	8	9	9
Precipitation mm	122	144	130	115	135	101
Precipitation inches	4.8	5.7	5.1	4.5	5.3	4.0
Daily hours of sunshine	8	7	5	4	2	1

SOLOMON ISLANDS

Official Name: Solomon Islands
(Independent nation; formerly British Solomon Islands)

Capital: Honiara (on island of Guadalcanal)
Languages: English, Melanesian pidgin, more than 50
indigenous languages

The larger islands are volcanic in origin, mountainous and
thickly forested. There are numerous small islands and
atolls.

Best time to visit: April to November.

April to November: Season of less rain. Hot, humid.
Average afternoon temperature, 30°C (86°F).
December to March: Wet season. Hot, humid. Cyclones may occur. Most rain usually falls in
January, 380mm (15in). Rain, when it occurs, usually comes late afternoon, and humidity increases.
Afternoon temperature, 31°C (88°F).
Sunshine throughout year averages 6 to 8 hours per day.

Tulaghi, (near Honiara), Solomon Islands:

	Jan	Feb	Mar	Apr	May	Jun
Sunrise ºC(ºF)	24(76)	24(76)	24(76)	24(76)	24(75)	24(75)
Mid–afternoon ºC(ºF)	31(88)	31(88)	31(88)	31(88)	31(88)	30(86)
Days with precipitation	15	14	12	14	14	13
Precipitation mm	381	407	373	256	214	174
Precipitation inches	15.0	16.0	14.7	10.1	8.4	6.9

	Jul	Aug	Sep	Oct	Nov	Dec
Sunrise ºC(ºF)	23(74)	23(74)	23(74)	23(74)	24(75)	24(75)
Mid–afternoon ºC(ºF)	29(85)	29(85)	30(87)	31(87)	31(87)	32(89)
Days with precipitation	13	14	13	14	12	14
Precipitation mm	195	219	208	221	258	264
Precipitation inches	7.7	8.6	8.2	8.7	10.2	10.4

SOMALIA

Official Name: Somali Democratic Republic

Capital: Mogadishu
Languages: Somali, Arabic, English, Italian

The land is arid. In the north there is desert with rugged mountains rising beyond 2100m (7000ft). In the south the desert is flat with scrub and there is a region of grassy plains.

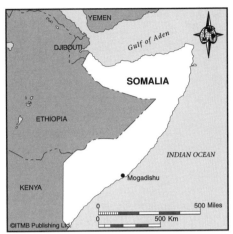

Best time to visit: November to March.

November to March: Sunny, humid, dry, dusty, hot, 30°C (86°F) on both coasts.

May to September: Main rainy season but rainfall is unreliable. Sunny, humid and hot. The cool waters of the offshore current maintain the air temperatures along the Indian Ocean coast at about 29°C (85°F) while the warm waters of the northern coast along the Gulf of Aden push air temperatures to beyond 40°C (104°F).

Mogadishu, Somalia: Altitude 12m (39ft)

	Jan	Feb	Mar	Apr	May	Jun
Sunrise °C(°F)	23(73)	23(73)	24(76)	26(78)	25(77)	23(73)
Mid–afternoon °C(°F)	30(86)	30(86)	31(88)	32(89)	32(89)	29(85)
Days with precipitation	0	0	0	5	7	14
Precipitation mm	0	0	0	58	58	97
Precipitation inches	0	0	0	2.3	2.3	3.8
Daily hours of sunshine	8	9	9	8	8	7

	Jul	Aug	Sep	Oct	Nov	Dec
Sunrise °C(°F)	23(73)	23(73)	23(73)	24(76)	24(76)	24(76)
Mid–afternoon °C(°F)	28(83)	28(83)	29(84)	30(86)	31(87)	30(86)
Days with precipitation	20	11	7	5	5	2
Precipitation mm	64	48	25	23	41	13
Precipitation inches	2.5	1.9	1.0	0.9	1.6	0.5
Daily hours of sunshine	7	8	9	9	8	8

SOUTH AFRICA

Official Name: Republic of
South Africa

Capital: Pretoria (administrative).
      Cape Town (legislative).
      Bloemfontein (judiciary).
Languages: Afrikaans, English,
Bantu languages

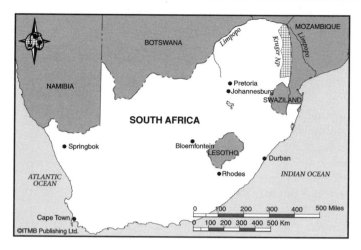

The entire country is on a large
plateau except for coastal land
that extends inland for an average
of 80km (50 miles). There are
high mountains in the east, the
Drakensbergs, that exceed 3000m (10000ft), and mountains along the south coast.

Weather in general: All months are generally good for travel. The weather is sunny and temperate without extremes of temperature. Winter, **June to August**, is generally mild, except in the Drakensberg Mountains where it snows. Summer, **October to March**, is hot and is when most rain, 90% of it, falls throughout the country. The exception is Cape Town and surrounding region which receives its rain in winter, May to August.

Best months for all of the country, except Cape Town: September & April.
Best time for Cape Town: October to March. (Dry, longer days.)
Best time for Kruger National Park: June to mid–October. (Cool, dry.)

October to March: Summer. Days are warm to hot, 21 to 27°C (70 to 80°F). Nights are comfortably cool except along the hot, humid, east coast, e.g. Durban.
October to March is the rainy season, except for Cape Town which has winter rains June to August. October to March is a pleasant time to visit Cape Town.
Beach season in Durban in KwaZulu–Natal province and along the southern coast is best in December and January.
April is a transitional month with pleasant weather of little or no rain, with afternoon temperatures of 23°C (73°F) and 7 to 8 hours of sunshine daily.
May to August: Winter. Throughout most of the country days are dry, sunny and mild to warm; nights are cold. Exceptions are Cape Town where it is wet with drizzly rain and cold westerly winds, and the Drakensberg Mountains where it snows. Skiing is at Tiffindell, 2800m (9000ft), near Rhodes.
September is a transitional month with pleasant weather of little or no rain, with afternoon temperatures of 23°C (73°F) and 8 to 9 hours of sunshine daily.

Natural attractions:
Wildlife viewing is best in winter, May to August, and into early October. Weather is pleasant. Grass is lower so animals can be seen more easily. Mosquitoes are absent.
Bird watching is best October to March during the rainy summer months. The grasses are greener and the bird population increases due to migratory birds from other parts of Africa, and Europe.
Kruger National Park, the country's most famous game reserve, is open year–round. June to mid–October is best. The wet season, October to March, has thunderstorms, and temperatures reach 30°C (86°F).

Wildflower season at Springbok in Namaqualand of Northern Cape Province: The semi–desert blooms from mid–August to mid–September. Daytime temperature is a pleasant 19°C (67°F), and rain is negligible.

Note about school holidays: Because most of South Africa's tourists are its own residents, accommodation is booked heavily in advance for school holidays particularly those from mid–December to mid–January.

Cape Town, southwest coast, South Africa: Altitude 17m (56ft)

	Jan	Feb	Mar	Apr	May	Jun
Sunrise °C(°F)	16(60)	16(60)	14(57)	12(53)	9(48)	8(46)
Mid–afternoon °C(°F)	26(78)	26(78)	25(77)	23(73)	20(68)	18(64)
Days with precipitation	3	3	3	6	8	10
Precipitation mm	14	16	21	41	68	93
Precipitation inches	0.6	0.6	0.8	1.6	2.7	3.7
Daily hours of sunshine	11	11	9	8	7	6

	Jul	Aug	Sep	Oct	Nov	Dec
Sunrise °C(°F)	7(44)	8(46)	9(48)	11(51)	13(55)	15(59)
Mid–afternoon °C(°F)	17(62)	18(64)	19(66)	21(69)	24(75)	25(77)
Days with precipitation	9	9	7	5	3	4
Precipitation mm	83	77	41	33	16	17
Precipitation inches	3.3	3.0	1.6	1.3	0.6	0.7
Daily hours of sunshine	6	7	7	9	10	11

Durban, east coast, South Africa: Altitude 5m (16ft)

	Jan	Feb	Mar	Apr	May	Jun
Sunrise °C(°F)	21(70)	21(70)	20(68)	17(62)	14(57)	11(51)
Mid–afternoon °C(°F)	28(82)	28(82)	28(82)	26(78)	25(77)	23(74)
Days with precipitation	10	9	9	6	4	3
Precipitation mm	134	113	126	73	59	28
Precipitation inches	5.3	4.4	5.0	2.9	2.3	1.1
Daily hours of sunshine	6	6	7	7	7	8

	Jul	Aug	Sep	Oct	Nov	Dec
Sunrise °C(°F)	11(51)	13(55)	15(59)	17(62)	18(64)	20(68)
Mid–afternoon °C(°F)	23(73)	23(73)	23(73)	24(75)	25(77)	27(80)
Days with precipitation	3	5	7	10	11	10
Precipitation mm	39	62	73	98	108	102
Precipitation inches	1.5	2.4	2.9	3.9	4.3	4.0
Daily hours of sunshine	7	7	6	5	6	6

Johannesburg, South Africa: Altitude 1665m (5463ft)

	Jan	Feb	Mar	Apr	May	Jun
Sunrise °C(°F)	15(59)	14(58)	13(55)	10(50)	7(44)	4(39)
Mid–afternoon °C(°F)	26(78)	25(77)	24(76)	21(71)	19(66)	16(61)
Days with precipitation	12	8	8	7	2	1
Precipitation mm	125	94	90	54	13	9
Precipitation inches	4.9	3.7	3.6	2.1	0.5	0.4
Daily hours of sunshine	8	8	8	8	9	9

	Jul	Aug	Sep	Oct	Nov	Dec
Sunrise °C(°F)	4(39)	6(42)	9(48)	11(51)	13(55)	14(57)
Mid–afternoon °C(°F)	17(62)	19(66)	23(73)	24(75)	24(75)	25(77)
Days with precipitation	1	1	3	7	10	11
Precipitation mm	4	6	27	76	117	103
Precipitation inches	0.1	0.2	1.1	3.0	4.6	4.1
Daily hours of sunshine	9	9	9	9	8	8

SOUTH KOREA, see KOREA (South)

SPAIN
Official Name: Kingdom of Spain

Capital: Madrid
Languages: Spanish, Catalan, Galician, Basque

Much of Spain's interior is a vast, almost treeless plateau with an average height of 600m (2000ft) above sea level. It is crossed by irregular mountain ranges.
(Balearic Islands and Canary Islands, which belong to Spain, are listed separately under **B** and **C**.)

Best time to visit, in general, is May to October.
We have divided the weather into three regions. Refer to map for corresponding numbers.

1. Central Plateau. (Includes Madrid, Zaragoza, Sevilla, Cordoba.)
Best time: May, September and October although June to August are good, but hotter.

May: Mild. Average afternoon temperatures range from 21°C (70°F) in the north to 29°C (85°F) in the south. Nights can be cool. Nine hours of sunshine daily. Light rains.
June to August: Summer. Hot winds. Low humidity. Average afternoon temperatures range from 24°C (75°F) in the north to 36°C (98°F) in the south. Eleven to 12 hours of sunshine daily. Occasional light rain.
September and October: Mild. Afternoon temperatures, 21°C (70°F) in north to 27°C (80°F) in the south. Eight hours of sunshine daily. Light rains.

November to April: Cool. Cold winds blow from the mountains. December and January are the coldest, 9°C (47°F), in the afternoons. Five hours of sunshine daily. This is the rainy season.

2. Mediterranean Coast.

Best time: April to October. (However, Costa del Sol in the south attracts tourist crowds all year–round because of warm weather.)

April and May: Mild, balmy weather. Average afternoon temperatures, 21°C (70°F). Eight to 9 hours of sunshine daily. Light rain.

June to August: Hot and balmy, but sea breezes keep the temperatures bearable. Average afternoon temperature, 27°C (80°F). This is the dry season with 10 to 11 hours of sunshine daily. August is a busy month; beaches are packed with European holidaymakers.

September and October: Warm and balmy. Average afternoon temperature, 21 to 27°C (70 to 80°F). Seven hours of sunshine daily. Light rain.

November to March: Mild in the north, e.g. Costa Brava. Average afternoon temperature, 14°C (57°F), with 4 to 6 hours of sunshine daily, and light rain. Warmer in the south, e.g. Costa del Sol. Average afternoon temperature, 17°C (62°F) with 5 to 7 hours of sunshine daily, and negligible rain.

3. Northwestern region. (Includes Santander.)

Best time: June to September.

June to September: Weather is changeable with warm, sunny days and cool days of fine rain, mist and cloud. Average afternoon temperature is 21°C (70°F) with 7 hours of sunshine daily.

October to May: Cool and cloudy. Afternoon temperatures drop to 13°C (55°F) during winter, December to February. Expect only 3 hours of sunshine daily. October to May is the rainy season. Most rain falls in December.

Cultural Event: The Fiesta de San Fermin, commonly known as **"Running of the Bulls"** is held annually in Pamplona, July 7 to 14.

Madrid, Spain: Altitude 667m (2188ft)

	Jan	Feb	Mar	Apr	May	Jun
Sunrise °C(°F)	2(35)	2(35)	5(41)	7(44)	10(50)	15(59)
Mid–afternoon °C(°F)	9(48)	11(51)	15(59)	18(64)	21(69)	27(80)
Days with precipitation	8	7	9	10	6	5
Precipitation mm	46	44	33	54	41	26
Precipitation inches	1.8	1.7	1.3	2.1	1.6	1.0
Daily hours of sunshine	5	6	7	8	9	11

	Jul	Aug	Sep	Oct	Nov	Dec
Sunrise °C(°F)	17(62)	17(62)	14(57)	10(50)	5(41)	2(35)
Mid–afternoon °C(°F)	31(87)	30(86)	25(77)	19(67)	13(56)	9(48)
Days with precipitation	2	2	6	8	9	9
Precipitation mm	13	9	30	45	64	51
Precipitation inches	0.5	0.4	1.2	1.8	2.5	2.0
Daily hours of sunshine	12	11	9	7	5	4

SRI LANKA

Official Name: Democratic Socialist Republic of Sri
Lanka

Capital: Colombo
Languages: Sinhalese, Tamil, English

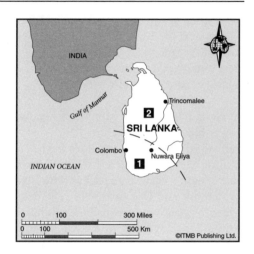

The south–central area consists of a large mountainous
mass with peaks around 2400m (8000ft). There are
extensive lowlands around the coast and in the north.

The main influences on weather on the island are the
southwest monsoon and the northeast monsoon. When
rain is falling in one region, the other region is dry. Rain
often comes as afternoon thunderstorms.

Best time to visit when the entire island is dry: February to March.
Best time to visit Colombo, the highlands and southwest coast: December to April. (Dry.)
Best time to visit the north, and the southeast lowlands: February to September. (Dry.)

We have divided the island into two weather regions. See map for corresponding numbers.
1. South–central and southwest highland areas, and southwest coast. (Includes Colombo.)
Best time: December to April.

December to April: Dry season. Average afternoon temperature, 31°C (87°F). Eight hours of sunshine
daily. High humidity, but periodic winds make the humidity bearable.
May to September: Rainy because of the southwest monsoon which brings rain from the Indian
Ocean. May receives the heaviest rainfall, then the rains gradually taper off each month towards
September. Afternoon temperatures remain a constant 29°C (85°F) each month. The sea is a constant
27°C (81°F) year–round, but during May to September coastal tides make swimming dangerous. Six
hours of sunshine daily. Humidity is high. Colombo's humidity is 70% to 80% daily.
October to November: Thunderstorms bring heavy rain. Afternoon temperatures average 29°C
(85°F). Humidity is high. Expect 6 hours of sunshine daily.

Cultural event: Esala Perahera in Kandy is held for 9 nights between mid–June and mid–July.
Includes parades of drummers, dancers and dozens of caparisoned elephants, one of which carries the
venerated tooth of Buddha.

Natural attraction: Tea estates in the highlands around Nuwara Eliya (pronounced locally as
Nu'reliya). Rain falls here year–round, but there is less rain January to May – a good time to visit.
Temperatures in these highlands average a comfortable 19 to 22°C (66 to 71°F) year–round.

Colombo, southwest coast, Sri Lanka: Altitude 7m (23ft)

	Jan	Feb	Mar	Apr	May	Jun
Sunrise ºC(ºF)	22(72)	23(73)	24(75)	25(77)	26(78)	26(78)
Mid–afternoon ºC(ºF)	31(87)	31(87)	32(89)	32(89)	31(87)	30(86)
Days with precipitation	7	7	8	14	19	14
Precipitation mm	62	69	130	253	382	186
Precipitation inches	2.4	2.7	5.1	10.0	15.0	7.3
Daily hours of sunshine	8	9	9	8	6	7

	Jul	Aug	Sep	Oct	Nov	Dec
Sunrise ºC(ºF)	25(77)	25(77)	25(77)	24(75)	23(74)	23(74)
Mid–afternoon ºC(ºF)	30(86)	30(86)	30(86)	30(86)	30(86)	30(86)
Days with precipitation	12	11	12	19	16	10
Precipitation mm	125	114	236	369	310	168
Precipitation inches	4.9	4.5	9.3	14.5	12.2	6.6
Daily hours of sunshine	6	6	6	6	7	7

2. The north, and the southeast lowlands. (Includes Trincomalee.)
Best time: February to September.

February to September: Dry season. Afternoon average temperature, 32ºC (90ºF). Seven to 9 hours of sunshine daily.
October to January: Rainy because of the northeast monsoons. Afternoon temperatures drop from 31ºC (88ºF) in October to 27ºC (80ºF) in January. Six hours of sunshine daily. Humidity is 60%, low when compared with Colombo's 70% to 80%.

Trincomalee, northeast coast, Sri Lanka: Altitude 7m (23ft)

	Jan	Feb	Mar	Apr	May	Jun
Sunrise ºC(ºF)	24(75)	25(77)	25(77)	26(78)	26(78)	26(78)
Mid–afternoon ºC(ºF)	28(82)	29(84)	31(88)	33(91)	35(95)	35(95)
Days with precipitation	10	5	4	5	5	2
Precipitation mm	132	100	54	50	52	26
Precipitation inches	5.2	3.9	2.1	2.0	2.0	1.0
Daily hours of sunshine	7	9	9	9	8	7

	Jul	Aug	Sep	Oct	Nov	Dec
Sunrise ºC(ºF)	26(78)	26(78)	25(77)	25(77)	24(75)	24(75)
Mid–afternoon ºC(ºF)	34(93)	34(93)	34(93)	32(89)	29(84)	28(82)
Days with precipitation	3	6	7	13	17	17
Precipitation mm	70	89	104	217	334	341
Precipitation inches	2.8	3.5	4.1	8.5	13.1	13.4
Daily hours of sunshine	7	7	8	6	6	6

SUDAN
Official Name: Republic of Sudan

Capital: Khartoum
Languages: Arabic, English, African languages

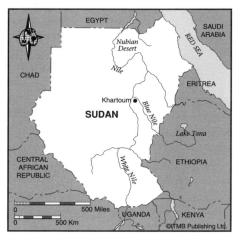

Along the Nile, which flows south to north, there are tropical forests and swamplands in the south, grassy plains in the centre and desert in the north. Western Sudan also consists of desert.

Sudan has two weather regions, the northern half (including Khartoum) which is dry and hot throughout most of the year, and the southern half where rainfall and humidity are greater, but temperatures slightly lower.

Best time to visit: November to March.

November to March: Winter. Dry season. Average afternoon temperatures range 32 to 38°C (90 to 100°F) throughout the country. Nights in the desert regions can be bitterly cold with temperatures near freezing. Expect 10 hours of sunshine daily throughout the country.
April to October: Hot, rainy season. In the northern region (including Khartoum) light rains fall July and August. Expect 10 hours of sunshine daily in the north, April to October. In the southern half of the country rainfall increases the farther south you go. Nine wet months, March to November, are possible. Expect high humidity and 7 hours of sunshine daily in the south.
Sandstorms (haboobs) can sweep in from the Sahara desert between April and November. They are more likely to occur near the beginning of the rainy season, e.g. April. They can last 3 or 4 days.

Khartoum, northern Sudan: Altitude 380m (1247ft)

	Jan	Feb	Mar	Apr	May	Jun
Sunrise °C(°F)	16(60)	17(62)	21(69)	24(76)	27(80)	27(80)
Mid–afternoon °C(°F)	31(87)	33(91)	37(98)	40(104)	42(107)	41(105)
Days with precipitation	0	0	0	0	1	1
Precipitation mm	0	0	0	0	4	5
Precipitation inches	0	0	0	0	0.1	0.2
Daily hours of sunshine	10	10	10	10	9	8

	Jul	Aug	Sep	Oct	Nov	Dec
Sunrise °C(°F)	26(78)	25(77)	26(78)	26(78)	21(70)	17(62)
Mid–afternoon °C(°F)	38(101)	37(98)	39(102)	39(102)	35(96)	32(89)
Days with precipitation	4	4	2	1	0	0
Precipitation mm	46	75	25	5	1	0
Precipitation inches	1.8	3.0	1.0	0.2	0.04	0
Daily hours of sunshine	8	8	8	9	10	10

SURINAME

Official Name: Republic of Suriname

Capital: Paramaribo
Languages: Dutch, English, Hindi, local languages

There is a swampy coastal plain that ranges up to 160km (100 miles) in width. Beyond the plain is a central plateau of grassland and woodland. Farther south is a densely forested mountainous region.

The weather in general is hot and damp year–round with humidity averaging about 82% daily. No season is very dry or very wet. Even in the wet seasons of which there are two, long periods of sunshine occur between the rains. Suriname escapes the Caribbean hurricanes. The prevailing tradewinds from the northeast keep the coastal temperatures down to a range of 23°C (73°F) in the morning to 31°C (87°F) in the afternoon.

Best time: December to April. January and February are the coolest with 29°C (85°F).

February to April: Minor dry season with occasional rain.
Mid–April to mid–August: Main rainy season. Cloudy.
Mid–August to mid–November: Main dry season with only a little rain. September and October are the hottest months, 33°C (91°F).
Mid–November to mid–February: Minor rainy season.

Paramaribo, Suriname: Altitude 4m (12ft)

	Jan	Feb	Mar	Apr	May	Jun
Sunrise °C(°F)	22(72)	22(72)	22(72)	23(73)	23(73)	23(73)
Mid–afternoon °C(°F)	29(85)	29(85)	29(85)	30(86)	30(86)	30(86)
Days with precipitation	18	13	14	16	23	23
Precipitation mm	213	165	201	229	310	302
Precipitation inches	8.4	6.5	7.9	9.0	12.2	11.9
Daily hours of sunshine	6	6	6	5	6	8

	Jul	Aug	Sep	Oct	Nov	Dec
Sunrise °C(°F)	23(73)	23(73)	23(73)	23(73)	23(73)	22(72)
Mid–afternoon °C(°F)	31(87)	32(89)	33(91)	33(91)	32(89)	30(86)
Days with precipitation	20	14	9	9	12	18
Precipitation mm	231	158	79	76	125	224
Precipitation inches	9.1	6.2	3.1	3.0	4.9	8.8
Daily hours of sunshine	8	9	9	9	8	6

SWAZILAND
Official Name: Kingdom of Swaziland

Capital: Mbabane (administrative)
        Lobamba (legislative)
Languages: English, Siswati

In the west are rugged hills, many with pine forests. In the centre and east are lowlands with scrub and grassland (the veld).

**Best time: Pleasant throughout the year but best times are April and May, and
August and September.** (Dry and warm.)

April and May: Warm, 21°C (70°F). Light rain.
June to August: Winter. Sunny, dry and mild, 19°C (67°F) in afternoons but nights may fall to 6°C (42°F) or lower. There are frosts in June and July.
September: Warm, 23°C (73°F). Light rains.
October to March: Summer. Rainy season. Most rain comes as thunderstorms, the bulk of it falling in the highlands in the west. Humidity is low. Average daily maximum temperature is a warm 25°C (77°F).

Mbabane, Swaziland: Altitude 1163m (3816ft)

	Jan	Feb	Mar	Apr	May	Jun
Sunrise °C(°F)	15(59)	15(59)	14(57)	12(53)	8(47)	6(42)
Mid–afternoon °C(°F)	25(77)	25(77)	24(75)	23(74)	21(70)	19(66)
Days with precipitation	15	14	13	8	4	3
Precipitation mm	254	213	193	71	33	20
Precipitation inches	10.0	8.4	7.6	2.8	1.3	0.8
Daily hours of sunshine	8	8	8	7	8	8

	Jul	Aug	Sep	Oct	Nov	Dec
Sunrise °C(°F)	6(42)	7(45)	9(49)	12(54)	13(56)	14(58)
Mid–afternoon °C(°F)	19(66)	21(70)	23(73)	24(75)	24(76)	25(77)
Days with precipitation	3	4	7	12	14	16
Precipitation mm	23	28	61	127	170	208
Precipitation inches	0.9	1.1	2.4	5.0	6.7	8.2
Daily hours of sunshine	8	8	9	9	8	7

SWEDEN

Official Name: Kingdom of Sweden
Capital: Stockholm
Language: Swedish

The northwest, along the Norwegian border, is mountainous. East of the mountains is a broad plateau that slopes down to the Gulf of Bothnia. South–central Sweden is a lowland of many lakes and there are uplands farther south. Forests cover more than half of the country.

Best time to visit: Late May to September.

Late May to September: Fairly sunny and warm with occasional rain. There can be a mix of hot and cold days, and dry and wet days. The heavy rains fall from mid–July to November. August is the wettest. In Stockholm and the south, mid–summer temperatures in July average 20°C (68°F) in the daytime. North of Stockholm, temperatures are only a few degrees lower because the long summer days tend to raise the temperature. Longer daylight hours are experienced in the higher latitudes. In mid–summer, 24 hours of twilight occur north of the Arctic Circle. Be aware that June and July are when mosquitoes are prevalent.

October to April: Cold, with temperatures dropping to freezing point, particularly in mid–winter, January. Rain falls year–round. In Stockholm and the south, both rain and snow fall. North of Stockholm the precipitation is mainly snow. In the far north, Lappland, winter runs from October to April, accompanied by long, dark nights and –40°C (–40°F) temperatures.

Rainfall in Sweden, although year–round, is moderate because the coastal mountains of Norway capture much of the rain coming from the Atlantic. However, rain that does arrive hits Sweden's west coast first (e.g. Gothenburg, Göteborg), making it the wettest coast.

Stockholm, Sweden: Altitude 44m (144ft)

	Jan	Feb	Mar	Apr	May	Jun
Sunrise °C(°F)	–5(23)	–5(23)	–3(27)	1(33)	6(42)	11(51)
Mid–afternoon °C(°F)	–1(30)	–1(30)	3(37)	9(48)	16(60)	21(69)
Days with precipitation	10	7	7	7	7	7
Precipitation mm	39	27	26	30	30	45
Precipitation inches	1.5	1.1	1.0	1.2	1.2	1.8
Daily hours of sunshine	1	3	4	6	9	10

	Jul	Aug	Sep	Oct	Nov	Dec
Sunrise °C(°F)	13(55)	13(55)	9(48)	5(41)	1(33)	–3(27)
Mid–afternoon °C(°F)	22(72)	20(68)	15(59)	10(50)	5(41)	1(33)
Days with precipitation	10	10	10	9	11	10
Precipitation mm	72	66	55	50	53	46
Precipitation inches	2.8	2.6	2.2	2.0	2.1	1.8
Daily hours of sunshine	8	7	5	3	2	1

SWITZERLAND
Official Name: Swiss Confederation

Capital: Bern
Languages: German, French, Italian, Romansch

Switzerland is mountainous with many peaks remaining snow–capped year–round. The Jura Mountains are in the northwest and the Alps are in the south. Between them stretches the 50km (30 miles) wide Swiss plateau from Lake Geneva in the southwest to Lake of Constance in the northeast. The plateau is studded with numerous hills.

Best time: May to September for general tourism.
December to April for winter sports.

May to October: Warm, wet. While valleys may enjoy clear, warm weather the mountains may be cloaked in cloud. July and August are usually the wettest months with thunderstorms bringing heavy rain. Higher elevations receive more rain. Precipitation is distributed unevenly because of differences in elevation and variations in dominant winds. For example, in summer as well as winter, Tichino, the canton in the south, is affected by warm air from the Mediterranean. It is the warmest region of the country. Valais, the canton in the southwest, is known for being the driest.

November to April: Cool to below freezing point. In these months, much of the precipitation comes as snow. Many mountain peaks retain a snow cover throughout the year. Valleys are often foggy while the resorts in the mountains enjoy cold but clear weather. A cold wind, the bise, from the north, predominates in winter. In spring, March to May, the föhn, a warm, dry, southeasterly wind comes down the northern slopes of mountains. Its strength, dryness and warmth can quicken the spring thaw and cause avalanches. They could blow for three days at a time.

Zurich, Switzerland: Altitude 569m (1867ft)

	Jan	Feb	Mar	Apr	May	Jun
Sunrise ºC(ºF)	–3(27)	–2(29)	1(33)	4(39)	8(46)	11(51)
Mid–afternoon ºC(ºF)	2(35)	4(39)	8(46)	12(53)	17(62)	20(68)
Days with precipitation	11	10	12	12	13	13
Precipitation mm	69	70	70	89	105	125
Precipitation inches	2.7	2.8	2.8	3.5	4.1	4.9
Daily hours of sunshine	1	3	4	5	5	6

	Jul	Aug	Sep	Oct	Nov	Dec
Sunrise ºC(ºF)	13(55)	12(53)	10(50)	6(42)	2(35)	–1(30)
Mid–afternoon ºC(ºF)	22(72)	21(71)	18(64)	13(55)	7(44)	3(37)
Days with precipitation	12	12	9	8	11	11
Precipitation mm	118	135	94	69	82	75
Precipitation inches	4.6	5.3	3.7	2.7	3.2	3.0
Daily hours of sunshine	7	6	5	3	2	1

SYRIA

Official Name: Syrian Arab Republic

Capital: Damascus
Languages: Arabic, Kurdish, Armenian

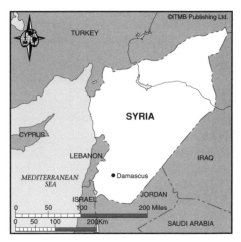

The short Mediterranean coastline has a narrow plain that rises abruptly to a narrow mountain range. Extending in a north–south line are the main cities of Aleppo, Hama, Homs and Damascus which are located in valleys and plains. To the east of them is the Syrian desert.

Syria's generally sunny climate varies from a Mediterranean type (mild, wet winters and hot, dry summers) in the west to a desert type (a wide temperature range between hot days and cold nights) in the east.

Best time: First choice is March to May (after the rains). **Second choice is September to November** (mild autumn).

March to May: Spring. Dry and warm. Temperatures begin to rise.
May to September: Long summer. Sunny, dry, hot. On the coast, temperatures range 30 to 35°C (85 to 95°F). In the desert, temperatures range around 40°C (104°F) but can reach 45°C (113°F). At the beginning and end of summer, in May and September, expect hot, dust laden winds to come from the Arabian Peninsula. These winds, khamsin in Arabic, sirocco in Italian, can push the temperature well over 40°C (104°F).
September to November: Autumn. Temperatures start to decrease and light rains start to fall.
December to February: Winter. This is the main rainy season when heavy rainstorms can be expected. However, winter can have its dry, sunny spells lasting many days.
Near the coast it is wet and mild with temperatures around 10°C (50°F).
In the mountains that run north–south from the northern coast to the region near Damascus there are snow falls.
In the eastern side of the mountains where Aleppo, Hama, Homs and Damascus are situated and in the desert which comprises most of Syria, afternoon winter temperatures average 12°C (54°F). The annual rainfall on the coast, most of which falls in winter, averages 500 to 1000mm (20 to 40in). As you travel east it decreases to 250 to 500mm (10 to 20in) in the region between Aleppo and Damascus and to 25 to 125 mm (1 to 5 in) in the desert (e.g. Palmyra, also called Tadmor, where impressive ruins stand). Desert rainfall is irregular, but sudden downpours can occur, causing flash floods.

Damascus, Syria: Altitude 720m (2362ft)

	Jan	Feb	Mar	Apr	May	Jun
Sunrise °C(°F)	3(37)	4(39)	6(42)	9(48)	13(55)	16(60)
Mid–afternoon °C(°F)	12(53)	14(57)	18(64)	23(73)	29(84)	33(91)
Days with precipitation	7	5	5	3	1	0
Precipitation mm	44	34	27	15	6	0
Precipitation inches	1.7	1.3	1.1	0.6	0.2	0
Daily hours of sunshine	5	7	8	9	11	12

Damascus, Syria: (continued)

	Jul	Aug	Sep	Oct	Nov	Dec
Sunrise ºC(ºF)	18(64)	17(62)	16(60)	13(55)	8(46)	4(39)
Mid–afternoon ºC(ºF)	36(96)	36(96)	32(89)	27(80)	20(68)	14(57)
Days with precipitation	0	0	0	2	3	6
Precipitation mm	0	0	0	11	27	40
Precipitation inches	0	0	0	0.4	1.1	1.6
Daily hours of sunshine	12	12	11	9	7	5

TAIWAN

Conventional Name: Taiwan

Capital: Taipei
Language: Mandarin (official language)

Taiwan, also called Republic of China, is an independent state, but recognized only as an island province by mainland China (People's Republic of China). The backbone of Taiwan is a high, forested mountain range. On its western side a plain slopes gently down to the Taiwan Strait. On the eastern side the land terminates at the coast as precipitous cliffs.

Best time: April and May, and October and November.

April and May: Clear skies, moderate days, cool nights.
Mid–May to mid–October: Summer. Hot and wet. Humidity can be 75%. Temperatures can exceed 30ºC (86ºF). Monsoon rains come from the southwest from early May to late September, bringing rain mainly to the south. The north receives less rain than the south. The typhoon season is from mid–August to early October. The winds come from the south and storm northwards towards Japan. As many as half–a–dozen typhoons may touch down or pass close to Taiwan.
October and November: Clear skies, moderate days, cool nights.
November to March: Winter. Cool, cloudy and damp. Temperatures do not usually go below 5ºC (41ºF). Monsoon rains come from the northeast, from late October to late March, affecting mainly north and east coasts of Taiwan. The south remains drier.
Rain: The rainfall in the mountains is five times that of the coast.

Taipei, Taiwan: Altitude 9m (30ft)

	Jan	Feb	Mar	Apr	May	Jun
Sunrise ºC(ºF)	12(53)	12(53)	14(57)	17(63)	21(69)	23(73)
Mid–afternoon ºC(ºF)	19(66)	18(65)	21(70)	25(77)	28(83)	32(89)
Days with precipitation	9	13	12	14	12	13
Precipitation mm	86	135	178	170	231	290
Precipitation inches	3.4	5.3	7.0	6.7	9.1	11.4
Daily hours of sunshine	3	3	3	4	5	6

Taipei, Taiwan: (continued)

	Jul	Aug	Sep	Oct	Nov	Dec
Sunrise ºC(ºF)	24(75)	24(75)	23(73)	19(67)	17(62)	14(57)
Mid–afternoon ºC(ºF)	33(92)	33(92)	31(88)	27(81)	24(75)	21(69)
Days with precipitation	10	12	10	9	7	8
Precipitation mm	231	305	244	122	66	71
Precipitation inches	9.1	12.0	9.6	4.8	2.6	2.8
Daily hours of sunshine	7	7	6	5	3	3

TAJIKISTAN
Official Name: Republic of Tajikistan

Capital: Dushanbe
Languages: Tajik, Russian

Tajikistan has both lowlands and mountains. The western one–third of the country consists mainly of lowlands. It is where Dushanbe is situated. Lowland weather is described below. The eastern two–thirds of the country consists mainly of mountains and high plateaus and has snowstorms occurring from October to May. This leaves June to September as the time to travel in the eastern region.

Best time for the lowland region in the west: March to May, and September and October. (Mild.)

March to May: Spring. Sunny, mild, 10ºC (50ºF) and higher as the season advances. Light rain but some falls as heavy downpours.
June to August: Summer. Sunny, dry, dusty and hot. Afternoon temperatures can exceed 35ºC (95ºF). Dry winds from the north can cause dust storms during the period June to October.
September to November: Autumn. September and October are mild with the chance of a dust storm. Light rain falls October and November. November is the start of the cold season.
December to February: Winter. Cold winds blow from the polar regions. Coldest months are January and February with morning and afternoon temperatures below freezing.

Dushanbe, Tajikistan: Altitude 800m (2625ft)

	Jan	Feb	Mar	Apr	May	Jun
Sunrise ºC(ºF)	–5(23)	–4(25)	3(37)	9(48)	14(57)	17(62)
Mid–afternoon ºC(ºF)	3(37)	8(46)	13(55)	19(66)	25(77)	27(80)
Days with precipitation	9	9	13	10	8	2
Precipitation mm	66	75	108	105	66	6
Precipitation inches	2.6	3.0	4.3	4.1	2.6	0.2
Daily hours of sunshine	4	4	5	7	9	11

Dushanbe, Tajikistan: (continued)

	Jul	Aug	Sep	Oct	Nov	Dec
Sunrise ºC(ºF)	18(64)	16(60)	12(53)	5(41)	3(37)	–2(29)
Mid–afternoon ºC(ºF)	32(89)	31(87)	27(80)	18(64)	13(55)	7(44)
Days with precipitation	1	0	1	4	5	8
Precipitation mm	3	1	3	31	45	60
Precipitation inches	0.1	0.04	0.1	1.2	1.8	2.4
Daily hours of sunshine	11	11	10	7	5	4

TANZANIA
Official Name: United Republic of Tanzania

Capital: Dar es Salaam
         Dodoma (legislative)
Languages: Swahili, English, other African languages

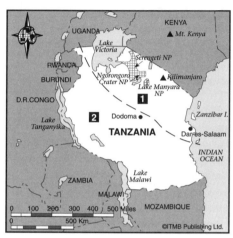

Along the coast is a low, generally flat, narrow plain.
Inland is a plateau which comprises most of the country.
Major features include Mt Kilimanjaro and Lakes
Victoria, Tanganyika and Malawi which are along the
country's borders. Zanzibar is a fairly flat coral island.

**Good time for the whole country: In the dry seasons of
January and February and June to October.**

We have divided the weather into two regions. Refer to map for corresponding numbers.
1. The north. (Includes Arusha, the game reserves of Serengeti, Lake Manyara, Ngorongoro
Crater and Tarangire, Dar es Salaam, the coast north of Dar es Salaam and the offshore islands, e.g.
Zanzibar.)
Inland temperatures are pleasantly hot in the daytime and cool at night. Coastal temperatures can be
oppressive, day and night, but sea breezes temper the heat. Inland humidity is low; coastal humidity is
high. Sunshine per day averages 9 hours in the dry season and 7 hours in the wet.
January and February: Dry, although January could receive a little rain. February is the hottest
month.
March to May: Wet. The "long rains."
June to October: Dry. August and September is the coolest time.
November and December: Wet. The "short rains."

2. The south. (Includes the interior plateau, and the coast south of Dar es Salaam.)
Along the south coast rain falls every month, but mostly March to May.
May or June to October: Dry. Afternoon temperatures, 27 to 30ºC (80 to 86ºF). Sunny, 8 hours daily.
November to April or May: Wet. Afternoon temperatures, 28 to 31ºC (82 to 87ºF). Seven hours of
sunshine daily.

Arusha, northern Tanzania: Altitude 1387m (4550ft)

	Jan	Feb	Mar	Apr	May	Jun
Sunrise ºC(ºF)	13(55)	14(57)	15(59)	16(60)	15(59)	13(55)
Mid–afternoon ºC(ºF)	28(82)	28(82)	27(80)	25(77)	23(73)	22(72)
Days with precipitation	7	7	11	16	10	3
Precipitation mm	66	77	138	223	83	17
Precipitation inches	2.6	3.0	5.4	8.8	3.3	0.7
Daily hours of sunshine	8	8	7	6	7	7

	Jul	Aug	Sep	Oct	Nov	Dec
Sunrise ºC(ºF)	12(53)	12(53)	13(55)	14(57)	14(57)	14(57)
Mid–afternoon ºC(ºF)	22(72)	23(73)	25(77)	27(80)	27(80)	27(80)
Days with precipitation	2	1	1	4	9	10
Precipitation mm	8	7	8	24	119	103
Precipitation inches	0.3	0.3	0.3	0.9	4.7	4.1
Daily hours of sunshine	7	8	8	8	7	8

Dar es Salaam, coastal Tanzania: Altitude 55m (180ft)

	Jan	Feb	Mar	Apr	May	Jun
Sunrise ºC(ºF)	25(77)	25(77)	24(75)	23(73)	22(72)	20(68)
Mid–afternoon ºC(ºF)	31(87)	31(87)	31(87)	30(86)	29(84)	28(82)
Days with precipitation	7	4	12	18	13	5
Precipitation mm	78	52	131	269	176	42
Precipitation inches	3.1	2.0	5.2	10.6	6.9	1.6
Daily hours of sunshine	8	7	7	5	6	7

	Jul	Aug	Sep	Oct	Nov	Dec
Sunrise ºC(ºF)	19(66)	19(66)	19(66)	21(69)	22(72)	24(75)
Mid–afternoon ºC(ºF)	28(82)	28(82)	28(82)	29(84)	30(86)	31(87)
Days with precipitation	5	4	5	6	8	10
Precipitation mm	31	27	28	66	132	116
Precipitation inches	1.2	1.1	1.1	2.6	5.2	4.6
Daily hours of sunshine	7	8	9	9	8	8

Natural attractions:

1. Mt Kilimanjaro. 5895m (19340ft).

Climbing season: July to October, and December to March. Outside these months there could be some rain and wind. Knowing this, you can climb any time of year. The climb, or more correctly an uphill trek, is 3 days up, 2 days down, but the length of time can vary.

2. Herd migration in the Serengeti.
Best time to see wildebeest in the Serengeti: December through May.

Tanzania and Kenya share a plain and woodlands called the Serengeti in Tanzania and the Masai Mara in Kenya. Each year tens of thousands of wildebeest migrate in search of fresh grazing pasture and water accompanied by zebras who use the wildebeest as water diviners. Wildebeest outnumber zebras six to one. As they migrate they are preyed upon by predators. A wildebeest is also called a gnu (pronounced noo; rhymes with zoo).

The migratory circuit is approximately 800km (500 miles), and the timetable is roughly as follows:

End of May, beginning of June: The herds of wildebeest and zebras are on the short–grass plains in the Serengeti National Park between Lake Ndutu and Seronera. (There are lodges at both places.) Surface water in hollows and depressions begins to dry up and the grass loses its freshness. This coincides with the rutting, or breeding, season when for three weeks wildebeest bulls engage in territorial battles and fill the plains with deep lowing. They mark out their territory by scraping the earth with hoofs and horns and try to herd as many females onto this ground as possible for the purpose of mating. Then great columns of animals begin to form and reform as the instinctive urge to migrate westwards seizes them.

Late May to July and August: Columns are sometimes 40km (25 miles) long. After heading west towards the Sabora Plain the herd splits; one group heads north and the other northeast in search of fresher grasses and permanent water. Many drown when crossing the broad Mara River in the north.

August and September: The herds are in Kenya in the Masai Mara National Reserve.

October: When the grazing in the north is exhausted the herds, with heavily pregnant wildebeest cows, leave the Masai Mara to trek southwards.

November: Herds continue southwards. This is the period of the "short rains."

December: Herds arrive on the short–grass plains near Lake Ndutu where the grass is fresh after the rains.

Late January to early February: Calving takes place on the open plains where the herds can watch for predators. Eighty to ninety percent of wildebeest are born during a three–week period. Within five minutes of birth the calves can run. Predators such as lions, cheetahs and hyenas prey on the wildebeest, zebras and gazelles. Thousands of new born calves swamp the plain, too many for predators to prey and glut upon. Preservation of the species is thus ensured. This is a dramatic time to be on safari near Lake Ndutu or Seronera. Also, the weather is dry at this time. Be aware that the birthing period could vary. It may extend into March.

February to May: Animals are on the plains moving back and forth in search of fresh grazing and water. March and April are when the "long rains" arrive, brought by the southeast monsoon. But the monsoon winds are not always dependable so the rains could be heavy or very light. Note that the early or late coming of the rains can vary the cycle slightly.

End of May to beginning of June: The cycle starts again when water becomes scarce and the grass loses its freshness. The animals mate and begin the migration.

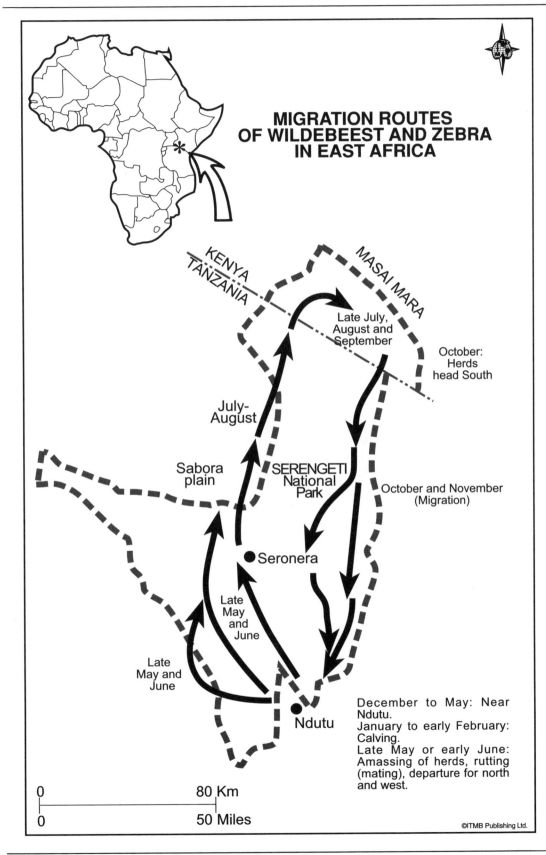

MIGRATION ROUTES OF WILDEBEEST AND ZEBRA IN EAST AFRICA

KENYA
TANZANIA

MASAI MARA

Late July, August and September

October: Herds head South

July-August

Sabora plain

SERENGETI National Park

October and November (Migration)

● Seronera

Late May and June

Late May and June

Late May and June

● Ndutu

December to May: Near Ndutu.
January to early February: Calving.
Late May or early June: Amassing of herds, rutting (mating), departure for north and west.

0 ⊢——————⊣ 80 Km
0 ⊢——————⊣ 50 Miles

©ITMB Publishing Ltd.

THAILAND
Official Name: Kingdom of Thailand

Capital: Bangkok
Languages: Thai, English, regional dialects

Mountain ranges extend from the north (e.g. around Chiang Mai) along the Myanmar border into the Malay Peninsula. Another range extends north–south through central Thailand. Between them are alluvial plains. The eastern half of the country is low–lying and barren with gentle hills.

Best time to travel, in general: November to February.
(Cooler, dry.)
The east and west coasts of the southern peninsula differ.
Best time for the southern peninsula's east coast: February to April.
Good time for the southern peninsula's west coast: November to May. Best is December to March.

We have divided the weather into three regions. Refer to map for corresponding numbers.
1. Central, north and northeast. (The bulk of Thailand; includes Bangkok and Chiang Mai.)
Best time: November to February.

November to February: Cool, dry. Dry winds coming out of wintry central Asia cool the country. Average daily maximum temperature is 31°C (88°F). Nine hours of sunshine daily. Virtually no rain. Low humidity, 65% to 70%. December and January are the coolest and best months.
March to May: Hottest months with intense heat, 35°C (95°F), in the afternoons. Compared with other times of the year the weather is unpleasant. Humidity is 95%. April and May are the hottest.
June to October: Hot with monsoon rains brought by winds that pick up moisture from the Indian Ocean and the Bay of Bengal. Expect violent thunderstorms. Afternoon temperatures reach 34°C (94°F). High humidity. Low sunshine, 5 hours daily.

Cultural event: Elephant Round–up. Held at Surin on third weekend of November.

2. Southern peninsula's east coast. (Includes resort island of Koh Samui.)
Best time: February to April.

February to September: Comparatively dry, but there is rain every month. Best months are February to April (less rain).
October to January: Rainy. The monsoon winds come from the northeast across the Gulf of Thailand.

3. Southern peninsula's west coast: (Includes resort island of Phuket, pronounced Poo–ket.)
Best months: December to March. November, April and May are also good.

November to May: Some rain, but outside the monsoon season. December to March are the best months. They have the least rain, about 5 rainy days per month. Temperatures are above 30°C (86°F).
May to October: Rainy. The monsoon comes from the southwest, picking up moisture over the Indian Ocean and Bay of Bengal. The monsoon downpours come once or twice a day, not as constant rain. Daily maximum temperatures are about 30°C (86°F).

Bangkok, central Thailand: Altitude 20m (66ft)

	Jan	Feb	Mar	Apr	May	Jun
Sunrise ºC(ºF)	21(69)	23(73)	25(77)	26(78)	26(78)	25(77)
Mid–afternoon ºC(ºF)	32(89)	33(91)	34(93)	35(95)	34(93)	33(91)
Days with precipitation	1	2	2	4	13	12
Precipitation mm	9	30	29	65	220	149
Precipitation inches	0.4	1.2	1.1	2.6	8.7	5.9
Daily hours of sunshine	9	9	9	9	7	6

	Jul	Aug	Sep	Oct	Nov	Dec
Sunrise ºC(ºF)	25(77)	25(77)	25(77)	24(75)	23(73)	21(69)
Mid–afternoon ºC(ºF)	33(91)	33(91)	32(89)	32(89)	32(89)	31(87)
Days with precipitation	13	15	18	14	5	1
Precipitation mm	155	197	344	242	48	10
Precipitation inches	6.1	7.8	13.6	9.5	1.9	0.4
Daily hours of sunshine	6	5	5	6	8	8

Chiang Mai, northern Thailand: Altitude 314m (1030ft)

	Jan	Feb	Mar	Apr	May	Jun
Sunrise ºC(ºF)	14(57)	15(59)	18(64)	22(72)	23(73)	24(75)
Mid–afternoon ºC(ºF)	29(84)	32(89)	35(95)	36(96)	34(93)	32(89)
Days with precipitation	1	1	1	5	12	12
Precipitation mm	7	5	13	50	158	132
Precipitation inches	0.3	0.2	0.5	2.0	6.2	5.2
Daily hours of sunshine	9	10	9	9	9	6

	Jul	Aug	Sep	Oct	Nov	Dec
Sunrise ºC(ºF)	24(75)	23(73)	23(73)	22(72)	19(66)	15(59)
Mid–afternoon ºC(ºF)	31(87)	31(87)	31(87)	31(87)	30(86)	28(82)
Days with precipitation	14	17	14	9	4	1
Precipitation mm	161	236	228	122	53	20
Precipitation inches	6.3	9.3	9.0	4.8	2.1	0.8
Daily hours of sunshine	5	5	6	7	8	8

Phuket, southern Thailand: Altitude 3m (9ft)

	Jan	Feb	Mar	Apr	May	Jun
Sunrise ºC(ºF)	23(73)	24(75)	24(75)	25(77)	25(77)	25(77)
Mid–afternoon ºC(ºF)	32(89)	33(91)	34(93)	33(91)	32(89)	32(89)
Days with precipitation	3	2	4	9	19	17
Precipitation mm	30	21	49	122	319	269
Precipitation inches	1.2	0.8	1.9	4.8	12.6	10.6
Daily hours of sunshine	9	10	9	8	6	5

Phuket, southern Thailand: (continued)

	Jul	Aug	Sep	Oct	Nov	Dec
Sunrise ºC(ºF)	24(75)	24(75)	24(75)	24(75)	24(75)	24(75)
Mid–afternoon ºC(ºF)	31(87)	31(87)	31(87)	31(87)	31(87)	31(87)
Days with precipitation	17	17	21	20	13	6
Precipitation mm	291	273	399	310	176	59
Precipitation inches	11.5	10.7	15.7	12.2	6.9	2.3
Daily hours of sunshine	6	6	5	6	7	8

TOGO

Official Name: Republic of Togo

Capital: Lomé
Languages: French, Kabye, Ewe and other African
languages

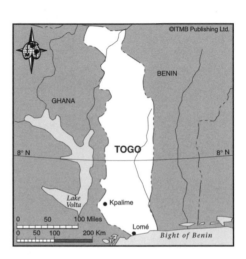

From its short coastline of 50km (31 miles) the country
extends inland to lagoons and lakes then to hills and
wooded savanna grasslands farther north.

**Best time for the whole country: November to
February.** (March also is a good month.)

We have divided the weather into two regions.
1. Coastal region. (Includes Lomé.)
Mid–November to March: Main dry season, although there could be a little rain on the coast during
these months.
March to mid–July: Rainy season with violent storms. Rainiest are May and June. Mid–February to
mid–April is the hottest period, 31ºC (88ºF), but temperatures can rise to 38ºC (100ºF).
August and September: Short dry season.
Late September to mid–November: Short rainy season with most rain in October.
Rain: The hills near Kpalimé in the southwest experience a longer rainy period from March to
October.

2. Northern region.
October to April: Single dry season. The hot, dry, harmattan wind from the northeast blows from
December to March. The harmattan brings dust from the Sahara which occasionally reduces visibility
to 1km. March is the hottest month when temperatures can reach 38ºC (100ºF).
April to October: Wet. Most rain falls in August. Humid and hot. August is the coolest month, 29ºC
(84ºF).

Lomé, coastal Togo: Altitude 25m (82ft)

	Jan	Feb	Mar	Apr	May	Jun
Sunrise ºC(ºF)	23(73)	24(75)	25(77)	24(75)	24(75)	23(73)
Mid–afternoon ºC(ºF)	32(89)	32(89)	33(91)	32(89)	31(87)	30(86)
Days with precipitation	1	2	4	6	9	11
Precipitation mm	9	23	53	96	153	252
Precipitation inches	0.4	0.9	2.1	3.8	6.0	9.9
Daily hours of sunshine	7	8	7	7	7	5

	Jul	Aug	Sep	Oct	Nov	Dec
Sunrise ºC(ºF)	23(73)	22(72)	23(73)	23(73)	23(73)	23(73)
Mid–afternoon ºC(ºF)	28(82)	28(82)	29(84)	30(86)	32(88)	32(88)
Days with precipitation	7	3	4	6	4	1
Precipitation mm	91	33	65	75	20	8
Precipitation inches	3.6	1.3	2.6	3.0	0.8	0.3
Daily hours of sunshine	5	5	6	7	8	7

TOKELAU

Official Name: Tokelau
(Overseas Territory of New Zealand)

Capital: None. Each atoll has its own administrative centre

Languages: Tokelauan, English

Tokelau, a dependency of New Zealand, is comprised of three coral atolls in the Pacific Ocean 480km (300 miles) north of Samoa. It has a tropical oceanic climate.

Best time to visit: April to November.

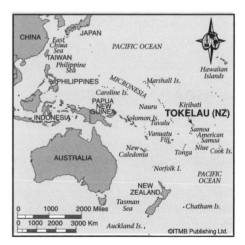

April to November: Season of less rain. Expect some brief, heavy showers. High humidity. Sea breezes offer some relief.
November to April: Wet. Rainstorms can last longer – a day or more – unlike the brief heavy showers of other months. Humidity is high. Sea breezes temper the heat and humidity.
Temperatures: Average daily maximum temperature throughout the year is about 29ºC (84ºF). The minimum is about 25ºC (77ºF).
Rainfall is irregular. Sometimes there is no large variation in rainfall from month to month. Cyclones are rare because the islands are largely out of range of the cyclones of the North Pacific and South Pacific.
Sunshine averages 6 to 8 hours daily throughout the year.

TONGA

Official Name: Kingdom of Tonga

Capital: Nuku'alofa
Languages: Tongan, English

Comprised of 170 islands, only 37 are inhabited. Some are hilly of volcanic origin; some are low–lying of coral formation. The largest island, Tongatapu, where the capital is located, is low–lying and fertile and studded with palm trees.

Best time to visit: April to November.

April to November: Season of less rain. Sunny, warm, humid. Tempered by the refreshing southeast tradewinds that sweep the South Pacific Ocean. Expect 10 days with rain per month. Average afternoon temperature, 29ºC (85ºF).
December to March: Wet season. Hot, humid. One or two cyclones are possible, December to March, and also in April. Rain, when it occurs, usually comes late afternoon, and humidity increases. Expect 17 rainy days a month. Afternoon temperature, 29ºC (85ºF).
Sunshine throughout the year averages 7 hours per day.

Note: For a table showing weather similar to Tonga's refer to Papeete, Tahiti. See French Polynesia.

TRINIDAD and TOBAGO

Official Name: Republic of Trinidad and Tobago

Capital: Port of Spain
Languages: English, French, Spanish, Chinese, Hindi

Trinidad has plains and mangrove swamps and is traversed by rainforested hills. Tobago is the top of a volcanic mountain mass which has rainforests and sandy beaches.

Best time: January to May.

January to May: Dry season.
June to December: Wet season. Heavy, short rainfalls with sunshine. August is the rainiest. Humidity is high. Hurricanes do not affect Trinidad and Tobago because the islands are south of their path.

Cultural event: Carnival. Monday and Tuesday before Ash Wednesday (around February). Parades, costumed bands and a torchlight procession at Port of Spain.

Port of Spain, Trinidad: Altitude 12m (39ft)

	Jan	Feb	Mar	Apr	May	Jun
Sunrise ºC(ºF)	20(68)	21(69)	21(69)	22(71)	23(73)	23(73)
Mid–afternoon ºC(ºF)	30(86)	30(86)	31(88)	32(89)	32(89)	31(87)
Days with precipitation	18	15	13	12	21	26

	Jul	Aug	Sep	Oct	Nov	Dec
Sunrise ºC(ºF)	23(73)	23(73)	23(73)	22(72)	22(72)	21(70)
Mid–afternoon ºC(ºF)	31(87)	31(87)	32(89)	32(89)	31(87)	30(86)
Days with precipitation	26	24	18	20	13	21

TRISTAN DA CUNHA
(A dependency of St. Helena, a British possession)

Main settlement: Edinburgh
Language: English

Tristan da Cunha is a remote island in the South Atlantic with an area of 98 sq. km (38 sq. miles). It is the cone of a volcano whose height is 2060m (6760ft). It is frequently snow–capped between June and October.

Best time: Any time of year.
The climate is temperate. Moderate rainfall is distributed evenly over the island. Winds are strong and persistent; there are few days without wind. Humidity throughout the year is high.

Tristan da Cunha, South Atlantic Ocean:

	Jan	Feb	Mar	Apr	May	Jun
Sunrise ºC(ºF)	15(59)	16(60)	14(57)	14(57)	12(53)	11(51)
Mid–afternoon ºC(ºF)	19(66)	20(68)	19(66)	18(64)	16(60)	14(57)
Days with precipitation	12	13	11	12	17	19

	Jul	Aug	Sep	Oct	Nov	Dec
Sunrise ºC(ºF)	10(50)	9(48)	9(48)	11(51)	12(53)	14(57)
Mid–afternoon ºC(ºF)	14(57)	13(55)	13(55)	15(59)	16(60)	18(64)
Days with precipitation	20	21	18	16	13	13

TUNISIA

Official Name: Republic of Tunisia

Capital: Tunis
Languages: Arabic, French

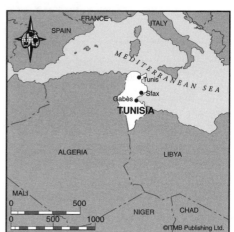

Proceeding from north to south there is, firstly, a narrow coastal strip; secondly, mountains with fertile valleys and plains; then a plateau of grazing land; then salt lakes or shotts. South of the shotts is desert which covers 40 percent of Tunisia.

Best time for northern and eastern regions for general travel and sightseeing:
Mid–March to early June, and September and October. (Pleasantly warm.)
Popular time for beaches: Late June to August. (Hot and humid.)
Best time for the Saharan south: December to February. (Cooler.)

The three climatic regions are:
1. Northern and eastern regions. (Includes Tunis.)
Best time: Mid–March to early June, and September and October.

Mid–March to early June: Sunny, pleasantly warm, light rain.
June to August: Summer. Sunny, dry, humid, very hot with daytime temperatures reaching 32°C (90°F). Nights can be uncomfortably warm.
September and October: Sunny, light rains, hot.
November to February: Rainy and cooler.
Rains fall September to April. The dry season is May to mid–September.

2. Western mountains and central plateau, a semi–arid steppe.
Best time: December to February.

December to February: Winter. Light rains. Afternoon temperatures are lower than at the coast at Gabes by 2°C (3°F).
June to August: Summer. Mainly dry. Afternoon temperatures are higher than at the coast at Gabès by 6°C (11°F).

3. Saharan south.
Best time: December to February.

December to February: Winter. Temperatures are cool to pleasantly warm. Rainfall is negligible.
May to July: Very hot with daytime temperatures exceeding 40°C (104°F). Hot, dry winds from the Sahara raise temperatures and bring dust storms, but these are rare. Nighttime temperatures drop dramatically in the desert. Away from the coast humidity is low. Rainfall is negligible during these months.

Tunis, northern coast, Tunisia: Altitude 66m (217ft)

	Jan	Feb	Mar	Apr	May	Jun
Sunrise ºC(ºF)	7(44)	7(44)	8(46)	10(50)	14(57)	17(62)
Mid–afternoon ºC(ºF)	16(60)	17(62)	18(64)	21(69)	25(77)	29(84)
Days with precipitation	12	12	11	9	6	5
Precipitation mm	59	57	47	38	23	10
Precipitation inches	2.3	2.2	1.9	1.5	0.9	0.4
Daily hours of sunshine	5	6	6	8	9	10

	Jul	Aug	Sep	Oct	Nov	Dec
Sunrise ºC(ºF)	20(68)	21(69)	19(66)	16(60)	11(51)	8(46)
Mid–afternoon ºC(ºF)	33(91)	33(91)	30(86)	25(77)	21(69)	17(62)
Days with precipitation	1	2	7	9	11	14
Precipitation mm	3	7	33	66	56	67
Precipitation inches	0.1	0.3	1.3	2.6	2.2	2.6
Daily hours of sunshine	11	11	9	7	6	5

Gabès, southern coast, Tunisia: Altitude 5m (16ft)

	Jan	Feb	Mar	Apr	May	Jun
Sunrise ºC(ºF)	8(46)	8(46)	10(50)	14(57)	17(62)	21(69)
Mid–afternoon ºC(ºF)	17(62)	18(64)	20(68)	22(72)	25(77)	27(80)
Days with precipitation	4	3	4	3	2	1
Precipitation mm	24	19	23	13	7	3
Precipitation inches	0.9	0.7	0.9	0.5	0.3	0.1
Daily hours of sunshine	7	8	8	9	10	11

	Jul	Aug	Sep	Oct	Nov	Dec
Sunrise ºC(ºF)	23(73)	24(75)	22(72)	17(62)	12(53)	8(46)
Mid–afternoon ºC(ºF)	31(87)	31(87)	30(86)	26(78)	22(72)	18(64)
Days with precipitation	0	0	3	4	4	4
Precipitation mm	0	1	23	44	32	33
Precipitation inches	0	0.04	0.9	1.7	1.3	1.3
Daily hours of sunshine	12	11	9	8	8	7

TURKEY

Official Name: Republic of Turkey

Capital: Ankara
Languages: Turkish, Kurdish, Arabic

The part of Turkey in Europe where
Istanbul is located is mostly gently
undulating terrain. The Asian part
comprises the high Anatolian plateau,
750 to 900m (2500 to 3000ft) above
sea level, enclosed by mountain ranges
in the north and south.

Best times to visit the whole country:
First choice: April to June. (Warm, dry, green landscapes after winter rains.)
Second choice: September and October. (Warm, dry, brown landscapes after dry summer.)
Third choice: July and August. (Hot, dry, dusty, peak season for tourism from Europe.)
Other months, November to March, are cold and wet.

We have divided the weather into five regions. Refer to map for corresponding numbers.

1. Northwest region. (Includes Istanbul, northern Aegean Sea and Sea of Marmara.)
April to mid–September: Dry and hot. July and August are hottest with afternoon temperatures, 28°C
(82°F). Beach weather is June to September.
November to February: Wet and cool.

Istanbul, Turkey: Altitude 18m (59ft)

	Jan	Feb	Mar	Apr	May	Jun
Sunrise °C(°F)	3(38)	3(38)	4(39)	8(46)	12(53)	16(60)
Mid–afternoon °C(°F)	9(48)	9(48)	12(53)	17(62)	22(72)	26(78)
Days with precipitation	12	10	9	7	5	3
Precipitation mm	99	67	62	49	31	21
Precipitation inches	3.9	2.6	2.4	1.9	1.2	0.8
Daily hours of sunshine	3	4	4	6	9	11

	Jul	Aug	Sep	Oct	Nov	Dec
Sunrise °C(°F)	19(66)	16(66)	16(60)	12(53)	9(48)	5(41)
Mid–afternoon °C(°F)	28(82)	28(82)	25(77)	20(68)	15(59)	11(51)
Days with precipitation	3	3	4	7	9	12
Precipitation mm	19	26	41	71	89	122
Precipitation inches	0.7	1.0	1.6	2.8	3.5	4.8
Daily hours of sunshine	12	11	8	6	4	3

2. Black Sea coast. (Includes Samsun.)
April to mid–September: Warm, humid. Temperatures rarely exceed 29°C (85°F). A little rain, but mostly dry. Beach weather is June to September.
November to March: Cool to mild. Rainy months.

Samsun, Black Sea coast, Turkey: Altitude 4m (13ft)

	Jan	Feb	Mar	Apr	May	Jun
Sunrise °C(°F)	4(39)	4(39)	5(41)	8(46)	12(53)	16(60)
Mid–afternoon °C(°F)	11(51)	11(51)	12(53)	16(60)	19(66)	23(73)
Days with precipitation	8	8	9	10	8	5
Precipitation mm	61	50	56	62	49	45
Precipitation inches	2.4	2.0	2.2	2.4	1.9	1.8
Daily hours of sunshine	3	3	4	5	6	8

	Jul	Aug	Sep	Oct	Nov	Dec
Sunrise °C(°F)	19(66)	19(66)	16(60)	13(55)	9(48)	6(42)
Mid–afternoon °C(°F)	26(78)	26(78)	24(75)	20(68)	17(62)	13(55)
Days with precipitation	4	4	5	8	8	9
Precipitation mm	29	34	50	85	89	82
Precipitation inches	1.1	1.3	2.0	3.4	3.5	3.2
Daily hours of sunshine	10	9	7	5	4	3

3. Central arid plateau. (Includes Ankara.)
This arid plateau, the Anatolian Plateau, is shielded in the north by the Pontine Mountains and in the south by the Taurus Mountains.
April to mid–September: Very warm, dry summers, June to August. April, May and September are pleasantly warm. Occasional thunderstorms. Evenings can be chilly.
November to March: Cold, wet winters with some snow. The eastern half of the plateau is colder and receives more snow which can lie on the ground for 3 to 4 months.

Ankara, central plateau, Turkey: Altitude 891m (2923ft)

	Jan	Feb	Mar	Apr	May	Jun
Sunrise °C(°F)	–3(27)	–2(29)	1(33)	5(41)	9(48)	13(55)
Mid–afternoon °C(°F)	4(39)	6(42)	12(53)	17(62)	21(70)	26(79)
Days with precipitation	8	7	8	8	9	6
Precipitation mm	47	36	36	48	55	37
Precipitation inches	1.9	1.4	1.4	1.9	2.2	1.5
Daily hours of sunshine	3	4	6	7	9	10

	Jul	Aug	Sep	Oct	Nov	Dec
Sunrise °C(°F)	15(59)	15(59)	11(51)	7(44)	3(37)	–1(30)
Mid–afternoon °C(°F)	30(86)	30(86)	26(78)	20(68)	13(55)	6(42)
Days with precipitation	3	2	2	5	6	8
Precipitation mm	14	12	19	27	33	49
Precipitation inches	0.6	0.5	0.7	1.1	1.3	1.9
Daily hours of sunshine	12	12	10	8	5	3

4. Southeastern Turkey.

April to mid–September: Hot, dry. Temperature ranges 25°C (77°F) to over 38°C (100°F). Hottest, July and August.

December to March: Warm, wet. Temperature ranges 15°C (59°F) in November and March down to 8°C (46°F) in January, the coolest month. Rainy period. January is the wettest.

5. Southern (Mediterranean) and western (Aegean) coasts. (Includes Antalya.)

April to October: Hot, dry. Water temperature remains above 16°C (60°F), even in winter. Beach weather is April to November.

November to March: Mild and wet. The south coast is protected from the cold winds from the north by the Taurus Mountains which keep temperatures mild, 14 to 17°C (57 to 63°F) in the afternoons. The western (Aegean) coast averages 2°C (4°F) cooler than the southern coast.

Antalya, southern coast, Turkey: Altitude 57m (187ft)

	Jan	Feb	Mar	Apr	May	Jun
Sunrise °C(°F)	6(42)	6(42)	8(46)	11(51)	15(59)	19(66)
Mid–afternoon °C(°F)	15(59)	15(59)	18(64)	21(69)	25(77)	30(86)
Days with precipitation	10	10	7	5	3	1
Precipitation mm	238	191	102	48	28	9
Precipitation inches	9.4	7.5	4.0	1.9	1.1	0.4
Daily hours of sunshine	5	6	7	8	10	12

	Jul	Aug	Sep	Oct	Nov	Dec
Sunrise °C(°F)	22(72)	22(72)	19(66)	15(59)	11(51)	8(46)
Mid–afternoon °C(°F)	34(93)	34(93)	31(87)	26(78)	21(69)	17(62)
Days with precipitation	1	0	1	4	6	10
Precipitation mm	5	2	13	70	150	223
Precipitation inches	0.2	0.08	0.5	2.8	5.9	8.8
Daily hours of sunshine	13	12	10	8	6	4

TURKMENISTAN

Official Name: Turkmenistan
(Independent republic)

Capital: Ashgabat (Ashkhabad)
Languages: Turkmen, Russian, Uzbek

Turkmenistan is mostly desert and steppe with a narrow
belt of mountains in the south. There is abundant
sunshine, lack of rainfall, and high temperatures in
summer.

Best time to visit: March and April (spring) **and
September and October** (autumn).

March to May: Spring. Sunny and warm. Light rains may fall.
June to August: Summer. Sunny, dry and hot with maximum daytime temperatures usually above
35°C (95°F). Humidity is low which makes the heat somewhat bearable.
September to November: Autumn. September and October are pleasant, sunny and dry. November is
the start of the cooler months.
December to February: Winter. Temperatures fall to freezing and sunshine is reduced to 3 to 4 hours
per day.

Ashgabat, Turkmenistan: Altitude 304m (997ft)

	Jan	Feb	Mar	Apr	May	Jun
Sunrise °C(°F)	−2(29)	0(32)	5(41)	11(51)	16(60)	21(69)
Mid–afternoon °C(°F)	7(44)	10(50)	16(60)	24(75)	30(86)	36(96)
Days with precipitation	9	8	11	10	7	2
Precipitation mm	22	27	39	44	28	4
Precipitation inches	0.9	1.1	1.5	1.7	1.1	0.1
Daily hours of sunshine	4	4	5	6	9	11

	Jul	Aug	Sep	Oct	Nov	Dec
Sunrise °C(°F)	23(73)	21(70)	15(59)	9(48)	5(41)	1(33)
Mid–afternoon °C(°F)	38(100)	37(98)	32(89)	23(73)	17(62)	10(50)
Days with precipitation	1	1	2	5	6	8
Precipitation mm	3	1	4	14	20	21
Precipitation inches	0.1	0.04	0.1	0.6	0.8	0.8
Daily hours of sunshine	11	11	9	7	5	3

TURKS and CAICOS

Official Name: The Turks and Caicos Islands
(Dependent Territory of the United Kingdom)

Capital: Cockburn Town (Grand Turk is the seat
of government.)
Language: English

The Turks and Caicos comprise more than a dozen islands
and islets, all of which are low–lying and generally flat.

Best time: December to April.

December to April: Relatively dry. Cooler. Average
afternoon temperature, 28°C (82°F).
May to November: Wet season. September to November are the rainiest months.
Sunshine: Sunny, 7 to 9 hours a day, year–round, even during the wet season.
Hurricanes: Possible, June to November, but they rarely touch down.

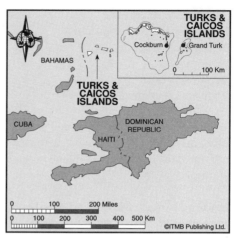

Note: See under Caribbean Islands for general weather information.

Grand Turk, Turks and Caicos: Altitude 3m (10ft)

	Jan	Feb	Mar	Apr	May	Jun
Sunrise ºC(ºF)	21(70)	21(70)	22(71)	23(73)	24(75)	25(77)
Mid–afternoon ºC(ºF)	27(81)	27(81)	28(82)	29(84)	30(86)	31(87)
Days with precipitation	13	8	8	6	8	9
Precipitation mm	56	36	28	38	66	41
Precipitation inches	2.2	1.4	1.1	1.5	2.6	1.6

	Jul	Aug	Sep	Oct	Nov	Dec
Sunrise ºC(ºF)	25(77)	26(78)	25(77)	24(76)	23(73)	22(71)
Mid–afternoon ºC(ºF)	31(87)	32(89)	31(87)	31(87)	29(84)	28(82)
Days with precipitation	10	12	12	13	13	13
Precipitation mm	43	51	81	102	114	69
Precipitation inches	1.7	2.0	3.2	4.0	4.5	2.7

TUVALU

Official Name: Tuvalu (pronounced too–va'loo)
(Independent nation; formerly a British possession)

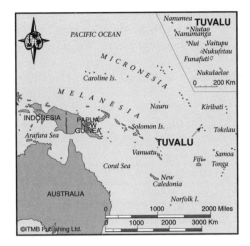

Capital: Funafuti
Languages: Tuvalu, English

Tuvalu, formerly Ellice Islands, consists of 9 low coral atolls no more than 4m (13ft) above sea level. The total land area is 25 sq. km (10 sq. miles).

Best time to visit: April to November.

April to September: Season of less rain. Sunny, warm, humid. Tempered by the refreshing southeast tradewinds that sweep the South Pacific Ocean. Expect 13 rainy days per month. Average afternoon temperature, 29°C (85°F).
October to March: Wet season. Hot, humid. Cyclones, although rare, may approach from the south. Strong westerly winds bring rainstorms. Rain, when it occurs, usually comes late afternoon, and humidity increases. Expect 18 days of rain a month. Afternoon temperature, 31°C (88°F).
Sunshine throughout the year averages 6 to 8 hours per day, including during the wet season.

Note: For a table showing weather similar to Tuvalu's, refer to Suva, Fiji.

UGANDA

Official Name: Republic of Uganda

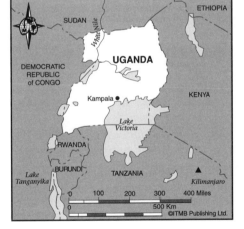

Capital: Kampala
Languages: English, Swahili, Luganda

Most of Uganda is a plateau more than 1000m (3300ft) above sea level. This helps give it a pleasant climate year–round. The region around Lake Victoria is rainier than other parts of the country during the wet season because of the presence of the lake as a source of moisture. The moisture is pulled into the atmosphere and falls as rain. The Ruwenzori Mountains in the southwest are always wet, even in the dry season. The northern region is mainly dry.

Best time to visit: End of May to early October, (dry, warm) **and late November to February** (dry, warm).

Following are the seasons of the plateau which comprises most of Uganda.
June to mid–September: Dry.
Mid–September to November: Wet.
Late November to February: Dry.
March to May: Wet.

Natural attractions:
1. Murchison Falls on the Victoria Nile River is a spectacular sight of water cascading through a gap.
2. Gorilla sanctuary in the Bwindi National Park.

Kampala, Uganda: Altitude 1312m (4304ft)

	Jan	Feb	Mar	Apr	May	Jun
Sunrise ºC(ºF)	18(65)	18(65)	18(65)	18(65)	17(63)	17(63)
Mid–afternoon ºC(ºF)	28(83)	28(83)	27(81)	26(79)	25(77)	25(77)
Days with precipitation	9	9	14	19	19	11
Precipitation mm	46	61	130	175	147	74
Precipitation inches	1.8	2.4	5.1	6.9	5.8	2.9
Daily hours of sunshine	5	6	5	4	4	6

	Jul	Aug	Sep	Oct	Nov	Dec
Sunrise ºC(ºF)	17(62)	16(61)	17(62)	17(62)	17(63)	17(63)
Mid–afternoon ºC(ºF)	25(77)	25(78)	27(80)	27(80)	27(80)	27(80)
Days with precipitation	10	14	12	14	16	12
Precipitation mm	46	86	91	97	122	99
Precipitation inches	1.8	3.4	3.6	3.8	4.8	3.9
Daily hours of sunshine	6	5	5	5	5	4

UKRAINE

Official Name: Ukraine
(Independent republic)

Capital: Kiev
Languages: Ukrainian, Russian, Romanian

Ukraine's dominant feature which covers much of the country is the steppe, the vast, fertile, undulating plains. In the far west of the country is part of the Carpathian range and in the Crimea peninsula there is a mountain range.

Best time for the whole country: May to September.
April and October are also mild, and pleasant for travel.

1. Plains region. (Includes Kiev.)
May to September: Temperatures exceed 20ºC (68ºF) most days. The hottest months are July and August but these are also the wettest months. The rain comes as heavy, torrential downpours.
October to April: Both October and April are mild, about 13ºC (56ºF), but snow flurries can start in October. The long winter is November to March. December to February stays below freezing point. Kiev's ground is snow–covered during these three months. Cold winds from Russia blow at this time.

2. Crimea peninsula. (Includes Simferopol.)
May to September: The sunny peninsula is a popular summer resort. July and August are dry and hot, 28ºC (82ºF).

October to April: The southern coast of the peninsula is mild but it may drop to below freezing point on some days in mid–January and February. The average January temperature at Yalta is 6°C (42°F). The rainiest months are November to January.

Kiev, Ukraine: Altitude 167m (548ft)

	Jan	Feb	Mar	Apr	May	Jun
Sunrise °C(°F)	–10(14)	–8(18)	–4(25)	5(41)	11(51)	14(57)
Mid–afternoon °C(°F)	–4(25)	–2(29)	3(37)	14(57)	21(69)	24(76)
Days with precipitation	9	8	8	8	8	10
Precipitation mm	47	46	39	49	53	73
Precipitation inches	1.9	1.8	1.5	1.9	2.1	2.9
Daily hours of sunshine	1	2	4	6	9	9

	Jul	Aug	Sep	Oct	Nov	Dec
Sunrise °C(°F)	15(59)	14(57)	10(50)	6(42)	0(32)	–6(21)
Mid–afternoon °C(°F)	25(77)	24(76)	20(68)	13(55)	6(42)	–1(30)
Days with precipitation	10	8	7	6	9	10
Precipitation mm	88	69	47	35	51	52
Precipitation inches	3.5	2.7	1.9	1.4	2.0	2.0
Daily hours of sunshine	10	8	7	5	2	1

Simferopol, Crimea, Ukraine: Altitude 181m (594ft)

	Jan	Feb	Mar	Apr	May	Jun
Sunrise °C(°F)	–5(23)	–3(27)	–1(30)	5(41)	10(50)	14(57)
Mid–afternoon °C(°F)	3(37)	5(41)	9(48)	16(60)	22(72)	25(77)
Days with precipitation	8	7	7	6	6	6
Precipitation mm	42	33	37	33	44	53
Precipitation inches	1.6	1.3	1.5	1.3	1.7	2.1
Daily hours of sunshine	3	4	5	7	9	10

	Jul	Aug	Sep	Oct	Nov	Dec
Sunrise °C(°F)	16(60)	15(59)	12(53)	7(44)	4(39)	0(32)
Mid–afternoon °C(°F)	28(82)	28(82)	23(73)	17(62)	12(53)	7(44)
Days with precipitation	5	4	5	5	8	9
Precipitation mm	55	41	37	32	44	54
Precipitation inches	2.2	1.6	1.5	1.3	1.7	2.1
Daily hours of sunshine	11	10	9	7	4	2

UNITED ARAB EMIRATES

Official Name: United Arab Emirates
The United Arab Emirates comprise seven sheikdoms or emirates, each named for their main town: Abu Dhabi, Dubai, Sharjah, Ajman, Umm Al–Qaiwain, Ras Al–Khaimah and Fujairah.

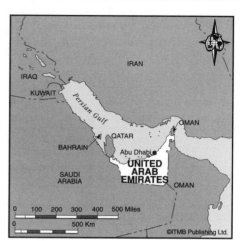

Capital: Abu Dhabi
Languages: Arabic (official), Farsi (Persian), English, Hindi, Urdu

The region is comprised of flat, sandy, rocky, unproductive desert. Eighty percent of the population live in the coastal cities and towns; the remainder live in oases in the hinterland.

Best time: November to March.

November to February: Warm on the coast and inland with pleasant temperatures, 25 to 30°C (77 to 87°F). It can be windy, and with light rains.
March to October: Dry, humid and hot, 35 to 40°C (95 to 104°F). Summer, July and August, has the most extreme, uncomfortable heat of 40°C (104°F) and higher.

Abu Dhabi, United Arab Emirates: Altitude 27m (89ft)

	Jan	Feb	Mar	Apr	May	Jun
Sunrise °C(°F)	12(53)	13(55)	16(60)	19(66)	23(73)	25(77)
Mid–afternoon °C(°F)	24(75)	25(77)	29(84)	33(91)	38(100)	40(104)
Days with precipitation	0	2	2	1	0	0
Precipitation mm	4	42	25	7	0	0
Precipitation inches	0.1	1.6	1.0	0.3	0	0
Daily hours of sunshine	9	9	9	10	11	11

	Jul	Aug	Sep	Oct	Nov	Dec
Sunrise °C(°F)	28(82)	29(84)	26(78)	22(72)	18(64)	14(57)
Mid–afternoon °C(°F)	42(107)	42(107)	40(104)	36(96)	31(87)	26(78)
Days with precipitation	0	0	0	0	0	1
Precipitation mm	0	0	0	0	2	9
Precipitation inches	0	0	0	0	0.08	0.4
Daily hours of sunshine	11	10	10	10	10	8

UNITED KINGDOM

Official Name: United Kingdom of Great Britain and
Northern Ireland
(Comprises England, Scotland, Wales, Northern Ireland)
Capital: London
Languages: English, Welsh, Gaelic

The eastern and southern coasts that face the Continent
both have plains along their coasts. The western coast that
faces the Atlantic Ocean has the country's highest hills and
an irregular coastline indented by wide and deep inlets.

Best time: June to August.

June to August: Summer. Long, warm days. The
southern half of the country is slightly warmer than the
north. June is the sunniest and driest month but, even so,
expect light rains.

September to November: Autumn. Average afternoon
temperatures begin falling and daily sunshine begins
diminishing. Expect light rains.

December to February: Winter. Short, cold days. Average afternoon temperatures throughout the
country average about 7°C (44°F) although the southwest region is a degree or two warmer, 8°C
(47°F). Rain, fog and low cloud reduce daily sunshine to one to three hours. Expect light snowfalls.

March to May: Spring. Average afternoon temperatures begin rising and hours of sunshine per day
begin increasing. Light snow is possible in March. Expect light rains throughout spring.

Rain falls throughout the country about two or three times a week.

Altitude affects weather in the hills and mountains of Scotland, Wales and northern England. There is
more rain, strong wind, snow and low cloud than at lower elevations.

Cultural event: Edinburgh International Festival. Last 2 weeks in August and first week of
September. Includes military tatoo performed nightly in Edinburgh Castle.

Belfast, Northern Ireland: Altitude 67m (217ft)

	Jan	Feb	Mar	Apr	May	Jun
Sunrise °C(°F)	1(33)	1(33)	2(35)	3(37)	6(42)	9(48)
Mid–afternoon °C(°F)	6(42)	7(44)	9(48)	11(51)	14(57)	17(62)
Days with precipitation	15	11	14	11	13	12
Precipitation mm	86	58	67	53	60	63
Precipitation inches	3.4	2.3	2.6	2.1	2.4	2.5
Daily hours of sunshine	1	2	3	5	6	6

	Jul	Aug	Sep	Oct	Nov	Dec
Sunrise °C(°F)	11(51)	11(51)	9(48)	7(44)	3(37)	2(35)
Mid–afternoon °C(°F)	18(64)	18(64)	16(60)	13(55)	9(48)	7(44)
Days with precipitation	11	13	13	14	13	14
Precipitation mm	64	80	85	88	78	78
Precipitation inches	2.5	3.2	3.4	3.5	3.1	3.1
Daily hours of sunshine	5	4	4	3	2	1

Cardiff, Wales: Altitude 62m (203ft)

	Jan	Feb	Mar	Apr	May	Jun
Sunrise °C(°F)	2(35)	2(35)	3(37)	4(39)	7(44)	10(50)
Mid–afternoon °C(°F)	7(44)	7(44)	9(48)	12(53)	15(59)	18(64)
Days with precipitation	15	10	12	10	11	9
Precipitation mm	91	67	76	57	64	66
Precipitation inches	3.6	2.6	3.0	2.2	2.5	2.6
Daily hours of sunshine	2	3	4	6	7	7

	Jul	Aug	Sep	Oct	Nov	Dec
Sunrise °C(°F)	12(53)	12(53)	10(50)	8(46)	4(39)	3(37)
Mid–afternoon °C(°F)	20(68)	20(68)	17(62)	14(57)	10(50)	8(46)
Days with precipitation	9	10	11	13	14	14
Precipitation mm	74	80	92	96	100	98
Precipitation inches	2.9	3.2	3.6	3.8	3.9	3.9
Daily hours of sunshine	7	6	5	3	2	2

London, England: Altitude 5m (16ft)

	Jan	Feb	Mar	Apr	May	Jun
Sunrise °C(°F)	0(32)	0(32)	1(33)	3(37)	6(42)	9(48)
Mid–afternoon °C(°F)	7(44)	7(44)	10(50)	13(55)	16(60)	20(68)
Days with precipitation	13	9	11	10	10	8
Precipitation mm	78	51	61	54	55	57
Precipitation inches	3.1	2.0	2.4	2.1	2.2	2.2
Daily hours of sunshine	2	3	4	5	7	7

	Jul	Aug	Sep	Oct	Nov	Dec
Sunrise °C(°F)	11(51)	11(51)	9(48)	6(42)	3(37)	1(33)
Mid–afternoon °C(°F)	22(72)	21(69)	19(66)	15(59)	10(50)	8(46)
Days with precipitation	7	9	9	10	11	12
Precipitation mm	45	56	68	73	77	79
Precipitation inches	1.8	2.2	2.7	2.9	3.0	3.1
Daily hours of sunshine	7	6	5	4	2	2

Edinburgh, Scotland (Glasgow is similar): Altitude 134m (440ft)

	Jan	Feb	Mar	Apr	May	Jun
Sunrise °C(°F)	0(32)	0(32)	1(33)	3(37)	6(42)	9(48)
Mid–afternoon °C(°F)	6(42)	6(42)	9(48)	11(51)	14(57)	17(62)
Days with precipitation	12	9	11	8	10	8
Precipitation mm	57	42	51	41	51	51
Precipitation inches	2.2	1.6	2.0	1.6	2.0	2.0
Daily hours of sunshine	1	2	3	4	5	6

Edinburgh, Scotland (Glasgow is similar): (continued)

	Jul	Aug	Sep	Oct	Nov	Dec
Sunrise °C(°F)	10(50)	10(50)	8(46)	6(42)	2(35)	1(33)
Mid–afternoon °C(°F)	19(66)	18(64)	16(60)	13(55)	9(48)	7(44)
Days with precipitation	9	10	11	12	12	11
Precipitation mm	57	65	67	65	63	58
Precipitation inches	2.2	2.6	2.6	2.6	2.5	2.3
Daily hours of sunshine	5	5	4	3	2	1

UNITED STATES OF AMERICA
Official Name: United States of America

Capital: Washington, DC (District of Columbia)

The Continental U.S. has four main physical divisions described here from west to east. They are the Cordillera, which includes the Rocky Mountains and other ranges; the Interior Plains which encompass half of the land mass of Continental U.S.; the Appalachian Highland that extends from Maine to central Alabama; and the combined coastal plain along the Atlantic seaboard and the Gulf of Mexico.
Alaska is mountainous with extensive interior lowlands.
The Hawaiian Islands are mountainous with active and extinct volcanoes.

The weather of the 50 states is described below. (Refer to the map on the next page.)

ALABAMA (Capital: Montgomery)
Good time to visit Alabama: Mid–March to April, and mid–September to mid–October.

March to May: Warm. Light rain. Colourful season when flowers are in bloom.
July and August: Hot, over 32°C (90°F). High humidity. Afternoon thunderstorms.
September and October: Warm, dry season.
November to February: Mild on the plains. Cool in the northeastern mountains which receive snow.

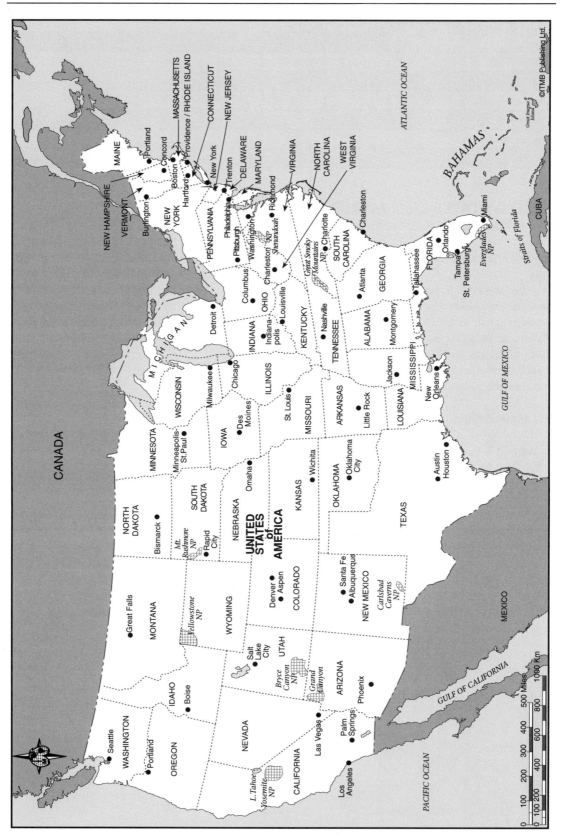

ALASKA (Capital: Juneau)

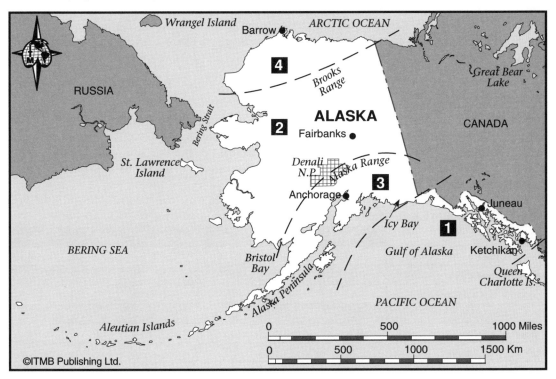

Best time for general travel in Alaska: June to August (warm). June is usually ideal (less rain).

Best time for cruising the "inside passage": Busiest time is mid–June to late August. Crowds at the ports of call may be avoided in part by taking a cruise in May, early June, late August, or September.

Natural attraction: Denali National Park.
Popular time: Late May to early September. Busiest, late June to late August. Snow arrives late September; roads are closed then reopened in May.

We have divided the weather into four regions. Refer to map for corresponding numbers.
1. Southeast. (Includes Juneau.)
This damp panhandle extends from Dixon Entrance south of Ketchikan to Icy Bay in the Gulf of Alaska. Cruise ships and Alaska State Ferries use the "inside passage" between the islands and the mainland.
June to August: Summer. Warm in afternoon, 10 to 16°C (50 to 60°F). Rains fall, especially late summer. Annual precipitation totals 2550mm (100in) in some places. Driest days are in May and June.
September to May: Starting in September, days are chilly; nights are cold. Water temperature usually stays above freezing September to May. Temperature differences are not extreme.

2. Interior. (Includes Fairbanks.)
Extends from the Alaska Range in the south to the Brooks Range in the north.
June to August: Summer. Warm and wet. Afternoon temperatures average 18 to 24°C (65 to 75°F). Daylight is 16 to 22 hours daily. Rainfall peaks in August. Precipitation totals about 280mm (11in) per year.
September to May: Winters are long and severe. Temperatures usually range –21 to –23°C (–5 to –10°F) but can drop to –40°C (–40°F).
Daylight is 4 to 6 hours daily in the middle of winter. Snow falls October to April.

3. South central (includes Anchorage) **and Southwest.** (Includes Alaskan Peninsula and Aleutian Islands.)
June to August: Summer. Warm. Rainfall is moderate but peaks in Anchorage in September.
September to May: Cold and chilly but has warmer temperatures than the Interior because of the stream of warm water, the Japan Current, which moves towards Alaska from the Pacific Ocean. Snow falls October to April.

4. Arctic. North of the Brooks Range. (Includes Barrow.)
June to August: Summer. Temperatures average 4°C (40°F). For eight weeks the sun never sets.
September to May: Temperatures average –23°C (–9°F) but may drop to –32°C (–25°F). Temperatures are not as cold as the interior because the Arctic Ocean waters have a moderating effect, keeping the temperatures higher. For two months in winter the sun does not rise. Snowfalls occur October to April.

Anchorage, Alaska: Altitude 35m (114ft)

	Jan	Feb	Mar	Apr	May	Jun
Sunrise °C(°F)	–13(8)	–11(13)	–8(18)	–2(29)	4(25)	8(18)
Mid–afternoon °C(°F)	–6(21)	–3(27)	1(33)	6(42)	12(53)	16(60)
Days with precipitation	6	9	8	7	7	8
Precipitation mm	20	20	18	17	19	29
Precipitation inches	0.8	0.8	0.7	0.7	0.7	1.1
Daily hours of sunshine	3	4	6	8	9	9
Snow mm	279	304	228	152	25	0
Snow inches	11	12	9	6	1	0

	Jul	Aug	Sep	Oct	Nov	Dec
Sunrise °C(°F)	11(51)	10(50)	5(41)	–2(29)	–9(16)	–12(11)
Mid–afternoon °C(°F)	18(64)	17(62)	13(55)	5(41)	–3(27)	–5(23)
Days with precipitation	11	12	13	11	10	11
Precipitation mm	43	62	69	52	28	28
Precipitation inches	1.7	2.4	2.7	2.0	1.1	1.1
Daily hours of sunshine	8	7	5	4	3	2
Snow mm	0	0	0	152	253	380
Snow inches	0	0	0	6	10	15

Barrow, Alaska: Altitude 4m (13ft)

	Jan	Feb	Mar	Apr	May	Jun
Sunrise °C(°F)	–28(–18)	–31(–24)	–29(–21)	–23(–10)	–10(14)	–1(30)
Mid–afternoon °C(°F)	–22(–8)	–24(–12)	–23(–10)	–15(5)	–4(25)	4(39)
Days with precipitation	3	3	3	3	3	4
Precipitation mm	4	4	4	5	4	7
Precipitation inches	0.1	0.1	0.1	0.2	0.1	0.3

Barrow, Alaska: (continued)

	Jul	Aug	Sep	Oct	Nov	Dec
Sunrise ºC(ºF)	1(33)	1(33)	–3(27)	–13(8)	–22(–8)	–27(–17)
Mid–afternoon ºC(ºF)	7(44)	6(42)	1(33)	–8(18)	–16(3)	–21(–6)
Days with precipitation	8	10	8	9	5	4
Precipitation mm	24	24	15	11	6	4
Precipitation inches	0.9	0.9	0.6	0.4	0.2	0.1

Fairbanks, Alaska: Altitude 138m (453ft)

	Jan	Feb	Mar	Apr	May	Jun
Sunrise ºC(ºF)	–28(–18)	–26(–15)	–19(–3)	–6(21)	3(37)	10(50)
Mid–afternoon ºC(ºF)	–19(–3)	–14(7)	–5(23)	5(41)	15(59)	21(70)
Days with precipitation	7	7	7	5	6	10
Precipitation mm	12	10	9	8	16	35
Precipitation inches	0.5	0.4	0.4	0.3	0.6	1.4
Daily hours of sunshine	2	4	8	11	11	13
Snow mm	279	228	202	101	25	0
Snow inches	11	9	8	4	1	0

	Jul	Aug	Sep	Oct	Nov	Dec
Sunrise ºC(ºF)	11(51)	8(46)	2(35)	–8(18)	–21(–5)	–26(–15)
Mid–afternoon ºC(ºF)	22(72)	19(66)	13(55)	0(32)	–12(11)	–17(1)
Days with precipitation	12	12	9	10	9	8
Precipitation mm	48	50	24	23	20	22
Precipitation inches	1.9	2.0	0.9	0.9	0.8	0.9
Daily hours of sunshine	9	5	5	3	2	1
Snow mm	0	0	25	253	329	304
Snow inches	0	0	1	10	13	12

Juneau, Alaska: Altitude 7m (23ft)

	Jan	Feb	Mar	Apr	May	Jun
Sunrise ºC(ºF)	–7(19)	–5(23)	–3(27)	0(32)	4(39)	7(44)
Mid–afternoon ºC(ºF)	–1(30)	1(33)	4(39)	8(46)	13(55)	16(60)
Precipitation mm	115	95	83	70	87	80
Precipitation inches	4.5	3.8	3.3	2.8	3.4	3.2
Daily hours of sunshine	3	3	4	6	7	6

	Jul	Aug	Sep	Oct	Nov	Dec
Sunrise ºC(ºF)	9(48)	8(46)	6(42)	3(37)	–3(27)	–5(23)
Mid–afternoon ºC(ºF)	18(64)	17(62)	13(55)	8(46)	3(37)	0(32)
Precipitation mm	106	135	171	199	125	113
Precipitation inches	4.2	5.3	6.7	7.8	4.9	4.4
Daily hours of sunshine	6	5	4	2	2	1

ARIZONA (Capital: Phoenix)
Best time for Arizona in general is April and May, and September and October. However, at any time of the year there is always somewhere in the state where the sky is clear and the weather pleasant.

Weather for Phoenix and the Grand Canyon is described below.

Phoenix
Best time: March to May, and September to November, particularly April, May, September and October. Rainfall during the year is very low.

March to May (spring) is sunny and warm.
June to August: Summer is sunny and very hot with many days over 38°C (100°F). Nighttime temperatures often hover around 30°C (86°F). Expect strong winds and thunderstorms in July and August.
September to November (autumn) is sunny and warm.
December to February: Winter is sunny and mild, 20°C (68°F), in the afternoons but can be freezing at night.

Phoenix, Arizona: Altitude 337m (1106ft)

	Jan	Feb	Mar	Apr	May	Jun
Sunrise °C(°F)	5(41)	7(44)	9(48)	13(55)	18(64)	23(73)
Mid–afternoon °C(°F)	19(66)	21(70)	24(75)	29(84)	34(93)	40(104)
Days with precipitation	3	4	3	2	1	1
Precipitation mm	17	16	20	7	3	3
Precipitation inches	0.7	0.6	0.8	0.3	0.1	0.1
Daily hours of sunshine	8	10	11	12	13	14

	Jul	Aug	Sep	Oct	Nov	Dec
Sunrise °C(°F)	27(81)	26(78)	22(72)	16(60)	9(48)	5(41)
Mid–afternoon °C(°F)	41(106)	40(104)	37(98)	31(88)	24(75)	19(66)
Days with precipitation	4	5	3	3	2	4
Precipitation mm	20	30	17	12	12	20
Precipitation inches	0.8	1.2	0.7	0.5	0.5	0.8
Daily hours of sunshine	13	12	12	10	9	9

Grand Canyon.
There are two rims, the South Rim, 2125m (6971ft), and the North Rim, 2500m (8200ft).
• **South Rim** is more easily accessible and receives most visitors. The visitor facilities are open all year.
  Good time to visit the South Rim is April to October.

April to June: Sunny, mild, relatively dry.
July and August: Sunny, pleasant, warm, 27°C (80°F) in the daytime, but rainy. The canyon floor, 1500m (5000ft) below the rim, has hotter daytime temperatures which sometimes exceed 38°C (100°F).
September and October: Sunny, pleasant, mild, relatively dry.
November to March: Snow. Clouds which can obscure views. Icy roads.

- **North Rim**, 16km (10 miles) north of the South Rim as the crow flies, is at a higher elevation, has lower temperatures and receives more snow. Visitor facilities are open May 15 to October 15. The road stays open until mid–December, or when heavy snow makes it impassable.
Good time to visit the North Rim is late May to early October.

Recreational activities in the canyon: River rafting trips are available April through October.

Grand Canyon, Arizona: Altitude 2125m (6971ft)

	Jan	Feb	Mar	Apr	May	Jun
Sunrise ºC(ºF)	–7(20)	–6(21)	–4(25)	–1(31)	4(39)	8(46)
Mid–afternoon ºC(ºF)	5(41)	7(45)	10(50)	16(60)	21(70)	27(81)
Days with precipitation	6	6	6	5	3	3
Precipitation mm	37	40	35	22	15	9
Precipitation inches	1.5	1.6	1.4	0.9	0.6	0.4
Snow mm	380	330	456	228	50	0
Snow inches	15	13	18	9	2	0

	Jul	Aug	Sep	Oct	Nov	Dec
Sunrise ºC(ºF)	12(54)	12(54)	8(47)	3(37)	–3(27)	–6(21)
Mid–afternoon ºC(ºF)	29(85)	28(82)	25(77)	18(65)	11(51)	6(43)
Days with precipitation	11	11	6	5	5	6
Precipitation mm	47	58	40	30	22	43
Precipitation inches	1.9	2.3	1.6	1.2	0.9	1.7
Snow mm	0	0	0	50	202	406
Snow inches	0	0	0	2	8	16

ARKANSAS (Capital: Little Rock)
General weather for **Little Rock**. (On the Arkansas River.)
June to August (summer) is warm and sometimes humid. The warm air from the Gulf of Mexico brings warm weather from May to September.
December to February (winter) is mild but winds from the polar region can bring severely cold temperatures. Rain falls year–round, but the months December to May are particularly rainy.

Little Rock, Arkansas: Altitude 165m (541ft)

	Jan	Feb	Mar	Apr	May	Jun
Sunrise ºC(ºF)	–2(29)	1(33)	6(42)	10(50)	15(59)	20(68)
Mid–afternoon ºC(ºF)	9(48)	12(53)	18(64)	23(73)	27(80)	32(89)
Days with precipitation	10	9	11	10	10	8
Precipitation mm	108	111	124	134	134	88
Precipitation inches	4.3	4.4	4.9	5.3	5.3	3.5
Daily hours of sunshine	4	5	6	8	9	10
Snow mm	50	25	25	0	0	0
Snow inches	2	1	1	0	0	0

Little Rock, Arkansas: (continued)

	Jul	Aug	Sep	Oct	Nov	Dec
Sunrise ºC(ºF)	22(72)	21(70)	17(62)	10(50)	5(41)	1(33)
Mid–afternoon ºC(ºF)	34(93)	33(91)	29(84)	24(75)	17(62)	11(51)
Days with precipitation	8	7	7	6	8	9
Precipitation mm	85	75	90	75	93	103
Precipitation inches	3.4	3.0	3.6	3.0	3.7	4.1
Daily hours of sunshine	10	10	9	8	6	5
Snow mm	0	0	0	0	0	25
Snow inches	0	0	0	0	0	1

CALIFORNIA (Capital: Sacramento)
Best time for California: April and May, and September and October when the fog has cleared and temperatures are warm.
Weather in general:
June to August (summer) is dry and hot, 30ºC (86ºF).
December to February (winter) is rainy and mild.

Lake Tahoe
Best time for hiking in the area is June to August (summer). Skiing is popular in winter.

Lake Tahoe, California: Altitude 1900m (6230ft)

	Jan	Feb	Mar	Apr	May	Jun
Sunrise ºC(ºF)	–9(17)	–8(18)	–6(22)	–3(27)	–1(31)	3(38)
Mid–afternoon ºC(ºF)	2(36)	3(38)	6(43)	11(51)	16(60)	20(68)
Days with precipitation	11	10	10	7	5	3
Precipitation mm	156	134	103	52	30	15
Precipitation inches	6.1	5.3	4.1	2.0	1.2	0.6
Snow mm	1400	1190	990	406	126	0
Snow inches	55	47	39	16	5	0

	Jul	Aug	Sep	Oct	Nov	Dec
Sunrise ºC(ºF)	6(43)	6(43)	3(38)	0(32)	–4(25)	–6(21)
Mid–afternoon ºC(ºF)	26(79)	26(79)	21(70)	14(58)	7(45)	4(39)
Days with precipitation	1	1	3	5	6	9
Precipitation mm	8	4	8	53	90	144
Precipitation inches	0.3	0.1	0.3	2.1	3.6	5.7
Snow mm	0	0	0	75	355	939
Snow inches	0	0	0	3	14	37

Los Angeles, on the Pacific Ocean coast.
Best time: April, May and September, October. (Mild, and fog has cleared.)

April to September has warm, dry, sunny afternoons but often cloudy mornings.
October to March has mild, sunny afternoons, cloudy mornings and light rain. Throughout the year sea breezes and cloud keep the coastal temperatures mild.

Los Angeles, California: Altitude 32m (105ft)

	Jan	Feb	Mar	Apr	May	Jun
Sunrise ºC(ºF)	9(48)	9(48)	10(50)	12(53)	13(55)	15(59)
Mid–afternoon ºC(ºF)	19(65)	19(66)	19(66)	20(68)	21(70)	22(72)
Days with precipitation	6	6	5	4	1	1
Precipitation mm	76	70	55	32	3	3
Precipitation inches	3.0	2.8	2.2	1.3	0.1	0.1
Daily hours of sunshine	7	8	9	9	9	10

	Jul	Aug	Sep	Oct	Nov	Dec
Sunrise ºC(ºF)	17(62)	18(64)	17(62)	15(59)	12(53)	9(48)
Mid–afternoon ºC(ºF)	24(75)	25(77)	25(77)	24(75)	21(70)	19(66)
Days with precipitation	1	0	1	2	3	5
Precipitation mm	0	0	5	7	50	53
Precipitation inches	0	0	0.2	0.3	2.0	2.1
Daily hours of sunshine	12	11	10	9	8	8

Palm Springs
The **season**, that is, the main season for tourism is **late October to early May. The best months to see the desert wildflowers are March and April**, but this is dependent on the rains.

Palm Springs, California: Altitude 125m (411ft)

	Jan	Feb	Mar	Apr	May	Jun
Sunrise ºC(ºF)	4(39)	6(43)	8(47)	12(53)	14(58)	17(63)
Mid–afternoon ºC(ºF)	20(68)	21(71)	26(79)	31(87)	34(94)	39(102)
Days with precipitation	4	4	3	2	1	1
Precipitation mm	30	32	20	7	0	0
Precipitation inches	1.2	1.3	0.8	0.3	0	0

	Jul	Aug	Sep	Oct	Nov	Dec
Sunrise ºC(ºF)	23(73)	21(71)	19(66)	14(57)	8(47)	5(41)
Mid–afternoon ºC(ºF)	42(108)	41(106)	39(102)	33(91)	26(79)	21(70)
Days with precipitation	2	2	2	2	2	5
Precipitation mm	7	7	9	7	12	43
Precipitation inches	0.3	0.3	0.4	0.3	0.5	1.7

Yosemite National Park

A good time to visit when it is less crowded is April to early June, and September to November.
The Yosemite Valley can look its best in early June when the waterfalls are full. July and August, with
their summer weather, is the busiest season.

Yosemite National Park, California: Altitude 1215m (3985ft)

	Jan	Feb	Mar	Apr	May	Jun
Sunrise °C(°F)	−4(26)	−3(28)	−1(31)	3(37)	6(43)	8(47)
Mid–afternoon °C(°F)	8(47)	11(52)	15(59)	19(67)	23(73)	27(80)
Days with precipitation	11	10	10	7	5	3
Precipitation mm	162	174	134	5	35	12
Precipitation inches	6.4	6.9	5.3	0.2	1.4	0.5
Snow mm	406	329	406	228	0	0
Snow inches	16	13	16	9	0	0

	Jul	Aug	Sep	Oct	Nov	Dec
Sunrise °C(°F)	12(54)	11(52)	8(47)	4(39)	−1(31)	−3(28)
Mid–afternoon °C(°F)	32(90)	32(90)	28(83)	21(71)	14(58)	8(47)
Days with precipitation	1	1	3	5	6	9
Precipitation mm	5	3	9	50	95	187
Precipitation inches	0.2	0.1	0.4	2.0	3.8	7.4
Snow mm	0	0	0	0	101	380
Snow inches	0	0	0	0	4	15

COLORADO (Capital: Denver)

Good time for general sightseeing in Colorado is July to October. July and August are the warmest
months and are the peak months for wildflowers. A popular month is September when the aspen
leaves turn to a golden hue. The **ski season** runs from mid–November to mid–April, although times
vary according to the location of ski resorts.

Aspen, Colorado: Altitude 2369m (7773ft)

	Jan	Feb	Mar	Apr	May	Jun
Sunrise °C(°F)	−15(6)	−13(8)	−10(15)	−4(25)	0(32)	3(38)
Mid–afternoon °C(°F)	1(34)	3(37)	6(43)	12(53)	18(64)	23(74)
Days with precipitation	8	8	8	8	8	6
Precipitation mm	45	45	45	43	40	27
Precipitation inches	1.8	1.8	1.8	1.7	1.6	1.1
Snow mm	685	635	610	279	75	0
Snow inches	27	25	24	11	3	0

Aspen, Colorado: (continued)

	Jul	Aug	Sep	Oct	Nov	Dec
Sunrise ºC(ºF)	7(44)	6(43)	2(36)	–3(28)	–9(16)	–13(9)
Mid–afternoon ºC(ºF)	27(80)	26(78)	21(71)	16(60)	7(45)	3(37)
Days with precipitation	7	9	8	7	7	6
Precipitation mm	37	40	35	35	35	37
Precipitation inches	1.5	1.6	1.4	1.4	1.4	1.5
Snow mm	0	0	25	126	431	533
Snow inches	0	0	1	5	17	21

Denver
Most pleasant season for travel is September and October. (Autumn.)

June to August: Summer is sunny, rainy and cool to warm.
September and October: Autumn is sunny, mild with little rain. Light snowfalls can fall in late September or early October.
December to February: Winter is mild with occasional cold, severe air masses coming from the north. Expect snowfalls. Many of the cold air masses are deflected eastwards by the protective Rocky Mountains.
March to May: Spring is cloudy and windy with some rain and snow. March and April have the heaviest snowfalls.

Denver, Colorado: Altitude 1626m (5335ft)

	Jan	Feb	Mar	Apr	May	Jun
Sunrise ºC(ºF)	–9(16)	–7(19)	–3(27)	1(33)	6(42)	11(51)
Mid–afternoon ºC(ºF)	6(42)	8(46)	11(51)	17(62)	22(72)	27(80)
Days with precipitation	6	6	9	9	10	9
Precipitation mm	16	17	30	47	68	47
Precipitation inches	0.6	0.7	1.2	1.9	2.7	1.9
Daily hours of sunshine	7	8	8	9	9	10
Snow mm	202	202	329	253	25	0
Snow inches	8	8	13	10	1	0

	Jul	Aug	Sep	Oct	Nov	Dec
Sunrise ºC(ºF)	15(59)	14(57)	9(48)	2(35)	–4(25)	–8(18)
Mid–afternoon ºC(ºF)	31(87)	30(86)	25(77)	19(66)	11(51)	7(44)
Days with precipitation	9	8	6	5	5	5
Precipitation mm	45	32	27	27	20	9
Precipitation inches	1.8	1.3	1.1	1.1	0.8	0.4
Daily hours of sunshine	10	10	9	8	6	6
Snow mm	0	0	50	101	202	152
Snow inches	0	0	2	4	8	6

CONNECTICUT (Capital: Hartford)
Best time for Connecticut: Late May and early June, and September and October. (Summer, July to August, is also a good time.)

Rainfall in the New England states, of which this is one, does not have a dominant rainy season. Rain is distributed fairly evenly throughout the year, and snow falls from December to March.

Connecticut's weather in brief:
April and May: Cool to mild, 16 to 21°C (60 to 70°F).
June to August: Summer. Days are warm, 21 to 32°C (70 to 90°F). Evenings are cooler, particularly in the mountains and along the coast. Summer can be humid as well as rainy and foggy. These are busy months, especially on the coast.
September to November: Autumn. Fairly dry, sunny days and cool nights. September and October are ideal months.
December to March: Light rain, snow and sleet.

Hartford, Connecticut: Altitude 55m (180ft)

	Jan	Feb	Mar	Apr	May	Jun
Sunrise °C(°F)	–9(16)	–7(19)	–2(29)	3(37)	9(48)	14(57)
Mid–afternoon °C(°F)	1(33)	3(37)	8(46)	15(59)	22(72)	27(80)
Days with precipitation	9	8	9	9	10	9
Precipitation mm	87	82	92	98	105	95
Precipitation inches	3.4	3.2	3.6	3.9	4.1	3.8
Daily hours of sunshine	5	6	7	7	8	9
Snow mm	279	329	304	50	0	0
Snow inches	11	13	12	2	0	0

	Jul	Aug	Sep	Oct	Nov	Dec
Sunrise °C(°F)	17(62)	16(60)	11(51)	5(41)	0(32)	–6(21)
Mid–afternoon °C(°F)	29(84)	28(82)	24(75)	18(64)	11(51)	3(37)
Days with precipitation	8	8	7	7	8	10
Precipitation mm	81	93	96	91	103	99
Precipitation inches	3.2	3.7	3.8	3.6	4.1	3.9
Daily hours of sunshine	9	9	7	6	5	4
Snow mm	0	0	0	0	50	329
Snow inches	0	0	0	0	2	13

DELAWARE (Capital: Dover)
Best time to visit Delaware: Late May and early June, and September. July and August are also good months but these summer months are hot and humid, sometimes over 30°C (86°F). The annual precipitation of 1150mm (45in) is fairly well distributed throughout the year but July and August are the rainiest months.

DISTRICT OF COLUMBIA
Washington
The best weather is April and May (spring) **and September and October** (autumn).
June to August (summer) has thunderstorms with lightning, strong winds and heavy rains. July is the warmest month.
December to February (winter) has snowfalls; the coldest time is January and early February. Rain falls year–round.

Washington, District of Columbia: Altitude 20m (66ft)

	Jan	Feb	Mar	Apr	May	Jun
Sunrise ºC(ºF)	–3(27)	–2(29)	3(37)	8(46)	14(57)	19(67)
Mid–afternoon ºC(ºF)	6(42)	8(46)	14(57)	19(66)	25(77)	29(84)
Days with precipitation	10	9	10	10	12	9
Precipitation mm	70	66	88	75	93	90
Precipitation inches	2.8	2.6	3.5	3.0	3.7	3.6
Daily hours of sunshine	5	6	7	8	9	9
Snow mm	126	177	75	0	0	0
Snow inches	5	7	3	0	0	0

	Jul	Aug	Sep	Oct	Nov	Dec
Sunrise ºC(ºF)	22(72)	21(71)	17(62)	10(50)	5(41)	0(32)
Mid–afternoon ºC(ºF)	31(87)	30(86)	27(80)	21(70)	15(59)	8(46)
Days with precipitation	10	9	8	7	8	10
Precipitation mm	103	106	83	68	78	88
Precipitation inches	4.1	4.2	3.3	2.7	3.1	3.5
Daily hours of sunshine	9	8	8	7	5	4
Snow mm	0	0	0	0	50	152
Snow inches	0	0	0	0	2	6

FLORIDA (Capital: Tallahassee)
This state is for all seasons. We have divided the state into the south and the north.
In the southern half, October to April is the busy tourist season, especially December to March which is mild and dry.
Great time to visit is October to November as it is not too hot and the crowds are less, but hurricanes can occur August to November.

In northern Florida and the panhandle the peak season is the warm summer, May to August. Average temperature in Tallahassee is 27°C (80°F). December to February, the coldest months in the north, is the off–season. Average daytime temperature in Tallahassee is 13°C (55°F).

Natural attraction: Everglades National Park, west of Homestead.
Best time for viewing wildlife is December to April. Busiest tourist months are February and March. Least crowded are June and September.

Miami

Miami is a year–round destination.

June to September (long summer) is the hottest time, 32ºC (90ºF) and also the rainiest.

October and November (mild) is a very good time to visit.

December to March (winter) is mild, 22ºC (72ºF) and dry.

Hurricanes can be expected September and October.

Miami, Florida: Altitude 5m (16ft)

	Jan	Feb	Mar	Apr	May	Jun
Sunrise ºC(ºF)	15(59)	16(60)	18(64)	20(68)	22(72)	24(75)
Mid–afternoon ºC(ºF)	24(75)	25(77)	26(78)	28(82)	29(84)	31(87)
Days with precipitation	7	6	6	6	10	15
Precipitation mm	55	50	53	91	154	228
Precipitation inches	2.2	2.0	2.1	3.6	6.1	9.0
Daily hours of sunshine	8	8	9	9	9	9

	Jul	Aug	Sep	Oct	Nov	Dec
Sunrise ºC(ºF)	25(77)	25(77)	24(75)	22(72)	19(66)	16(60)
Mid–afternoon ºC(ºF)	32(89)	32(89)	31(87)	29(84)	27(80)	25(77)
Days with precipitation	16	17	18	15	8	7
Precipitation mm	174	169	220	207	68	40
Precipitation inches	6.9	6.7	8.7	8.2	2.7	1.6
Daily hours of sunshine	9	8	7	6	7	7

Orlando

Orlando is a year–round destination.

June to September (summer) is hot, 32ºC (90ºF). The air is humid because of the profusion of lakes on the surrounding flat land. June to September is the rainy season with afternoon rainstorms occurring daily. Rain falls in all other months, but is lighter.

November to April has bright, clear, sunny days. Although nighttime winter temperatures may drop to freezing, snow is extremely rare.

Orlando, Florida: Altitude 33m (108ft)

	Jan	Feb	Mar	Apr	May	Jun
Sunrise ºC(ºF)	9(48)	10(50)	13(55)	15(59)	19(66)	22(72)
Mid–afternoon ºC(ºF)	22(72)	23(73)	26(78)	28(82)	31(87)	32(89)
Days with precipitation	6	7	8	5	9	14
Precipitation mm	58	73	88	68	73	180
Precipitation inches	2.3	2.9	3.5	2.7	2.9	7.1

	Jul	Aug	Sep	Oct	Nov	Dec
Sunrise ºC(ºF)	23(73)	23(73)	22(72)	19(66)	14(57)	11(51)
Mid–afternoon ºC(ºF)	33(91)	33(91)	32(89)	29(84)	26(78)	23(73)
Days with precipitation	18	16	14	9	5	6
Precipitation mm	210	169	182	103	40	47
Precipitation inches	8.3	6.7	7.2	4.1	1.6	1.9

Tampa–St Petersburg
This is a year–round destination.
June to September (summer) is hot, 32°C (90°F). This is the rainy season with frequent rainstorms during the afternoons. The rains tend to cool the temperature. Temperatures throughout the year are modified by the waters of the Gulf of Mexico.
December to March (winter) is pleasantly dry and cool in the daytime, 22°C (72°F). Snow is rare.

Tampa–St Petersburg, Florida: Altitude 3m (10ft)

	Jan	Feb	Mar	Apr	May	Jun
Sunrise °C(°F)	10(50)	11(51)	14(57)	16(60)	20(68)	23(73)
Mid–afternoon °C(°F)	21(69)	22(72)	25(77)	28(82)	31(87)	32(89)
Days with precipitation	6	7	7	5	6	12
Precipitation mm	58	73	98	53	60	164
Precipitation inches	2.3	2.9	3.9	2.1	2.4	6.5
Daily hours of sunshine	6	7	9	10	10	9

	Jul	Aug	Sep	Oct	Nov	Dec
Sunrise °C(°F)	24(75)	24(75)	23(73)	18(64)	14(57)	11(51)
Mid–afternoon °C(°F)	32(89)	32(89)	32(89)	29(84)	25(77)	22(72)
Days with precipitation	16	16	13	7	5	6
Precipitation mm	213	202	162	63	45	55
Precipitation inches	8.4	8.0	6.4	2.5	1.8	2.2
Daily hours of sunshine	9	8	7	8	7	6

GEORGIA (Capital: Atlanta)
Good time to visit Georgia: Mid–March to April (spring) **and mid–September to mid–October** (autumn).

Georgia's weather in brief:
Mid–March to mid–April: Spring afternoon temperatures are a mild 15 to 20°C (59 to 70°F). Expect some rain.
June to August: Summer. Daily afternoon thunderstorms. Humidity is high. Temperatures reach an uncomfortable 35°C (95°F) but can be less along the coast and in the mountains.
Mid–September to mid–October: Pleasantly warm with an "Indian summer." Afternoon temperatures range 21 to 27°C (70 to 80°F). Foliage is changing colour; it is especially spectacular in the mountains.
November: Temperatures drop dramatically.
December to February: Snow falls in the northern mountains.

Atlanta, in the foothills of the Blue Ridge Mountains.
Atlanta's weather in brief:
June to August (summer) is very hot with daytime temperatures over 30°C (in the high 80s°F).
December to February (winter) is mild with light snow that disappears quickly from the ground.
Rain falls year–round, but less falls September to November (autumn).

Atlanta, Georgia: Altitude 315m (1033ft)

	Jan	Feb	Mar	Apr	May	Jun
Sunrise ºC(ºF)	–3(27)	1(33)	6(42)	10(50)	15(59)	19(66)
Mid–afternoon ºC(ºF)	10(50)	13(55)	18(64)	22(72)	26(78)	30(86)
Days with precipitation	11	10	12	9	9	10
Precipitation mm	108	111	147	116	93	96
Precipitation inches	4.3	4.4	5.8	4.6	3.7	3.8
Daily hours of sunshine	5	5	6	8	9	10
Snow mm	25	0	0	0	0	0
Snow inches	1	0	0	0	0	0

	Jul	Aug	Sep	Oct	Nov	Dec
Sunrise ºC(ºF)	21(70)	21(70)	17(62)	11(51)	6(42)	2(35)
Mid–afternoon ºC(ºF)	31(87)	31(87)	28(82)	23(73)	17(62)	12(53)
Days with precipitation	12	9	7	6	8	10
Precipitation mm	124	88	80	63	85	106
Precipitation inches	4.9	3.5	3.2	2.5	3.4	4.2
Daily hours of sunshine	9	9	8	7	6	5
Snow mm	0	0	0	0	0	0
Snow inches	0	0	0	0	0	0

HAWAII (Capital: Honolulu)
Hawaii is a year–round destination but months vary.

Temperatures throughout the year average 27ºC (80ºF), but summer (May to October) is a few degrees hotter than winter (November to April).

Rainfall is the main consideration, not temperature. There is less rain in summer, May to October.

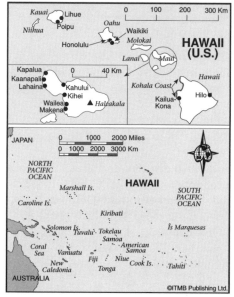

Best time to visit: April to mid–July, and September and October. May is usually ideal. Other months through out the year are also good, particularly on the drier west and southwest coasts of all the islands which are usually hot and dry. North and northeast coasts of all the islands are cooler and wet. See below under **Rain** and **Beaches**.

Below is described the general weather of the Hawaiian Islands.

Mid–April to mid–July: Part of summer. Sunny, less rain, not too windy, not too humid. The northeast tradewinds blow almost daily. They have a pleasing, cooling effect and keep down humidity. Rain showers are brief, usually lasting a few minutes. Although these months have excellent weather they are not part of the busy season which is November to April.
Mid–July to August: Part of summer. Weather is the same as April to mid–July, except that August is the hottest month, 32ºF (90ºF). This is a busy time when family vacationers add to the crowds, especially on Oahu.

September and October: Part of summer. Weather is the same as mid–April to mid–July.
November to April: Winter. Periods of fine, sunny weather with breezes. There is more chance of cloudy, humid days with little wind and an increase in rainfall. Most rain falls in these months. The northeast tradewinds that bring cooling relief are less frequent. When they stop blowing, the unpleasant kona winds from the south can blow, bringing thunderstorms, cloudiness and stickiness. They can blow intermittently from October to April or, in some years, not blow at all. Hurricanes are rare but if one were to touch down it would usually be between November and April. February is an unreliable month in that if rain were going to fall for a few days, say three in a row, it could happen in February. However, November to April is the peak season for tourism, mainly because weather elsewhere (e.g. North American mainland) is inclement.

Winds

Because of the cooling affect of the prevailing northwest tradewinds that blow for 300 days a year, afternooon temperatures in the islands remain fairly constant, around 27°C (80°F). They also keep down humidity. Honolulu's humidity is only 50 to 60%. They blow almost daily May to October (summer) and less frequently November to April (winter). From October to April (winter) when the cooling northwest winds are less frequent, hot moist winds from the southwest will take over. These unpleasant kona winds bring cloudiness, thunderstorms, and humid weather.

Rain

November to April are the rainiest months. May to October are the driest.
All islands have a wet side and a dry side.
Wet side (north and east coasts): Called the windward side because the coasts face the incoming northeast tradewinds. The winds collect moisture as they travel over the Pacific Ocean and dump some on the coasts. As these moisture–laden winds attempt to climb over the interior mountains they form clouds and release more moisture on the windward slopes. The rain falls at or below 900m (3000ft), therefore the upper slopes of high mountains (e.g. Haleakala, Mauna Loa and Mauna Kea) remain quite dry, while the lower slopes get saturated.
Dry side (south and west coasts): Called the leeward (i.e. sheltered) side because little rain goes over the mountains. Hence the south and west coasts are drier.

Beaches

Beaches that lie on the leeward side, in the rain shadow of interior mountains, are drier and offer the best beach weather. The main islands and their hot, dry, popular, leeward beaches are:
- **Oahu:** Waikiki
- **Maui:** Kapalua, Kaanapali, Kihei, Wailea and Makena. The Kihei–Wailea coast offers the best chances for year–round sun. If it is raining on one beach, move along to another.
- **Hawaii** (The Big Island): The Kohala coast is usually always clear and is the best bet for year–round sun. The town of Kailua–Kona on the leeward side receives only 635mm (25in) of rain annually. Compare this with Hilo on the windward side which receives 3300mm (130in), more than five times as much rain.
- **Kauai:** Poipu and west of Poipu are the driest beaches and the best bet for year–round sun.
- **Lanai:** The leeward side and the basins on the island are dry and hot with water shortages. Even the windward side receives only 1000mm (40in) of rain annually.
- **Molokai:** The western part of the island is drier than the east. The east receives only 750mm (30in) of rain annually.

Natural attraction:

On Maui is **Haleakala**, over 3000m (10000ft) above sea level, which many people drive up for the sunrise. The summit is 9°C (49°F) compared with 27°C (80°F) on the coast. Take a blanket with you if you go at sunrise. Air is "thinner" at this altitude due to lower atmospheric pressure. Exertion can make you breathless. Busiest time is July and August. Least crowded is November and December.

Recreational activities:
1. Hiking. The closer you are to the mountains, the wetter it will be. Hikers should choose summer (May to October) because it is drier. Temperatures decrease the higher you go.
2. Surfing. The surfing season is October to April when high surf is more common.

Hilo on Hawaii, "The Big Island": Altitude 11m (36ft)

	Jan	Feb	Mar	Apr	May	Jun
Sunrise ºC(ºF)	18(64)	18(64)	18(64)	19(66)	19(66)	20(68)
Mid–afternoon ºC(ºF)	27(80)	27(80)	27(80)	27(80)	27(80)	28(82)
Days with precipitation	14	14	20	22	22	20
Precipitation mm	251	261	354	388	252	158
Precipitation inches	9.9	10.3	13.9	15.3	9.9	6.2
Daily hours of sunshine	5	5	5	5	5	6

	Jul	Aug	Sep	Oct	Nov	Dec
Sunrise ºC(ºF)	20(68)	21(70)	20(68)	20(68)	19(66)	18(64)
Mid–afternoon ºC(ºF)	28(82)	29(85)	29(85)	28(82)	27(80)	27(80)
Days with precipitation	24	22	20	20	20	17
Precipitation mm	247	237	217	244	369	306
Precipitation inches	9.7	9.3	8.5	9.6	14.5	12.1
Daily hours of sunshine	5	6	5	4	4	4

Honolulu, island of Oahu, Hawaii: Altitude 5m (16ft)

	Jan	Feb	Mar	Apr	May	Jun
Sunrise ºC(ºF)	19(66)	19(66)	20(68)	20(68)	21(70)	22(72)
Mid–afternoon ºC(ºF)	27(80)	27(80)	28(83)	28(83)	29(84)	30(86)
Days with precipitation	7	5	6	5	3	2
Precipitation mm	90	56	56	39	29	13
Precipitation inches	3.6	2.2	2.2	1.5	1.1	0.5
Daily hours of sunshine	7	8	8	8	9	10

	Jul	Aug	Sep	Oct	Nov	Dec
Sunrise ºC(ºF)	23(73)	23(73)	23(73)	22(72)	21(69)	19(66)
Mid–afternoon ºC(ºF)	31(88)	32(89)	31(88)	31(88)	29(84)	27(81)
Days with precipitation	3	3	4	5	6	7
Precipitation mm	15	11	20	58	76	97
Precipitation inches	0.6	0.4	0.8	2.3	3.0	3.8
Daily hours of sunshine	10	10	9	8	7	6

Kahului, island of Maui, Hawaii: Altitude 20m (67ft)

	Jan	Feb	Mar	Apr	May	Jun
Sunrise ºC(ºF)	18(64)	18(64)	18(64)	19(66)	19(66)	21(70)
Mid–afternoon ºC(ºF)	27(80)	27(80)	27(80)	28(82)	29(84)	30(86)
Days with precipitation	8	6	7	6	3	2
Precipitation mm	105	73	69	47	20	7
Precipitation inches	4.1	2.9	2.7	1.9	0.8	0.3
Daily hours of sunshine	7	8	8	8	9	10

	Jul	Aug	Sep	Oct	Nov	Dec
Sunrise ºC(ºF)	21(70)	22(72)	21(70)	21(70)	20(68)	18(64)
Mid–afternoon ºC(ºF)	30(86)	31(87)	31(87)	30(86)	29(85)	27(80)
Days with precipitation	3	3	2	4	7	8
Precipitation mm	10	12	9	31	66	83
Precipitation inches	0.4	0.5	0.4	1.2	2.6	3.3
Daily hours of sunshine	9	9	9	8	7	7

Kailua–Kona, Hawaii, "The Big Island": Altitude 5m (18ft)

	Jan	Feb	Mar	Apr	May	Jun
Sunrise ºC(ºF)	18(65)	18(65)	18(65)	19(66)	20(68)	21(69)
Mid–afternoon ºC(ºF)	27(81)	27(81)	27(81)	28(82)	28(82)	28(82)
Days with precipitation	10	7	8	7	8	7
Precipitation mm	78	43	53	40	58	55
Precipitation inches	3.1	1.7	2.1	1.6	2.3	2.2

	Jul	Aug	Sep	Oct	Nov	Dec
Sunrise ºC(ºF)	21(69)	21(69)	21(69)	21(69)	20(68)	18(65)
Mid–afternoon ºC(ºF)	29(84)	29(84)	29(84)	29(84)	28(82)	28(82)
Days with precipitation	8	8	7	6	7	7
Precipitation mm	63	60	43	43	45	43
Precipitation inches	2.5	2.4	1.7	1.7	1.8	1.7

Lahaina, island of Maui, Hawaii: Altitude 4m (12ft)

	Jan	Feb	Mar	Apr	May	Jun
Sunrise ºC(ºF)	17(62)	17(62)	17(62)	18(64)	19(66)	20(68)
Mid–afternoon ºC(ºF)	27(80)	27(80)	28(82)	28(82)	30(86)	31(88)
Days with precipitation	10	12	8	9	5	5
Precipitation mm	70	58	58	32	12	4
Precipitation inches	2.8	2.3	2.3	1.3	0.5	0.1

Lahaina, island of Maui, Hawaii: (continued)

	Jul	Aug	Sep	Oct	Nov	Dec
Sunrise ºC(ºF)	21(69)	21(69)	21(69)	20(68)	19(66)	18(64)
Mid–afternoon ºC(ºF)	31(88)	32(89)	32(89)	31(88)	29(85)	28(82)
Days with precipitation	7	6	5	7	9	10
Precipitation mm	5	14	7	30	40	68
Precipitation inches	0.2	0.6	0.3	1.2	1.6	2.7

Lihue, island of Kauai, Hawaii: Altitude 45m (147ft)

	Jan	Feb	Mar	Apr	May	Jun
Sunrise ºC(ºF)	18(65)	18(65)	19(66)	20(68)	21(70)	22(72)
Mid–afternoon ºC(ºF)	26(78)	26(78)	26(78)	26(78)	27(81)	28(83)
Days with precipitation	11	9	11	12	10	9
Precipitation mm	126	75	75	75	75	25
Precipitation inches	5.0	3.0	3.0	3.0	3.0	1.0
Daily hours of sunshine	6	6	7	7	8	8

	Jul	Aug	Sep	Oct	Nov	Dec
Sunrise ºC(ºF)	23(73)	23(73)	23(73)	22(72)	21(70)	19(67)
Mid–afternoon ºC(ºF)	29(84)	29(84)	29(84)	28(83)	27(81)	26(78)
Days with precipitation	13	11	10	12	13	12
Precipitation mm	50	50	50	101	126	101
Precipitation inches	2.0	2.0	2.0	4.0	5.0	4.0
Daily hours of sunshine	8	8	8	7	5	5

IDAHO (Capital: Boise)
Idaho's summer tourist season runs from Memorial Day in late May to Labor Day in early September. **Best time to visit Idaho for general sightseeing is September and October.** (Dry, pleasant, foliage changes colour.) June to August (summer) is also good.

Late May to early September: Mild days and cool nights with occasional short, afternoon rainstorms, especially in the mountains. The plains in July and August can be dry and hot, 30 to 40ºC (approximately 85 to 100ºF) but are subject to occasional thunderstorms.
October to February: Starting in October, snow can be expected at higher elevations.
March to May: Spring. Cold and windy. Occasional avalanches.

Recreational activity: Ski season runs from Thanksgiving Day (late November) to March.

Boise
June to September is mostly dry with low humidity and afternoon temperatures ranging 27 to 32ºC (80 to 90ºF).
December to March is mild, 4 to 10ºC (40 to 50ºF), with heavy rainstorms and cloudy conditions. These are caused by chinook winds, the warm, moisture–laden winds that blow from the Pacific Ocean. Snow also falls during these winter months, but the amount is kept small by the warm chinook winds.

Boise, Idaho: Altitude 874m (2867ft)

	Jan	Feb	Mar	Apr	May	Jun
Sunrise ºC(ºF)	–6(21)	–3(27)	–1(30)	3(37)	7(44)	11(51)
Mid–afternoon ºC(ºF)	3(37)	7(44)	12(53)	16(60)	22(72)	27(80)
Days with precipitation	12	10	9	8	8	7
Precipitation mm	38	30	25	27	32	27
Precipitation inches	1.5	1.2	1.0	1.1	1.3	1.1
Daily hours of sunshine	3	5	7	9	11	12
Snow mm	202	101	50	25	0	0
Snow inches	8	4	2	1	0	0

	Jul	Aug	Sep	Oct	Nov	Dec
Sunrise ºC(ºF)	14(57)	14(57)	9(48)	4(39)	–1(30)	–5(23)
Mid–afternoon ºC(ºF)	32(89)	31(87)	25(77)	18(64)	9(48)	3(37)
Days with precipitation	2	3	4	6	10	12
Precipitation mm	3	7	10	20	32	35
Precipitation inches	0.1	0.3	0.4	0.8	1.3	1.4
Daily hours of sunshine	14	12	11	8	5	4
Snow mm	0	0	0	0	50	126
Snow inches	0	0	0	0	2	5

ILLINOIS (Capital: Springfield)

Chicago, on Lake Michigan.

Pleasant month for visiting Chicago is September.

Chicago's weather in brief:

June to August (summer) is warm to hot with periods of high humidity which may last four to five days. Wind shifts, combined with heavy rainstorms, can suddenly end a hot, humid period. Lake Michigan causes summer temperatures by the lakeside to be a few degrees cooler than in the city. Winds are often stronger along the shore.

December to March (winter) is cold with snowfalls.

Chicago, Illinois: Altitude 205m (672ft)

	Jan	Feb	Mar	Apr	May	Jun
Sunrise ºC(ºF)	–11(13)	–8(18)	–2(29)	4(39)	9(48)	14(57)
Mid–afternoon ºC(ºF)	–2(29)	1(33)	8(46)	15(59)	21(69)	26(78)
Days with precipitation	11	10	13	12	11	11
Precipitation mm	43	32	63	85	85	106
Precipitation inches	1.7	1.3	2.5	3.4	3.4	4.2
Daily hours of sunshine	4	5	7	7	9	10
Snow mm	253	202	202	50	0	0
Snow inches	10	8	8	2	0	0

Chicago, Illinois: (continued)

	Jul	Aug	Sep	Oct	Nov	Dec
Sunrise ºC(ºF)	17(62)	16(60)	12(53)	6(42)	0(32)	–7(19)
Mid–afternoon ºC(ºF)	28(82)	28(82)	24(75)	17(62)	9(48)	1(33)
Days with precipitation	10	8	10	9	10	11
Precipitation mm	88	68	75	58	53	40
Precipitation inches	3.5	2.7	3.0	2.3	2.1	1.6
Daily hours of sunshine	10	9	8	7	5	4
Snow mm	0	0	0	0	50	202
Snow inches	0	0	0	0	2	8

INDIANA (Capital: Indianapolis)
Good month to visit Indianapolis is September.

Weather in brief for Indianapolis:
June to August (summer) is warm. Occasionally sticky weather is brought by warm air arriving from the distant Gulf of Mexico. Occasionally hot, dry weather is brought by southwest winds.
December to March (winter) is cool with small snowfalls.
Rain is distributed fairly evenly throughout the year.

Indianapolis, Indiana: Altitude 246m (807ft)

	Jan	Feb	Mar	Apr	May	Jun
Sunrise ºC(ºF)	–8(18)	–6(21)	0(32)	5(41)	11(51)	16(60)
Mid–afternoon ºC(ºF)	1(33)	3(37)	10(50)	17(62)	23(73)	28(82)
Days with precipitation	11	10	13	12	12	10
Precipitation mm	70	60	93	98	103	106
Precipitation inches	2.8	2.4	3.7	3.9	4.1	4.2
Daily hours of sunshine	4	5	7	7	9	10
Snow mm	126	126	101	0	0	0
Snow inches	5	5	4	0	0	0

	Jul	Aug	Sep	Oct	Nov	Dec
Sunrise ºC(ºF)	18(64)	17(62)	13(55)	6(42)	1(33)	–5(23)
Mid–afternoon ºC(ºF)	30(86)	29(84)	25(77)	19(66)	11(51)	4(39)
Days with precipitation	9	8	8	8	10	12
Precipitation mm	93	72	73	63	78	68
Precipitation inches	3.7	2.8	2.9	2.5	3.1	2.7
Daily hours of sunshine	10	10	9	7	5	4
Snow mm	0	0	0	0	50	126
Snow inches	0	0	0	0	2	5

IOWA (Capital: Des Moines)
Best time to visit Iowa: September.

Iowa's weather in brief:
June to August: Summer. Warm and sunny. Expect the occasional hailstorm and thunderstorm.
September and October: Warm and sunny, light rain.
November to March: Cold with snowfalls.
April and May: Mild with rain, brought by southerly winds.
Sunshine is abundant. An average of 215 days per year are sunny.

Des Moines, at the confluence of the Des Moines and Racoon Rivers.
Des Moines' weather in brief:
June to August (summer) is hot and sunny with occasional thunderstorms that occur from May to October. The rains taper off particularly in October and November (autumn). September is usually an excellent month to visit because it is warm and sunny with diminishing rain.
December to March is the long winter period when cold winds blow over the flat land.

Des Moines, Iowa: Altitude 294m (965ft)

	Jan	Feb	Mar	Apr	May	Jun
Sunrise ºC(ºF)	–12(11)	–9(16)	–2(29)	4(39)	11(51)	16(60)
Mid–afternoon ºC(ºF)	–2(29)	1(33)	8(46)	17(62)	23(73)	28(82)
Days with precipitation	7	7	10	10	11	11
Precipitation mm	27	27	58	75	106	124
Precipitation inches	1.1	1.1	2.3	3.0	4.2	4.9
Daily hours of sunshine	5	6	6	8	9	10
Snow mm	202	177	177	50	0	0
Snow inches	8	7	7	2	0	0

	Jul	Aug	Sep	Oct	Nov	Dec
Sunrise ºC(ºF)	19(66)	18(64)	12(53)	6(42)	–1(30)	–9(16)
Mid–afternoon ºC(ºF)	30(86)	29(84)	24(75)	18(64)	9(48)	0(32)
Days with precipitation	9	9	9	7	6	7
Precipitation mm	83	83	78	53	35	27
Precipitation inches	3.3	3.3	3.1	2.1	1.4	1.1
Daily hours of sunshine	11	10	9	8	6	4
Snow mm	0	0	0	0	75	152
Snow inches	0	0	0	0	3	6

KANSAS (Capital: Topeka)
Best time for Kansas: September.
Kansas lies midway between the Pacific and the Atlantic. It is affected by cold winds from the north and warm winds from the south. The western third of Kansas is the windiest region in the country.

September and October: Warm with diminishing rain. 27°C (80°F) in the afternoons.
November to March: Cold. Snow falls, but does not stay on the ground for more than a few days at a time. January is the coldest month. Strong winds cause erosion by blowing loose soil into dust storms.
April: Cloudiest month. Sky is overcast 60% of the time, especially in the northeast.
May and June: There is a chance of tornadoes. Touchdowns are more likely to occur in the eastern part of Kansas than the western part.
July and August: Hot with heavy rainfall. Although skies are overcast 35% of the time, June to August are the sunniest months with 11 to 12 hours per day.

Wichita, on the Arkansas River.
Wichita's weather in brief:
June to August (summer) is hot with most days above 30°C (86°F). From March to July expect heavy rainstorms with strong southerly winds and tornadoes.
December to March (winter) is mild with light snowfalls.

Wichita, Kansas: Altitude 409m (1342ft)

	Jan	Feb	Mar	Apr	May	Jun
Sunrise °C(°F)	–7(19)	–5(23)	1(32)	7(44)	12(53)	18(64)
Mid–afternoon °C(°F)	24(75)	24(75)	26(78)	28(82)	30(86)	31(87)
Days with precipitation	5	5	7	8	10	9
Precipitation mm	20	25	45	73	90	114
Precipitation inches	0.8	1.0	1.8	2.9	3.6	4.5
Daily hours of sunshine	6	7	7	9	9	10
Snow mm	101	101	75	0	0	0
Snow inches	4	4	3	0	0	0

	Jul	Aug	Sep	Oct	Nov	Dec
Sunrise °C(°F)	21(70)	20(68)	15(59)	8(46)	1(33)	–5(23)
Mid–afternoon °C(°F)	32(89)	32(89)	31(87)	29(84)	27(80)	24(75)
Days with precipitation	8	7	8	6	5	6
Precipitation mm	111	78	93	63	30	27
Precipitation inches	4.4	3.1	3.7	2.5	1.2	1.1
Daily hours of sunshine	11	10	8	7	6	5
Snow mm	0	0	0	0	25	75
Snow inches	0	0	0	0	1	3

KENTUCKY (Capital: Frankfort)
Good time to visit Kentucky: April and May, and September and October.

April and May: Days are warm, nights are cool.
June: Usually sunny and pleasant but is sometimes a hot 30°C (86°F).
July and August can always be expected to be humid and hot with daytime temperatures remaining in the 30s°C (90s°F) for weeks at a time. In spite of the heat, summer (June to August) is the "tourist season."

September and October: Days are warm, nights are cool. Mid–October is the peak time for the changing colours of autumn foliage.
December to February is cold and wet with snow.
March has strong winds and driving rain.

Louisville, on the Ohio River.
Louisville's weather in brief:
June to August (summer) is hot with temperatures reaching 32°C (90°F).
December to March (winter) is cold with light snow each month.
April and May is springtime with heavy rainstorms that continue to the end of summer. The air is humid at this time.

Louisville, Kentucky: Altitude 149m (489ft)

	Jan	Feb	Mar	Apr	May	Jun
Sunrise °C(°F)	–5(23)	–3(27)	2(35)	7(44)	13(55)	17(62)
Mid–afternoon °C(°F)	5(41)	7(44)	13(55)	20(68)	24(75)	29(84)
Days with precipitation	12	11	13	12	11	10
Precipitation mm	88	88	126	103	106	103
Precipitation inches	3.5	3.5	5.0	4.1	4.2	4.1
Daily hours of sunshine	3	5	6	7	9	10
Snow mm	126	101	101	0	0	0
Snow inches	5	4	4	0	0	0

	Jul	Aug	Sep	Oct	Nov	Dec
Sunrise °C(°F)	20(68)	19(66)	15(59)	8(46)	3(37)	–2(29)
Mid–afternoon °C(°F)	31(87)	30(86)	27(80)	21(69)	14(57)	7(44)
Days with precipitation	11	8	8	7	10	11
Precipitation mm	95	75	73	60	83	83
Precipitation inches	3.8	3.0	2.9	2.4	3.3	3.3
Daily hours of sunshine	10	9	9	7	5	4
Snow mm	0	0	0	0	25	50
Snow inches	0	0	0	0	1	2

LOUISIANA (Capital: Baton Rouge)
New Orleans, on the Mississippi River.
Good month to visit New Orleans is October.

New Orleans' weather in brief:
June to August (summer) is hot and wet with daytime temperatures reaching 32°C (90°F). Heavy afternoon thunderstorms can be expected daily from mid–June to the end of September. New Orleans is in the hurricane belt. The **hurricane season extends from June to October.** If a hurricane were to strike, it would be more likely to do so in August or September. From **December to March** rains are lighter but can fall continually for two to three days at a time. This cold winter rain, combined with warm air over the Gulf waters, causes fog, particularly December to April. This may affect travellers because flights and river transport may be disrupted.

Cultural event: Mardi Gras carnival. Street parades with floats for two weeks leading up to Ash Wednesday. In New Orleans, Louisiana. February or March.

New Orleans, Louisiana: Altitude 9m (30ft)

	Jan	Feb	Mar	Apr	May	Jun
Sunrise ºC(ºF)	7(44)	8(46)	11(51)	15(59)	18(65)	21(71)
Mid–afternoon ºC(ºF)	17(62)	18(65)	21(70)	26(78)	29(85)	32(90)
Days with precipitation	10	9	9	7	8	10
Precipitation mm	114	121	139	106	106	119
Precipitation inches	4.5	4.8	5.5	4.2	4.2	4.7
Daily hours of sunshine	5	6	7	8	9	9

	Jul	Aug	Sep	Oct	Nov	Dec
Sunrise ºC(ºF)	23(73)	23(73)	21(70)	16(60)	10(50)	7(45)
Mid–afternoon ºC(ºF)	32(90)	33(91)	31(87)	27(80)	21(70)	18(64)
Days with precipitation	15	13	10	6	7	10
Precipitation mm	169	131	141	58	98	129
Precipitation inches	6.7	5.2	5.6	2.3	3.9	5.1
Daily hours of sunshine	8	8	8	8	6	5

MAINE (Capital: Augusta)
Portland, on the Atlantic coast.
General weather for Portland:
Best time for sunny weather is June to October (summer and autumn).
December to February (winter) is cold with snow.
March to April (spring) is wet and cold. Rain falls year–round.

Portland, Maine: Altitude 19m (62ft)

	Jan	Feb	Mar	Apr	May	Jun
Sunrise ºC(ºF)	–11(13)	–10(14)	–4(25)	1(33)	6(42)	11(51)
Mid–afternoon ºC(ºF)	–1(30)	–1(30)	5(41)	11(51)	17(62)	23(73)
Days with precipitation	11	10	11	12	13	11
Precipitation mm	85	88	90	88	83	78
Precipitation inches	3.4	3.5	3.6	3.5	3.3	3.1
Daily hours of sunshine	5	6	6	7	8	10
Snow mm	456	508	355	75	0	0
Snow inches	18	20	14	3	0	0

	Jul	Aug	Sep	Oct	Nov	Dec
Sunrise ºC(ºF)	15(59)	14(57)	9(48)	3(37)	–1(30)	–8(18)
Mid–afternoon ºC(ºF)	26(78)	25(77)	21(70)	15(59)	8(46)	2(35)
Days with precipitation	9	9	8	9	12	12
Precipitation mm	65	65	78	83	125	103
Precipitation inches	2.6	2.6	3.1	3.3	4.9	4.1
Daily hours of sunshine	10	9	8	7	5	5
Snow mm	0	0	0	0	75	406
Snow inches	0	0	0	0	3	16

MARYLAND (Capital: Annapolis)
Best time to visit the state: Late May and early June, and September. July and August are also good months but the summer months are hot and humid.

Baltimore, on the western shore of Chesapeake Bay.
Best months for Baltimore are May to September. Hot summers, June to August, are humid but are tempered by bay breezes. Rain falls year–round but most falls June to September. Thunderstorms and hurricanes are also possible, June to September.
December to February (winter) is cold and rainy but with minimal snow.

Baltimore, Maryland: Altitude 47m (154ft)

	Jan	Feb	Mar	Apr	May	Jun
Sunrise ºC(ºF)	–5(23)	–3(27)	1(33)	6(42)	11(51)	17(62)
Mid–afternoon ºC(ºF)	5(41)	6(42)	12(53)	18(64)	23(73)	28(82)
Days with precipitation	10	9	11	11	11	9
Precipitation mm	73	70	93	78	90	95
Precipitation inches	2.9	2.8	3.7	3.1	3.6	3.8
Daily hours of sunshine	5	6	7	8	8	9
Snow mm	126	152	126	0	0	0
Snow inches	5	6	5	0	0	0

	Jul	Aug	Sep	Oct	Nov	Dec
Sunrise ºC(ºF)	19(66)	19(66)	15(59)	8(46)	3(37)	–2(29)
Mid–afternoon ºC(ºF)	31(87)	30(86)	26(78)	20(68)	14(57)	7(44)
Days with precipitation	9	10	8	7	9	9
Precipitation mm	103	106	78	70	78	83
Precipitation inches	4.1	4.2	3.1	2.8	3.1	3.3
Daily hours of sunshine	9	9	7	7	5	5
Snow mm	0	0	0	0	25	126
Snow inches	0	0	0	0	1	5

MASSACHUSETTS (Capital: Boston)
Best time for Massachusetts: Late May and early June, and September and October. (Summer, July to August, is also a good time.)

Massachusetts' weather in brief:
April and May: Cool to mild, 16 to 21ºC (60 to 70ºF).
June to August: Summer. Days are warm, 21 to 32ºC (70 to 90ºF). Evenings are cooler, particularly along the coast. Summer can be humid as well as rainy and foggy. These are busy months, especially on the coast. The hottest summer temperatures occur in the dry valley of the Connecticut River in central Massachusetts.
September to November: Autumn. Fairly dry, sunny days and cool nights. September and October are ideal months. Afternoon temperatures range 16 to 21ºC (60 to 70ºF).
December to March: Light rain, snow and sleet.
Rainfall in the New England states, of which this is one, does not have a dominant rainy season. Rain is distributed fairly evenly throughout the year, and snow falls from December to March.

Boston, Massachusetts: Altitude 9m (29ft)

	Jan	Feb	Mar	Apr	May	Jun
Sunrise ºC(ºF)	–6(21)	–5(23)	–1(30)	5(41)	10(50)	15(59)
Mid–afternoon ºC(ºF)	2(35)	3(37)	8(46)	13(55)	19(66)	25(77)
Days with precipitation	9	8	9	9	9	8
Precipitation mm	91	92	94	91	83	79
Precipitation inches	3.6	3.6	3.7	3.6	3.3	3.1
Daily hours of sunshine	5	6	7	8	9	10
Snow mm	304	304	202	25	0	0
Snow inches	12	12	8	1	0	0

	Jul	Aug	Sep	Oct	Nov	Dec
Sunrise ºC(ºF)	18(64)	18(64)	14(57)	8(46)	4(39)	–3(27)
Mid–afternoon ºC(ºF)	28(82)	27(80)	23(73)	17(62)	11(51)	5(41)
Days with precipitation	7	8	7	7	9	10
Precipitation mm	72	82	78	84	107	102
Precipitation inches	2.8	3.2	3.1	3.3	4.2	4.0
Daily hours of sunshine	10	9	8	7	5	5
Snow mm	0	0	0	0	25	202
Snow inches	0	0	0	0	1	8

MICHIGAN (Capital: Lansing)
Detroit
Pleasant month to visit Detroit is September.

Detroit's weather in brief:
June to August (summer) is sunny and warm with intermittent brief showers. Near Detroit are the Great Lakes, the waters of which retain warmth from the summer sunshine.
From **November to March** cold polar air which passes over the lakes is modified, saving Detroit from experiencing bitterly cold winters, but bringing heavy clouds. A mix of rain and snow is common in winter.

Detroit, Michigan: Altitude 189m (619ft)

	Jan	Feb	Mar	Apr	May	Jun
Sunrise ºC(ºF)	–9(16)	–8(18)	–3(27)	3(37)	8(46)	13(55)
Mid–afternoon ºC(ºF)	0(32)	1(33)	7(44)	14(57)	21(70)	26(78)
Days with precipitation	13	12	13	12	12	11
Precipitation mm	47	45	58	78	85	78
Precipitation inches	1.9	1.8	2.3	3.1	3.4	3.1
Daily hours of sunshine	4	5	6	7	9	10
Snow mm	202	202	126	25	0	0
Snow inches	8	8	5	1	0	0

Detroit, Michigan: (continued)

	Jul	Aug	Sep	Oct	Nov	Dec
Sunrise ºC(ºF)	16(60)	15(59)	11(51)	5(41)	0(32)	–6(21)
Mid–afternoon ºC(ºF)	28(82)	27(80)	23(73)	16(60)	9(48)	2(35)
Days with precipitation	9	9	9	9	11	13
Precipitation mm	75	75	58	63	58	55
Precipitation inches	3.0	3.0	2.3	2.5	2.3	2.2
Daily hours of sunshine	10	9	8	6	4	3
Snow mm	0	0	0	0	93	177
Snow inches	0	0	0	0	4	7

MINNESOTA (Capital: St Paul)
Minneapolis–St Paul
Pleasant month to visit Minneapolis–St Paul is September.

Weather in Minneapolis–St Paul in brief:
June to August (summer) is warm and wet, with more rain than in winter. The region of flat and rolling grasslands is subject to wide swings of temperature, from afternoon temperatures of –6ºC (21ºF) in January to 29ºC (84ºF) in July.

Minneapolis–St Paul, Minnesota: Altitude 255m (837ft)

	Jan	Feb	Mar	Apr	May	Jun
Sunrise ºC(ºF)	–16(3)	–13(8)	–5(23)	2(35)	9(48)	14(57)
Mid–afternoon ºC(ºF)	–6(21)	–3(27)	4(39)	14(57)	21(69)	26(78)
Days with precipitation	9	7	10	10	12	12
Precipitation mm	17	20	43	50	85	98
Precipitation inches	0.7	0.8	1.7	2.0	3.4	3.9
Daily hours of sunshine	4	6	6	7	8	9
Snow mm	228	202	279	75	0	0
Snow inches	9	8	11	3	0	0

	Jul	Aug	Sep	Oct	Nov	Dec
Sunrise ºC(ºF)	17(62)	16(60)	10(50)	4(39)	–4(25)	–12(11)
Mid–afternoon ºC(ºF)	29(84)	27(80)	21(69)	15(59)	5(41)	–4(25)
Days with precipitation	10	9	9	8	8	9
Precipitation mm	93	78	68	45	30	22
Precipitation inches	3.7	3.1	2.7	1.8	1.2	0.9
Daily hours of sunshine	10	9	8	7	4	4
Snow mm	0	0	0	0	152	228
Snow inches	0	0	0	0	6	9

MISSISSIPPI (Capital: Jackson)
Good month for visiting Jackson, on the Pearl River, **is October**.

Jackson's weather in brief:
June to August (summer) is hot and humid. Warm, moist, southerly winds blow from the Gulf of Mexico giving Jackson a long period of warmth, April to September.
October to March is cooler because of the cool air arriving from the north.
Rain falls year–round, but September to November has less rain.

Jackson, Mississippi: Altitude 101m (331ft)

	Jan	Feb	Mar	Apr	May	Jun
Sunrise ºC(ºF)	0(32)	2(35)	7(44)	11(51)	16(60)	19(66)
Mid–afternoon ºC(ºF)	13(55)	16(60)	21(69)	25(77)	29(84)	33(91)
Days with precipitation	11	9	11	9	9	8
Precipitation mm	114	116	141	119	111	85
Precipitation inches	4.5	4.6	5.6	4.7	4.4	3.4
Daily hours of sunshine	5	6	7	8	9	10

	Jul	Aug	Sep	Oct	Nov	Dec
Sunrise ºC(ºF)	21(69)	21(69)	18(64)	10(50)	6(42)	2(35)
Mid–afternoon ºC(ºF)	34(93)	33(91)	31(87)	26(78)	21(69)	15(59)
Days with precipitation	11	11	9	6	8	11
Precipitation mm	108	90	75	55	98	126
Precipitation inches	4.3	3.6	3.0	2.2	3.9	5.0
Daily hours of sunshine	9	9	8	8	6	5

MISSOURI (Capital: Jefferson City)
St Louis, on the Mississippi River.
An ideal month to visit St Louis is September.

St Louis' weather in brief:
June to August (summer) is warm and wet.
December to March (winter) has 460mm (18in) of snow, which is not severe, caused by polar air from Canada.
Rain falls year–round.

St Louis, Missouri: Altitude 172m (564ft)

	Jan	Feb	Mar	Apr	May	Jun
Sunrise ºC(ºF)	–6(21)	–4(25)	2(35)	8(46)	13(55)	19(66)
Mid–afternoon ºC(ºF)	3(37)	6(42)	13(55)	19(66)	24(75)	30(86)
Days with precipitation	8	8	11	11	11	9
Precipitation mm	45	53	75	98	111	93
Precipitation inches	1.8	2.1	3.0	3.9	4.4	3.7
Daily hours of sunshine	4	6	7	8	9	10
Snow mm	101	101	126	0	0	0
Snow inches	4	4	5	0	0	0

St Louis, Missouri: (continued)

	Jul	Aug	Sep	Oct	Nov	Dec
Sunrise °C(°F)	21(70)	20(68)	16(60)	9(48)	3(37)	−3(27)
Mid–afternoon °C(°F)	32(89)	31(87)	27(80)	20(68)	13(55)	5(41)
Days with precipitation	9	7	9	8	8	10
Precipitation mm	73	73	73	70	63	50
Precipitation inches	2.9	2.9	2.9	2.8	2.5	2.0
Daily hours of sunshine	10	9	9	8	6	4
Snow mm	0	0	0	0	25	101
Snow inches	0	0	0	0	1	4

MONTANA (Capital: Helena)
Best time to visit Montana for general sightseeing is June to September.

Great Falls, at the confluence of the Missouri and Sun rivers.
Weather for Great Falls in brief:
June to September is sunny and mild. Most rain falls between April and September; May and June are the rainiest. July to September has pleasant travelling weather.
December to February and March is cold and snowy, but the amount of snow is lessened by the warming affect of the chinook winds from the Pacific Ocean.

Great Falls, Montana: Altitude 1116m (3662ft)

	Jan	Feb	Mar	Apr	May	Jun
Sunrise °C(°F)	−11(13)	−8(18)	−5(23)	0(32)	5(41)	9(48)
Mid–afternoon °C(°F)	−1(30)	3(37)	6(42)	13(55)	18(64)	24(75)
Days with precipitation	9	8	9	9	11	12
Precipitation mm	22	17	25	30	60	78
Precipitation inches	0.9	0.7	1.0	1.2	2.4	3.1
Daily hours of sunshine	4	5	8	8	9	11
Snow mm	253	202	253	202	25	0
Snow inches	10	8	10	8	1	0

	Jul	Aug	Sep	Oct	Nov	Dec
Sunrise °C(°F)	12(53)	11(51)	6(42)	2(35)	−4(25)	−10(14)
Mid–afternoon °C(°F)	28(82)	28(82)	21(69)	15(59)	6(42)	1(33)
Days with precipitation	7	7	7	6	7	7
Precipitation mm	32	27	30	17	20	17
Precipitation inches	1.3	1.1	1.2	0.7	0.8	0.7
Daily hours of sunshine	12	11	9	6	4	3
Snow mm	0	0	25	75	177	228
Snow inches	0	0	1	3	7	9

NEBRASKA (Capital: Lincoln)
Omaha, on the west bank of the Missouri River.
The most pleasant month to visit Omaha is September for warm temperatures and diminishing rain.
Omaha's weather in brief:
June to August (summer) is sunny, warm and wet. Most rain falls May to August.
December to February (winter) is dry but cold with afternoon temperatures hovering just above freezing. Winter storms that traverse the country affect Nebraska. Snow falls in winter.
Omaha, Nebraska: Altitude 406m (1332ft)

	Jan	Feb	Mar	Apr	May	Jun
Sunrise ºC(ºF)	−12(11)	−8(18)	−2(29)	4(39)	10(50)	16(60)
Mid–afternoon ºC(ºF)	−1(30)	2(35)	9(48)	17(62)	23(73)	28(82)
Days with precipitation	7	7	9	9	12	11
Precipitation mm	20	25	40	75	103	124
Precipitation inches	0.8	1.0	1.6	3.0	4.1	4.9
Daily hours of sunshine	5	6	6	8	9	10
Snow mm	202	177	177	25	0	0
Snow inches	8	7	7	1	0	0

	Jul	Aug	Sep	Oct	Nov	Dec
Sunrise ºC(ºF)	19(66)	17(62)	12(53)	5(41)	−2(29)	−9(16)
Mid–afternoon ºC(ºF)	30(86)	29(84)	24(75)	18(64)	9(48)	1(33)
Days with precipitation	9	9	8	6	5	6
Precipitation mm	93	101	83	47	27	20
Precipitation inches	3.7	4.0	3.3	1.9	1.1	0.8
Daily hours of sunshine	11	9	9	8	6	5
Snow mm	0	0	0	0	0	152
Snow inches	0	0	0	0	0	6

NEVADA (Capital: Carson City)
Las Vegas
The best months to visit Las Vegas are April, May, September and October. Throughout the year there are few rainy and overcast days.
Las Vegas' weather in brief:
June to August (summer) is sunny with low humidity, dry and hot, 38ºC (100ºF). Nights are cool.
December to February (winter) has very low humidity, is sunny, dry and warm.
Las Vegas, Nevada: Altitude 664m (2178ft)

	Jan	Feb	Mar	Apr	May	Jun
Sunrise ºC(ºF)	1(32)	4(39)	7(44)	10(50)	16(60)	21(69)
Mid–afternoon ºC(ºF)	14(57)	17(62)	20(68)	25(77)	31(87)	38(100)
Days with precipitation	3	2	3	2	1	1
Precipitation mm	12	7	7	7	3	3
Precipitation inches	0.5	0.3	0.3	0.3	0.1	0.1
Daily hours of sunshine	8	9	10	11	12	14
Snow mm	25	0	0	0	0	0
Snow inches	1	0	0	0	0	0

Las Vegas, Nevada: (continued)

	Jul	Aug	Sep	Oct	Nov	Dec
Sunrise ºC(ºF)	25(77)	23(73)	19(66)	12(53)	6(42)	1(33)
Mid–afternoon ºC(ºF)	41(105)	40(104)	35(95)	28(82)	20(68)	14(57)
Days with precipitation	3	3	2	2	2	2
Precipitation mm	9	12	7	5	9	9
Precipitation inches	0.4	0.5	0.3	0.2	0.4	0.4
Daily hours of sunshine	12	12	12	10	9	10
Snow mm	0	0	0	0	0	0
Snow inches	0	0	0	0	0	0

NEW HAMPSHIRE (Capital: Concord)

Best time for New Hampshire: Late May and early June, and September and October. (Summer, July to August, is also a good time.)

New Hampshire's weather in brief:

April and May: Cool to mild, 16 to 21ºC (60 to 70ºF).
June to August: Summer. Days are warm, 21 to 32ºC (70 to 90ºF). Evenings are cooler, particularly in the mountains and along the coast. Summer can be humid as well as rainy and foggy. These are busy months, especially on the coast.
September to November: Autumn. Fairly dry, sunny days and cool nights. Afternoon temperatures range 16 to 21ºC (60 to 70ºF).
December to March: Light rain, snow and sleet.
Rainfall in the New England states, of which this is one, does not have a dominant rainy season. Rain is distributed fairly evenly throughout the year and, as indicated above, snow falls from December to March.

Concord, New Hampshire: Altitude 104m (342ft)

	Jan	Feb	Mar	Apr	May	Jun
Sunrise ºC(ºF)	−13(10)	−12(11)	−6(22)	0(32)	6(42)	11(52)
Mid–afternoon ºC(ºF)	0(31)	1(34)	6(42)	14(57)	21(69)	26(78)
Days with precipitation	11	10	11	11	12	11
Precipitation mm	68	60	70	73	76	83
Precipitation inches	2.7	2.4	2.8	2.9	3.0	3.3
Snow mm	431	406	279	50	0	0
Snow inches	17	16	11	2	0	0

	Jul	Aug	Sep	Oct	Nov	Dec
Sunrise ºC(ºF)	14(57)	12(54)	8(47)	2(36)	−3(28)	−10(15)
Mid–afternoon ºC(ºF)	28(83)	27(80)	22(72)	17(62)	9(48)	2(35)
Days with precipitation	10	10	9	8	11	11
Precipitation mm	78	73	78	68	101	83
Precipitation inches	3.1	2.9	3.1	2.7	4.0	3.3
Snow mm	0	0	0	0	101	355
Snow inches	0	0	0	0	4	14

NEW JERSEY (Capital: Trenton)
Best time to visit New Jersey: Late May and early June, and September. July and August (summer) are also good months but they are hot and humid, reaching 30ºC (86ºF). They are the rainiest months, although rain falls year–round.

NEW MEXICO (Capital: Santa Fé)
Best time to visit New Mexico: September and October.
New Mexico, with its mountains and desert is a year–round destination. Seventy percent of the days are sunny.

New Mexico's weather in brief:
March and early April: Winds are chilly, sandstorms are possible, rivers are high.
June: Hottest month, 38ºC (100ºF).
July and August: Hot with thunderstorms that often come in the afternoons. In most years most rain falls in these two months.
September and October: Pleasant temperatures. Foliage is changing colour.
November to February: Cold with snow. Santa Fé, at 1934m (6344ft) is a ski area.

Natural attraction: Carlsbad Caverns National Park, near Carlsbad. Best time is March to late October to see the bats. Busiest, June and July. Least crowded, November and January.

Albuquerque
Weather in brief in Albuquerque:
July to September is sunny and warm with short, violent thunderstorms. Long periods of steady rain are unknown, hence disruption of open air activities is negligible.
Other months are sunny and mild with minimal rainfall.

Albuquerque, New Mexico: Altitude 1619m (5311ft)

	Jan	Feb	Mar	Apr	May	Jun
Sunrise ºC(ºF)	–6(21)	–3(27)	0(32)	4(39)	9(48)	15(59)
Mid–afternoon ºC(ºF)	8(46)	12(53)	16(60)	22(72)	26(78)	32(89)
Days with precipitation	3	4	4	3	4	4
Precipitation mm	7	9	12	12	12	12
Precipitation inches	0.3	0.4	0.5	0.5	0.5	0.5
Daily hours of sunshine	8	8	9	9	11	12
Snow mm	50	50	50	25	0	0
Snow inches	2	2	2	1	0	0

	Jul	Aug	Sep	Oct	Nov	Dec
Sunrise ºC(ºF)	18(64)	17(62)	13(55)	6(42)	0(32)	–5(23)
Mid–afternoon ºC(ºF)	34(93)	32(89)	28(82)	22(72)	14(57)	9(48)
Days with precipitation	9	9	6	5	3	4
Precipitation mm	35	32	20	20	7	12
Precipitation inches	1.4	1.3	0.8	0.8	0.3	0.5
Daily hours of sunshine	11	10	10	9	8	7
Snow mm	0	0	0	0	25	75
Snow inches	0	0	0	0	1	3

NEW YORK (Capital: Albany)
Buffalo–Niagara Falls

Weather in brief for Buffalo–Niagara Falls:
June to August (summer) is mild and sunny.
September to November (autumn) has long dry periods. Frosts start in mid–October.
December to March (winter) experiences heavy snowfalls, almost 2500mm (100in). The weather is affected by the nearby lakes, Lake Ontario and Lake Erie. The cold water and the late thawing of ice in Lake Erie delays the coming of spring (April and May). Ice can remain until mid–May.

Buffalo–Niagara Falls, New York: Altitude 216m (710ft)

	Jan	Feb	Mar	Apr	May	Jun
Sunrise ºC(ºF)	–8(18)	–8(18)	–3(27)	2(35)	8(46)	14(57)
Mid–afternoon ºC(ºF)	–1(30)	0(32)	5(41)	12(53)	19(66)	24(75)
Days with precipitation	20	17	16	14	13	10
Precipitation mm	73	63	73	80	75	55
Precipitation inches	2.9	2.5	2.9	3.2	3.0	2.2
Daily hours of sunshine	3	4	5	7	8	10
Snow mm	559	456	302	75	0	0
Snow inches	22	18	12	3	0	0

	Jul	Aug	Sep	Oct	Nov	Dec
Sunrise ºC(ºF)	17(62)	16(60)	12(53)	6(42)	1(33)	–5(23)
Mid–afternoon ºC(ºF)	27(80)	25(77)	22(72)	15(59)	8(46)	2(35)
Days with precipitation	10	10	10	11	16	20
Precipitation mm	73	88	83	75	93	75
Precipitation inches	2.9	3.5	3.3	3.0	3.7	3.0
Daily hours of sunshine	10	9	7	5	3	2
Snow mm	0	0	0	0	329	559
Snow inches	0	0	0	0	13	22

New York City, on the Hudson River.

Best times to visit New York City are June and September: Mild, pleasant. Other good months are April and May, and October and November. A less pleasant time to visit is mid–July to mid–August when temperatures reach 32ºC (90ºF) and humidity hits 90%. June to August (summer) is sunny and hot, but the afternoon heat is tempered by sea breezes. Because of the close proximity of the mild Atlantic waters, there is a long frost–free period, mid–April to mid–November, and the arrival of winter snow is delayed until December.

New York City, New York: Altitude 40m (130ft)

	Jan	Feb	Mar	Apr	May	Jun
Sunrise ºC(ºF)	–4(25)	–3(27)	1(33)	6(42)	11(51)	16(60)
Mid–afternoon ºC(ºF)	3(37)	4(39)	9(48)	15(59)	20(68)	25(77)
Days with precipitation	11	10	12	11	11	10
Precipitation mm	68	73	93	83	88	75
Precipitation inches	2.7	2.9	3.7	3.3	3.5	3.0
Daily hours of sunshine	5	6	7	7	8	10
Snow mm	177	228	126	25	0	0
Snow inches	7	9	5	1	0	0

	Jul	Aug	Sep	Oct	Nov	Dec
Sunrise ºC(ºF)	20(68)	20(68)	16(60)	10(50)	5(41)	–1(30)
Mid–afternoon ºC(ºF)	28(82)	28(82)	24(75)	18(64)	12(53)	6(42)
Days with precipitation	11	10	8	8	9	10
Precipitation mm	93	101	83	70	95	88
Precipitation inches	3.7	4.0	3.3	2.8	3.8	3.5
Daily hours of sunshine	10	9	8	7	6	5
Snow mm	0	0	0	0	25	152
Snow inches	0	0	0	0	1	6

NORTH CAROLINA (Capital: Raleigh)

Best time to visit North Carolina: April, May (spring) **and September, October** (autumn).
North Carolina's weather in brief:
April and May: Mild with afternoon temperatures 22 to 26ºC (72 to 78ºF). Expect light rains. Flowers are in bloom.
June to August: Brief afternoon thunderstorms. High humidity. Afternoon temperatures reach 32ºC (90ºF).
September and October: Pleasantly warm. Afternoon temperatures reach 27ºC (80ºF). Foliage changes colour at this time.
November to March: Cold with light snowfalls. Morning temperatures from December to February are below freezing but rise to 10ºC (50ºF) by mid–afternoon.
The hurricane season is mainly September and October, especially along the coastline. The torrential downpours and strong winds become less intense as a hurricane travels inland.

Charlotte
Charlotte's weather in brief:
May to September are warm months where temperatures can exceed 32ºC (90ºF) in July and August.
December to February (winter) is mild to cool with a chance of two or three light falls of snow.
Rain falls year–round but is lighter from September to November.

Charlotte, North Carolina: Altitude 234m (768ft)

	Jan	Feb	Mar	Apr	May	Jun
Sunrise ºC(ºF)	–1(30)	0(32)	4(39)	7(44)	14(57)	19(66)
Mid–afternoon ºC(ºF)	9(48)	12(53)	17(62)	22(72)	26(78)	30(86)
Days with precipitation	10	10	12	9	9	10
Precipitation mm	88	95	114	85	73	93
Precipitation inches	3.5	3.8	4.5	3.4	2.9	3.7
Daily hours of sunshine	6	6	8	9	9	10
Snow mm	50	25	25	0	0	0
Snow inches	2	1	1	0	0	0

	Jul	Aug	Sep	Oct	Nov	Dec
Sunrise ºC(ºF)	21(70)	20(68)	17(62)	10(50)	5(41)	0(32)
Mid–afternoon ºC(ºF)	32(89)	31(87)	28(82)	22(72)	17(62)	11(51)
Days with precipitation	12	9	7	7	7	10
Precipitation mm	116	101	88	68	68	85
Precipitation inches	4.6	4.0	3.5	2.7	2.7	3.4
Daily hours of sunshine	9	9	8	7	6	5
Snow mm	0	0	0	0	0	25
Snow inches	0	0	0	0	0	1

NORTH DAKOTA (Capital: Bismarck)
Best time for North Dakota: June to September.

North Dakota's weather in brief:
July and August (summer) is sunny with about 10 hours of sunshine daily, and hot with temperatures nearing 38ºC (100ºF). Rains fall mainly May to August.
November to March is a long, severe winter with below freezing temperatures.

Bismarck, North Dakota: Altitude 506m (1660ft)

	Jan	Feb	Mar	Apr	May	Jun
Sunrise ºC(ºF)	–19(–2)	–15(5)	–8(18)	–1(30)	6(42)	11(51)
Mid–afternoon ºC(ºF)	–7(19)	–3(26)	4(39)	13(55)	20(68)	25(77)
Days with precipitation	4	3	4	6	7	8
Precipitation mm	11	11	20	42	55	69
Precipitation inches	0.4	0.4	0.8	1.6	2.2	2.7
Daily hours of sunshine	5	5	7	8	10	11

	Jul	Aug	Sep	Oct	Nov	Dec
Sunrise ºC(ºF)	14(57)	12(53)	6(42)	1(33)	–8(18)	–16(3)
Mid–afternoon ºC(ºF)	29(84)	28(82)	22(72)	15(59)	4(39)	–4(25)
Days with precipitation	7	5	5	3	3	4
Precipitation mm	54	44	38	23	12	13
Precipitation inches	2.1	1.7	1.5	0.9	0.5	0.5
Daily hours of sunshine	11	10	8	6	4	4

OHIO (Capital: Columbus)
Columbus
An ideal month to visit Columbus is September with its warm temperatures and low rainfall. June to August (summer) has 10 hours of sunshine daily. Warm air from the Gulf of Mexico gives a warm daytime temperature of 29°C (84°F). The close proximity to rivers contributes to ground fog in the morning in summer and in the autumn months of September to November. Winters are kept cool by polar air from Canada. Snow falls mainly from December to March.

Columbus, Ohio: Altitude 254m (833ft)

	Jan	Feb	Mar	Apr	May	Jun
Sunrise °C(°F)	−7(19)	−6(21)	0(32)	4(39)	10(50)	14(57)
Mid–afternoon °C(°F)	1(33)	3(37)	10(50)	17(62)	22(72)	27(80)
Days with precipitation	13	12	14	13	13	11
Precipitation mm	73	58	85	93	103	103
Precipitation inches	2.9	2.3	3.4	3.7	4.1	4.1
Daily hours of sunshine	3	4	6	7	8	10
Snow mm	177	152	126	25	0	0
Snow inches	7	6	5	1	0	0

	Jul	Aug	Sep	Oct	Nov	Dec
Sunrise °C(°F)	17(62)	16(60)	13(55)	6(42)	1(33)	−4(25)
Mid–afternoon °C(°F)	29(84)	28(82)	25(77)	18(65)	11(51)	4(39)
Days with precipitation	11	9	9	8	11	12
Precipitation mm	106	73	60	47	68	60
Precipitation inches	4.2	2.9	2.4	1.9	2.7	2.4
Daily hours of sunshine	10	10	9	7	5	3
Snow mm	0	0	0	0	75	152
Snow inches	0	0	0	0	3	6

OKLAHOMA (Capital: Oklahoma City)
Oklahoma City's weather in brief:
June to August (summer) is sunny and hot with intermittent showers, thunderstorms and strong winds. Summer–like weather stretches from May to October. **December to February** is a short winter, dry and mild with occasional sleet caused by cool moisture from the north.

Oklahoma City, Oklahoma: Altitude 398m (1306ft)

	Jan	Feb	Mar	Apr	May	Jun
Sunrise °C(°F)	−4(25)	−1(30)	4(39)	9(48)	14(57)	19(66)
Mid–afternoon °C(°F)	8(46)	11(51)	17(62)	22(72)	26(78)	31(87)
Days with precipitation	5	6	7	8	10	9
Precipitation mm	27	32	50	88	131	106
Precipitation inches	1.1	1.3	2.0	3.5	5.2	4.2
Daily hours of sunshine	5	7	7	8	9	11
Snow mm	75	50	50	0	0	0
Snow inches	3	2	2	0	0	0

Oklahoma City, Oklahoma: (continued)

	Jul	Aug	Sep	Oct	Nov	Dec
Sunrise ºC(ºF)	21(69)	21(69)	17(62)	10(50)	4(39)	2(35)
Mid–afternoon ºC(ºF)	34(93)	34(93)	29(85)	23(73)	16(60)	10(50)
Days with precipitation	7	6	7	6	5	5
Precipitation mm	68	65	88	65	35	32
Precipitation inches	2.7	2.6	3.5	2.6	1.4	1.3
Daily hours of sunshine	11	11	10	8	7	6
Snow mm	0	0	0	0	0	50
Snow inches	0	0	0	0	0	2

OREGON (Capital: Salem)
Best time for Oregon: June to September.

Oregon's weather in brief:
June to September: Dry, sunny and warm throughout the state. In the Cascade Mountains, and in the coastal valleys where towns are located, afternoon temperatures climb beyond 27ºC (80ºF). East of the Cascades is eastern Oregon which occupies more than half the state. Temperatures there reach beyond 32ºC (90ºF), and it is drier. The mountains form a barrier against moisture coming from the Pacific Ocean.
October and November: Transitional months when temperatures start dropping to a mild 10ºC (50ºF) and rains become heavy.
December to February: Winter. The coast is damp, overcast and mild. Snow falls at higher elevations, allowing for winter sports.
March to May: Spring. Temperatures start rising to a mild 17ºC (63ºF). In early spring it is still rainy in the mountains.

Portland
Portland's weather in brief:
July and August (summer) are pleasantly mild months with little rainfall.
November to March is when most rain falls. Fog also occurs during these months. April, May, September and October are partly sunny and cool to mild with rain.

Portland, Oregon: Altitude 12m (39ft)

	Jan	Feb	Mar	Apr	May	Jun
Sunrise ºC(ºF)	1(33)	2(35)	4(39)	5(41)	8(46)	12(53)
Mid–afternoon ºC(ºF)	7(44)	11(51)	13(55)	16(60)	19(66)	23(73)
Days with precipitation	19	16	17	14	12	9
Precipitation mm	149	104	90	55	53	40
Precipitation inches	5.9	4.1	3.6	2.2	2.1	1.6
Daily hours of sunshine	2	3	4	6	7	7
Snow mm	101	25	25	0	0	0
Snow inches	4	1	1	0	0	0

Portland, Oregon: (continued)

	Jul	Aug	Sep	Oct	Nov	Dec
Sunrise ºC(ºF)	14(57)	14(57)	11(51)	7(44)	4(39)	2(35)
Mid–afternoon ºC(ºF)	27(80)	27(80)	24(75)	18(64)	11(51)	8(46)
Days with precipitation	4	5	7	13	17	19
Precipitation mm	13	20	40	90	141	152
Precipitation inches	0.5	0.8	1.6	3.6	5.6	6.0
Daily hours of sunshine	10	8	7	4	3	2
Snow mm	0	0	0	0	0	25
Snow inches	0	0	0	0	0	1

PENNSYLVANIA (Capital: Harrisburg)
Best time for Pennsylvania: Late May and early June, and September.
Pennsylvania's weather in brief:
March to May: Mild and wet.
June to August: Hot, humid, wet.
September to November: Cool. Some rain.
December to February: Cold, windy, snowfalls.

Philadelphia
Weather in brief for Philadelphia:
June to August (summer) is warm and occasionally humid.
December to March (winter) has strong winds and snowfalls.
Rain falls year–round.

Philadelphia, Pennsylvania: Altitude 8m (26ft)

	Jan	Feb	Mar	Apr	May	Jun
Sunrise ºC(ºF)	–5(23)	–4(25)	1(33)	6(42)	11(51)	17(62)
Mid–afternoon ºC(ºF)	3(37)	5(41)	11(51)	17(62)	23(73)	28(82)
Days with precipitation	11	9	11	11	11	10
Precipitation mm	70	65	93	83	85	93
Precipitation inches	2.8	2.6	3.7	3.3	3.4	3.7
Daily hours of sunshine	5	6	7	8	8	10
Snow mm	126	152	101	0	0	0
Snow inches	5	6	4	0	0	0

	Jul	Aug	Sep	Oct	Nov	Dec
Sunrise ºC(ºF)	20(68)	19(66)	15(59)	8(46)	3(37)	–2(29)
Mid–afternoon ºC(ºF)	30(86)	29(84)	25(77)	19(66)	13(55)	6(42)
Days with precipitation	9	9	8	7	8	10
Precipitation mm	103	103	75	63	85	83
Precipitation inches	4.1	4.1	3.0	2.5	3.4	3.3
Daily hours of sunshine	10	8	8	7	5	5
Snow mm	0	0	0	0	25	101
Snow inches	0	0	0	0	1	4

Pittsburgh
Weather in brief in Pittsburgh:
June to August (summer) is warm. Warm air from the distant Gulf of Mexico increases humidity.
December to March (winter) is influenced by cold polar air that comes down through Canada, causing snowfalls.
Rain falls throughout the year.

Pittsburgh, Pennsylvania: Altitude 373m (1224ft)

	Jan	Feb	Mar	Apr	May	Jun
Sunrise ºC(ºF)	–7(19)	–6(21)	–1(30)	4(39)	9(48)	14(57)
Mid–afternoon ºC(ºF)	1(33)	3(37)	9(48)	16(60)	21(69)	26(78)
Days with precipitation	15	14	15	14	13	12
Precipitation mm	65	58	90	85	90	93
Precipitation inches	2.6	2.3	3.6	3.4	3.6	3.7
Daily hours of sunshine	3	4	5	6	7	8
Snow mm	178	178	152	25	0	0
Snow inches	7	7	6	1	0	0

	Jul	Aug	Sep	Oct	Nov	Dec
Sunrise ºC(ºF)	16(60)	16(60)	12(53)	6(42)	1(33)	–4(25)
Mid–afternoon ºC(ºF)	28(82)	27(80)	23(73)	17(62)	10(50)	4(39)
Days with precipitation	11	9	9	10	12	14
Precipitation mm	95	80	63	63	63	63
Precipitation inches	3.8	3.2	2.5	2.5	2.5	2.5
Daily hours of sunshine	8	7	7	5	3	2
Snow mm	0	0	0	0	70	152
Snow inches	0	0	0	0	3	6

RHODE ISLAND (Capital: Providence)
Best time to visit Rhode Island: Late May and early June, and September and October. Summer, July to August, is also a good time.

Rhode Island's weather in brief:
April and May: Cool to mild, 16 to 21°C (60 to 70°F).
June to August: Summer. Days are warm, 21 to 32°C (70 to 90°F). Summer can be humid as well as rainy and foggy. These are busy months, especially on the coast.
September to November: Autumn. Fairly dry, sunny days and cool nights. September and October are ideal months. Afternoon temperatures range 16 to 21°C (60 to 70°F).
December to March: Light rain, snow and sleet.
Rainfall in the New England states, of which this is one, does not have a dominant rainy season. Rain is distributed fairly evenly throughout the year and, as mentioned above, snow falls from December to March.

Providence, Rhode Island: Altitude 19m (62ft)

	Jan	Feb	Mar	Apr	May	Jun
Sunrise ºC(ºF)	–7(19)	–6(21)	–2(29)	3(37)	8(46)	14(57)
Mid–afternoon ºC(ºF)	3(37)	4(39)	8(46)	14(57)	20(68)	25(77)
Days with precipitation	9	8	9	8	9	8
Precipitation mm	99	92	103	104	96	85
Precipitation inches	3.9	3.3	4.1	4.1	3.8	3.4
Daily hours of sunshine	6	6	7	7	8	9
Snow mm	228	253	228	25	0	0
Snow inches	9	10	9	1	0	0

	Jul	Aug	Sep	Oct	Nov	Dec
Sunrise ºC(ºF)	17(62)	17(62)	12(53)	6(42)	2(35)	–4(25)
Mid–afternoon ºC(ºF)	28(82)	27(80)	24(75)	18(64)	12(53)	5(41)
Days with precipitation	7	7	7	7	9	10
Precipitation mm	81	92	88	94	113	111
Precipitation inches	3.2	3.6	3.5	3.7	4.4	4.4
Daily hours of sunshine	9	8	8	7	5	5
Snow mm	0	0	0	0	0	202
Snow inches	0	0	0	0	0	8

SOUTH CAROLINA (Capital: Columbia)
Best time to visit: April, May and September, October.

Weather in brief in South Carolina:
April and May: Mild with light rain. Flowers are in bloom.
June to August: Hot; temperatures can reach 32ºC (90ºF). Occasional brief thunderstorms. Humidity is high. The mountains and the barrier islands are a few degrees lower.
September and October: Sunny and mild.
November to March: Cool to cold.

Hurricane season extends from June to October but September and October are the more susceptible months. A hurricane brings torrential downpours and powerful winds, especially to coastlines. It will weaken as it travels inland.

Charleston, on the Atlantic Ocean coast.
Weather in brief in Charleston:
March to May (spring) is wet with winds and storms occurring, but the temperature is mild, being modified by the ocean.
June to August (summer) has rainy, humid, warm days which touch 32ºC (90ºF). Almost half of the annual rainfall falls in these months.
September to November (autumn) is sunny and mild, but it starts getting cool in early November.
December to February (winter) is cool but with a negligible chance of snow.

Charleston, South Carolina: Altitude 15m (49ft)

	Jan	Feb	Mar	Apr	May	Jun
Sunrise ºC(ºF)	3(37)	4(39)	9(48)	12(53)	17(62)	21(69)
Mid–afternoon ºC(ºF)	14(57)	16(60)	20(68)	24(75)	28(82)	31(87)
Days with precipitation	10	9	11	7	9	11
Precipitation mm	73	83	121	75	95	159
Precipitation inches	2.9	3.3	4.8	3.0	3.8	6.3
Daily hours of sunshine	6	7	8	10	10	11

	Jul	Aug	Sep	Oct	Nov	Dec
Sunrise ºC(ºF)	23(73)	22(72)	20(68)	13(55)	8(46)	5(41)
Mid–afternoon ºC(ºF)	32(89)	32(89)	29(84)	25(77)	21(69)	16(60)
Days with precipitation	14	13	9	6	7	8
Precipitation mm	207	162	131	75	53	78
Precipitation inches	8.2	6.4	5.2	3.0	2.1	3.1
Daily hours of sunshine	10	9	8	7	7	6

SOUTH DAKOTA (Capital: Pierre)
Best time for South Dakota: June to September.
The rainiest months are April to September but the days are sunny.
July is the hottest month and January, the coldest.

Tourist attraction: Mount Rushmore National Park, near Keystone. Busiest, July and August. Least crowded, December and January. For the best light, view the sculptures in early morning.

Rapid City, on Rapid Creek near the Black Hills.
Weather in brief for Rapid City:
June to August (summer) has warm days and cool nights.
December to April has light snowfalls. The Black Hills deflect some cold winter storms, enabling the city to have warmer winters than other South Dakota cities.
April to June are the wettest months.

Rapid City, South Dakota: Altitude 966m (3169ft)

	Jan	Feb	Mar	Apr	May	Jun
Sunrise ºC(ºF)	–12(11)	–9(16)	–5(23)	0(32)	6(42)	11(51)
Mid–afternoon ºC(ºF)	1(33)	3(37)	8(46)	14(57)	20(68)	25(77)
Days with precipitation	7	8	9	10	12	13
Precipitation mm	12	14	25	53	70	93
Precipitation inches	0.5	0.6	1.0	2.1	2.8	3.7
Daily hours of sunshine	5	6	8	8	9	10
Snow mm	126	152	228	152	25	0
Snow inches	5	6	9	6	1	0

Rapid City, South Dakota: (continued)

	Jul	Aug	Sep	Oct	Nov	Dec
Sunrise ºC(ºF)	15(59)	13(55)	7(44)	2(35)	–5(23)	–11(13)
Mid–afternoon ºC(ºF)	30(86)	29(84)	24(75)	17(62)	8(46)	2(35)
Days with precipitation	9	7	6	4	6	6
Precipitation mm	53	37	30	22	12	9
Precipitation inches	2.1	1.5	1.2	0.9	0.5	0.4
Daily hours of sunshine	11	10	9	7	5	5
Snow mm	0	0	0	50	101	126
Snow inches	0	0	0	2	4	5

TENNESSEE (Capital: Nashville)

Good time to visit Tennessee is April and May (spring), although it can be rainy. Other good months are **September and October** (autumn) when days are warm and relatively dry but with cool evenings. **June to August** (summer) is hot with temperatures in the low 30sºC (over 90ºF).

December to February (winter) is cold, particularly in eastern Tennessee which receives heavy snowfalls which cause closure of mountain roads, especially in the Great Smoky Mountains National Park.

Natural attraction: Great Smoky Mountains National Park, near Gatlinburg.

Popular time, mid–April to October. Driest weather is September and October. Busiest time is July and August; least crowded is January and February.

Nashville, on the Cumberland River.

Weather in brief for Nashville: **May to September** has sunny, warm days with temperatures touching 32ºC (90ºF) in July, the hottest month. Thunderstorms occur throughout the year, but less rain falls **September to November**. **December to March** experiences snowfalls.

Nashville, Tennessee: Altitude 180m (590ft)

	Jan	Feb	Mar	Apr	May	Jun
Sunrise ºC(ºF)	–3(27)	–1(30)	4(39)	9(48)	14(57)	18(64)
Mid–afternoon ºC(ºF)	8(46)	10(50)	16(60)	22(72)	26(78)	30(86)
Days with precipitation	11	11	12	11	11	10
Precipitation mm	121	111	126	103	103	85
Precipitation inches	4.8	4.4	5.0	4.1	4.1	3.4
Daily hours of sunshine	4	5	6	8	8	10
Snow mm	75	75	50	0	0	0
Snow inches	3	3	2	0	0	0

	Jul	Aug	Sep	Oct	Nov	Dec
Sunrise ºC(ºF)	20(68)	20(68)	16(60)	9(48)	4(39)	0(32)
Mid–afternoon ºC(ºF)	32(89)	31(87)	28(82)	22(72)	16(60)	10(50)
Days with precipitation	10	9	8	7	9	11
Precipitation mm	95	80	78	55	88	111
Precipitation inches	3.8	3.2	3.1	2.2	3.5	4.4
Daily hours of sunshine	10	10	8	7	6	4
Snow mm	0	0	0	0	25	50
Snow inches	0	0	0	0	1	2

TEXAS (Capital: Austin)
Best time to visit Texas in general: April and May, and September and October. (Warm, pleasant.)

Weather in brief for Texas:
March to May: Spring. Warm, but can be stormy with big temperature variations.
June to August: Summer. Hot, often over 35°C (95°F). The Gulf coast may top 38°C (100°F) and receive tropical storms between May and September.
September to November: Autumn. Warm, but can be stormy with large variations in temperature.
December to February: Winter. Cold. Light snow is possible in mid–winter, but it is not uncommon to have warm days.
Tornadoes are probable in northern and central Texas from April to June.

Austin, on the Colorado River.
Weather in brief in Austin:
May to October is warm to hot reaching 36°C (96°F) with occasional thunderstorms and accompanying humidity. Although rainfall is fairly evenly distributed throughout the year there are peaks of rainfall in May and September.
November to April is mild but can become cool for a few days when cold winds blow from the north. Rain during these months is light but constant. Snow is negligible; there may be a light fall in January.

Austin, Texas: Altitude 189m (620ft)

	Jan	Feb	Mar	Apr	May	Jun
Sunrise °C(°F)	4(39)	6(42)	11(51)	15(59)	19(66)	22(72)
Mid–afternoon °C(°F)	15(59)	17(62)	22(72)	26(78)	29(84)	33(91)
Days with precipitation	8	8	7	7	8	6
Precipitation mm	47	78	47	88	101	78
Precipitation inches	1.9	3.1	1.9	3.5	4.0	3.1
Daily hours of sunshine	5	6	7	7	7	10
Snow mm	25	0	0	0	0	0
Snow inches	1	0	0	0	0	0

	Jul	Aug	Sep	Oct	Nov	Dec
Sunrise °C(°F)	23(73)	23(73)	21(69)	16(60)	10(50)	5(41)
Mid–afternoon °C(°F)	35(95)	35(95)	32(89)	28(82)	22(72)	17(62)
Days with precipitation	5	6	7	6	7	7
Precipitation mm	47	55	93	75	50	55
Precipitation inches	1.9	2.2	3.7	3.0	2.0	2.2
Daily hours of sunshine	10	10	8	7	6	5
Snow mm	0	0	0	0	0	0
Snow inches	0	0	0	0	0	0

Houston, near the Gulf of Mexico.
Weather in brief in Houston:
May to October is hot and humid with some thunderstorms. Close proximity to the Gulf ensures year–round humidity brought by sea breezes.
November to April is mild. Rain is uniformly distributed throughout the year.

Houston, Texas: Altitude 33m (108ft)

	Jan	Feb	Mar	Apr	May	Jun
Sunrise ºC(ºF)	4(39)	6(42)	10(50)	14(57)	18(64)	21(70)
Mid–afternoon ºC(ºF)	16(60)	18(64)	22(72)	26(78)	29(84)	32(89)
Days with precipitation	11	6	10	7	9	8
Precipitation mm	95	88	68	88	129	114
Precipitation inches	3.8	3.5	2.7	3.5	5.1	4.5
Daily hours of sunshine	5	6	7	7	9	11

	Jul	Aug	Sep	Oct	Nov	Dec
Sunrise ºC(ºF)	22(72)	22(72)	20(68)	14(57)	10(50)	6(42)
Mid–afternoon ºC(ºF)	34(93)	34(93)	31(87)	28(82)	22(72)	18(64)
Days with precipitation	10	10	10	8	8	9
Precipitation mm	103	111	119	103	101	101
Precipitation inches	4.1	4.4	4.7	4.1	4.0	4.0
Daily hours of sunshine	10	10	9	8	6	5

UTAH   (Capital: Salt Lake City)
Utah's summer tourist season runs from Memorial Day in late May to Labor Day in early September.
Best time to visit Utah for general sightseeing is **September and October** (dry, pleasant).
Least pleasant time to visit northern Utah, where Salt Lake City is located, is mid–April to early June. This is known locally as the "mud season" because of melting snow, unpredictable spring rain and mild to very cold temperatures.

Best time for ski enthusiasts is between January and early April.

Natural attraction: Bryce Canyon National Park, near Tropic.
Best time: Late May to September. Busiest, August and September. Least crowded, January and February.

Salt Lake City, on the Jordan River.
Weather in brief for Salt Lake City:
June to September: Summer is sunny with very little rain, and hot, 32ºC (90ºF).
October and November: Autumn is partly sunny with little rain and mild temperatures. Frosts start around mid–October and snowfalls are experienced from November to April.
The long winter from **December to March** is cold with heavy snow that stays on the ground during the season.
April to May: Spring is sunny and mild but is prone to storms.

Salt Lake City, Utah: Altitude 1288m (4226ft)

	Jan	Feb	Mar	Apr	May	Jun
Sunrise ºC(ºF)	–7(19)	–4(25)	0(32)	3(37)	8(46)	13(55)
Mid–afternoon ºC(ºF)	2(35)	6(42)	11(51)	16(60)	22(72)	28(82)
Days with precipitation	10	9	9	10	7	6
Precipitation mm	32	30	40	53	37	32
Precipitation inches	1.3	1.2	1.6	2.1	1.5	1.3
Daily hours of sunshine	4	6	7	9	11	12
Snow mm	329	253	253	126	25	0
Snow inches	13	10	10	5	1	0

	Jul	Aug	Sep	Oct	Nov	Dec
Sunrise ºC(ºF)	18(64)	17(62)	11(51)	5(41)	0(32)	–6(21)
Mid–afternoon ºC(ºF)	33(91)	32(89)	26(78)	19(66)	10(50)	3(37)
Days with precipitation	4	5	5	6	7	9
Precipitation mm	17	23	17	30	32	35
Precipitation inches	0.7	0.9	0.7	1.2	1.3	1.4
Daily hours of sunshine	12	11	10	8	6	4
Snow mm	0	0	0	25	152	304
Snow inches	0	0	0	1	6	12

VERMONT (Capital: Montpelier)

Best time for Vermont: Late May and early June, and September and October. Summer, July to August, is also a good time but these are the rainiest months. Rain falls in all other months, and snow falls from December to March.

Burlington, on eastern shore of Lake Champlain.
Weather in brief for Burlington:
June to August is a brief, mild summer.
September to November (autumn) is cool with the first frosts occurring in September.
December to February (winter) is cold with polar air coming down through Canada. Expect cloudy conditions throughout the year.

Burlington, Vermont: Altitude 104m (341ft)

	Jan	Feb	Mar	Apr	May	Jun
Sunrise ºC(ºF)	–14(7)	–13(8)	–6(21)	1(33)	7(44)	13(55)
Mid–afternoon ºC(ºF)	–4(25)	–2(29)	4(39)	12(53)	20(68)	24(75)
Days with precipitation	14	12	13	12	14	12
Precipitation mm	43	43	47	65	75	88
Precipitation inches	1.7	1.7	1.9	2.6	3.0	3.5
Daily hours of sunshine	4	5	6	7	8	9
Snow mm	456	456	304	101	0	0
Snow inches	18	18	12	4	0	0

Burlington, Vermont: (continued)

	Jul	Aug	Sep	Oct	Nov	Dec
Sunrise ºC(ºF)	15(59)	14(57)	9(48)	4(39)	–1(30)	–9(16)
Mid–afternoon ºC(ºF)	27(80)	25(77)	21(70)	14(57)	7(44)	0(32)
Days with precipitation	12	12	12	11	14	15
Precipitation mm	88	93	78	68	73	55
Precipitation inches	3.5	3.7	3.1	2.7	2.9	2.2
Daily hours of sunshine	10	8	7	5	3	3
Snow mm	0	0	0	0	178	508
Snow inches	0	0	0	0	7	20

VIRGINIA (Capital: Richmond)
Best time to visit Virginia is April, May and September and October.

Virginia's weather in brief:
April and May: Spring. Mild with light rain. Afternoons range 20 to 27ºC (67 to 80ºF).
June to August: Summer. Hot, humid. Afternoons reach 30ºC (86ºF). Rain comes in brief thunderstorms.
September and October: Autumn. Mild with light rain. Afternoons range 20 to 27ºC (67 to 80ºF).
December to February: Winter. Cold. Snow falls in the mountains.

Natural attraction: Shenandoah National Park, near Luray.
Popular time, May to October. Busiest, July and October. Least crowded, January and February.

Richmond, on the James River.
Weather in brief in Richmond:
June to August: Summer has humid, warm days, 30ºC (86ºF).
September to November: Autumn is the drier season with mild, sunny weather.
December to February is cold with morning temperatures below freezing point but days are mild.
March to May are transitional months when snow melts and when rain and temperatures increase.

Richmond, Virginia: Altitude 54m (177ft)

	Jan	Feb	Mar	Apr	May	Jun
Sunrise ºC(ºF)	–3(27)	–2(29)	2(35)	7(44)	12(53)	17(62)
Mid–afternoon ºC(ºF)	8(46)	10(50)	15(59)	21(70)	25(77)	29(84)
Days with precipitation	10	9	11	9	11	10
Precipitation mm	73	75	85	70	85	88
Precipitation inches	2.9	3.0	3.4	2.8	3.4	3.5
Daily hours of sunshine	6	6	8	9	9	10
Snow mm	126	75	75	0	0	0
Snow inches	5	3	3	0	0	0

Richmond, Virginia: (continued)

	Jul	Aug	Sep	Oct	Nov	Dec
Sunrise ºC(ºF)	20(68)	19(66)	15(59)	8(46)	3(37)	–1(30)
Mid–afternoon ºC(ºF)	31(87)	31(87)	27(80)	21(69)	16(60)	10(50)
Days with precipitation	11	10	8	7	8	9
Precipitation mm	141	129	90	73	80	80
Precipitation inches	5.6	5.1	3.6	2.9	3.2	3.2
Daily hours of sunshine	10	9	8	7	6	5
Snow mm	0	0	0	0	0	50
Snow inches	0	0	0	0	0	2

WASHINGTON (Capital: Olympia)

Good time for general travel in Washington: June to October. Best months are September and October. (Pleasant, dry.) For ski enthusiasts: November to March.

We have divided the weather into two regions. Western Washington, west of the Cascade Mountains, is described below. Eastern Washington follows as a **Footnote**.

June to August: Summer. Dry and warm, 21ºC (70ºF). Skies are often cloudless in July and August, but light rain is possible.
September to November: Autumn. September and October are very pleasant months. Light rains start in October and can drizzle on and off to early July. Sunshine and rain can alternate several times daily. Most precipitation occurs November to April.
December to February: Winter. Wet and cool, 8ºC (47ºF) in afternoons. The wettest months are December and January. Arctic air brings light snowfalls which melt quickly.
March to May: Spring. Wet, March and April, with mild and partly sunny and cloudy days. May is drier and warmer, 18ºC (64ºF).

Footnote: Eastern Washington, east of the Cascade Mountains, has higher afternoon summer (June to August) temperatures, 32ºC (90ºF) and more snow in winter (December to February), 255 to 760mm (10 to 30in).

Seattle
Weather in brief in Seattle, western Washington:
June to August (summer) is sunny and pleasantly warm with little rain.
November to March is the cool, wet season with a mix of cloudy skies and limited sunshine. Rainstorms sometimes arrive from the north. The nearby Pacific Ocean has a moderating influence, precluding wide swings of temperatures. Light snowfalls are mainly confined to December and January.

Seattle, Washington: Altitude 38m (125ft)

	Jan	Feb	Mar	Apr	May	Jun
Sunrise ºC(ºF)	2(35)	3(37)	4(39)	6(42)	9(48)	12(53)
Mid–afternoon ºC(ºF)	7(44)	10(50)	11(51)	14(57)	18(64)	21(69)
Days with precipitation	20	16	17	14	10	9
Precipitation mm	131	98	80	60	43	40
Precipitation inches	5.2	3.9	3.2	2.4	1.7	1.6
Daily hours of sunshine	2	4	5	7	8	8
Snow mm	101	25	25	0	0	0
Snow inches	4	1	1	0	0	0

	Jul	Aug	Sep	Oct	Nov	Dec
Sunrise ºC(ºF)	14(57)	14(57)	12(53)	8(46)	5(41)	3(37)
Mid–afternoon ºC(ºF)	24(75)	24(75)	21(69)	15(59)	10(50)	7(44)
Days with precipitation	5	6	8	10	18	20
Precipitation mm	22	22	45	85	134	136
Precipitation inches	0.9	0.9	1.8	3.4	5.3	5.4
Daily hours of sunshine	10	8	7	4	3	2
Snow mm	0	0	0	0	26	50
Snow inches	0	0	0	0	1	2

WEST VIRGINIA (Capital: Charleston)
Best time to visit West Virginia: April, May and September, October.
West Virginia's weather in brief:
April and May: Mild with light rain. Afternoons range 20 to 27ºC (67 to 80ºF).
June to August: Summers are hot and humid. Average afternoon maximum is 29ºC (85ºF). Expect brief thunderstorms.
September and October: Mild with light rain. Afternoons range 20 to 27ºC (67 to 80ºF).
December to February: Cold with heavy snowfalls exceeding 3m (10ft) in some areas.

Charleston
Weather in brief in Charleston:
May to September is warm. Rain falls throughout the year. It falls as thunderstorms in June and July. July is the wettest month and October, the driest.
November to March is cold with most snow falling in January and February. Fog can be expected on more than 230 days per year, making Charleston the foggiest city in the country.

Charleston, West Virginia: Altitude 299m (981ft)

	Jan	Feb	Mar	Apr	May	Jun
Sunrise ºC(ºF)	–5(23)	–4(25)	2(35)	6(42)	11(51)	15(59)
Mid–afternoon ºC(ºF)	5(41)	7(44)	14(57)	19(66)	24(75)	28(82)
Days with precipitation	15	14	15	14	13	11
Precipitation mm	85	78	101	83	88	83
Precipitation inches	3.4	3.1	4.0	3.3	3.5	3.3
Snow mm	228	202	101	0	0	0
Snow inches	9	8	4	0	0	0

Charleston, West Virginia: (continued)

	Jul	Aug	Sep	Oct	Nov	Dec
Sunrise ºC(ºF)	18(64)	17(62)	14(57)	7(44)	2(35)	–2(29)
Mid–afternoon ºC(ºF)	30(86)	29(84)	26(78)	20(68)	14(57)	9(48)
Days with precipitation	13	10	9	9	12	14
Precipitation mm	126	93	73	63	70	80
Precipitation inches	5.0	3.7	2.9	2.5	2.8	3.2
Snow mm	0	0	0	0	75	126
Snow inches	0	0	0	0	3	5

WISCONSIN (Capital: Madison)
Milwaukee, on Lake Michigan

Weather in brief in Milwaukee:
June to August (summer) is sunny, clear and warm. The waters of Lake Michigan cool the lake shore in summer and warm it in winter, **December to February**. However, winters are cold with afternoon temperatures hovering around freezing point. Snow falls mainly December to March, often coming as severe storms.

Milwaukee, Wisconsin: Altitude 211m (692ft)

	Jan	Feb	Mar	Apr	May	Jun
Sunrise ºC(ºF)	–11(13)	–9(16)	–3(27)	2(35)	7(44)	13(55)
Mid–afternoon ºC(ºF)	–3(27)	–1(30)	5(41)	12(53)	18(64)	24(75)
Days with precipitation	11	9	12	12	11	9
Precipitation mm	40	27	55	70	72	90
Precipitation inches	1.6	1.1	2.2	2.8	2.9	3.6
Daily hours of sunshine	5	5	6	7	9	10
Snow mm	304	228	228	50	0	0
Snow inches	12	9	9	2	0	0

	Jul	Aug	Sep	Oct	Nov	Dec
Sunrise ºC(ºF)	17(62)	16(60)	12(53)	5(41)	0(32)	–8(18)
Mid–afternoon ºC(ºF)	27(80)	25(77)	21(69)	15(59)	7(44)	0(32)
Days with precipitation	11	9	9	8	10	11
Precipitation mm	85	68	75	50	50	45
Precipitation inches	3.4	2.7	3.0	2.0	2.0	1.8
Daily hours of sunshine	10	9	7	6	4	3
Snow mm	0	0	0	0	75	253
Snow inches	0	0	0	0	3	10

WYOMING (Capital: Cheyenne)
Best time to visit Wyoming for general sightseeing is June to October.

Weather in brief for Wyoming:
June to August: Summer. Sunny and hot with temperatures to 35ºC (95ºF). Occasional thunderstorms.
September to November: Autumn. Pleasant, warm days and cool evenings in September and October. November is cooler.
December to February: Winter. Cold with strong winds, blizzards and snow.
March to May: Windy, rainy, cold, but becoming mild by May.

Yellowstone National Park
Weather in brief:
June to September is sunny and pleasantly warm. Rain is well distributed throughout the year.
November to early April are the cold winter months of heavy snowfalls. Popular time, mid–April to late October. Busiest, July and August. Least crowded, November and December.

Yellowstone National Park, Wyoming: Altitude 1900m (6233ft)

	Jan	Feb	Mar	Apr	May	Jun
Sunrise ºC(ºF)	–13(10)	–13(10)	–9(17)	–4(26)	1(34)	5(41)
Mid–afternoon ºC(ºF)	–3(26)	–2(29)	2(36)	9(48)	14(58)	19(67)
Days with precipitation	13	11	12	10	13	12
Precipitation mm	40	32	43	32	50	43
Precipitation inches	1.6	1.3	1.7	1.3	2.0	1.7
Snow mm	762	584	584	254	101	25
Snow inches	30	23	23	10	4	1

	Jul	Aug	Sep	Oct	Nov	Dec
Sunrise ºC(ºF)	8(46)	7(45)	3(37)	–2(29)	–7(20)	–12(11)
Mid–afternoon ºC(ºF)	25(77)	24(76)	18(65)	11(52)	3(38)	–3(28)
Days with precipitation	10	9	8	9	10	12
Precipitation mm	32	30	30	35	35	35
Precipitation inches	1.3	1.2	1.2	1.4	1.4	1.4
Snow mm	0	0	25	177	456	660
Snow inches	0	0	1	7	18	26

URUGUAY

Official Name: Oriental Republic of Uruguay

Capital: Montevideo
Language: Spanish

Most of Uruguay is low–lying and consists of gently
rolling grasslands. Woodland occurs along river banks.

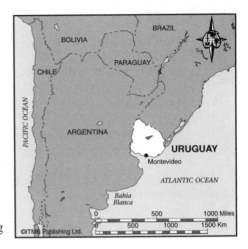

Best time to visit: November to March. (But weather is
pleasant throughout year.)

November to March: Warm. Average afternoon
temperature, December to March, is 27°C (80°F). Cooling
breezes from the sea temper the climate. Nights are
pleasantly mild, about 17°C (63°F). Occasional thunderstorms occur December to February.
April to October: Chilly winds blow in July and August, making Montevideo uncomfortably cold.
Coolest months are June, July and August, 15°C (59°F). Rain falls throughout the year but is usually
heaviest in April and May.

Montevideo, Uruguay: Altitude 22m (72ft)

	Jan	Feb	Mar	Apr	May	Jun
Sunrise °C(°F)	17(62)	16(61)	15(59)	12(53)	9(48)	6(43)
Mid–afternoon °C(°F)	28(82)	28(82)	26(78)	22(71)	18(64)	15(59)
Days with precipitation	6	5	5	6	6	5
Precipitation mm	74	66	99	99	84	81
Precipitation inches	2.9	2.6	3.9	3.9	3.3	3.2
Daily hours of sunshine	11	10	9	8	6	5

	Jul	Aug	Sep	Oct	Nov	Dec
Sunrise °C(°F)	6(43)	6(43)	8(46)	9(49)	12(54)	15(59)
Mid–afternoon °C(°F)	14(58)	15(59)	17(63)	20(68)	23(74)	26(79)
Days with precipitation	6	7	6	6	6	7
Precipitation mm	74	79	76	66	74	79
Precipitation inches	2.9	3.1	3.0	2.6	2.9	3.1
Daily hours of sunshine	5	6	7	8	10	10

UZBEKISTAN
Official Name: Republic of Uzbekistan

Capital: Tashkent
Languages: Uzbek, Russian, Tajik

The country is part of a vast lowland plain consisting of desert and semi–arid grasslands. Mountains on its eastern border shelter it from rain, leaving it a dry country.

Best time to visit: May to end of June, and September to early November.

March to May: Spring. Sunny, mild, light rain. March and April are the wettest months.
June to August: Summer. Sunny, dry, hot, 32°C (90°F), but humidity is low. Hottest time is mid–July to end of August.
September to November: Autumn. Sunny, warm and mainly dry. Light rains and frost occur towards October and November.
December to February: Winter. Harsh, cold winds. Sunny and mainly dry but with light rains and some snow in the mountains in the east. Coldest time is January and early February when the temperature can drop to freezing.

Tashkent, Uzbekistan: Altitude 488m (1601ft)

	Jan	Feb	Mar	Apr	May	Jun
Sunrise °C(°F)	–3(27)	–2(29)	4(39)	10(50)	14(57)	18(64)
Mid–afternoon °C(°F)	6(42)	8(46)	14(57)	22(72)	27(80)	33(91)
Days with precipitation	8	7	9	8	5	1
Precipitation mm	55	47	72	64	32	7
Precipitation inches	2.2	1.9	2.8	2.5	1.3	0.3
Daily hours of sunshine	4	4	5	7	10	12

	Jul	Aug	Sep	Oct	Nov	Dec
Sunrise °C(°F)	19(66)	17(62)	12(53)	7(44)	3(37)	0(32)
Mid–afternoon °C(°F)	36(97)	34(94)	29(84)	21(70)	14(57)	9(48)
Days with precipitation	1	0	1	4	6	8
Precipitation mm	4	2	5	34	45	53
Precipitation inches	0.1	0.08	0.2	1.3	1.8	2.1
Daily hours of sunshine	12	12	10	7	5	3

VANUATU

Official Name: Republic of Vanuatu (pronounced va–noo–ah'too)

Capital: Port–Vila
Languages: English, French, Bislama (a form of pidgin English), Melanesian dialects

More than 80 islands and islets comprise Vanuatu. The 12 largest islands are mountainous and hilly.

Best time to visit: April to November.

April to November: Season of less rain. Sunny, warm, humid. Tempered by the refreshing southeast tradewinds that sweep the South Pacific Ocean.
December to March: Wet season. Hot, humid. Cyclones may develop. Rain, when it occurs, usually comes late afternoon, and humidity increases.
Sunshine throughout the year averages 7 hours per day.

Port–Vila, Vanuatu:

	Jan	Feb	Mar	Apr	May	Jun
Sunrise ºC(ºF)	23(73)	23(73)	23(73)	22(72)	21(70)	19(67)
Mid–afternoon ºC(ºF)	28(83)	29(84)	29(84)	28(82)	26(79)	25(77)
Days with precipitation	12	12	11	13	9	9
Precipitation mm	272	260	312	239	148	129
Precipitation inches	10.7	10.2	12.3	9.4	5.8	5.1

	Jul	Aug	Sep	Oct	Nov	Dec
Sunrise ºC(ºF)	19(67)	19(67)	19(67)	20(68)	21(70)	22(72)
Mid–afternoon ºC(ºF)	24(76)	24(76)	24(76)	26(78)	27(80)	28(82)
Days with precipitation	9	5	7	8	7	10
Precipitation mm	103	93	104	103	161	183
Precipitation inches	4.1	3.7	4.1	4.1	6.3	7.2

VATICAN
Official Name: State of the Vatican City (also called The Holy See)

Capital: Vatican City
Languages: Italian, Latin

Vatican City, only 44 hectares (108.7 acres), lies within the city of Rome, on Vatican Hill just west of the Tiber River.

Best time: Late April to June, and September to mid–October. These months avoid the summer crowds of July and August. For the weather table, refer to Rome, Italy.

March to May: Spring. Mild with light rain.
June to August: Summer. Warm, dry season. July and August are muggy and temperatures reach 30°C (87°F).
September to November (Autumn) and **December to February** (Winter). Mild. The rainy season is September to March with most rain falling in November. The rains, brought by westerly winds, seem to be endless.

VENEZUELA
Official Name: Republic of Venezuela

Capital: Caracas
Language: Spanish

Much of Venezuela is mountainous. There are high ranges of the Andes in the northwest and low ranges parallel to the Caribbean coast. South of the ranges is the vast, grassy, lowland region in the Orinoco river valley known as Los Llanos. In the south and southeast is a forested plateau with rounded hills. In the northwest is Lake Maracaibo and lowlands with extensive marshes.

Best time to visit: December to April. (But anytime is good for the coast.)

December to April: Dry season. Temperatures depend on elevation. Afternoon temperatures in Caracas, at an elevation of 945m (3100ft), average 28°C (82°F). Evenings are cool. Coastal temperatures average 33°C (91°F). Expect 7 to 8 hours of sunshine daily throughout the country. Humidity is moderate.
May to November: Wet season. Hot and humid. Average afternoon temperature in Caracas is 28°C (82°F). Coastal temperatures, e.g. Maracaibo, average 34°C (93°F) in the afternoons. Expect 6 to 8 hours of sunshine daily throughout the country. In the north of the country (Caracas and Maracaibo) rain consists of short downpours in the afternoon, then the sky clears quickly.
Snow: Highest points in the Andes mountains are covered with snow year–round. It is cold at night even if days are hot.

Natural attractions:

1. Wildlife: December to April is a good time to visit the rolling, grassy plains called Los Llanos to observe birds (over 300 species) and wildlife (capybaras, monkeys, reptiles) which gather at receding water holes. Los Llanos is prone to flooding in the wet season, May to November.

2. Climbing: December to April, the dry season, is a good time to climb Auyántepui, the mountain–top from which spills Angel Falls, highest falls in the world.

3. Angel Falls is best viewed in the wet season, May to November. In the dry season there is less water. Note that the time to **view** the falls is different from the time to **climb** the mountain.

4. Snorkeling, scuba diving at, for example, Puerto La Cruz, east of Caracas: Best time is July to November when underwater visibility is at its best.

Caracas, Venezuela: Altitude 945m (3100ft)

	Jan	Feb	Mar	Apr	May	Jun
Sunrise °C(°F)	16(60)	16(60)	17(62)	19(66)	20(68)	19(66)
Mid–afternoon °C(°F)	27(80)	28(82)	29(84)	29(84)	29(84)	28(82)
Days with precipitation	3	2	1	4	9	14
Precipitation mm	16	13	12	59	80	139
Precipitation inches	0.6	0.5	0.5	2.3	3.2	5.5
Daily hours of sunshine	7	8	8	6	6	6

	Jul	Aug	Sep	Oct	Nov	Dec
Sunrise °C(°F)	19(66)	19(66)	19(66)	18(64)	18(64)	17(62)
Mid–afternoon °C(°F)	28(82)	27(80)	28(82)	28(82)	28(82)	27(80)
Days with precipitation	13	13	11	12	9	6
Precipitation mm	121	124	114	123	73	42
Precipitation inches	4.8	4.9	4.5	4.8	2.9	1.6
Daily hours of sunshine	7	7	7	7	7	7

Maracaibo, Venezuela: Altitude 65m (213ft)

	Jan	Feb	Mar	Apr	May	Jun
Sunrise °C(°F)	23(73)	23(73)	24(75)	25(77)	25(77)	25(77)
Mid–afternoon °C(°F)	32(89)	33(91)	33(91)	33(91)	33(91)	34(93)
Days with precipitation	1	0	1	4	6	5
Precipitation mm	5	3	6	52	67	55
Precipitation inches	0.2	0.1	0.2	2.0	2.6	2.2
Daily hours of sunshine	9	9	8	6	6	7

	Jul	Aug	Sep	Oct	Nov	Dec
Sunrise °C(°F)	25(77)	25(77)	25(77)	24(75)	24(75)	23(73)
Mid–afternoon °C(°F)	34(93)	34(93)	34(93)	32(89)	32(89)	32(89)
Days with precipitation	4	6	8	9	5	2
Precipitation mm	26	60	104	114	71	17
Precipitation inches	1.0	2.4	4.1	4.5	2.8	0.7
Daily hours of sunshine	8	7	6	6	7	8

VIETNAM
Official Name: Socialist Republic of Vietnam

Capital: Hanoi
Languages: Vietnamese, Chinese, English, French,
Khmer, tribal languages

In the northwest are rugged highlands that reach 2450m
(8000ft). They extend along most of the length of
Vietnam. In the north there are lowlands around the delta
of the Red River (Song Coi). In the south, around Ho
Chi Minh City, lowlands comprise a vast plain and the
Mekong River delta.

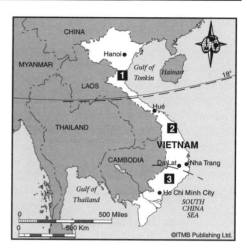

Best time to visit north, e.g. Hanoi: **Late September to
December, and March to April.** (Dry.) January and February are cool and drizzly.
Best time to visit south, e.g. Ho Chi Minh City: **December to April.** (Warm, mainly dry.)

We have divided the weather into three regions. Refer to map for corresponding numbers.
1. Northern region, north of 18th parallel. (Includes Hanoi.)
Best time: Late September to December, and March to April.
October to December: Dry season. Cool. Afternoon temperatures range 30°C (85°F) in October down
to 21°C (70°F) in December.
January to mid–March: Dry season but chilly with light, continuous drizzle. January is the coldest
month, 17°C (62°F). Statistically, March has the highest probability for clear skies in the north during
these cold months. However, expect only one hour of sunshine daily. Afternoon temperatures average
21°C (70°F).
Mid–March to April: Dry. Hot winds blow in from Laos. Good time to visit. Afternoon temperatures,
24 to 29°C (75 to 85°F). Humidity is high.
May to September: Rainy season. Weather is brought by moisture–laden monsoon winds. Most
rain falls in July and August. Flooding can occur. Unpredictable typhoons are possible. Heat can be
oppressive; can be over 38°C (100°F). Humidity is highest in August.

2. Central region. Comprises a) the central mountains and b) the central coast.
a) Central mountains. A mountain chain forms the backbone of Vietnam.
A representative town is Da Lat, 1500m (4900ft).
Best time: December to February.

December to February: Dry in mountains. Temperature is cool year–round.
April and May to October: Wet, cool. The mountains capture the moisture of the southwest monsoon
from the Indian Ocean. Not a good time to visit. October is wettest. Temperature is cool year–round.

b) Central coast. A representative town is Nha Trang.
Best time: May to October, except for Da Nang and Hué when April is best.

May to October: Dry, hot. The coast, sheltered by the mountains, is denied the precipitation of the
southwest monsoon. Exceptions are Da Nang and Hué which are farther north and near the central
mountains. They are deluged with monsoon rain from the southwest in October. Best time for Da
Nang and Hué is around April when it is drier and cooler.
December to February: Rain. Brought by northeast monsoons which collect moisture over the
South China Sea.

3. Southern region, south of Nha Trang. (Includes Ho Chi Minh City.)
Best time: December to April.

December to April: Dry season but with occasional rain. Always hot; 32°C (90°F) is common. April is the hottest and most humid month.
May to October and November: Wet season. Rains are brought by the southwest monsoon. Rainiest, June to September. Showers are sporadic but are often in early afternoon, and come almost daily. Flooding can occur in Mekong Delta, making travel challenging. Humidity is high, July to October.

Hanoi, northern Vietnam: Altitude 16m (53ft)

	Jan	Feb	Mar	Apr	May	Jun
Sunrise °C(°F)	13(56)	14(58)	17(63)	20(69)	23(74)	26(78)
Mid–afternoon °C(°F)	20(68)	21(69)	23(74)	28(82)	32(90)	33(92)
Days with precipitation	7	13	15	14	15	14
Precipitation mm	18	28	38	81	196	239
Precipitation inches	0.7	1.1	1.5	3.2	7.7	9.4
Daily hours of sunshine	1	1	1	2	4	5

	Jul	Aug	Sep	Oct	Nov	Dec
Sunrise °C(°F)	26(78)	26(78)	24(76)	22(71)	18(64)	15(59)
Mid–afternoon °C(°F)	33(91)	32(90)	31(88)	29(84)	26(78)	22(72)
Days with precipitation	15	16	14	9	7	7
Precipitation mm	323	343	254	99	43	20
Precipitation inches	12.7	13.5	10.0	3.9	1.7	0.8
Daily hours of sunshine	5	4	4	4	3	2

Ho Chi Minh City, southern Vietnam: Altitude 9m (30ft)

	Jan	Feb	Mar	Apr	May	Jun
Sunrise °C(°F)	21(70)	22(71)	23(74)	24(75)	24(75)	24(75)
Mid–afternoon °C(°F)	32(89)	33(91)	34(93)	35(95)	33(92)	32(89)
Days with precipitation	2	1	2	4	16	21
Precipitation mm	15	10	13	43	221	330
Precipitation inches	0.6	0.4	0.5	1.7	8.7	13.0
Daily hours of sunshine	5	6	5	6	4	4

	Jul	Aug	Sep	Oct	Nov	Dec
Sunrise °C(°F)	24(75)	24(75)	23(74)	23(74)	23(74)	22(71)
Mid–afternoon °C(°F)	31(87)	31(87)	31(87)	31(87)	31(87)	31(87)
Days with precipitation	23	21	21	20	11	7
Precipitation mm	315	269	335	269	114	56
Precipitation inches	12.4	10.6	13.2	10.6	4.5	2.2
Daily hours of sunshine	4	5	5	4	4	4

Da Nang, central coast, Vietnam: Altitude 3m (10ft)

	Jan	Feb	Mar	Apr	May	Jun
Sunrise ºC(ºF)	19(66)	20(68)	21(69)	23(73)	24(75)	25(77)
Mid–afternoon ºC(ºF)	24(75)	26(78)	27(81)	30(86)	33(91)	34(93)
Days with precipitation	15	7	4	4	8	7
Precipitation mm	102	31	12	18	47	42
Precipitation inches	4.0	1.2	0.5	0.7	1.9	1.7

	Jul	Aug	Sep	Oct	Nov	Dec
Sunrise ºC(ºF)	25(77)	25(77)	24(75)	23(73)	22(71)	20(68)
Mid–afternoon ºC(ºF)	34(93)	34(93)	31(88)	28(83)	27(80)	25(77)
Days with precipitation	11	12	17	21	21	20
Precipitation mm	99	117	447	530	221	209
Precipitation inches	3.9	4.6	17.6	20.9	8.7	8.2

VIRGIN ISLANDS (BRITISH)

Official Name: British Virgin Islands
(Dependent Territory of the United Kingdom)
Capital: Road Town (on Tortola Island)
Language: English

The British Virgin Islands include dozens of islands, islets and rocks. The main islands are Tortola and Virgin Gorda. Tortola is mountainous with shimmering white sand beaches. Its volcanic peak rises to 540m (1780ft). Virgin Gorda, 11km (7 miles) long, is mountainous in the northern half and relatively flat in the south.

Best time to visit: January to May, but pleasant weather year–round.
January to March: Winter. Driest months are February and March. Average afternoon temperature, 28ºC (83ºF).
April to September: Summer. Rains increase month by month, peaking in September.
October to December: Rains begin to decrease.
Sunshine: Expect 8 hours per day throughout the year.
Humid all year, particularly August to October.
Hurricanes are possible June through November, particularly September, but touchdowns are infrequent.
Note: See under Caribbean Islands for general weather information.

Road Town, British Virgin Islands: Altitude: sea level

	Jan	Feb	Mar	Apr	May	Jun
Sunrise ºC(ºF)	23(73)	23(73)	23(74)	24(75)	24(76)	25(77)
Mid–afternoon ºC(ºF)	28(83)	28(83)	29(84)	29(85)	30(86)	31(87)
Days with precipitation	10	8	7	9	11	10
Precipitation mm	63	48	48	76	102	76
Precipitation inches	2.6	1.9	1.9	3.0	4.0	3.0

Road Town, British Virgin Islands: (continued)

	Jul	Aug	Sep	Oct	Nov	Dec
Sunrise ºC(ºF)	25(78)	25(78)	25(78)	25(77)	24(76)	23(74)
Mid–afternoon ºC(ºF)	31(88)	31(88)	31(88)	31(87)	30(86)	29(84)
Days with precipitation	11	13	15	14	11	11
Precipitation mm	84	104	127	124	102	89
Precipitation inches	3.3	4.2	5.0	4.9	4.0	3.5

VIRGIN ISLANDS (UNITED STATES)

Official Name: Virgin Islands of the United States
(Dependent Territory of the U.S.A.)

Capital: Charlotte Amalie (pronounced a–mahl–yah) on
St Thomas Island
Languages: English with some Spanish and Creole

Of the dozens of small islands in the group, there are 3
main islands, St Thomas, St Croix (pronounced Croy) and
St John, all of which are hilly with forests.

Best time to visit: January to May. (But pleasant
weather year–round.)

See Virgin Islands (British) for a description of the monthly weather.

Note: See under Caribbean Islands for general weather information.

St Thomas and St Croix islands:

	Jan	Feb	Mar	Apr	May	Jun
Sunrise ºC(ºF)	22(71)	22(71)	22(72)	23(74)	24(75)	25(77)
Mid–afternoon ºC(ºF)	28(82)	28(82)	29(84)	29(85)	30(86)	31(88)
Days with precipitation	9	7	6	8	10	9
Precipitation mm	63	48	43	56	116	81
Precipitation inches	2.5	1.9	1.7	2.2	4.6	3.2

	Jul	Aug	Sep	Oct	Nov	Dec
Sunrise ºC(ºF)	25(77)	25(77)	24(76)	24(76)	23(74)	23(73)
Mid–afternoon ºC(ºF)	31(88)	31(88)	31(88)	31(88)	30(86)	29(84)
Days with precipitation	10	12	14	13	10	10
Precipitation mm	84	104	175	142	99	99
Precipitation inches	3.3	4.1	6.9	5.6	3.9	3.9

WALLIS and FUTUNA

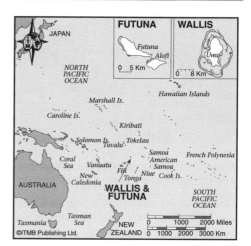

Official Name: Territory of the Wallis and Futuna Islands
(Overseas Territory of France)

Capital: Mata Utu (on Wallis)
Languages: Polynesian, French

The islands, located between Samoa and Fiji, have a
tropical oceanic climate.

Best time to visit: May to October.

May to October: Season of less rain. Hot, humid. Sea
breezes temper the climate. Average daily maximum
temperature is 27°C (81°F).
November to April: Rainy. This is the cyclone season. Humid and hotter, 30°C (86°F).
Sunshine throughout the year ranges 6 to 8 hours per day.

WESTERN SAHARA

Official Name: Western Sahara
(United with Morocco)

Principal town: Al–aiun (La'youn)
Languages: Spanish, French, Arabic

The country is a vast, flat desert.

Best time: November to April. (Comparatively cool.)

November to April: Sunny, dry. Hot during the day, in
the 30s°C (90s°F). Cold at night. Sandstorms may occur
during March, April and May.
June to September: Summer. Daytime temperatures rise
above 45°C (113°F). Nights are cool. Virtually rainless.

YEMEN
Official Name: Republic of Yemen

Capital: San'a
Language: Arabic

Yemen consists of mountainous uplands and a low–lying
coastal strip. The coastal strip, where the port of Aden is
situated, is hot, humid and subject to fog.
The mountainous uplands, where San'a is located at
2250m (7400ft), have a temperate climate. The monsoon
rains which come from the south and southwest are
unreliable. Occasionally they bypass Yemen. Long
droughts are common.

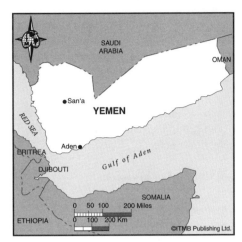

Best time: April and May, and September and October. (After the rainy seasons.)

March to May: The season of light rains is in March and April. May is dry. Temperatures are
moderate, 25 to 35°C (77 to 95°F).
June to September: Summer. In the uplands, June to August is hot and sunny. Upland temperatures
are about 30°C (86°F) in the daytime and 10°C (50°F) at night. The heavy monsoon season affects the
uplands late July to September. On the south coast and Red Sea coast the rainfall is low, humidity is
high, daytime temperatures can top 40°C (104°F) but drop to about 30°C (86°F) at night. Sea breezes
help temper the heat.
Late October to early February: Dry and dusty. In the uplands during winter, December to February,
daytime temperatures are mild, 25°C (77°F) but nights are cold and can drop to freezing point. Frosts
are possible. Coastal temperatures, October to February, can reach 32°C (90°F) in the day but can drop
to 21°C (70°F) at night.

Aden, Yemen: Altitude 7m (22ft)

	Jan	Feb	Mar	Apr	May	Jun
Sunrise °C(°F)	22(72)	23(73)	24(76)	25(77)	27(81)	29(84)
Mid–afternoon °C(°F)	28(82)	28(82)	30(86)	32(89)	34(93)	37(98)
Days with precipitation	1	0	1	0	0	0
Precipitation mm	5	0	5	0	0	0
Precipitation inches	0.2	0	0.2	0	0	0
Daily hours of sunshine	9	9	9	10	10	9

	Jul	Aug	Sep	Oct	Nov	Dec
Sunrise °C(°F)	28(82)	28(82)	28(82)	24(76)	23(73)	23(73)
Mid–afternoon °C(°F)	36(96)	36(96)	36(96)	33(91)	30(86)	28(82)
Days with precipitation	1	1	0	0	0	2
Precipitation mm	5	3	0	0	0	5
Precipitation inches	0.2	0.1	0	0	0	0.2
Daily hours of sunshine	7	8	9	10	10	9

ZAMBIA
Official Name: Republic of Zambia

Capital: Lusaka
Languages: English, Bantu languages

Most of Zambia is situated on plateaus from 600 to 2100m (2000 to 7000ft) above sea level. This gives it a pleasant climate.

Best time: May to October.

May to August: Dry and pleasant 25°C (77°F) in the afternoons. Above 1500m (5000ft) nighttime temperatures can fall to freezing.

September to late November: Dry, but gets progressively hotter. October is the hottest month, 32°C (90°F) on the plateaus but in excess of 40°C (104°F) in the low–lying valleys of Lower Zambezi and Luangwa.

Late November to April: Hot, wet. Thunderstorms are common in the afternoons but sometimes rain falls continuously for two or three days. The heaviest rainfalls occur in January in most areas. The north is wetter than the south. Uncomfortably high humidity is a result of the rain.

Natural attractions:
1. South Luangwa National Park, a superb wildlife park. **The best time to visit is June to October**, during the dry season. In the dry season animals concentrate around the diminishing waterholes and the grass is shorter. Both conditions make game viewing easier.
2. Victoria Falls, on the Zambezi River. Refer to the information under Zimbabwe.

Lusaka, Zambia: Altitude 1154m (3786ft)

	Jan	Feb	Mar	Apr	May	Jun
Sunrise °C(°F)	17(62)	17(62)	16(60)	16(60)	12(53)	11(51)
Mid–afternoon °C(°F)	26(78)	26(78)	29(84)	26(78)	24(75)	23(73)
Days with precipitation	17	17	10	3	0	0
Precipitation mm	264	236	131	48	4	0
Precipitation inches	10.4	9.3	5.2	1.9	0.1	0
Daily hours of sunshine	5	5	8	8	9	8

	Jul	Aug	Sep	Oct	Nov	Dec
Sunrise °C(°F)	9(48)	11(51)	14(57)	19(66)	18(64)	17(62)
Mid–afternoon °C(°F)	22(72)	25(77)	29(85)	30(86)	29(85)	26(78)
Days with precipitation	0	0	0	2	8	17
Precipitation mm	0	0	1	16	102	275
Precipitation inches	0	0	0.04	0.6	4.0	10.8
Daily hours of sunshine	9	9	9	9	6	6

ZIMBABWE
Official Name: Republic of Zimbabwe

Capital: Harare
Languages: English, Shona, Ndebele

Zimbabwe consists of plateaus, hills and lowlands.
Altitude determines the temperature. The lowland region
which includes Victoria Falls, Zambezi River Valley and
Lake Kariba is hotter than the plateau cities of Harare and
Bulawayo.

Best time: May to October (dry season; good for
observing wildlife). April is a good month for general
travel but not for viewing animals because grass is long
after the rains and the animals have moved to the many new depressions containing surface water.

Mid–May to mid–August: Winter. Mild to warm, dry, sunny with clear skies.
Mid–August to November: Spring. Warm, dry, sunny. October is the hottest month. Rains can start
sometime in November.
November to mid–March: Summer. Hot, rainy with thunderstorms. November is the beginning of
the wet season which lasts until March. Most rain falls as afternoon thunderstorms.
Mid–March to mid–May: Autumn. Becomes cooler. Rainfall is less.

Natural attractions:
1. Hwange National Park, a wildlife preserve.
Best time to visit: May to October. This is the dry season when animals congregate at the sparse
waterbeds. An ideal month is September because of the combination of good animal viewing and
the spring flowering season. During the rainy season, November to March, animals are hard to spot
because, with the greater availability of surface water, they disperse throughout the park. The best
time of day to observe wildlife is early morning and late afternoon or dusk when they are active, either
hunting, eating or drinking.
2. Victoria Falls, on the Zambezi River.
The falls can be enjoyed at any time of the year.
Best months to visit, in our view, are June to October when the falls are not at full volume. Best
time to visit for photography is morning and late afternoon when the light is softer. To capture
rainbows, use a polarizing filter on your camera lens.

June to October: From late June onwards water is diminishing, meaning less mist and therefore
clearer views. September and October have clear views, but more rock–face is visible because of the
lower volume. Even so, these are very good months.
November and early December: Views are clear but temperatures are rising. Some rain falls.
January and February and into March: This is the rainy season when thunderstorms can obscure
the views. Humidity is high. Temperature can reach 38°C (100°F).
April and May: The volume of water tumbling over the falls is at its greatest and is most impressive
at this time. Clouds of spray shoot skywards but they can obscure the views. Volume of water may
also be great at end of March and beginning of June.

Harare, Zimbabwe: Altitude 1473m (4831ft)

	Jan	Feb	Mar	Apr	May	Jun
Sunrise ºC(ºF)	16(60)	15(59)	15(59)	12(53)	9(48)	6(42)
Mid–afternoon ºC(ºF)	26(78)	26(78)	26(78)	25(77)	23(73)	21(69)
Days with precipitation	18	14	12	6	2	1
Precipitation mm	191	144	95	41	10	2
Precipitation inches	7.5	5.7	3.8	1.6	0.4	0.08
Daily hours of sunshine	7	7	7	8	8	9

	Jul	Aug	Sep	Oct	Nov	Dec
Sunrise ºC(ºF)	6(42)	7(44)	11(51)	13(55)	15(59)	16(60)
Mid–afternoon ºC(ºF)	21(69)	24(75)	27(80)	28(82)	27(80)	26(78)
Days with precipitation	1	1	1	4	11	16
Precipitation mm	2	2	9	37	101	170
Precipitation inches	0.08	0.08	0.4	1.5	4.0	6.7
Daily hours of sunshine	9	10	10	9	8	6

CRUISING: WHEN TO GO (continued from page 11)

North American Region

Alaska's Inside Passage: May to September. May is when wildflowers bloom. June to August is best for seeing migrating whales. September is when foliage changes colour.

Bermuda: May to October.

Canada's Northwest Passage: July and August.

Hawaii: Year round.

Mexican riviera (Pacific coast) and U.S. West Coast: October or November to April.

New England states and Canada's Atlantic provinces: Season is June to October. August to October are the best months.

U.S. east coast: June to October.

U.S. west coast: November to April.

South Pacific Islands (e.g. Tahiti, Fiji)

Mostly year–round. April to September is the popular season. The weather from December to February is unpredictable due to potential cyclones.

DIVING: WHEN TO GO (continued from page 12)

Cozumel (see Mexico)

Cuba Year–round. Best is February to May. December to May has good visibility and slightly cooler weather. June to November has storms. Whale sharks can be seen consistently from August to November. A seasonal hazard is the presence of stinging jellyfish, June to September.

Curaçao (Netherlands Antilles) Good year–round.

Dominica Best is May to November. For whale and dolphin watching, choose October to April.

Egypt
Red Sea: May to September is best but any other time is good.

Fiji Year–round. Best time is April through November. (Less rain, cooler.)

French Polynesia (Includes Bora Bora and Tahiti.) Good all year. Best between April and November.

Galapagos Islands Best is October to May. June to December is also good; it is a few degrees cooler.

Grenada Good year–round. Best time is December to May. (Driest and calmest.)

The Grenadines Year–round.

Hawaii (see United States of America)

Honduras (Includes the Bay Islands of Roatan, Guanaja and Utila.) Best months are February to September, especially June to September. October to January is rainy, underwater visibility is reduced and there are mosquitoes.

India
Andaman and Nicobar Islands: Good year–round. Best is October to May.
Lakshadweep Archipelago: Good year–round.

Indonesia Good year–round. Good months are April to October. The best are April, May and September.

Israel
Eilat: Best is January to August.

Kenya Best is September through March. Expect to see whale sharks and manta rays December through March.

Maldives Prime season is October to April. March, April and November have better visibility. Best time for whale sharks and manta rays is August to November.

Mexico
Baja California: Best time is August through October. Unfortunately this is the period when hurricanes may occur. Caribbean coast (Includes Cozumel.) Good year–round. Best is May to September. (Warm air, calm seas.) For cave diving, best is November to March. Rainy, September to November.

DIVING: WHEN TO GO (continued)

Micronesia (Includes Chuuk Lagoon.) Good all year. Best time is October to June. July to September is also good with a flat sea and good visibility.

New Zealand December to May is the best time for cave diving at Poor Knights Islands.

Palau Good year–round. Best is December through March.

Papua New Guinea Good year–round. Best is October through June.

Philippines
Subic Bay and Coron Bay: Best is April, May.
Visayas (central Philippines): Best is October to March.

Roatan (see Honduras)

Tahiti (see French Polynesia)

Saba (Netherlands Antilles) Best months are May through October. Winter (December to March) is cold but has better visibility.

Seychelles Best weather with calm seas is March to May, and September to October. Wet season is November to February.

St Kitts and Nevis Good year–round.

St Lucia Good year–round.

Solomon Islands Good year–round. Better months are July through September when rainfall, heat and humidity are lowest, and November when the sea is flat.

South Africa Good year–round. (Sharks are present August to November.)

Tanzania Best is December through March. Manta rays and whale sharks visit at this time.

Thailand
West coast of peninsula: Best is November to April. (Calm seas.) It is rainy from May to September or October, making diving difficult.
East coast of peninsula: Best is May to October.

Tobago Good year–round. Better from November to June, especially March to June. Sea can be rough in December.

Turks and Caicos Year–round. Better months, March to June. Storms are possible from July to November.

DIVING: WHEN TO GO (continued)

United States of America
California: Santa Catalina and Monterey. Best months are July through October. (Good visibility and warmth.)
Florida: Miami Beach. Best months are March to May, and September to November. (Warm, calm water and less chance of storms.)
Hawaii: Good year–round. Disruptive storms can occur in winter, December to February.
North Carolina: The Outer Banks. Best months are May through early October. Outside these months winter storms cause a reduction in visibility.

Vanuatu Best is May to November. (Drier, cooler.)

Virgin Islands, British and U.S. Good year–round but October to June is best. Note that June to December is the hurricane season.

Countries and major islands are shown in **bold–faced** type.

Z

NOTES

NOTES

NOTES

ORDER FORM
for the TRAVEL PLANNER'S WEATHER GUIDE

Name _____

Address _____

City _____ Province / State _____

Country _____ Postal / Zip code _____

Home phone _____

Fax number _____

Email _____

	Canadian Orders	US Orders	International Orders
Book price	Cdn $34.95	US $24.95	US $24.95
Shipping & Handling	9.86	8.00	15.00
Sub–total	44.81	32.95	39.95
GST	3.14	0.00	0.00
Total	**Cdn $47.95**	**US $32.95**	**US $39.95**

HOW TO ORDER
Mail or fax this page or email us.
Pay by money order or check to OPEN ROAD PUBLISHERS drawn on a Canadian or US bank, or pay by VISA card. We accept only VISA. If our policy changes it will be posted on our web site.

SEND TO:
OPEN ROAD PUBLISHERS
3316 WEST 8TH AVENUE
VANCOUVER, BC, V6R 1Y4
CANADA
FAX: +1 604 734 1586
EMAIL: sales@worldweatherguide.com
www.worldweatherguide.com

If you are paying by VISA* we need the following information:

Exact name on card _____

Card number _____

Expiry date _____ Signature _____

* We accept only VISA. If our policy changes it will be posted on our web site.

ORDER FORM
for the TRAVEL PLANNER'S WEATHER GUIDE

Name _____

Address _____

City _____ Province / State _____

Country _____ Postal / Zip code _____

Home phone _____

Fax number _____

Email _____

	Canadian Orders	US Orders	International Orders
Book price	Cdn $34.95	US $24.95	US $24.95
Shipping & Handling	9.86	8.00	15.00
Sub–total	44.81	32.95	39.95
GST	3.14	0.00	0.00
Total	**Cdn $47.95**	**US $32.95**	**US $39.95**

HOW TO ORDER
Mail or fax this page or email us.
Pay by money order or check to OPEN ROAD PUBLISHERS drawn on a Canadian or US bank, or pay by VISA card. We accept only VISA. If our policy changes it will be posted on our web site.

SEND TO:
OPEN ROAD PUBLISHERS
3316 WEST 8TH AVENUE
VANCOUVER, BC, V6R 1Y4
CANADA
FAX: +1 604 734 1586
EMAIL: sales@worldweatherguide.com
www.worldweatherguide.com

If you are paying by VISA* we need the following information:

Exact name on card _____

Card number _____

Expiry date _____ Signature _____

* We accept only VISA. If our policy changes it will be posted on our web site.

ABOUT THE AUTHORS

Russell and Penny Jennings have travelled throughout Africa, Asia, North and South America, Europe, the Middle East, the South Pacific and the Russian Federation. When planning their independent travels and arranging and escorting their tours to various destinations, choosing a good time to travel has always been of major importance.

In their travel agency business, when consulting with clients, they found it imperative to have weather information available immediately. The information in their previous weather books, combined with additional research, has resulted in this weather guide.

For more about the authors, refer to the PREFACE.